An Introduction

to the

Mathematics of
Financial Derivatives

◆

An Introduction

to the

Mathematics of
Financial Derivatives

◆

Salih N. Neftci

CUNY Graduate Center
New York, New York
and
Graduate Institute of International Studies
Geneva, Switzerland

Academic Press

San Diego   London   Boston   New York   Sydney   Tokyo   Toronto

This book is printed on acid-free paper. ∞

Copyright © 1996 by ACADEMIC PRESS

Academic Press
525 B Street, Suite 1900, San Diego, California 92101-4495, USA
http://www.apnet.com

Academic Press Limited
24-28 Oval Road, London NW1 7DX, UK
http://www.hbuk.co.uk/ap/

Library of Congress Cataloging-in-Publication Data

Neftci, Salih N.
    An introduction to the mathematics of financial derivatives / by
Salih N. Neftci.
        p.   cm.
    Includes bibliographical references and index.
    ISBN 0-12-515390-2
    1. Derivative securities--Mathematics.   I. Title.
HG6024.A3N44   1996
332.63'2--dc20   96-13492
                                                      CIP

Printed in the United States of America
98 99 BB 7 6 5

CONTENTS

CHAPTER · 2   A Primer on the Arbitrage Theorem

CHAPTER · 3   Calculus in Deterministic and Stochastic Environments

CHAPTER · 6   Martingales and Martingale Representations

CHAPTER · 11   The Dynamics of Derivative Prices
Stochastic Differential Equations

CHAPTER · 12   Pricing Derivative Products
Partial Differential Equations

CHAPTER · 13   The Black–Scholes PDE
An Application

CHAPTER · 14   Pricing Derivative Products
Equivalent Martingale Measures

CHAPTER · 15   Equivalent Martingale Measures
Applications

PREFACE

This book grew from the courses that I have been teaching at the Graduate Institute of International Studies at the International Center for Money and Banking in Geneva, Switzerland.

This book is intended for beginning graduate students and for practitioners in financial markets. It deals with a heuristic explanation of the major mathematical tools found useful in asset pricing theory. It is not a book on mathematics. It has very few proofs, and even those are sketchy. To learn stochastic calculus and martingale arithmetic, one must go to the technical manuals. Yet I hope that this book will be useful to those beginning to read such material. On the other hand, any student of finance who intends to work with continuous-time asset pricing models should find this material useful.

Several colleagues and students read the original manuscript. I especially thank Hans Genberg, Li Li, Michael Chen, Graham Davis, and an anonymous referee who provided useful comments. The remaining errors are of course mine.

Geneva
February 1996

INTRODUCTION

This book is intended as background reading for modern asset pricing theory as outlined by Jarrow (1996), Hull (1993), Duffie (1996), Ingersoll (1987), and other excellent sources.

Pricing models for financial derivatives require, by their very nature, utilization of continuous-time stochastic processes. A good understanding of the tools of stochastic calculus and of some deep theorems in the theory of stochastic processes is necessary for practical asset valuation.

There are several excellent technical sources dealing with this mathematical theory. Karatzas and Shreve (1991) and Revuz and Yor (1994) are the first that come to mind. Others are discussed in the references. Yet even to a mathematically well-trained reader, these sources are not easy to follow. Sometimes, the material discussed has no direct applications in finance. At other times, the practical relevance of the assumptions is difficult to understand.

The purpose of this text is to provide an introduction to the mathematics utilized in the pricing models of derivative instruments. The text approaches the mathematics behind continuous-time finance informally. Examples are given and relevance to financial markets is provided.

Such an approach may be found imprecise by a technical reader. We simply hope that the informal treatment provides enough intuition about some of these difficult concepts to compensate for this shortcoming. Unfortunately, by providing a descriptive treatment of these concepts, it is difficult to emphasize technicalities. This would defeat the purpose of the book. Further, there are excellent sources at a technical level. What seems to be missing is a text that explains the assumptions and concepts behind

xviii

these mathematical tools and then relates them to dynamic asset pricing theory.

1 Audience

The text is directed toward a reader with some background in finance. A strong background in calculus or stochastic processes is not needed, although previous courses in these fields will certainly be helpful. One chapter will review some basic concepts in calculus, but it is best if the reader has already fulfilled some minimum calculus requirements. It is hoped that strong practitioners in financial markets as well as beginning graduate students will find the text useful.

2 New Developments

During the past two decades, some major developments have occurred in the theoretical understanding of how derivative asset prices are determined and how these prices move over time. There were also some recent institutional changes that indirectly make the methods discussed in the following pages popular.

The past two decades saw the freeing of exchange and capital controls. This made the exchange rates significantly more variable. In the meantime, world trade grew significantly. This made the elimination of currency risk a much higher priority.

During this time, interest rate controls were eliminated. This coincided with increases in the government budget deficits, which in turn led to large new issues of government debt in all industrialized nations. For this (and other) reasons, the need to eliminate the interest-rate risk became more urgent. Interest-rate derivatives became very popular.

It is mainly the need to hedge interest-rate and currency risks that is at the origin of the recent prolific increase in markets for derivative products. This need was partially met by financial markets. New products were developed and offered, but the conceptual understanding of the structure, functioning, and pricing of these derivative products also played an important role. Because theoretical valuation models were directly applicable to these new products, financial intermediaries were able to "correctly" price and successfully market them. Without such a clear understanding of the conceptual framework, it is not clear to what extent a similar development might have occurred.

As a result of these needs, new exchanges and marketplaces came into existence. Introduction of new products became easier and less costly.

Trading became cheaper. The deregulation of the financial services that gathered steam during the 1980s was also an important factor here.

Three major steps in the theoretical revolution led to the use of advanced mathematical methods that we discuss in this book:

- The *arbitrage theorem*[1] gives the formal conditions under which "arbitrage" profits can or cannot exist. It is shown that if asset prices satisfy a simple condition, then arbitrage cannot exist. This was a major development that eventually permitted the calculation of the arbitrage-free price of any "new" derivative product. Arbitrage pricing must be contrasted with *equilibrium pricing*, which takes into consideration conditions other than arbitrage that are imposed by general equilibrium.

- The *Black–Scholes model* (Black and Scholes, 1973) used the method of arbitrage-free pricing. But the paper was also influential because of the technical steps introduced in obtaining a closed-form formula for options prices. For an approach that used abstract notions such as Ito calculus, the formula was accurate enough to win the attention of market participants.

- The methodology of using *equivalent martingale measures* was developed later. This method dramatically simplified and generalized the original approach of Black and Scholes. With these tools, a general method could be used to price any derivative product. Hence, arbitrage-free prices under more realistic conditions could be obtained.

Finally, derivative products have a property that makes them especially suitable for a mathematical approach. Despite their apparent complexity, derivative products are in fact extremely simple instruments. Often their value depends only on the underlying asset, some interest rates, and a few parameters to be calculated. It is significantly easier to model such an instrument mathematically[2] than, say, to model stocks. The latter are titles on private companies, and in general, hundreds of factors influence the performance of a company and, hence, of the stock itself.

3 Objectives

We have the following plan for learning the mathematics of derivative products.

[1]Sometimes called "the fundamental theorem of finance."

[2]Especially if one is armed with the arbitrage theorem.

3.1 The Arbitrage Theorem

The meaning and the relevance of the *arbitrage theorem* will be introduced first. This is a major result of the theory of finance. Without a good understanding of the conditions under which arbitrage, and hence infinite profits, is ruled out, it would be difficult to motivate the mathematics that we intend to discuss.

3.2 Risk-Neutral Probabilities

The arbitrage theorem, by itself, is sufficient to introduce some of the main mathematical concepts that we discuss later. In particular, the arbitrage theorem provides a *mathematical framework* and, more importantly, justifies the existence and utilization of risk-neutral probabilities. The latter are "synthetic" probabilities utilized in valuing assets. They make it possible to bypass issues related to risk premiums.

3.3 Wiener and Poisson Processes

All of this requires an introductory discussion of Wiener processes from a practical point of view, which means learning the "economic assumptions" behind notions such as Wiener processes, stochastic calculus, and differential equations.

3.4 New Calculus

In doing this, some familiarity with the *new* calculus needs to be developed. Hence, we go over some of the basic results and discuss some simple examples.

3.5 Martingales

At this point, the notion of martingales and their uses in asset valuation should be introduced. *Martingale measures* and the way they are utilized in valuing asset prices are discussed with examples.

3.6 Partial Differential Equations

Derivative asset valuation utilizes the notion of arbitrage to obtain *partial differential equations* (PDEs) that must be satisfied by the prices of these products. We present the mathematics of partial differential equations and their numerical estimation.

3.7 The Girsanov Theorem

The Girsanov theorem permits changing means of random processes by varying the underlying probability distribution. The theorem is in the background of some of the most important pricing methods.

3.8 The Feyman–Kac Formula

The Feyman–Kac formula and its simpler versions, give a correspondence between classes of partial differential equations and certain conditional expectations. These expectations are in the form of discounted future asset prices, where the discount rate is *random*. This correspondence is useful in pricing interest-rate derivatives.

3.9 Examples

The text gives as many examples as possible. Some of these examples have relevance to financial markets; others simply illustrate the mathematical concept under study.

CHAPTER 1

Financial Derivatives

A Brief Introduction

1 Introduction

This book is an introduction to quantitative tools used in pricing financial derivatives. Hence, it is mainly about mathematics. It is a simple and heuristic introduction to mathematical concepts that have practical use in financial markets.

Such an introduction requires a discussion of the logic behind asset pricing. In addition, at various points we provide examples that also require an understanding of formal asset pricing methods. All this necessitates a brief discussion of the securities under consideration. This introductory chapter has that aim. Readers can consult other books to obtain more background on derivatives. Hull (1993) is an excellent source for derivatives. Jarrow and Turnbull (1996) gives another approach. The more advanced books by Ingersoll (1987) and Duffie (1996) provide strong links to the underlying theory. The manual by Das (1994) provides a summary of the practical issues associated with derivative contracts.

This chapter first deals with the two basic building blocks of financial derivatives: options and forwards (futures). Next, we introduce the more complicated class of derivatives known as swaps. The chapter concludes by showing that a complicated swap can be decomposed into a number of forwards and options. This decomposition is very practical. If one succeeds in pricing forwards and options, one can then reconstitute any swap and obtain its price. This chapter also introduces some formal notation that will be used throughout the book.

2 Definitions

In the words of practitioners, "Derivative securities are financial contracts that 'derive' their value from the *cash market* instruments such as stocks, bonds, currencies and commodities."[1]

The academic definition of a "derivative instrument" is more precise:

> **DEFINITION:** A financial contract is a *derivative security*, or a *contingent claim* if its value at expiration date T is determined *exactly* by the market price of the underlying cash instrument at time T (Ingersoll, 1987).

Hence, at the time of the expiration of the derivative contract, denoted by T, the price $F(T)$ of a derivative asset is completely determined by S_T, the value of the "underlying asset." After that date the security ceases to exist. This simple characteristic of derivative assets plays a very important role in their valuation.

In the rest of this book the symbols $F(t)$ and $F(S_t, t)$ will be used alternately to denote the price of a derivative product written on the underlying asset S_t at time t. The financial derivative is sometimes assumed to yield a payout d_t. At other times the payout is zero. T will always denote expiration date.

3 Types of Derivatives

We can group derivative securities under three general headings:

1. Futures and forwards
2. Options
3. Swaps

Forwards and options are considered *basic building blocks*. Swaps and some other complicated structures are considered hybrid securities, which can eventually be decomposed into sets of basic forwards and options.

We let S_t denote the price of the relevant cash instrument, and we call this the *underlying security*.

We can list five main groups of underlying assets:

1. Stocks: These are claims to "real" returns generated in the production sector for goods and services.

2. Currencies: These are liabilities of governments or, sometimes, banks. They are not direct claims on real assets.

---

[1]See pages 2–3, Klein and Lederman (1994).

3. Interest rates: Interest rates are not assets. Hence, a *notional* asset is devised so that one can take a position on the direction of future interest rates.

In this category we can also include derivatives on bonds, notes, and T-bills, these are government debt instruments. They are promises by governments to pay certain sums of money on set dates. By dealing with derivatives on bonds, notes and T-bills, one takes positions on the direction of various interest rates. However, in most cases[2] these derivative instruments are not *notionals* and can result in actual delivery of the underlying asset. Note that in the case of an interest rate derivative, one cannot *deliver* the interest rate itself. The settlement must be done with cash.

4. Indexes: The S&P-500 and the FT-SE100 are two examples of stock indexes. The CRB commodity index is an index of commodity prices. Again, these are not "assets" themselves. However, derivative contracts can be written on notional amounts, and a position can be taken with respect to the direction of the underlying index.

5. Commodities: The main classes are:

- Soft commodities: cocoa, coffee, sugar
- Grains and oilseeds: barley, corn, cotton, oats, palm oil, potato, soybean, winter wheat, spring wheat, and others
- Metals: copper, nickel, tin, and others
- Precious metals: gold, platinum, silver
- Livestock: cattle, hogs, pork bellies and others
- Energy: Crude oil, fuel oil, and others

These underlying commodities are not *financial* assets. They are goods in kind. Hence, in most cases they can be physically purchased and stored.

There is another way one can classify the underlying asset which is important for our purposes.

3.1 Cash-and-Carry Markets

Some derivative products are written on products of *cash-and-carry* markets. Gold, silver, currencies, and T-bonds are some examples of cash-and-carry products.

In these markets, one can *borrow* at risk-free rates (by collateralizing the underlying physical asset), *buy* and *store* the product, and *insure* it until the expiration date of any derivative contract. Hence, one can easily build an alternative to holding a forward or futures contract on these commodities.

---

[2]There is a significant amount of trading on "notional" French government bonds in Paris.

For example, one can borrow at risk free rates, buy a T-bond, and hold it until the delivery date of a futures contract on T-bonds. This is equivalent to buying a futures contract and accepting the delivery of the underlying instrument at expiration. One can construct similar examples with currencies, gold, silver, crude oil, etc.[3]

Pure cash-and-carry markets have one more property. Information about future demand and supplies of the underlying instrument should not influence the "spread" between cash and futures (forward) prices. After all, this spread will depend mostly on the level of risk-free interest rates, storage, and insurance costs. Any relevant information concerning future supplies and demands of the underlying instrument is expected to make the cash price and the future price change by the same amount.

3.2 Price-Discovery Markets

The second type of underlying asset comes from *price discovery* markets. Here, it is physically impossible to buy the underlying instrument for cash and store it until some future expiration date. Such goods either are too *perishable* to be stored or may not have a cash market at the time the derivative is trading. One example is a contract on spring wheat. When the futures contracts for this commodity is traded in the exchange, the corresponding cash market may not exist.

The strategy of borrowing, buying, and storing it until some later expiration date is not applicable to price-discovery markets. Under these conditions any information about the *future* supply and demand of the underlying commodity cannot influence the corresponding cash price. However, such information can be *discovered* in the futures market, hence the terminology.

3.3 Expiration Date

The relationship between $F(t)$, the price of the derivative, and S_t is known exactly (or deterministically) only at the expiration date T. In the case of forwards or futures, we naturally expect

$$F(T) = S_T; \tag{1}$$

that is, at expiration the value of the futures contract should be equal to its cash equivalent.

For example, the (exchange traded) futures contract of promising the delivery of 100 troy ounces of gold cannot have a value different from the

---

[3]However, as in the case of crude oil, the storage process may end up being very costly. Environmental and other effects make it very expensive to store crude oil.

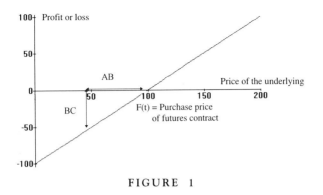

FIGURE 1

actual market value of 100 troy ounces of gold on the *expiration date* of the contract. They both represent the same thing at time T. So, in the case of gold futures we can indeed say that the equality in (1) holds at expiration.

At other times, $t \le T$, $F(t)$ may not equal S_t. Yet we can determine a *function* that ties S_t to $F(t)$.

4 Forwards and Futures

Futures and forwards are linear instruments. This section will discuss forwards; their differences from futures will be briefly indicated at the end.

DEFINITION: A forward contract is an obligation to buy (sell) an underlying asset at a specified *forward price* on a known date.

The expiration date of the contract and the forward price are written when the contract is entered into. If a forward purchase is made, the holder of such a contract is said to be *long* in the underlying asset. If at expiration the cash price is higher than the forward price, the long position makes a profit; otherwise there is a loss.

The payoff diagram for a simplified long position is shown in Figure 1. The contract is purchased for $F(t)$ at time t. It is assumed that the contract expires at time $t + 1$. The upward-sloping line indicates the profit or loss of the purchaser at expiration. The slope of the line is one.

If S_{t+1} exceeds $F(t)$, then the long position ends up with a profit.[4] Given that the line has unitary slope, the segment AB equals the vertical line BC. Hence, at time $t + 1$ the gain or loss can be read directly as the vertical distance between the line and the horizontal axis.

---

[4]Note that because the contract expires at $t + 1$, S_{t+1} will equal $F(t + 1)$.

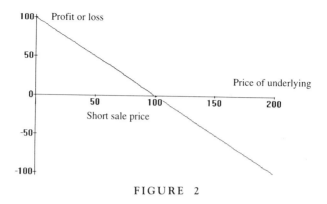

FIGURE   2

Figure 2 displays the payoff diagram of a *short position* under similar circumstances.

Such payoff diagrams are useful in understanding the mechanics of derivative products. In this book we treat them briefly. The reader can consult Hull (1993) for an extensive discussion.

4.1 Futures

Futures and forwards are similar instruments. The major differences can be stated briefly as follows.

Futures are traded in formalized *exchanges*. The exchange designs a standard contract and sets some specific expiration dates. Forwards are "custom made" and are traded *over-the-counter*.

Futures exchanges are cleared through exchange clearing houses, and there is an intricate mechanism designed to reduce the default risk.

Finally, futures contracts are *marked to market*. That is, every day the contract is settled and simultaneously a new contract is written. Any profit or loss during the day is recorded accordingly in the account of the contract holder.

5   Options

Options constitute the second basic building block of asset pricing. In later chapters we often use pricing models for standard call options as a major example to introduce concepts of stochastic calculus.

Forwards and futures *obligate* the contract holder to deliver or accept delivery of the underlying instrument at expiration. Options, on the other hand, give the owner the *right* but not the obligation to purchase or sell an asset.

There are two types of options.

DEFINITION: A European-type call option on a security S_t is the *right* to buy the security at a preset *strike price K*. This right may be exercised *at the expiration date T* of the option. The call option can be purchased for a price of C_t dollars called the *premium*.

A European *put option* is similar, but gives the owner the right to *sell* an asset at a specified price at expiration.

In contrast to European options, *American* options can be exercised *any* time between the writing and the expiration of the contract.

There are several reasons that traders and investors may want to calculate the arbitrage-free price, C_t, of a call option. Before the option is first *written* at time t, C_t is not known. A trader may want to obtain some estimate of what this price will be if the option is written. If the option is an exchange-traded security, it will start trading and a market price will emerge. If the option trades over-the-counter, it may again trade heavily and a price can be observed.

However, the option may be traded infrequently. Then, a trader may want to know the daily value of C_t in order to evaluate its risks. Another trader may think that the market is mispricing the call option, and the extent of this mispricing may be of interest. Again, the arbitrage-free value of C_t needs to be determined.

5.1 Some Notation

The most desirable way of pricing a call option is to find a *closed-form* formula for C_t that expresses the latter as a function of the underlying asset's price and the relevant parameters.

At time t, the only known "formula" concerning C_t is the one that determines its value at the time of expiration denoted by T. In fact,

- if there are no commissions and/or fees
- if the bid–ask spreads on S_t and C_t are zero

then at the expiration, C_T can assume only two possible values.

If the option is expiring *out-of-money*, that is, if at expiration the option holder faces

$$S_T < K, \tag{2}$$

then the option will have no value. The underlying asset can be purchased in the market for S_T, and this is less than the strike price K. No option holder will exercise his or her right to buy the underlying asset at K. Thus,

$$S_T < K \Rightarrow C_T = 0. \tag{3}$$

But, if the option expires *in-the-money*, that is, if at time T,

$$S_T > K, \tag{4}$$

the option will have some value. One should clearly exercise the option. One can buy the underlying security at price K and sell it at a higher price S_T. Since, there are no commissions or bid–ask spreads, the net profit will be $S_T - K$. Market participants, being aware of this, will place a value of $S_T - K$ on the option, and we have

$$S_T > K \Rightarrow C_T = S_T - K. \tag{5}$$

We can use a shorthand notation to express both of these possibilities by writing

$$C_T = \max\left[S_T - K, 0\right]. \tag{6}$$

This means that the C_T will equal the *greater* of the two values inside the brackets. In later chapters this notation will be used frequently.

Equation (6), which gives the relation between S_T and C_T, can be graphed easily. Figure 3 shows this relationship. Note that for $S_T \leq K$, the C_T is zero. For values of S_T such that $K < S_T$, the C_T increases at the same rate as S_T. Hence, for this range of values, the graph of Equation (6) is a straight line with unitary slope. Options are *nonlinear* instruments.

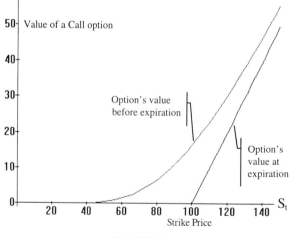

FIGURE 3

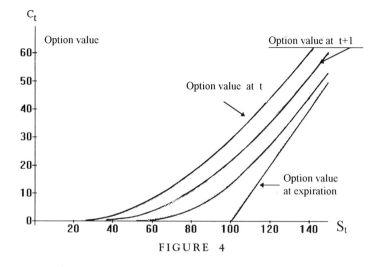

FIGURE 4

Figure 4 displays the value of a call option at various times before expiration. Note that for $t < T$ the value of the function can be represented by a smooth continuous curve. Only at expiration does the option value become a piecewise linear function with a kink at strike price.

6 Swaps

Swaps are more complicated instruments. They are among some of the most common types of derivatives. But this is not the reason that we are interested in them. It turns out that one method for pricing swaps is to *decompose* them into forwards and options. This illustrates the special role played by forwards and options as basic building blocks and justifies the special emphasis put on them in following chapters.

First a general definition of swaps.

DEFINITION: A swap is the simultaneous selling and purchasing of cash flows involving various currencies, interest rates, and a number of other financial assets.

Even a brief summary of swap instruments is outside the scope of this book. As mentioned earlier, our intention is to provide a heuristic introduction of the mathematics behind derivative asset pricing, and not to discuss the derivative products themselves. We limit our discussion to a typical example that illustrates the main points.

6.1 A Simple Interest Rate Swap

Decomposing a swap into its constituent components is a potent example of financial engineering and derivative asset pricing. It also illustrates the special role played by simple forwards and options. We discuss an interest rate swap in detail. Das (1994) can be consulted for more advanced swap structures.[5]

In its simplest form, an interest rate swap between two *counterparties A* and *B* is created as a result of the following steps:

1. Counterparty *A* needs a $1 million floating-rate loan. Counterparty *B* needs a $1 million fixed-rate loan. But, because of market conditions and their relationships with various banks, *B* has a comparative advantage in borrowing at a floating rate.[6]

2. *A* and *B* decide to exploit this comparative advantage. Each counterparty borrows at the market where they have a comparative advantage, and then they decide to exchange the interest payments.

3. Counterparty *A* borrows $1 million at a fixed rate. The interest payments will be received from counterparty *B* and paid back to the lending bank.

4. Counterparty *B* borrows $1 million at the floating rate. Interest payments[7] will be received from counterparty *A* and will be repaid to the lending bank.

5. Note that the initial sums, each being $1 million, are identical. Hence, they do not have to be exchanged. They are called *notional principals*. The interest payments are also in the same currency. Hence, the counterparties exchange only the interest *differentials*. This concludes the interest rate swap.

This very basic interest rate swap consists of exchanges of interest payments. The counterparties borrow in sectors where they have an advantage and then exchange the interest payments. At the end both counterparties will secure lower rates and the *swap dealer* will earn a fee.

It is always possible to decompose simple swap deals into a basket of simpler forward and/or options contracts. Then, the basket will replicate the swap. The forwards and options can then be priced separately, and the corresponding value of the swap can be determined from these num-

---

[5]Other recent sources on practical applications of swaps are Dattatreya *et al.* (1994) and Kapner and Marshall (1992).

[6]This means that *A* has a comparative advantage in borrowing at a fixed rate.

[7]For example, 6-month Libor + 2.

bers. This decomposition into building blocks of forwards will significantly facilitate the valuation of the swap contract.

7 Conclusions

In this chapter we have reviewed some basic derivative instruments. Our purpose was twofold: first, to give a brief treatment of the basic derivative securities so that we can use them in examples; and second, to discuss some notation in derivative asset pricing, where one first develops pricing formulas for simple building blocks, such as options and forwards, and then decomposes more complicated structures into baskets of forwards and options. This way, pricing formulas for simpler structures can be used to value more complicated structured products.

8 References

Hull (1993) is an excellent source on derivatives that is unique in many ways. Practitioners use it as a manual; beginning graduate students utilize it as a textbook. Hence, it is both practical and carefully done. Jarrow and Turnbull (1996) is a welcome addition to books on derivatives. Duffie (1996) is an excellent source on dynamic asset pricing theory. However, it is not a source on the details of actual instruments traded in the markets. Yet, practitioners with a very strong math background may find it useful. Das (1995) is a good manual on the practical aspects of derivative instruments.

CHAPTER 2

A Primer on the Arbitrage Theorem

1 Introduction

All current methods of pricing derivative assets utilize the notion of *arbitrage*. In *arbitrage pricing methods* this utilization is direct. Asset prices are obtained from conditions that preclude arbitrage opportunities. In *equilibrium pricing methods*, lack of arbitrage opportunities is part of general equilibrium conditions.

In its simplest form, arbitrage means taking simultaneous positions in different assets so that one guarantees a riskless profit higher than the riskless return given by U.S. Treasury bills. If such profits exist, we say that there is an *arbitrage opportunity*.

Arbitrage opportunities can arise in two different fashions. In the first way, one can make a series of investments with no current net commitment, yet expect to make a positive profit. For example, one can short-sell a stock and then use these proceeds to buy call options written on the same security. In this portfolio one finances a long position in call options with short positions in the underlying stock. If this is done properly, unpredictable movements in the short and long positions will cancel out, and the portfolio will be riskless. Once commissions and fees are deducted, such investment opportunities should not yield any excess profits. Otherwise, we say that there are *arbitrage opportunities* of the first kind.

In arbitrage opportunities of the *second kind*, a portfolio can ensure a negative net commitment today, while yielding nonnegative profits in the future.

We use these concepts to obtain a practical definition of a "fair price" for a financial asset. We say that the price of a security is at a "fair" level, or that the security is *correctly priced*, if there are no arbitrage opportunities of the first or second kind at those prices. Such *arbitrage-free* asset prices will be utilized as benchmarks. Deviations from these indicate opportunities for excess profits.

Of course, in practice, arbitrage opportunities may exist. This, however, would not reduce our interest in "arbitrage-free" prices. In fact, determining arbitrage-free prices is at the center of valuing derivative assets. We can imagine at least four possible utilizations of arbitrage-free prices.

A derivatives house may decide to engineer a *new* financial product. Because the product is new, the price at which it should be sold cannot be obtained by observing actual trading in financial markets. Under these conditions, calculating the arbitrage-free price will be very helpful in determining a market price for this product.

A second example is from *risk management*. Often, risk managers would like to measure the risks associated with their portfolios by running some "worst case" scenarios. These simulations are repeated periodically. Each time, some benchmark price needs to be utilized, given that what is in question is a hypothetical event that has not been observed.[1]

A third example is *marking to market* of assets held in portfolios: A treasurer may want to know the current market value of a nonliquid asset for which no trades have been observed lately. Calculating the corresponding arbitrage-free price may provide a solution.

Finally, arbitrage-free benchmark prices can be *compared* with prices observed in actual trading. Significant differences between observed and arbitrage-free values might indicate excess profit opportunities. This way arbitrage-free prices can be used to detect mispricings that may occur during short intervals. If the arbitrage-free price is *above* the observed price, the derivative is *cheap*. A *long* position may be called for. When the opposite occurs, the derivative instrument is *overvalued*.

The mathematical environment provided by the no-arbitrage theorem is the major tool used to calculate such benchmark prices.

2 Notation

We begin with some formalism and start developing the notation that is an integral part of every mathematical approach. A correct understand-

---

[1] Note that devising such scenarios is not at all straightforward. For example, it is not clear that markets will have the necessary liquidity to secure no-arbitrage conditions if they are hit by some extreme shock.

ing of the notation is sometimes as important as an understanding of the underlying mathematical logic.

2.1 Asset Prices

The index t will represent time. Securities such as options, futures, forwards, and stocks will be represented by a *vector* of asset prices denoted by S_t. This array groups all securities in financial markets under one symbol:

$$S_t = \begin{pmatrix} S_1(t) \\ \vdots \\ S_N(t) \end{pmatrix}. \tag{1}$$

Here, $S_1(t)$ may be riskless borrowing or lending, $S_2(t)$ may denote a particular stock, $S_3(t)$ may be a call option written on this stock, $S_4(t)$ may represent the corresponding put option, and so on. The t subscript in S_t means that prices belong to time represented by the value of t. In *discrete* time securities prices can be expressed as $S_0, S_1, \ldots, S_t, S_{t+1}, \ldots$. However, in continuous time the t subscript can assume any value between zero and infinity. We formally write this as

$$t \in [0, \infty). \tag{2}$$

In general, 0 denotes the *initial point*, and t represents the *present*. If we write

$$t < s, \tag{3}$$

then s is meant to be a *future* date.

2.2 States of the World

To proceed with the rest of this chapter, we need one more concept—a concept that, at the outset, may appear to be very abstract. Yet it has significant practical relevance.

We let the vector W denote all the possible *states of the world*,

$$W = \begin{pmatrix} w_1 \\ \vdots \\ w_K \end{pmatrix}, \tag{4}$$

where each w_i represents a distinct outcome that may occur. These states are *mutually exclusive*, and at least one of them is guaranteed to occur.

In general, financial assets will have different values and give different payouts at different states of the world w_i. It is assumed that there are a finite number K of such possible states.

It is not very difficult to visualize this concept. Suppose that from a trader's point of view, the only time of interest is the "next" instant. Clearly, securities prices may change, and we do not necessarily know how. Yet, in a small time interval securities prices may have an "uptick" or a "downtick," or may not show any movement at all. Hence, there are a total of three possible states of the world.

2.3 Returns and Payoffs

The states of the world w_i matter because in different states of the world returns to securities would be different. We let the symbol d_{ij} denote the number of units of account paid by one unit of security i in state j. These *payoffs* will have two components.

The first component is capital gains or losses. Asset values appreciate or depreciate. For an investor who is "long" in the asset, an appreciation leads to a capital gain and a depreciation to a capital loss. For somebody who is "short" in the asset, capital gains and losses will be reversed.[2]

The second component of the d_{ij} is *payouts* such as dividends or coupon interest payments. Some assets do not have such payouts. Call and put options and discount bonds are among these. But others do have payouts.[3]

The existence of several assets, along with the assumption of many states of the world means that for each asset there are several possible d_{ij}. *Matrices* are used to represent such arrays.

Thus, for the N assets under consideration, the payoffs d_{ij} can be grouped in a matrix D:

$$ D = \begin{pmatrix} d_{11} & \cdots & d_{1K} \\ \vdots & \vdots & \vdots \\ d_{N1} & \cdots & d_{NK} \end{pmatrix}. \tag{5} $$

There are two different ways one can visualize such a matrix. One can look at the matrix D as if each row represents payoffs to one unit of a given security in different states of the world. Or, conversely, one can look at D

---

[2]Note that to realize a capital gain, one must unwind the position.

[3]Another example, besides dividend-paying stocks and coupon bonds, is the investment in futures. The practice of "marking to the market" leads to daily payouts to a contract holder. However, in the case of futures these payouts may be negative or positive.

columnwise. Each column of D represents payoffs to different assets in a given state of the world.

If current prices of all assets are nonzero, then one can divide the ith row of D by the corresponding S_i and obtain the gross *returns* in different states of the world. The D will have a t subscript in case payoffs depend on time.

2.4 Portfolio

A portfolio is a particular combination of assets in question. To form a portfolio one needs to know the positions taken in each asset under consideration. The symbol θ_i represents the commitment with respect to the ith asset. Specifying all $\{\theta_i, i = 1 \ldots N\}$ specifies the portfolio.

A positive θ_i implies a long position in that asset, while a negative θ_i implies a short position. If an asset is not included in the portfolio, the corresponding θ_i is zero.

If a portfolio delivers the same payoff in all states of the world, then its value is known exactly and the portfolio is *riskless*.

3 A Basic Example of Asset Pricing

We use a simple model to explain most of the important results in pricing derivative assets. With this example we first intend to illustrate the *logic* used in derivative asset pricing. Second, we hope to introduce the *mathematical tools* needed to carry out this logic in practical applications. The model is kept simple on purpose. A more general case is discussed at the end of the chapter.

We assume that time consists of "now" and a "next period" and that these two periods are separated by an interval of length Δ. Throughout this book Δ will represent a "small" but noninfinitesimal interval.

We consider a case where the market participant is interested only in three assets:

1. A risk-free asset such as a Treasury bill, whose gross return until next period is $(1 + r\Delta)$.[4] This return is "risk-free" in the sense that it is constant regardless of the realized state of the world.

2. The second security is an *underlying asset*, for example, a stock $S(t)$. We assume that during the small interval Δ, the $S(t)$ can assume one of only *two* possible values. This means a minimum of *two* states of the world. $S(t)$ is risky because its payoff is different in the two states of the world.

---

[4]Note that we *must* multiply the r by the time that elapses, Δ, to get the proper return.

3. The third security is a derivative asset, a call option with premium $C(t)$ and a strike price C_o. The option expires "next" period. Given that the underlying asset has two possible values, the call option will assume two possible values as well.

This setup is fairly simple. There are three assets ($N = 3$), and two states of the world ($K = 2$). One of the assets is the underlying security; the other is the option. The third asset is risk-free borrowing or lending.

Yet the example is not altogether unrealistic. A trader operating in real (continuous) time may contemplate taking a (covered) position in a particular option. If the time interval under consideration is "small," prices of these assets may not change by more than an up- or downtick. Hence, the assumption of two states of the world may be a reasonable approximation.[5]

We summarize this information in terms of the formal notation discussed earlier. Asset prices will form a vector S_t of three elements only,

$$
S_t = \begin{bmatrix} B(t) \\ S(t) \\ C(t) \end{bmatrix}, \tag{6}
$$

where $B(t)$ is riskless borrowing or lending. $S(t)$ is a stock and $C(t)$ is the value of a call option written on this stock. The t indicates the time for which these prices apply.

Payoffs will be grouped in a matrix D_t, as discussed earlier. There are three assets, which means that matrix D_t will have three rows. Also, there are two states of the world. Hence, the D_t matrix will have two columns. The $B(t)$ is riskless borrowing or lending. Its payoff will be the same regardless of the state of the world that applies in the "next instant." The $S(t)$ is risky and its value may go either up to $S_1(t + \Delta)$ or down to $S_2(t + \Delta)$. Finally, the market value of the call option $C(t)$ will change in line with changes in the underlying asset price $S(t)$. Thus, in this particular case the D_t will be given by:

$$
D_t = \begin{bmatrix} (1 + r\Delta)B(t) & (1 + r\Delta)B(t) \\ S_1(t + \Delta) & S_2(t + \Delta) \\ C_1(t + \Delta) & C_2(t + \Delta) \end{bmatrix}, \tag{7}
$$

where r is the riskless rate of return.

---

[5]In fact, we show later that a continuous-time Wiener process, or Brownian motion, can be approximated arbitrarily well by such two-state processes, as we let the Δ go toward zero.

3.1 A First Glance at the Arbitrage Theorem

We are now ready to introduce a fundamental result in financial theory that can be used in calculating fair market values of derivative assets. But first we will simplify the notation even further. The amount of risk-free borrowing and lending is selected by the investor. Hence, we can always let

$$B(t) = 1. \tag{8}$$

Earlier, the time that elapses was called Δ. In this particular example we let

$$\Delta = 1. \tag{9}$$

The arbitrage theorem can now be stated:

THEOREM: Given the S_t, D_t defined in (6) and (7) and that the two states have positive probabilities of occurrence,

1. if *positive* constants ψ_1, ψ_2 can be found such that asset prices satisfy

$$\begin{bmatrix} 1 \\ S(t) \\ C(t) \end{bmatrix} = \begin{bmatrix} (1+r) & (1+r) \\ S_1(t+1) & S_2(t+1) \\ C_1(t+1) & C_2(t+1) \end{bmatrix} \begin{bmatrix} \psi_1 \\ \psi_2 \end{bmatrix}, \tag{10}$$

then there are no arbitrage possibilities;[6] and

2. if there are no arbitrage opportunities, then positive constants ψ_1, ψ_2 satisfying (10) can be found.

The relationship in (10) is called a *representation*. It is not a relation that can be observed in reality. In fact, $S_1(t+1)$ and $S_2(t+1)$ are "possible" future values of the underlying asset. Only one of them—namely, the one that belongs to the state that is realized—will be observed.

What do the constants ψ_1, ψ_2 represent? According to the representation implied by the arbitrage theorem, if a security pays 1 in state 1, and 0 in state 2, then

$$S(t) = (1)\psi_1. \tag{11}$$

Thus, investors are willing to pay ψ_1 (current) units for an "insurance policy" that offers one unit of account in state 1 and nothing in state 2. Similarly, ψ_2 indicates how much investors would like to pay for an "insurance

---

[6]Note that if $1 + r > 1$, we need to have $\psi_1 + \psi_2 < 1$ as well. This obtains from the first row of the matrix equation.

policy" that pays 1 in state 2 and nothing in state 1. Clearly, by spending $\psi_1 + \psi_2$ one can guarantee 1 unit of account in the future, regardless of which state is realized. This is indeed what the first row of representation (10) shows. Consistent with this interpretation, $\psi_i, i = 1, 2$ are called *state prices.*

At this point there are several other issues that may not be clear. One can in fact ask the following questions:

- How does one obtain this result?
- What does the existence of ψ_1, ψ_2 have to do with no arbitrage?
- Why is this result relevant for asset pricing?

For the moment, let us put the first two questions aside and answer the third question: What types of practical results (if any) does one obtain from the existence of ψ_1, ψ_2?

It turns out that the representation given by the arbitrage theorem is very important for practical asset pricing.

3.2 Relevance of the Arbitrage Theorem

The arbitrage theorem provides a very elegant and general method for pricing derivative assets.

Consider again the representation:

$$\begin{bmatrix} 1 \\ S(t) \\ C(t) \end{bmatrix} = \begin{bmatrix} (1+r) & (1+r) \\ S_1(t+1) & S_2(t+1) \\ C_1(t+1) & C_2(t+1) \end{bmatrix} \begin{bmatrix} \psi_1 \\ \psi_2 \end{bmatrix}. \tag{12}$$

Multiplying the first row of the dividend matrix D_t by the vector of ψ_1, ψ_2, we get

$$1 = (1+r)\psi_1 + (1+r)\psi_2. \tag{13}$$

Define:

$$\begin{aligned} \tilde{P}_1 &= (1+r)\psi_1 \\ \tilde{P}_2 &= (1+r)\psi_2 \end{aligned} \tag{14}$$

Because of the positivity of state prices and because of (13),

$$0 < \tilde{P}_i \leq 1$$
$$\tilde{P}_1 + \tilde{P}_2 = 1.$$

Hence, $\tilde{P}_i$'s are positive numbers, and they sum to one. As such, they can be interpreted as two *probabilities* associated with the two states under consideration. We say "interpreted" because the true probabilities that govern the occurrence of the two states of the world will in general be different from the $\tilde{P}_1$ and $\tilde{P}_2$. These are *defined* by Equation (14) and provide no direct information concerning the true probabilities associated with the two states of the world. For this reason, $\{\tilde{P}_1, \tilde{P}_2\}$ are called *risk-adjusted* synthetic probabilities.

3.3 The Use of Synthetic Probabilities

Risk-adjusted probabilities exist if there are no arbitrage opportunities. In other words, if there are no "mispriced assets," we are guaranteed to find positive constants $\{\psi_1, \psi_2\}$. Multiplying these by the riskless gross return $1 + r$ guarantees the existence of $\{\tilde{P}_1, \tilde{P}_2\}$.[7]

The importance of risk-adjusted probabilities for asset pricing stems from the following: Expectations calculated with them, once discounted by the risk-free rate r, equal the current value of the asset.

Consider the equality implied by the arbitrage theorem again. Note that the representation (10) implies three separate equalities:

$$1 = (1 + r)\psi_1 + (1 + r)\psi_2 \tag{15}$$

$$S(t) = \psi_1 S_1(t + 1) + \psi_2 S_2(t + 1) \tag{16}$$

$$C(t) = \psi_1 C_1(t + 1) + \psi_2 C_2(t + 1). \tag{17}$$

Now multiply the right-hand side of the last two equations by

$$\frac{1 + r}{1 + r} \tag{18}$$

to obtain[8]

$$S(t) = \frac{1}{(1 + r)}[(1 + r)\psi_1 S_1(t + 1) + (1 + r)\psi_2 S_2(t + 1)] \tag{19}$$

$$C(t) = \frac{1}{(1 + r)}[(1 + r)\psi_1 C_1(t + 1) + (1 + r)\psi_2 C_2(t + 1)]. \tag{20}$$

But, we can replace $(1 + r)\psi_i$, $i = 1, 2$ with the corresponding $\tilde{P}_i$, $i = 1, 2$. This means that the two equations become

$$S(t) = \frac{1}{(1 + r)}\left[\tilde{P}_1 S_1(t + 1) + \tilde{P}_2 S_2(t + 1)\right] \tag{21}$$

---

[7]This is the case with *finite* states of the world. With *uncountably* many states one needs further conditions for the existence of risk-adjusted probabilities.

[8]As long as r is not equal to -1, we can always do this.

$$C(t) = \frac{1}{(1+r)} \left[\tilde{P}_1 C_1(t+1) + \tilde{P}_2 C_2(t+1) \right]. \tag{22}$$

Now consider how these expressions can be interpreted. The expression on the right-hand side multiplies the term in the brackets by $1/(1+r)$, which is a riskless one-period discount factor. On the other hand, the term inside the brackets can be interpreted as some sort of *expected value*. It is the sum of possible future values of $S(t)$ or $C(t)$ weighted by the "probabilities" $\tilde{P}_1, \tilde{P}_2$. Hence, the terms in the brackets are expectations calculated using the risk-adjusted probabilities.

As such, the equalities in (21) and (22) do not represent "true" expected values. Yet as long as there is no arbitrage, these equalities are valid, and they can be used in practical calculations. We can use them in asset pricing, as long as the underlying probabilities are explicitly specified.

With this interpretation of $\tilde{P}_1, \tilde{P}_2$, the *current prices of all assets under consideration become equal to their discounted expected payoffs*. Further, the discounting is done using the risk-free rate, although the assets themselves are risky.

In order to emphasize the important role played by risk-adjusted probabilities, consider what happens when one uses the "true" probabilities dictated by their nature.

First, we obtain the "true" expected values by using the true probabilities denoted by P_1, P_2:

$$E^{true}[S(t+1)] = [P_1 S_1(t+1) + P_2 S_2(t+1)] \tag{23}$$

$$E^{true}[C(t+1)] = [P_1 C_1(t+1) + P_2 C_2(t+1)]. \tag{24}$$

Because these are "risky" assets, when discounted by the risk-free rate these expectations will in general[9] satisfy

$$S(t) < \frac{1}{(1+r)} E^{true}[S(t+1)] \tag{25}$$

$$C(t) < \frac{1}{(1+r)} E^{true}[C(t+1)]. \tag{26}$$

To see why one obtains such inequalities, assume otherwise:

$$S(t) = \frac{1}{(1+r)} E^{true}[S(t+1)] \tag{27}$$

$$C(t) = \frac{1}{(1+r)} E^{true}[C(t+1)]. \tag{28}$$

[9]We say "in general" because one can imagine risky assets that are negatively correlated with the "market." Such assets may have negative risk premiums and are called "negative beta" assets.

Rearranging, and assuming that asset prices are nonzero

$$(1+r) = \frac{E^{true}[S(t+1)]}{S(t)} \tag{29}$$

$$(1+r) = \frac{E^{true}[C(t+1)]}{C(t)}. \tag{30}$$

But this means that (true) expected returns from the risky assets equal risk-less return. This, however, is a contradiction, because in general risky assets will command a positive risk premium. If there is no such compensation for risk, no investor would hold them. Thus, for risky assets we generally have

$$(1+r+\text{risk premium for } S(t)) = \frac{E^{true}[S(t+1)]}{S(t)} \tag{31}$$

$$(1+r+\text{risk premium for } C(t)) = \frac{E^{true}[C(t+1)]}{C(t)}. \tag{32}$$

This implies, in general, the following inequalities for risky assets:[10]

$$S(t) < \frac{1}{(1+r)} E^{true}[S(t+1)] \tag{33}$$

$$C(t) < \frac{1}{(1+r)} E^{true}[C(t+1)]. \tag{34}$$

The importance of the no-arbitrage assumption in asset pricing should become clear at this point. If no-arbitrage implies the existence of positive constants such as ψ_1, ψ_2, then we can always obtain from these constants the risk-adjusted probabilities $\tilde{P}_1, \tilde{P}_2$ and work with "synthetic" expectations that satisfy

$$\frac{1}{(1+r)} E^{\tilde{P}}[S(t+1)] = S(t) \tag{35}$$

$$\frac{1}{(1+r)} E^{\tilde{P}}[C(t+1)] = C(t). \tag{36}$$

These equations are very convenient to use, and they internalize any risk premiums. Indeed, one does not need to calculate the risk premiums if one uses synthetic expectations. The corresponding discounting is done using the risk-free rate, which is easily observable.

---

[10] For negative beta assets, the inequalities are reversed.

3.4 Martingales and Submartingales

This is the right time to introduce a concept that is at the foundation of pricing financial assets. We give a simple definition of the terms and leave technicalities for later chapters.

Suppose at time t one has information summarized by I_t. A random variable X_t that satisfies the equality

$$E^P\left[X_{t+s}|I_t\right] = X_t \qquad \text{for all } s > 0, \tag{37}$$

is called a *martingale with respect to the probability P*.[11]

If instead we have

$$E^Q\left[X_{t+s}|I_t\right] \geq X_t \qquad \text{for all } s > 0, \tag{38}$$

then X_t is called a *submartingale* with respect to probability Q.

Here is why these concepts are fundamental.

According to the discussion in the previous section, asset prices discounted by the risk-free rate will be submartingales under the true probabilities, but become martingales under the risk-adjusted probabilities. Thus, as long as we utilize the latter, the tools available to martingale theory become applicable, and "fair market values" of the assets under consideration can be obtained by exploiting the martingale equality

$$X_t = E^{\tilde{P}}\left[X_{t+s}|I_t\right], \tag{39}$$

where $s > 0$, and where X_{t+s} is defined by

$$X_{t+s} = \frac{1}{(1+r)^s}S_{t+s}. \tag{40}$$

Here S_{t+s} and r are the security price and risk-free return, respectively. $\tilde{P}$ is the risk-adjusted probability. According to this, utilization of risk-adjusted probabilities will convert *all* (discounted) asset prices into martingales.

3.5 Equalization of Rates of Return

In fact, by using risk-adjusted probabilities we can derive another important result useful in asset pricing.

In the arbitrage-free representation given in (10), divide both sides of the equality by the current price of the asset and multiply both sides by

---

[11]There are other conditions that a martingale must satisfy. In later chapters we discuss them in detail. In the meantime, we assume implicitly that these conditional expectations exist—that is, they are finite.

$(1+r)$, the gross rate of riskless return. Assuming nonzero asset prices, we obtain

$$\tilde{P}_1 \frac{S_1(t+1)}{S(t)} + \tilde{P}_2 \frac{S_2(t+1)}{S(t)} = (1+r) \tag{41}$$

$$\tilde{P}_1 \frac{C_1(t+1)}{C(t)} + \tilde{P}_2 \frac{C_2(t+1)}{C(t)} = (1+r). \tag{42}$$

First note that ratios such as

$$\frac{S_1(t+1)}{S(t)}, \quad \frac{S_2(t+1)}{S(t)} \tag{43}$$

are the gross rates of return of $S(t)$ in states 1 and 2, respectively. The equalities (41) and (42) imply that if one uses $\tilde{P}_1, \tilde{P}_2$ in calculating the expected values, all assets would have the same expected return. According to this new result, "under $\tilde{P}_1, \tilde{P}_2$" all expected returns equal the risk-free return r.[12]

This is another widely used result in pricing financial assets.

4 A Numerical Example

A simple example needs to be discussed. Let the current value of a stock be given by

$$S_t = 100. \tag{44}$$

The stock can assume only two possible values in the next instant:

$$S(t+1) = 100 \tag{45}$$

and

$$S(t+1) = 150. \tag{46}$$

Hence, there are only *two* states of the world.

There is a call option with premium C, and strike price 100. The option expires next period.

Finally, it is assumed that 1 unit of account is invested in the risk-free asset with a return of 10%.

---

[12]In probability theory, the term "under $\tilde{P}_1, \tilde{P}_2$," means "if one uses the probabilities $\tilde{P}_1$ and $\tilde{P}_2$."

We obtain the following representation under no arbitrage:

$$
\begin{pmatrix} 1 \\ 100 \\ C \end{pmatrix} = \begin{pmatrix} 1.1 & 1.1 \\ 100 & 150 \\ 0 & 50 \end{pmatrix} \begin{pmatrix} \psi_1 \\ \psi_2 \end{pmatrix}. \tag{47}
$$

Note that the numerical value of the call premium C is left unspecified. Using this as a variable, we intend to show the role played by ψ_i in the arbitrage theorem.

4.1 Case 1: Arbitrage Possibilities

Multiplying the dividend matrix with the vector of ψ_i's yields three equations:

$$
1 = (1.1)\psi_1 + (1.1)\psi_2 \tag{48}
$$
$$
100 = 100\psi_1 + 150\psi_2 \tag{49}
$$
$$
C = 0\psi_1 + 50\psi_2. \tag{50}
$$

Now suppose a premium $C = 25$ is observed in financial markets. Then the last equation yields

$$
50\psi_2 = 25 \tag{51}
$$

or

$$
\psi_2 = \frac{1}{2}. \tag{52}
$$

Substituting this in (49) gives

$$
\psi_1 = .25. \tag{53}
$$

But at these values of ψ_1 and ψ_2, the first equation is not satisfied:

$$
1.1(.25) + 1.1(1.5) \neq 1. \tag{54}
$$

Clearly, at the observed value for the call premium, $C = 25$, it is impossible to find ψ_1, ψ_2 that satisfies all three equations given by the arbitrage-free representation.

There are arbitrage opportunities.

4.2 Case 2: Arbitrage-Free Prices

Consider the same system as before

$$
\begin{pmatrix} 1 \\ 100 \\ C \end{pmatrix} = \begin{pmatrix} 1.1 & 1.1 \\ 100 & 150 \\ 0 & 50 \end{pmatrix} \begin{pmatrix} \psi_1 \\ \psi_2 \end{pmatrix}. \tag{55}
$$

However, instead of starting with an observed value of C, solve the first two equations for ψ_1, ψ_2. These form a system of two equations in two unknowns. The unique solution gives

$$
\psi_1 = .7273, \qquad \psi_2 = .1818. \tag{56}
$$

Now use the third equation to calculate a value of C consistent with this solution:

$$
C = 9.09. \tag{57}
$$

At this price, arbitrage profits do not exist.

Note that using the constants ψ_1, ψ_2, we *derived* the arbitrage-free price $C = 9.09$. In this sense, we used the arbitrage theorem as an asset-pricing tool.

It turns out that in this particular case, the representation given by the arbitrage theorem is satisfied with positive and unique ψ_i. This may not always be true.

4.3 An Indeterminacy

The same method of determining the unique arbitrage-free value of the call option would not work if there were more than two states of the world. For example, consider the system

$$
\begin{pmatrix} 1 \\ 100 \\ C \end{pmatrix} = \begin{pmatrix} 1.1 & 1.1 & 1.1 \\ 100 & 50 & 150 \\ 0 & 0 & 50 \end{pmatrix} \begin{pmatrix} \psi_1 \\ \psi_2 \\ \psi_3 \end{pmatrix}. \tag{58}
$$

Here, the first two equations cannot be used to determine a *unique* set of $\psi_i > 0$ that can be plugged into the third equation to obtain a C. There are many such sets of ψ_i's.

In order to determine the arbitrage-free value of the call premium C, one would need to select the "correct" ψ_i. This can be done using the underlying economic equilibrium.

5 An Application: Lattice Models

Simple as it is, the example just discussed gives the logic behind one of the most common asset pricing methods, namely the so-called *lattice models*.[13] The binomial model is the simplest example.

We briefly show how this pricing methodology uses the results of arbitrage theorem.

Consider a call option C_t written on the underlying asset S_t. The call option has strike price C_0 and expires at time T, $t < T$. It is known that at expiration the value of the option is given by

$$C_T = \max[S_T - C_0, 0].\qquad(59)$$

We first divide the time interval $(T - t)$ into n smaller intervals, each of size Δ. We choose a "small" Δ, in the sense that the variations of S_t during Δ can be approximated reasonably well by an *up* or *down* movement only. That is, we hope that for small enough Δ the underlying asset price S_t cannot wander too far from the currently observed price S_t.

Accordingly, we assume that during Δ the only possible changes in S_t are an *up* movement by $\sigma\sqrt{\Delta}$ or a *down* movement by $-\sigma\sqrt{\Delta}$:

$$S_{t+\Delta} = \begin{cases} S_t + \sigma\sqrt{\Delta} \\ S_t - \sigma\sqrt{\Delta} \end{cases}.\qquad(60)$$

Clearly, the size of the parameter σ determines how far $S_{t+\Delta}$ can wander during a time interval of length Δ. For that reason it is called the *volatility* parameter. Note that regardless of σ, in smaller intervals, S_t will change less. The σ is known.

The dynamics described by Equation (60) represents a *lattice* or a *binomial tree*. Figure 1 displays these dynamics in the case of *multiplicative* up and down movements.

Suppose now that we are given the risk-free rate r for the period Δ. Can we determine the risk-adjusted probabilities?

We know from arbitrage theorem that the risk-adjusted probabilities $\tilde{P}_{up}$ and $\tilde{P}_{down}$ must satisfy

$$S_t = \frac{1}{1+r}\left[\tilde{P}_{up}(S_t + \sigma\sqrt{\Delta}) + \tilde{P}_{down}(S_t - \sigma\sqrt{\Delta})\right].\qquad(61)$$

In this equation, r, S_t, σ, and Δ are known. The first two are observed in the markets, while Δ is selected by us. Thus, the only unknown is the $\tilde{P}_{up}$, which can be determined easily.[14]

---

[13] Also called *tree models*.

[14] Remember that $\tilde{P}_{down} = 1 - \tilde{P}_{up}$.

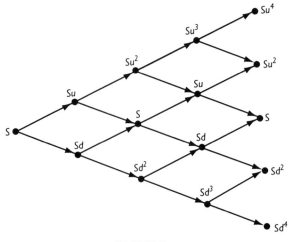

FIGURE 1

Once this is done, the $\tilde{P}_{up}$ can be used to calculate the current arbitrage-free value of the call option. In fact, the equation

$$C_t = \frac{1}{(1+r)}\left[\tilde{P}_{up}C^{up}_{t+\Delta} + \tilde{P}_{down}C^{down}_{t+\Delta}\right] \qquad (62)$$

"ties" two (arbitrage-free) values of the call option at any time $t + \Delta$ to the (arbitrage-free) value of the option as of time t. The P_{up} is known at this point. In order to make the equation usable, we need the two values $C^{up}_{t+\Delta}$ and $C^{down}_{t+\Delta}$. Given these, one could indeed calculate the value of the call option C_t at time t.

Figure 2 shows the multiplicative lattice for the option price C_t. The arbitrage-free values of C_t are at this point indeterminate, except for the expiration "nodes." In fact, given the lattice for S_t, we can determine the values of C_t at the expiration using the *boundary condition*

$$C_T = \max\left[S_T - C_0, 0\right]. \qquad (63)$$

Once this is done, one can go *backward* using

$$C_t = \frac{1}{(1+r)}\left[\tilde{P}_{up}C^{up}_{t+\Delta} + \tilde{P}_{down}C^{down}_{t+\Delta}\right]. \qquad (64)$$

Repeating this several times, one eventually reaches the initial node that gives the current value of the option.

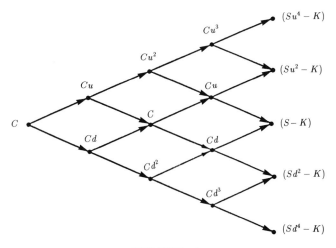

$$\text{FIGURE} \quad 2$$

Hence, the procedure is to use the dynamics of S_t to go *forward* and determine the expiration date values of the call option. Then, using the risk-adjusted probabilities, one works *backward* with the lattice for the call option to determine the current value C_t.

It is the arbitrage theorem and the implied martingale equalities that make it possible to calculate the risk-adjusted probabilities $\tilde{P}_{up}$ and $\tilde{P}_{down}$.

In this procedure Figure 1 gives an approximation of all the possible paths that S_t may take during the period $T - t$. The tree in Figure 2 gives an approximation of all possible paths that can be taken by the price of the call option written on S_t. If Δ is small, then the lattices will be close approximations to the true paths followed by S_t and C_t.

6 Some Generalizations

Up to this point the setup has been very simple. In general, such simple examples cannot be used to price real-life financial assets. Let us briefly consider some generalizations that are needed to do so.

6.1 Time Index

Up to this point we considered discrete time with $t = 1, 2, 3, \ldots$. In continuous-time asset pricing models, this will change. We have to assume that t is continuous:

$$t \in [0, \infty). \tag{65}$$

This way, in addition to the "small" time interval Δ dealt with in this chapter, we can consider *infinitesimal* intervals denoted by the symbol dt.

6.2 States of the World

In continuous time, the values that an asset can assume are not limited to two. There may be *uncountably many* possibilities and a continuum of states of the world.

To capture such generalizations, we need to introduce *stochastic differential equations*. For example, increments in security prices S_t may be modeled using

$$dS_t = \mu_t S_t \, dt + \sigma_t S_t \, dW_t, \qquad (66)$$

where the symbol dS_t represents an infinitesimal change in the price of the security, the $\mu_t S_t \, dt$ is the predicted movement during an infinitesimal interval dt, and $\sigma_t S_t \, dW_t$ is an unpredictable, infinitesimal random shock.

It is obvious that most of the concepts used in defining stochastic differential equations need to be developed step by step.

6.3 Discounting

Using continuous-time models leads to a change in the way *discounting* is done. In fact, if t is continuous, then the discount factor for an interval of length Δ will be given by the *exponential function*

$$e^{-r\Delta}. \qquad (67)$$

The r becomes the continuously compounded interest rate.

7 Conclusions: A Methodology for Pricing Assets

The arbitrage theorem provides a powerful methodology for determining fair market values of financial assets in practice. The major steps of this methodology as applied to financial derivatives can be summarized as follows:

1. Obtain a (approximate) model to track the dynamics of the underlying asset's price.
2. Calculate how the derivative asset price relates to the price of the underlying asset *at expiration* or at other *boundaries.*
3. Obtain risk-adjusted probabilities.
4. Calculate expected payoffs of derivatives *at expiration* using these risk-adjusted probabilities.

5. Discount this expectation using risk-free return.

In order to be able to apply this pricing methodology, one needs familiarity with the following types of mathematical tools.

First, the notion of time needs to be defined carefully. Tools for handling changes in asset prices during "infinitesimal" time periods must be developed. This requires *continuous-time analysis.*

Second, we need to handle the notion of "randomness" during such infinitesimal periods. Concepts such as probability, expectation, average value, and volatility during infinitesimal periods need to be carefully defined. This requires the study of the so-called *stochastic calculus.* We try to discuss the intuition behind the assumptions that lead to major results in stochastic calculus.

Third, we need to understand how to obtain risk-adjusted probabilities and how to determine the correct discounting factor. The *Girsanov theorem* states the conditions under which such risk-adjusted probabilities can be used. The theorem also gives the form of these probability distributions.

The notion of *martingales* is essential to Girsanov theorem, and consequently to the understanding of the "risk-neutral" world.

Finally, there is the question of how to relate the movements of various quantities to each other over time. In standard calculus, this is done using differential equations. In a random environment, the equivalent concept is a *stochastic differential equation* (SDE).

Needless to say, in order to attack these topics in turn, one must have some notion of the well-known concepts and results of "standard" calculus. There are basically three: (1) the notion of derivative, (2) the notion of integral, and (3) the Taylor series expansion.

8 References

In this chapter arbitrage theorem was treated in a simple way. Ingersoll (1987) provides a much more detailed treatment that would be quite accessible even to a beginner. Readers with a strong quantitative background may prefer Duffie (1996). The original article by Harrison and Kreps (1979) may also be consulted. Other related material can be found in Harrison and Pliska (1981).

9 Appendix: Generalization of the Arbitrage Theorem

According to the arbitrage theorem, if there are no arbitrage possibilities, then there are "supporting" state prices, $\{\psi_i\}$ such that each asset's price today equals a linear combination of possible future values. The theorem is also true in reverse. If there are such (supporting) state prices then there are no arbitrage opportunities.

In this section we state the general form of the arbitrage theorem. First we briefly define the underlying symbols.

- Define a matrix of payoffs, D:

$$D_t = \begin{pmatrix} d_{11} & \cdots & d_{1K} \\ \vdots & \vdots & \vdots \\ d_{N1} & \cdots & d_{NK} \end{pmatrix}. \tag{68}$$

N is the total number of securities and K is the total number of states of the world.

- Now define a *portfolio*, θ, as the vector of commitments to each asset:

$$\theta = \begin{pmatrix} \theta_1 \\ \vdots \\ \theta_N \end{pmatrix}. \tag{69}$$

In dealer's terminology, θ gives the *positions* taken at a certain time. Multiplying the θ by S_t, we obtain the value of portfolio θ:

$$S_t'\theta = \sum_{i=1}^{N} S_i(t)\theta_i. \tag{70}$$

This is total investment in portfolio θ at time t.

- Payoff to portfolio θ in state j is $\sum_{i=1}^{N} d_{ij}\theta_i$.[15]
  In matrix form this is expressed as

$$D'\theta = \begin{pmatrix} d_{11} & \cdots & d_{N1} \\ \vdots & \vdots & \vdots \\ d_{1K} & \cdots & d_{NK} \end{pmatrix} \begin{pmatrix} \theta_1 \\ \vdots \\ \theta_N \end{pmatrix}. \tag{71}$$

- We can now define an *arbitrage portfolio:*

---

[15]Note the difference between summation with respect to i and summation with respect to j.

DEFINITION: θ is an arbitrage portfolio, or simply an arbitrage, if either one of the following conditions is satisfied:

1. $S'\theta \leq 0$ and $D'\theta > 0$
2. $S'\theta < 0$ and $D'\theta \geq 0$.

According to this, the portfolio θ guarantees some positive return in all states, yet it costs nothing to purchase. Or it guarantees a nonnegative return while having a negative cost today.

The following theorem is the generalization of the arbitrage conditions discussed earlier.

THEOREM:

1. If there are no arbitrage opportunities, then there exists a $\psi > 0$ such that

$$S = D\psi. \tag{72}$$

2. If the condition in (1) is true, then there are no arbitrage opportunities.

This means that in an arbitrage-free world there exists ψ_i such that

$$\begin{pmatrix} S_1 \\ \vdots \\ S_N \end{pmatrix} = \begin{pmatrix} d_{11} & \cdots & d_{1K} \\ \vdots & \vdots & \vdots \\ d_{N1} & \cdots & d_{NK} \end{pmatrix} \begin{pmatrix} \psi_1 \\ \vdots \\ \psi_K \end{pmatrix}. \tag{73}$$

Note that according to the theorem we must have

$$\psi_i > 0 \text{ for all } i$$

if each state under consideration has a nonzero probability of occurrence.

Now suppose we consider a special type of return matrix where

$$D = \begin{pmatrix} 1 & \cdots & 1 \\ d_{21} & \cdots & d_{2K} \\ \vdots & \vdots & \vdots \\ d_{N1} & \cdots & d_{NK} \end{pmatrix}. \tag{74}$$

In this matrix D, the first row is constant and equals 1. This implies that the return for the first asset is the same no matter which state of the world is realized. So, the first security is riskless.

Using the arbitrage theorem, and multiplying the first row of D with the state price vector ψ, we obtain

$$S_1 = \psi_1 + \ldots + \psi_K, \tag{75}$$

or defining

$$\sum_{i=1}^{K} \psi_i = \psi_0. \tag{76}$$

The ψ_0 is the *discount in riskless borrowing*.

CHAPTER 3

Calculus in Deterministic and Stochastic Environments

1 Introduction

The mathematics of derivative assets assumes that time passes continuously. As a result, new information is revealed continuously, and decision-makers may face instantaneous changes in randomness.[1] Hence, technical tools for pricing derivative products require ways of handling random variables over infinitesimal time intervals. The mathematics of such random variables is known as *stochastic calculus.*

Stochastic calculus is an internally consistent set of operational rules that are different from the tools of "standard" calculus in some fundamental ways.

At the outset, stochastic calculus may appear too abstract to be of any use to a practitioner. This first impression is not correct. Continuous time finance is both *simpler* and *richer*. Once a market participant gets some practice, it is easier to work with continuous-time tools than their discrete-time equivalents.

In fact, sometimes there are no equivalent results in discrete time. In this sense stochastic calculus offers a wider variety of tools to the financial analyst. For example, continuous time permits infinitesimal adjustments in portfolio weights. This way, replicating "nonlinear" assets with "simple" portfolios becomes possible. In order to *replicate* an option, the underlying

---

[1] "New" is used here in the sense of being "unpredictable."

asset and risk-free borrowing may be used. Such an *exact* replication will be impossible in discrete time.[2]

1.1 Information Flows

It may be argued that the manner in which information flows in financial markets is more consistent with stochastic calculus than with "standard calculus."

For example, the relevant "time interval" may be different on different trading days. During some days an analyst may face more volatile markets, in others less. Changing volatility may require changing the basic "observation period," i.e., the Δ of the previous chapter.

Also, numerical methods used in pricing securities are costly in terms of computer time. Hence, the pace of activity may make the analyst choose coarser or finer time intervals depending on the level of volatility. Such approximations can best be accomplished using random variables defined over continuous time. The tools of stochastic calculus will be needed to define these models.

1.2 Modeling Random Behavior

A more technical advantage of stochastic calculus is that a complicated random variable can have a very simple structure in continuous time, once the attention is focused on infinitesimal intervals. For example, if the time period under consideration is denoted by dt, and if dt is "infinitesimal," then asset prices may safely be assumed to have two likely movements: uptick or downtick.

Under some conditions, such a "binomial" structure may be a good approximation to reality during an infinitesimal interval dt, but not necessarily in a large "discrete time" interval denoted by Δ.[3]

Finally, the main tool of stochastic calculus—namely, the Ito integral—may be more appropriate to use in financial markets than the Riemann integral used in standard calculus.

These are some reasons behind developing a new calculus. Before doing this, however, a review of standard calculus will be helpful. After all, although the rules of stochastic calculus are different, the reasons for developing such rules are the same as in standard calculus:

---

[2]Unless, of course, the underlying state space is itself discrete. This would be the case when the underlying asset price can assume only a finite number of possible values in the future.

[3]A binomial random variable can assume one of the two possible values, and it may be significantly easier to work with them than with, say, a random variable that may assume any one of an uncountable number of possible values.

• We would like to calculate the response of one variable to a (random) change in another variable. That is to say, we would like to be able to *differentiate* various functions of interest.

• We would like to calculate sums of random increments that are of interest to us. This leads to the notion of (stochastic) *integral*.

• We would like to *approximate* an arbitrary function by using simpler functions. This leads us to (stochastic) Taylor series approximations.

• Finally, we would like to model the dynamic behavior of continuous-time random variables. This leads to *stochastic differential equations.*

2 Some Tools of Standard Calculus

In this section we review the major concepts of *standard* (deterministic) calculus. Even if the reader is familiar with elementary concepts of standard calculus discussed here, it may still be worthwhile to go over the examples in this section. The examples are devised to highlight exactly those points at which standard calculus will fail to be a good approximation in case underlying variables are stochastic.

3 Functions

Suppose A and B are two sets, and let f be a rule which associates to every element x of A, exactly one element y in B.[4] Such a rule is called a *function* or a *mapping*. In mathematical analysis, functions are denoted by

$$f : A \to B \qquad (1)$$

or by

$$y = f(x), \qquad x \in A. \qquad (2)$$

If the set B is made of real numbers, then we say that f is a *real-valued function* and write

$$f : A \to R. \qquad (3)$$

If the sets A and B are themselves collections of functions, then f transforms a function into another function, and is called an *operator.*

Most readers will be familiar with the standard notion of functions. Fewer readers may have had exposure to *random* functions.

---

[4]The set A is called the *domain*, and the set B is called the *range* of f.

3.1 Random Functions

In the function

$$y = f(x), \qquad x \in A, \tag{4}$$

once the value of x is given, we get the element y. Often y is assumed to be a *real number*. Now consider the following significant alteration.

There is a set W where $w \in W$ denotes a *state of the world*. The function f depends on $x \in R$, *and* on $w \in W$:

$$f : R \times W \to R \tag{5}$$

or

$$y = f(x, w), \qquad x \in R, w \in W, \tag{6}$$

where the notation $R \times W$ implies that one has to "plug in" to $f(\cdot)$ two variables, one from the set W, and the other from R.

The function $f(x, w)$ has the following property: Given a $w \in W$, the $f(\cdot, w)$ becomes a function of x only. Thus, for different values of $w \in W$ we get different functions of x. Two such cases are shown in Figure 1. $f(x, w_1)$ and $f(x, w_2)$ are two functions of x that are different because the second element w is different.

When x represents time, we can interpret $f(x, w_1)$ and $f(x, w_2)$ as two different *trajectories* that depend on different states of the world.

Hence, if w represents the underlying randomness, the function $f(x, w)$ can be called a *random function*. Another name for random functions is

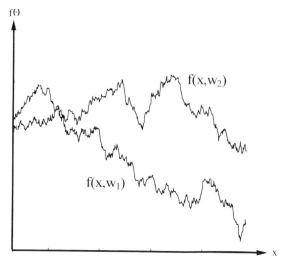

FIGURE 1

stochastic processes. With stochastic processes, x will represent time, and we often limit our attention to the set $x \geq 0$.

Note this fundamental point. Randomness of a stochastic process is in terms of the trajectory as a whole, rather than a particular value at a specific point in time. In other words, the random drawing is done from a collection of trajectories. Choosing the state of the world w determines the complete trajectory.

3.2 Examples of Functions

There are some important functions that play special roles in our discussion. We will briefly review them.

3.2.1 The Exponential Function
The infinite sum

$$1 + \frac{1}{2!} + \frac{1}{3!} + \cdots + \frac{1}{n!} + \cdots \tag{7}$$

converges to an irrational number between 2 and 3 as $n \to \infty$. This number is denoted by the letter e. The *exponential function* is obtained by raising e to a power of x:

$$y = e^x, \qquad x \in R. \tag{8}$$

This function is generally used in discounting asset prices in continuous time.

The exponential function has a number of important properties. It is infinitely differentiable. That is to say, the following operation can be repeated infinitely:

$$\frac{dy}{dx} = e^{f(x)} \frac{df(x)}{dx}. \tag{9}$$

The exponential function also has an interesting multiplicative property:

$$e^x e^z = e^{x+z}. \tag{10}$$

Finally, if x is a random variable, then $y = e^x$ will be random as well.

3.2.2 The Logarithmic Function
The logarithmic function is defined as the inverse of the exponential function. Given

$$y = e^x, \qquad x \in R, \tag{11}$$

the natural logarithm of y is given by

$$\log_e(y) = x, \qquad y > 0. \tag{12}$$

A practitioner may sometimes work with the logarithm of asset prices. Note that while y is always positive, there is no such restriction on x. Hence, the logarithm of an asset price may extend from minus to plus infinity.

3.2.3 Functions of Bounded Variation

The following construction will be used several times during later chapters.

Suppose a time interval is given by $[0, T]$. We *partition* this interval into n subintervals by selecting the t_i, $i = 1, \ldots, n$, as

$$0 = t_0 \leq t_1 \leq t_2 \leq \cdots \leq t_n = T. \tag{13}$$

The $[t_i - t_{i-1}]$ represents the length of the ith subinterval.

Now consider a function of time $f(t)$, defined on the interval $[0, T]$:

$$f:[0, T] \rightarrow R. \tag{14}$$

We form the sum

$$\sum_{i=1}^{n} |f(t_i) - f(t_{i-1})|. \tag{15}$$

This is the sum of the absolute values of all changes in $f(\cdot)$ from one t_i to the next.

Clearly for each partition of the interval $[0, T]$, we can form such a sum. Given that uncountably many partitions are possible, the sum can assume uncountably many values. If these sums are bounded from above, the function $f(\cdot)$ is said to be of *bounded variation*. Thus, bounded variation implies

$$V_0 = \max \sum_{i=1}^{n} |f(t_i) - f(t_{i-1})| < \infty, \tag{16}$$

where the maximum is taken over all possible partitions of the interval $[0, T]$. In this sense, V_0 is the maximum of all possible variations in $f(\cdot)$, and it is finite.

The V_0 is called *total variation* of f on $[0, T]$.

Heuristically speaking, functions of bounded variation are not excessively "irregular." In fact, any "smooth" function will be of bounded variation.[5]

---

[5]It can be shown that if a function has a derivative everywhere on $[0, T]$, then the function is of bounded variation.

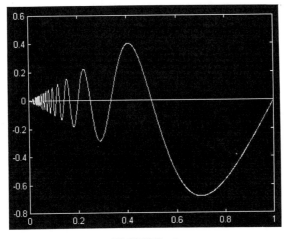

FIGURE 2

3.2.4 An Example
Consider the function

$$f(t) = \begin{cases} t\sin\left(\dfrac{\pi}{t}\right) & \text{when } 0 < t \le 1 \\ 0 & \text{when } t = 0 \end{cases} \tag{17}$$

It can be shown that $f(t)$ is not of bounded variation.[6]

That this is the case is shown in Figure 2. Note that as $t \to 0$, f becomes excessively "irregular."

The concept of bounded variation will play an important role in our discussions later. One reason is the following: asset prices in continuous time will have some unpredictable part. No matter how finely we slice the time interval, they will still be partially unpredictable. But this means that trajectories of asset prices will have to be very irregular.

As will be seen later, continuous-time processes that we use to represent asset prices have trajectories with unbounded variation.

---

[6]To show this formally, choose the partition

$$0, < \frac{2}{2n+1} < \frac{2}{2n-1} < \cdots < \frac{2}{5} < \frac{2}{3} < 1. \tag{18}$$

Then the variation is

$$\sum_{i=1}^{n} |f(t_i) - f(t_{i-1})| = 4\left[\frac{1}{3} + \frac{1}{5} + \frac{1}{7} + \cdots + \frac{1}{2n+1}\right]. \tag{19}$$

The right-hand side of this equality can be made arbitrarily large as $n \to \infty$.

4 Convergence and Limit

Suppose we are given a *sequence*

$$x_0, x_1, x_2, \ldots, x_n, \ldots, \tag{20}$$

where x_n represents an object that changes as n is increased. This "object" can be a sequence of numbers, a sequence of functions, or a sequence of operations. The essential point is that we are observing successive versions of x_n.

The notion of *convergence* of a sequence has to do with the "eventual" value of x_n as $n \to \infty$. In the case where x_n represents real numbers, we can state this more formally:

DEFINITION: We say that a sequence of real numbers x_n converges to $x^* < \infty$ if for arbitrary $\epsilon > 0$, there exists a $N < \infty$ such that

$$|x_n - x^*| < \epsilon \qquad \text{for all} \quad n > N. \tag{21}$$

We call x^* the *limit* of x_n.

In words, x_n converges to x^* if x_n stays arbitrarily close to the point x^* after a finite number of steps. Two important questions can be asked.

Can we deal with convergence of x_n if these were *random* variables, instead of being deterministic numbers? This question is relevant, since a random number x_n can conceivably assume an extreme value and suddenly may fall very far from any x^* even if $n > N$.

Secondly, since one can define different measures of "closeness," we should in principle be able to define convergence in different ways as well. Are these definitions all equivalent?

We will answer these questions later. However, convergence is clearly a very important concept in approximating a quantity that does not easily lend itself to direct calculation. For example, we may want to define the notion of integral as the limit of a sequence.

4.1 The Derivative

The notion of the derivative[7] can be looked at in (at least) two different ways. First of all, the derivative is a way of dealing with the "smoothness" of functions. It is a way of defining *rates* of change of variables under consideration. In particular, if trajectories of asset prices are "too irregular," then their derivative with respect to time may not exist.

---

[7]The reader should not confuse the mathematical operation of differentiation or taking a *derivative* with the term "derivative securities" used in finance.

Second, the derivative is a way of calculating how one variable *responds* to a change in another variable. For example, given a change in the price of the underlying asset, we may want to know how the market value of an option written on it may move. These types of derivatives are usually taken using the *chain rule*.

The derivative is a *rate* of change. But it is a rate of change for infinitesimal movements. We give a formal definition first.

DEFINITION: Let

$$y = f(x) \tag{22}$$

be a function of $x \in R$. Then the derivative of $f(x)$ with respect to x, if it exists, is formally denoted by the symbol f_x and is given by

$$f_x = \lim_{\Delta \to 0} \frac{f(x + \Delta) - f(x)}{\Delta}, \tag{23}$$

where Δ is an increment in x.

The variable x can represent any real-life phenomenon. Suppose it represents *time*.[8] Then Δ would correspond to a finite time interval. The $f(x)$ would be the value of y at time x, and the $f(x + \Delta)$ would represent the value of y at time $x + \Delta$. Hence, the numerator in (23) is the change in y during a time interval Δ. The ratio itself becomes the *rate of change* in y during the same interval. For example, if y is the price of a certain asset at time x, the ratio in (23) would represent the rate at which the price changes during an interval Δ.

Why is a limit being taken in (23)? In defining the derivative, the limit has a practical use. It is taken to make the ratio in (23) independent of the size of Δ, the time interval that passes.

For making the ratio independent of the size of Δ, one pays a price. The derivative is defined for *infinitesimal* intervals. For larger intervals, the derivative becomes an *approximation* that deteriorates as Δ gets larger and larger.

4.1.1 Example: The Exponential Function
As an example of derivatives, consider the exponential function:

$$f(x) = Ae^{rx}, \qquad x \in R. \tag{24}$$

---

[8]Note that time is one of the few deterministic variables one can imagine.

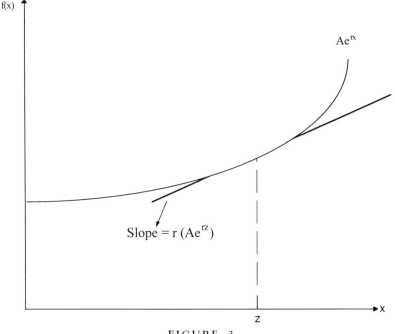

FIGURE 3

A graph of this function with $r > 0$ is shown in Figure 3. Taking the derivative with respect to x formally:

$$f_x = \frac{df(x)}{dx} = r[Ae^{rx}]$$

(25)

$$= rf(x).$$

The quantity f_x is the rate of change of $f(x)$ at point x. Note that as x gets larger, the term e^{rx} increases. This can be seen in Figure 3 from the increasing growth the $f(\cdot)$ exhibits. The ratio

$$\frac{f_x}{f(x)} = r$$

(26)

is the *percentage* rate of change. In particular, we see that an exponential function has a constant percentage rate of change with respect to x.

4.1.2 Example: The Derivative as an Approximation

To see an example of how derivatives can be used in approximations, consider the following argument.

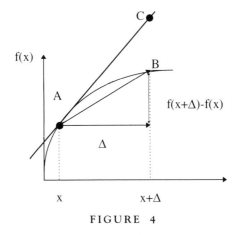

FIGURE 4

Let Δ be a finite interval. Then using the the definition of derivative in (23), and note that if Δ is "small," we can write approximately

$$f(x + \Delta) \simeq f(x) + f_x \cdot \Delta. \qquad (27)$$

This equality means that the value assumed by $f(\cdot)$ at point $x + \Delta$, can be approximated by the value of $f(\cdot)$ at point x, *plus* the derivative f_x multiplied by Δ. Note that when one does not know the *exact* value of $f(x + \Delta)$, the knowledge of $f(x)$, f_x, and Δ is sufficient to obtain an approximation.[9]

This result is shown in Figure 4, where the ratio

$$\frac{f(x + \Delta) - f(x)}{\Delta} \qquad (28)$$

represents the slope of the segment denoted by AB. As Δ becomes smaller and smaller, with A fixed, the segment AB converges towards the tangent at the point A. Hence, the derivative f_x is the slope of this tangent.

When we add the product $f_x \Delta$ to $f(x)$ we obtain the point C. This point can be taken as an approximation of B. Whether this will be a "good" or a "bad" approximation depends on the size of Δ and on the shape of the function $f(\cdot)$.

Two simple examples will illustrate these points. First consider Figure 5. Here Δ is large. As expected, the approximation $f(x) + f_x \cdot \Delta$ is not very near $f(x + \Delta)$.

---

[9]If x represents time, and if x is the "present" then $f(x + \Delta)$ will belong to the "future." However, $f(x)$, f_x, and Δ are all quantities that relate to the "present." In this sense, they can be used for obtaining a crude "prediction" of $f(x + \Delta)$ in real time. This prediction requires having a numerical value for f_x, the value of the derivative at the point x.

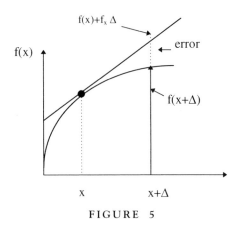

FIGURE   5

Figure 6 illustrates a more relevant example. We consider a function $f(\cdot)$ that is not very smooth. The approximating $\hat{f}(x + \Delta)$ obtained from

$$\hat{f}(x + \Delta) \simeq f(x) + f_x \cdot \Delta \tag{29}$$

may end up being a very unsatisfactory approximation to the true $f(x + \Delta)$. Clearly, the more "irregular" the function $f(\cdot)$ becomes, the more such approximations are likely to fail.

Consider an extreme case in the next example.

4.1.3 Example: High Variation

Consider Figure 7, where the function $f(x)$ is continuous, but exhibits extreme variations even in small intervals Δ. Here, not only is the prediction

$$f(x + \Delta) \simeq f(x) + f_x \cdot \Delta \tag{30}$$

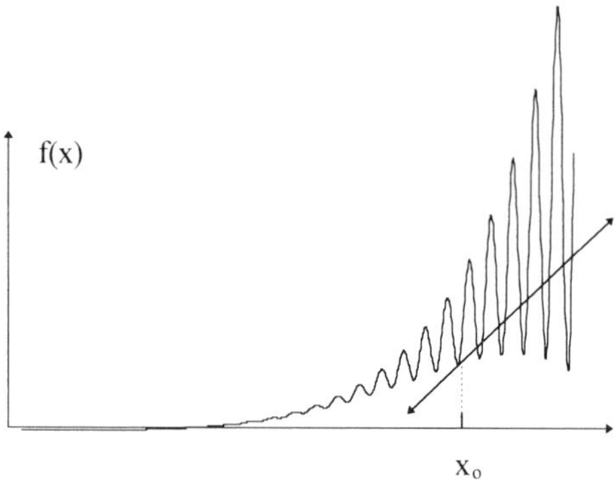

FIGURE   6

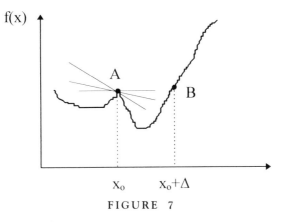

FIGURE 7

likely to fail, but even a satisfactory definition of f_x may not be obtained. Take, for example, the point x_0. What is the rate of change of the function $f(x)$ at the point x_0? It is difficult to answer. Indeed, one can draw many tangents with differing slopes to $f(x)$ at that particular point.

It appears that the function $f(x)$ is not differentiable.

4.2 The Chain Rule

The second use of the derivative is the chain rule. In the examples discussed earlier, $f(x)$ was a function of x, and x was assumed to represent the time. The derivative was introduced as the response of a variable to a variation in time.

In pricing derivative securities, we face a somewhat different problem. The price of a derivative asset, e.g., a call option, will depend on the price of the underlying asset, and the price of the underlying asset depends on time.[10]

Hence, there is a chain effect. Time passes, new (small) events occur, the price of the underlying asset changes, and this affects the derivative asset's price. In standard calculus, the tool used to analyze these sorts of chain effects is known as the "chain rule."

Suppose in the example just given x was not itself the time, but a deterministic function of time, denoted by the symbol $t \geq 0$:

$$x_t = g(t). \tag{31}$$

---

[10]Note that as time passes, the expiration date of a contract comes closer, and even if the underlying asset's price remains constant, price of the call option will fall.

Then the function $f(\cdot)$ is called a *composite function* and is expressed as

$$y_t = f(g(t)). \tag{32}$$

The question is how to obtain a formula that gives the ultimate effect of a change in t on the y_t?

In standard calculus the chain rule is defined as follows.

DEFINITION: For f and g defined as above we have

$$\frac{dy}{dt} = \frac{df(g(t))}{dg(t)} \frac{dg(t)}{dt}. \tag{33}$$

According to this, the chain rule is the product of two derivatives. First, the derivative of $f(g(t))$ is taken with respect to $g(t)$. Second, the derivative of $g(t)$ is taken with respect to t. The final effect of t on y_t is then equal to the product of these two expressions.

The chain rule is a useful tool in approximating the responses of one variable to changes in other variables.

Take the case of derivative asset prices. A trader observes the price of the underlying asset continuously and wants to know how the valuation of the complex derivative products written on this asset would change. If the derivative is an exchange-traded product, these changes can be observed from the markets directly.[11] However, if the derivative is a "structured" product, its valuation needs to be calculated in-house, using theoretical pricing models. These pricing models will use some tool such as the "chain rule" shown in (33).

In the example just given, $f(x)$ was a function of x_t, and x_t was a deterministic variable. There was no randomness associated with x_t. What would happen if x_t is random, or if the function $f(\cdot)$ depends on some random variable z_t as well? In other words,

1. Can we still use the *same* chain rule formula?
2. How does the chain rule formula change in stochastic environments?

The answer to the first question is no. The chain rule formula given in (33) cannot be used in a continuous-time stochastic environment. In fact, by "stochastic calculus" we mean a set of methods that yield the formulas equivalent to the chain rule and that approximate the laws of motion of random variables in continuous time.

The *purpose* of stochastic calculus is the same as that of standard calculus. The rules, though, are different.

---

[11] Of course, there is always the question of whether the markets are correctly pricing the security at that instant.

4.3 The Integral

The integral is the mathematical tool used for calculating sums. In contrast to the $\sum$ operator, which is used for sums of a countable number of objects, integrals denote sums of *uncountably infinite* objects. Since it is not clear how one could "sum" objects that are not even countable, a formal definition of integral has to be derived.

The general approach in defining integrals is, in a sense, obvious. One would first begin with an approximation involving a countable number of objects, and then take some limit and move into uncountable objects. Given that different types of limits may be taken, the integral can be defined in various ways. In standard calculus the most common form is the Riemann integral. A somewhat more general integral defined similarly is the Riemann–Stieltjes integral.

In this section we will review these definitions.

4.3.1 The Riemann Integral

We are given a deterministic function $f(t)$ of time $t \in [0, T]$. Suppose we are interested in integrating this function over an interval $[0, T]$

$$\int_0^T f(s)\,ds, \tag{34}$$

which corresponds to the area shown in Figure 8.

In order to calculate the Riemann integral, we *partition* the interval $[0, T]$ into n disjoint subintervals

$$t_0 = 0 < t_1 < \cdots < t_n = T, \tag{35}$$

then consider the approximating sum

$$\sum_{i=1}^{n} f\left(\frac{t_i + t_{i-1}}{2}\right)(t_i - t_{i-1}). \tag{36}$$

DEFINITION: Given that

$$\max_i |t_i - t_{i-1}| \to 0,$$

the Riemann integral will be defined by the limit

$$\sum_{i=1}^{n} f\left(\frac{t_i + t_{i-1}}{2}\right)(t_i - t_{i-1}) \to \int_0^T f(s)\,ds, \tag{37}$$

where the limit is taken in a standard fashion.

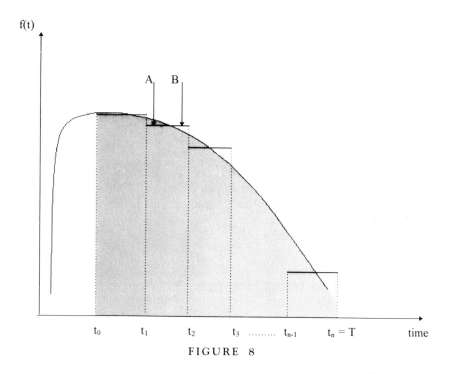

FIGURE 8

The term on the left-hand side of (37) involves adding the surfaces of n rectangles constructed using $(t_i - t_{i-1})$ as the base and $f((t_i + t_{i-1})/2)$ as the height. Figure 8 displays this construction. Note that the small area A is approximately equal to the area B. This is especially true if the base of the rectangles is small *and* if the function $f(t)$ is smooth—that is, does not vary heavily in small intervals.

In case the sum of the rectangles fails to approximate the area under the curve, we may be able to correct this by considering a *finer* partition. As the $|t_i - t_{i-1}|$'s get smaller, the base of the rectangles will get smaller. More rectangles will be available, and the area can be approximated "better."

Obviously, the condition that $f(t)$ should be smooth plays an important role during this process. In fact, a very "irregular" path followed by $f(t)$ may be much more difficult to approximate by this method. Using the terminology discussed before, in order for this method to work the function $f(t)$ must be *Riemann-integrable*.

A counterexample is shown in Figure 9. Here, the function $f(t)$ shows steep variations. If such variations do not smooth out as the base of the rectangles gets smaller, the approximation by rectangles may fail.

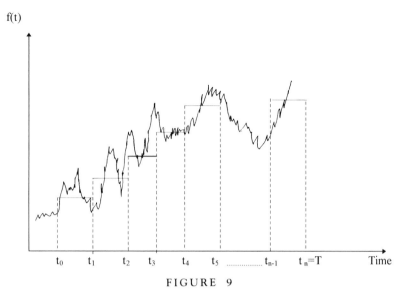

f(t)

t_0 t_1 t_2 t_3 t_4 t_5 .... t_{n-1} $t_n{=}T$ Time

FIGURE   9

We have one more comment that will be important in dealing with the Ito integral later in the text. The rectangles used to approximate the area under the curve were constructed in a particular way. To do this, we used the value of $f(t)$ evaluated at the *midpoint* of the intervals $t_i - t_{i-1}$. Would the same approximation be valid if the rectangles were defined in a different fashion? For example, if one defined the rectangles either by

$$f(t_i)(t_i - t_{i-1}) \qquad\qquad (38)$$

or by

$$f(t_{i-1})(t_i - t_{i-1}), \qquad\qquad (39)$$

would the integral be different? To answer this question, consider Figure 10. Note that as the partitions get finer and finer, rectangles defined either way would eventually approximate the same area. Hence, at the limit, the approximation by rectangles would not give a different integral even when one uses different heights for defining the rectangles.

It turns out that a similar conclusion cannot be reached in stochastic environments.

Suppose $f(W_t)$ is a function of a random variable W_t and that we are interested in calculating

$$\int_{t_0}^{T} f(W_s)dW_s. \qquad\qquad (40)$$

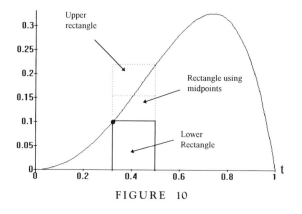

Unlike the deterministic case, the choice of rectangles defined by

$$f(W_{t_i})(W_{t_i} - W_{t_{i-1}}) \qquad (41)$$

will in general result in a different expression from the rectangles:

$$f(W_{t_{i-1}})(W_{t_i} - W_{t_{i-1}}). \qquad (42)$$

To see the reason behind this fundamental point, consider the case where W_t is a *martingale*. Then the expectation of the term in (42), conditional on information at time t_{i-1}, will vanish. This will be the case because, by definition, future increments of a martingale will be unrelated to the current information set.

On the other hand, the same conditional expectation of the term in (41) will in general be nonzero.[12] Clearly, in stochastic calculus, expressions that utilize different definitions of approximating rectangles may lead to different results.

Finally, we would like to emphasize an important result in passing. Note that when $f(\cdot)$ depends on a random variable, the resulting integral itself will be a random variable. In this sense we will be dealing with *random integrals*.

4.3.2 The Stieltjes Integral
The Stieltjes integral is a different definition of the integral. Define the *differential df* as a small variation in the function $f(x)$ due to an infinitesimal variation in x:

$$df(x) = f(x + dx) - f(x). \qquad (43)$$

---

[12]Note that $(W_{t_i} - W_{t_{i-1}})$ and W_{t_i} are correlated.

We already discussed the approximation

$$df(x) \cong f_x(x)\,dx. \tag{44}$$

(Note that according to the notation used here, the derivative $f_x(x)$ is a function of x as well.) Now suppose we want to integrate a function $h(x)$ with respect to x:

$$\int_{x_0}^{x_n} h(x)\,dx, \tag{45}$$

where the function $h(x)$ is given by

$$h(x) = g(x)f_x(x). \tag{46}$$

Then Stieltjes integral is defined as

$$\int_{x_0}^{x_n} g(x)\,df(x) \tag{47}$$

with

$$df(x) = f_x(x)\,dx. \tag{48}$$

This definition is not very different from that of the Riemann integral. In fact, similar approximating sums are used in both cases.

If x represents time t, the Stieltjes integral over a partitioned interval $[0, T]$ is given by

$$\int_0^T g(s)\,df(s) \cong \sum_{i=1}^n g\left(\frac{t_i + t_{i-1}}{2}\right)(f(t_i) - f(t_{i-1})). \tag{49}$$

Because of these similarities, the limit as $\max_i |t_i - t_{i-1}| \to 0$ of the right-hand side is known as the Riemann–Stieltjes integral.

The Riemann–Stieltjes integral is useful when the integration is with respect to increments in $f(x)$ rather than the x itself. Clearly, in dealing with financial derivatives this is often the case. The price of the derivative asset depends on the underlying asset's price, which in turn depends on time. Hence, it may appear that the Riemann–Stieltjes integral is a more appropriate tool for dealing with derivative asset prices.

However, before coming to such a conclusion, note that all the discussion thus far involved deterministic functions of time. Would the same definitions be valid in a stochastic environment? Can we use the same rectangles to approximate integrals in random environments? Would the choice of the rectangle make a difference?

The answers to these questions are in general no. It turns out that in stochastic environments the functions to be integrated may vary too much for a straightforward extension of the Riemann integral to the stochastic case. A new definition of integral will be needed.

4.3.3 Example

In this section we would like to discuss an example of a Riemann–Stieltjes integral. We do this by using a simple function. We let

$$g(S_t) = aS_t, \tag{50}$$

where a is a constant. This makes $g(\cdot)$ a *linear* function of S_t.[13] What is the value of the integral

$$\int_0^T aS_t \, dS(t) \tag{51}$$

if the Riemann–Stieltjes definition is used?

Directly "taking" the integral gives

$$\int_0^T aS_t \, dS(t) = a\left[\frac{1}{2}S_t^2\right]_0^T \tag{52}$$

or

$$\int_0^T aS_t \, dS(t) = a\left[\frac{1}{2}S_T^2 - \frac{1}{2}S_0^2\right]. \tag{53}$$

Now, let us try to see if we can we get the same result using the approximation by rectangles.

Because $g(\cdot)$ is linear, in this particular case the approximation by rectangles works well. This is especially true if we evaluate the height of the rectangle at the midpoint of the base. Figure 11 shows this setup, with $a = 4$.

Due to the linearity of $g(\cdot)$, a single rectangle whose height is measured at the midpoint of the interval $S_0 - S_T$ is sufficient to replicate the shaded area. In fact, the area of the rectangle $S_0 A B S_T$ is

$$a\left[\frac{S_T + S_0}{2}\right][S_T - S_0] = a\left[\frac{1}{2}S_T^2 - \frac{1}{2}S_0^2\right]. \tag{54}$$

The Riemann–Stieltjes approximating sums measure the area under the rectangle exactly, with no need to augment the number of approximating rectangles.

---

[13] Note that S_t is a function of time.

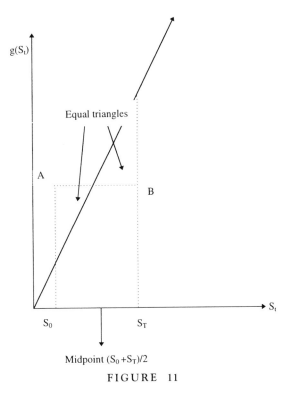

FIGURE   11

4.4 Integration by Parts

In standard calculus there is a useful result known as integration by parts. It can be used to transform some integrals into a form more convenient to deal with. A similar result is also very useful in stochastic calculus, even though the resulting formula is different.

Consider two differentiable functions $f(t)$ and $h(t)$, where $t \in [0, T]$ represents time. Then it can be shown that

$$\int_0^T f_t(t)h(t)\,dt = [f(T)h(T) - f(0)h(0)] - \int_0^T h_t(t)f(t)\,dt, \qquad (55)$$

where $h_t(t)$ and $f_t(t)$ are the derivatives of the corresponding functions with respect to time. They are themselves functions of time t.

In the notation of the Stieltjes integral, this transformation means that an expression that involves an integral

$$\int_0^T h(t)\,df(t) \tag{56}$$

can now be transformed so that it ends up containing the integral

$$\int_0^T f(t)\,dh(t). \tag{57}$$

The stochastic version of this transformation is very useful in evaluating Ito integrals. In fact, imagine that $f(\cdot)$ was *random* while $h(\cdot)$ was (conditionally) a deterministic function of time. Then, using integration by parts, we can express *stochastic integrals* as a function of integrals with respect to a deterministic variable. In stochastic calculus this important role will be played by *Ito's formula*.

5 Partial Derivatives

Consider a call option. Time to expiration affects the price (premium) of the call in two different ways. First, as time passes the expiration date will approach, and the remaining life of the option gets shorter. This lowers the premium. But at the same time, as time passes the price of the underlying asset will change. This will also affect the premium. Hence, the price of a call is a function of two variables. It is more appropriate to write

$$C_t = F(S_t, t), \tag{58}$$

where C_t is the call premium, S_t is the price of the underlying asset, and t, time.

Now suppose we "fix" the time variable t and differentiate $F(S_t, t)$ with respect to S_t. The resulting *partial* derivative,

$$\frac{\partial F(S_t, t)}{\partial S_t} = F_s, \tag{59}$$

would represent the (theoretical) effect of a change in the price of the underlying asset when time is kept fixed. This effect is an abstraction, because in practice one needs *some* time to pass before S_t can change.

The partial derivative with respect to time variable can be defined similarly as

$$\frac{\partial F(S_t, t)}{\partial t} = F_t. \tag{60}$$

Note that even though S_t is a function of time, we are acting as if it doesn't change. Again, this shows the abstract character of the partial derivative. As t changes, S_t will change as well. But in taking partial derivatives, we behave as if it is a constant.

Because of this abstract nature of partial derivatives, this type of differentiation cannot be used directly in representing actual changes of asset price in financial markets. However, partial derivatives are very useful as intermediary tools. They are useful in taking a *total* change and then splitting it into components that come from different sources, and they are useful in *total differentiations.*

Before dealing with total differentiation, we have one last comment on partial derivatives. Because the latter do not represent "observed" changes, there is no difference between their use in stochastic or deterministic environments. We do not have to develop a new theory of partial differentiation in stochastic environments.

To make this more clear, consider the following example.

5.1 Example

Consider the function of two variables

$$F(S_t, t) = .3S_t + t^2, \tag{61}$$

where S_t is the (random) price of a financial asset and t is time.

Taking the partial with respect to S_t involves simply differentiating $F(\cdot)$ with respect to S_t:

$$\frac{\partial F(S_t, t)}{\partial S_t} = .3. \tag{62}$$

Here ∂S_t is an abstract increment in S_t and does not imply a similar actual change in reality. In fact, the partial derivative F_s is simply "how much the function $F(\cdot)$ would have changed if we changed the S_t by one unit." The F_s is just a multiplier.

5.2 Total Differentials

Suppose we observe a small change in the price of a call option at time t. Let this total change be denoted by the differential dC_t. How much of this variation is due to a change in the underlying asset's price? How much of the variation is the result of the expiration date getting nearer as time passes? Total differentiation is used to answer such questions.

Let $f(s_t, t)$ be a function of the two variables. Then the total differential is defined as

$$df = \left[\frac{\partial f(S_t, t)}{\partial S_t} \right] dS_t + \left[\frac{\partial f(S_t, t)}{\partial t} \right] dt. \tag{63}$$

In other words, we take the total change in S_t and multiply this by the *partial* derivative f_s. We take the total change in time dt and multiply this by the partial derivative f_t. The total change in $f(\cdot)$ is the sum of these two products.

According to this, total differentiation is calculated by splitting an observed change into different abstract components.

5.3 Taylor Series Expansion

Let $f(x)$ be an infinitely differentiable function of $x \in R$, and pick an arbitrary value of x; call this x_0.

DEFINITION: The Taylor series expansion of $f(x)$ *around* $x_0 \in R$ is defined as

$$f(x) = f(x_0) + f_x(x_0)(x - x_0) + \frac{1}{2} f_{xx}(x_0)(x - x_0)^2$$
$$+ \frac{1}{3!} f_{xxx}(x_0)(x - x_0)^3 + \cdots \tag{64}$$
$$= \sum_{i=0}^{\infty} \frac{1}{i!} f^i(x_0)(x - x_0)^i,$$

where $f^i(x_0)$ is the ith order derivative of $f(x)$ with respect to x *evaluated* at the point x_0.[14]

We are not going to elaborate on why the expansion in (64) is valid if $f(x)$ is continuous and smooth enough. Taylor series expansion is taken for granted. We will, however, discuss some implications of Taylor series expansion.

First, note that at this point the expression in (64) is *not* an approximation. The right-hand side involves an *infinite* series. Each element involves "simple" powers of x only, but there are an infinite number of such elements. Because of this, Taylor series *expansion* is not very useful in practice.

---

[14]This last point implies that once x_0 is plugged in $f^i(\cdot)$, the latter become constants, independent of x.

Yet the expansion in (64) can be used to obtain useful approximations. Suppose we consider Equation (64) and only look at those x's *near* the x_0. That is, suppose

$$(x - x_0) \cong \text{"small"}. \tag{65}$$

Then, we surely have

$$|x_1 - x_0| > |x_1 - x_0|^2 > |x_1 - x_0|^3 > \cdots. \tag{66}$$

(Each time we raise $|(x_1 - x_0)|$ to a higher power, we multiply it by a "small" number and make the result even "smaller.")

Under these conditions we may want to drop some of the terms on the right-hand side of (64) *if* we can argue that they are negligible. To do this, we must adopt a "convention" for smallness and then eliminate all terms that are "negligible" according to this criterion.

But when is a term "small" enough to be negligible?

The convention in calculus is that, in general, terms of order $(dx)^2$ or higher are assumed to be negligible if x is a *deterministic* variable.[15]

Thus, if we assume that x is deterministic, and let $(x - x_0)$ be small, then we could use the first-order Taylor series approximation:

$$f(x) \cong f(x_0) + f_x(x_0)(x - x_0). \tag{67}$$

This becomes an equality if the $f(x)$ has a derivative at x_0 and if we let

$$(x - x_0) \to 0. \tag{68}$$

Under these conditions the infinitesimal variation $(x - x_0)$ is denoted by

$$dx \simeq (x - x_0) \tag{69}$$

and the one in $f(\cdot)$ by

$$df(x) = f(x) - f(x_0). \tag{70}$$

As a result we obtain the familiar notation in terms of the differentials dx and df:

$$df(x) = f_x(x)\, dx. \tag{71}$$

Here, the $f_x(x)$ is written as a function of x instead of the usual $f_x(x_0)$, since we are considering the limit when x approaches x_0.

---

[15]Note that, if so, the terms $(dx)^3, (dx)^4, \ldots$ will be smaller than $(dx)^2$.

5.3.1 Second-Order Approximations
The equation

$$f(x) \simeq f(x_0) + f_x(x - x_0) \tag{72}$$

was called the first-order Taylor series approximation. Often, a better approximation can be obtained by including the second-order term:

$$f(x) \simeq f(x_0) + f_x(x_0)(x - x_0) + \frac{1}{2} f_{xx}(x_0)(x - x_0)^2. \tag{73}$$

This point is quite relevant for the later discussion of stochastic calculus. In fact, in order to prepare the groundwork for Ito's lemma, we would like to consider a specific example.

5.3.2 Example: Duration and Convexity
Consider the exponential function where t denotes time and where $r > 0$ and $t \in [0, T]$:

$$B_t = 100e^{-r(T-t)}. \tag{74}$$

This function begins at $t = 0$ with a value of $B_0 = 100e^{-rT}$. Then it increases at a constant percentage rate r. As $t \to T$, the value of B_t approaches 100. Hence, B_t could be visualized as the value, as of time t, of 100 to be paid at time T. It is the present value of a zero-coupon bond that matures at time T, and r is the corresponding continuously compounding *yield to maturity*.

We are interested in the Taylor series approximation of B_t with respect to t, assuming that r, T remain constant. A first-order Taylor series expansion around $t = t_0$ will be given by

$$y_t \cong 100e^{-r(T-t_0)} + (r)100e^{-r(T-t_0)}(t - t_0), \quad t \in [0, T], \tag{75}$$

where the first term on the right-hand side is B_t evaluated at $t = t_0$. The second term on the right-hand side is the first derivative of B_t with respect to t, evaluated at t_0, times the increment, $t - t_0$.

Figure 12 displays this approximation. The equation is represented by a convex curve that increases as $t \to T$. The first-order Taylor series approximation is shown as a straight line tangent to the curve at point A. Note that as we go away from t_0 in either direction, the line becomes a worse approximation of the exponential curve. At t's near t_0, on the other hand, the approximation is quite close.

Figure 13 plots the exponential curve with the second-order Taylor series approximation:

$$B_t \cong 100e^{-r(T-t_0)} + (r)100e^{-r(T-t_0)}(t - t_0)$$
$$+ \frac{1}{2}(r^2)100e^{-r(T-t_0)}(t - t_0)^2, \quad t \in [0, T]. \tag{76}$$

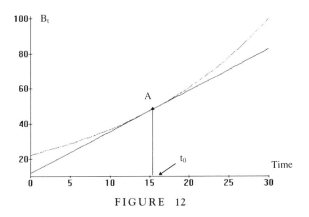

FIGURE 12

The right-hand side of this equation is a *parabola* that touches the exponential curve at point A. Because of the curvature of the parabola near t_0,
we expect this curve to be nearer to the exponential function.

Note that the difference between the first-order and second-order Taylor
series approximations hinges on the size of the term $(t - t_0)^2$. As t gets
nearer t_0, this terms becomes smaller. More importantly, it becomes smaller
faster than the term $(t - t_0)$.

These Taylor series approximations show how the valuation of a discount
bond would change as the *maturity date* gets nearer and nearer.

A second set of Taylor series approximations can be obtained by expanding B_t with respect to r with t, T fixed. Consider a second-order approxi-

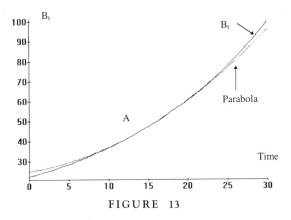

FIGURE 13

mation around the rate r_0:

$$B_t \cong (100e^{-r_0(T-t)})\left[1-(T-t)(r-r_0)+\frac{1}{2}(T-t)^2(r-r_0)^2\right] \quad t \in [0, T], r > 0.$$

Dividing by $(100e^{-r_0(T-t)})$:

$$\frac{dB_t}{B_t} \cong -(T-t)(r-r_0) + \frac{1}{2}(T-t)^2(r-r_0)^2, \quad t \in [0, T], r > 0.$$

This expression provides a second-order Taylor series expansion for the percentage rate of change in the value of a zero coupon bond as r changes infinitesimally. The right-hand side measures the percentage rate of change in the bond price as r changes by $r - r_0$, where r_0 can be interpreted as the current rate. We see two terms containing $r - r_0$ on the right-hand side. In financial markets the coefficient of the first term is called modified *duration*. The second term is positive and has a coefficient of $(T - t)^2$. It represents the so-called *convexity* of the bond. Overall, the second-order Taylor series expansion of B_t with respect to r shows that, as interest rates increase (decrease), the value of the bond decreases (increases). The "convexity" of the bond implies that the bigger these changes, the smaller their *relative* effects.

5.4 Ordinary Differential Equations

The third major notion from standard calculus that we would like to review is the concept of an ordinary differential equation (ODE). For example consider the expression

$$dB_t = -r_t B_t \, dt \quad \text{with known} \quad B_0, r_t > 0. \tag{77}$$

This expression states that B_t is a quantity that varies with t—i.e., changes in B_t are a function of t and of B_t. The equation is called an *ordinary differential equation*.

Here, the percentage variation in B_t is proportional to some factor r_t times dt:

$$\frac{dB_t}{B_t} = -r_t \, dt. \tag{78}$$

Now, we say that the function B_t defined by

$$B_t = e^{-\int_0^t r_u \, du} \tag{79}$$

solves the ODE in (77) in the sense that plugging in the quantity in (79) will satisfy the equality (77).

Thus, an ordinary differential equation is first of all an *equation*. That is, it is an equality where there exist one or more *unknowns* that need to be determined.

A very simple analogy may be useful. In a *simple equation*,

$$3x + 1 = x, \tag{80}$$

the unknown is x. x is a number to be determined. The solution is $-1/2$.

In a *matrix equation*,

$$Ax - b = 0, \tag{81}$$

the unknown is a vector. Under appropriate conditions the solution would be $A^{-1}b$—i.e., the inverse of A multiplied by the vector b.

In an *ordinary differential equation*,

$$\frac{dx_t}{dt} = ax_t + b, \tag{82}$$

the unknown is x_t a *function*. More precisely, it is a function of t:

$$x_t = f(t).$$

In the case of the ODE

$$dB_t = -r_t B_t \, dt, \tag{83}$$

the solution was

$$B_t = e^{-\int_0^t r_u du}. \tag{84}$$

Readers will recognize this as the valuation function for a zero-coupon bond. This is an example showing that the pricing functions for fixed income securities can be characterized as solutions of some appropriate differential equations. In stochastic settings we will obtain more complex versions of this result.

Finally, we need to define the *integral equation*,

$$\int_0^t (ax_s + b)ds = x_t, \tag{85}$$

where the unknown x_t is again a function of t.

6 Conclusions

This chapter reviewed basic notions in calculus. Most of these concepts were elementary. The notions of derivative, integral, and Taylor series may all be well known. However, it is important to review them for later purposes.

Stochastic calculus is an attempt to perform similar operations when the underlying phenomena are continuous-time random processes. It turns out that in such an environment, the usual definitions of derivative, integral, and Taylor series approximations do not apply. In order to understand stochastic versions of such concepts, one first has to understand their deterministic equivalents.

The other important concept of the chapter was the notion of "smallness." In particular, we need a convention to decide when an increment is small enough to be ignored.

7 References

The reader may at this point prefer to skim through an elementary calculus book. A review of basic differentiation and integration rules may especially help. Solving some exercises might also be useful.

CHAPTER 4

Pricing Derivatives

Models and Notation

1 Introduction

There are some aspects of pricing derivative instruments that sets them apart from the general theory of asset valuation. Under simplifying assumptions, one can express the arbitrage-free price of a derivative as a function of some "basic" securities, and then obtain a set of *formulas* that can be used to price the asset without having to consider any linkages to other financial markets or to the real side of the economy.

There are some specific ways one obtains such formulas. One method was discussed in Chapter 2. The notion of *arbitrage* can be used to determine a probability measure under which financial assets behave as *martingales* once discounted properly. The tools of martingale arithmetic become available, and one can calculate arbitrage-free prices easily by evaluating the implied expectations. This approach to pricing derivatives is called the *method of equivalent martingale measures*.

The second pricing method that utilizes arbitrage takes a somewhat more direct approach. One first constructs a risk-free portfolio, and then obtains a *partial differential equation* (PDE) that is implied by the lack of arbitrage opportunities. This PDE is either solved analytically or evaluated numerically.

In either case, the problem of pricing derivatives is to find a function $F(S_t, t)$ that relates the price of the derivative product to S_t, the price of the underlying asset, and possibly to some other market risk factors. When a *closed-form* formula is impossible to determine, one finds numerical ways to describe the dynamics of $F(S_t, t)$.

This chapter provides examples of how to determine such pricing functions $F(S_t, t)$ for *linear* and *nonlinear* derivatives. These concepts are clarified, and an example of partial differential equation methods is given. This discussion provides some motivation for the fundamental tools of stochastic calculus that we introduce later.

2 Pricing Functions

The unknown of a derivative pricing problem is a *function* $F(S_t, t)$, where S_t is the price of the underlying asset and t is time. Ideally, the financial analyst will try to obtain a *closed-form* formula for $F(S_t, t)$. The Black–Scholes formula that gives the price of a call option in terms of the underlying asset and some other relevant parameters is perhaps the best-known case. There are, however, many other examples, some considerably simpler.

In cases in which a closed-form formula does not exist, the analyst tries to obtain an equation that governs the *dynamics* of $F(S_t, t)$.[1]

In this section we show examples of how to determine such $F(S_t, t)$. The discussion is intended to introduce new mathematical tools and concepts that have common use in pricing derivative products.

2.1 Forwards

Consider the class of cash-and-carry goods.[2] We would like to show how a pricing function $F(S_t, t)$, where S_t is the underlying asset, can be obtained for *forward* contracts. In particular, we would like to consider a forward contract with the following provisions:

- At some future date T,

$$t < T, \tag{1}$$

   F dollars will be paid to receive one unit of gold.
- The contract is signed at time t, but no payment changes hands until time T.

Hence, we have a contract that imposes an *obligation* on both counterparties—the one that delivers the gold, and the one that accepts the delivery.

---

[1]The nonexistence of a *closed-form* formula does not necessarily imply the nonexistence of a pricing function. It may simply mean that we are not able to *express* the pricing function in terms of a simple formula. For example, all continuous and "smooth" functions can be expanded as an infinite Taylor series expansion. At the same time, truncating Taylor series in order to obtain a closed-form formula would in general lead to an approximation error.

[2]See Chapter 1 for definition.

How can one determine a *function* $F(S_t, t)$ that gives the fair market value of such a contract at time t in terms of the underlying parameters?[3]

We use an *arbitrage* argument.

Suppose one buys one unit of physical gold at time t for S_t dollars using funds borrowed at the continuously compounding risk-free rate r_t. The r_t is assumed to be fixed during the contract period. Let the insurance and storage costs per time unit be c dollars. The total cost of *holding* this gold during a period of length $T - t$ will be given by

$$e^{r_t(T-t)}S_t + (T - t)c, \tag{2}$$

where the first term is the principal and interest to be returned to the bank at time T, and the second represents *total* storage and insurance costs paid at time T.

This is one way of securing one unit of physical gold at time T. One borrows the necessary funds, buys the underlying commodity, and stores it until time T.

The forward contract is another way of securing one unit of gold at time T. One signs a contract now for delivery of one unit of gold at time T, with the understanding that all payments will be made at expiration.

Hence, the outcome of the two sets of transactions is identical.[4] This means that they must cost the same. Otherwise there will be arbitrage opportunities. An astute player will enter into two separate contracts, buying the cheaper gold and selling the expensive gold simultaneously.

Mathematically, this gives the equality

$$F(S_t, t) = e^{r_t(T-t)}S_t + (T - t)c. \tag{3}$$

Thus we used the possibility of exploiting any arbitrage opportunities and obtained an equality that expresses the price of a forward contract $F(S_t, t)$ as a function of S_t, t and other parameters. In fact, we determined a *function* $F(S_t, t)$ that gives the value of the forward contract at any time t.

Of the arguments in $F(S_t, t)$, S_t and t are *variables*. They may change during the life of the contract. On the other hand, c, r_t, and T are *parameters*. It is assumed that they will remain constant during $T - t$.

---

[3]Note the sense in which this is a *derivative* contract. Once the contract is signed, it becomes a separate security and can be traded on its own. To trade the forward contract, one need not have in possession any physical gold. In fact, such instruments can be derived from "notional" underlying assets that do not even exist concretely. Derivatives written on equity indices are one such class.

[4]Note that behind this statement there are assumptions such as zero default risk of the forward contract.

Note that the function $F(S_t, t)$ in (3) is *linear* in S_t. Thus, forward contracts are called *linear products*. Later we will derive the Black–Scholes formula which provides a pricing function $F(S_t, t)$ for call options. This formula will be *nonlinear* in S_t. Instruments that have optionlike characteristics are called *nonlinear* products.

2.1.1 Boundary Conditions
Here we have to mention briefly what a *boundary condition* is.

Suppose we want to express formally, the notion that the "expiration date gets nearer." To do this, we use the concept of limits. We let

$$t \to T. \tag{4}$$

Note that as this happens,

$$\lim_{t \to T} e^{r_t(T-t)} = 1. \tag{5}$$

One question here is the presence of r_t. In reality, this is a *random* variable, and one may ask if the use of a standard *limit* concept is valid. Ignoring this and applying the limit to the left-hand side of the expression in (3), we obtain

$$S_T = F(S_T, T). \tag{6}$$

According to this, at expiration the cash price of the underlying asset and the price of the forward contract will be equal.

This is an example of a boundary condition. At the expiration date—i.e., at the boundary for time variable t—the pricing function $F(S_t, t)$ assumes a special value, S_T. The boundary condition is known at time t.

2.2 Options

Determining the pricing function $F(S_t, t)$ for nonlinear assets is not as easy as in the case of forward contracts. This will be done in later chapters. At this point we only introduce an important property that the $F(S_t, t)$ should satisfy in the case of nonlinear products. This will prepare the ground for further mathematical tools.

Suppose C_t is a call option written on the stock S_t. Let r be the constant risk-free rate. K is the strike price, and T, $t < T$ is the expiration date. Then the price of the call can be expressed as[5]

$$C_t = F(S_t, t). \tag{7}$$

[5]Note that the interest rate r is constant and hence dropped as an argument of $F(\cdot)$.

The pricing function $F(S_t, t)$ for options will have a fundamental property. Under simplifying conditions the S_t will be the only source of randomness affecting the option's price. Hence, unpredictable movements in S_t can be offset by opposite positions taken simultaneously in C_t. This property imposes some conditions on the way $F(S_t, t)$ can change over time *once* the time path of S_t is given.

To see how this property can be made more explicit, consider Figure 1. The lower part of this figure displays a payoff diagram for a short position in S_t. A unit of the underlying asset is borrowed and sold at a price S_t.

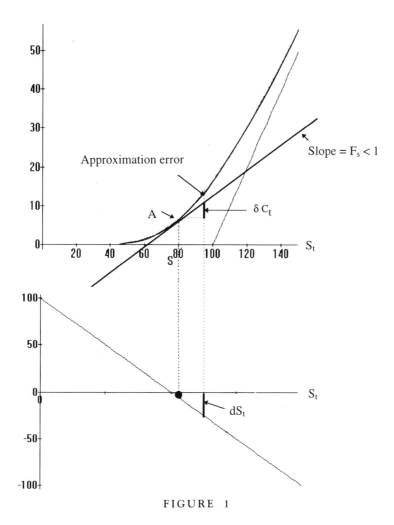

FIGURE 1

The upper part of Figure 1 displays the price $F(S_t, t)$ of a call option written on S_t. At this point we leave aside how the formula for $F(S_t, t)$ is obtained and graphed. [6]

Suppose originally the underlying asset's price is at S_t. That is, originally we are at point A on the $F(S_t, t)$ curve. If the stock price increases by dS_t, the short position will lose exactly the amount dS_t. But the option position gains.

However, we see a critical point. According to Figure 1, when S_t increases by dS_t, the price of the call will increase only by dC_t; and this latter change is smaller because the slope of the curve is less than one:

$$dC_t < dS_t. \tag{8}$$

Hence, if we owned one call option and sold one stock, a price increase equal to dS_t would lead to a net loss.

But this reasoning suggests that with careful adjustments of positions, such losses could be eliminated. Consider the slope of the tangent to $F(S_t, t)$ at point A. This slope is given by

$$\frac{\partial F(S_t, t)}{\partial S_t} = F_s. \tag{9}$$

Now, suppose we are short not *one*, but F_s units of the underlying stock. Then, as S_t increases by dS_t, the total loss on the short position will be $F_s dS_t$. But according to Figure 1, this amount is very close to dC_t. It is indicated by ∂C_t.

Clearly, if dS_t is a small incremental change, then the ∂C_t will be a very good approximation of the actual change dC_t. As a result, the gain in the option position will (approximately) offset the loss in the short position. Such a portfolio will not move unpredictably.

Thus, incremental movements in $F(S_t, t)$ and S_t should be related by some equation such as

$$d[F_s S_t] + d[F(S_t, t)] = g(t),$$

where $g(t)$ is a completely predictable function of time t.[7]

If we learn how to calculate such differentials, the equation above can be used in finding a closed-form formula for $F(S_t, t)$. When such closed-form formulae do not exist, *numerical methods* can be used to trace the trajectories followed by $F(S_t, t)$.

The following definition formalizes some of the concepts discussed in this section.

---

[6] It comes from the Black–Scholes formula that we prove later.

[7] And of other possible parameters of the problem.

DEFINITION: Offsetting changes in C_t by taking the opposite position in F_s units of the underlying asset is called *delta hedging*. Such a portfolio is *delta neutral*, and the parameter F_s is called the *delta*.

It is important to realize that when dS_t is "large," the approximation

$$\partial C_t \cong dC_t \tag{10}$$

will fail. With an extreme movement, the "hedge" does not hold. This can be seen in Figure 2. If the change in S_t is equal to dS_t, then the corresponding dC_t would far exceed the loss $-F_s\, dS_t$.

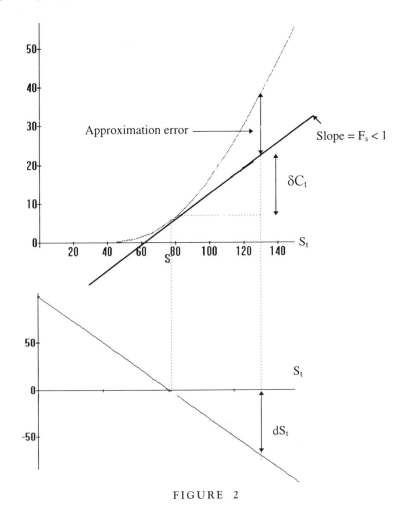

FIGURE 2

Clearly, the assumption of *continuous time* implicitly plays a fundamental role in asset pricing. In fact, we were able to replicate the movements in the option position by infinitesimally adjusting our short position in the underlying asset. The ability to make such infinitesimal adjustments in the portfolio clearly hinges on the assumption of continuous time. As shown earlier, with "large" increments such approximations will deteriorate quickly.

3 Application: Another Pricing Method

This book deals with the *mathematics* of derivative asset pricing. It is not a text on asset pricing per se. However, a discussion of general methods of pricing derivative assets is unavoidable. This is needed to illustrate the type of mathematics that we intend to discuss and in order to provide examples.

We use the discussion of the previous section to summarize the pricing method that uses partial differential equations (PDEs).

1. Assume that an analyst observes the current price of a derivative product $F(S_t, t)$ and the underlying asset price S_t in real time. Suppose the analyst would like to calculate the change in derivative asset's price $dF(S_t, t)$, given a change in the price of the underlying asset dS_t.

2. Here the notions that we introduced in Chapter 3 start to become useful. Remember that the concept of differentiation is a tool that one can use to approximate small *changes* in a function. In this particular case, we indeed have a function $F(\cdot)$ that depends on S_t, t. Thus, *if* we can use the standard calculus, we could write

$$dF(S_t, t) = F_s \, dS_t + F_t \, dt, \tag{11}$$

where the F_i's are *partial* derivatives,[8]

$$F_s = \frac{\partial F}{\partial S_t}, \qquad F_t = \frac{\partial F}{\partial t}, \tag{12}$$

and where $dF(S_t, t)$ denotes the total change.

3. Equation (11), called the total differential of $F(\cdot)$, gives the change in derivative product's price in terms of changes in its determinants. Hence, one might think of an analyst who first obtains estimates of dS_t and then uses the equation for total differential to evaluate the $dF(S_t, t)$. Equation

---

[8]Note the important difference between $F(S_t, t)$ which denotes the price of the derivative at time t, and F_t, which denotes the *partial derivative* of $F(S_t, t)$ with respect to t.

(11) can be used once the partial derivatives F_s, F_t are evaluated numerically. This, on the other hand, requires that the functional form of $F(S_t, t)$ be known.

However, all this depends on our ability to take total differentials as in (11). Can this be done in a straightforward fashion, if underlying variables are continuous-time *stochastic processes?*

The answer to this question is no. Yet with the new tools of *stochastic* calculus it can be done.

4. Once the stochastic version of Equation (11) is determined, one can complete the "program" for valuing a derivative asset in the following way:

Using delta-hedging and risk-free portfolios, one can obtain additional relationships among $dF(S_t, t)$, dS_t, and dt. These additional relationships can be used to eliminate all differentials from 11.

5. One would then obtain a relationship that ties only the partial derivatives of $F(\cdot)$ to each other. Such equations are called partial differential equations and can be solved for $F(S_t, t)$ if one has enough boundary conditions and if a closed-form solution exists.

Thus, we are led to a problem where the *unknown* is a *function*. This argument shows that partial differential equations and their solutions are topics that need to be studied.

An example might be helpful at this point.

3.1 Example

Suppose you know that the partial derivative of $F(x)$ with respect to $x \in [0, X]$ is a known constant, b:

$$F_x = b. \tag{13}$$

This equation is a trivial PDE. It is an expression involving a partial derivative of $F(x)$, a term with unknown functional form.

Using this PDE, can we tell the *form* of the function $F(x)$? The answer is yes. Only linear relationships have a property such as (13). Thus, $F(x)$ must be given by

$$F(x) = a + bx. \tag{14}$$

Hence, the *form* of $F(x)$ is pinned down. However, the parameter a is still unknown. It is found by using the so called "boundary conditions."

For example, if we knew that at the *boundary* $x = X$,

$$F(X) = 10, \tag{15}$$

then *a* can be determined by

$$a = 10 - bX. \tag{16}$$

Remember that in the case of derivative products, one generally has some information about the form of $F(\cdot)$ at the expiration date. Such information can sometimes be used to determine the function $F(\cdot)$ explicitly, given a PDE.

4 The Problem

The program discussed earlier may appear quite technical at the outset, but, in fact, it is a straightforward approach to follow. However, there is a fundamental problem.[9]

Financial market data are not *deterministic*. In fact, all the variables under consideration, with the exception of the time variable t, are likely to be *random*. Since time is continuous, we observe uncountably many random variables as time passes. Hence, $F(S_t, t)$, S_t, and possibly the risk-free rate r_t are all *continuous-time stochastic processes*.

Can we, then, apply the same reasoning and use the same tools as in standard calculus to write

$$dF(t) = F_s \, dS_t + F_r \, dr_t + F_t \, dt \, ? \tag{18}$$

The answer to this question is no. It turns out that one needs a "new" calculus and a different formula when the variables under consideration are random processes. The following is a first look at some of these difficulties.

4.1 A First Look at Ito's Lemma

In standard calculus, variables under consideration are deterministic. Hence, to get a relation such as

$$dF(t) = F_s \, dS_t + F_r \, dr_t + F_t \, dt, \tag{19}$$

one uses total differentiation. The change in $F(.)$ is given by the relation on the right-hand side of (19). But according to the rules of calculus, this

---

[9]In fact, at this point, there are *two* problems. For one, given the equation

$$dF(t) = F_s \, dS_t + F_r \, dr_t + F_t \, dt, \tag{17}$$

we still do not know how arbitrage can be used to eliminate the terms such as $dt, dF(t), dS_t$, and dr_t. We will leave this aside for the time being.

equation holds exactly only during infinitesimal intervals.[10] In *finite* time intervals, Equation (19) will hold only as an approximation.

Consider the univariate Taylor series expansion again.

Let $f(x)$ be an infinitely differentiable function of $x \in R$. One can then write the Taylor series expansion of $f(x)$ around $x_0 \in R$ as

$$f(x) = f(x_0) + f_x(x_0)(x - x_0) + \frac{1}{2}f_{xx}(x_0)(x - x_0)^2$$

$$+ \frac{1}{3!}f_{xxx}(x_0)(x - x_0)^3 + \cdots \tag{20}$$

$$= \sum_{i=0}^{\infty} \frac{1}{i!}f^i(x_0)(x - x_0)^i,$$

where $f^i(x_0)$ is the ith-order partial derivative of $f(x)$ with respect to x, evaluated at x_0.

We can reinterpret $df(x)$ using the approximation

$$df(x) \cong f(x) - f(x_0) \tag{21}$$

and dx as

$$dx \cong (x - x_0) \tag{22}$$

Thus, an expression such as

$$dF(t) = F_s \, dS_t + F_r \, dr_t + F_t \, dt \tag{23}$$

depends on the assumption that the terms $(dt)^2$, $(dS_t)^2$, and $(dr_t)^2$, and those of higher order, are "small" enough that they can be omitted from a multivariate Taylor series expansion.[11] Because of such an approximation, higher powers of the differentials dS_t, dt, or dr_t do not show up on the right-hand side of (23).

Now, dt is a small deterministic change in t. So, to say that $(dt)^2$, $(dt)^3, \ldots$ are "small" with respect to dt is an internally consistent statement.

However, the same argument cannot be used for $(dS_t)^2$, and possibly, for $(dr_t)^2$.[12]

---

[10] An *infinitesimal* time period is an infinitely small time interval. In fact, it has zero "mass."

[11] This would make the expression a Taylor series *approximation*.

[12] For that matter, it may not be true for the cross-product term $(dS_t dr_t)$ either.

First of all, it is maintained that $(dS_t)^2$ and $(dr_t)^2$ are random during small intervals.[13] Thus, they have *nonzero* variances during dt.

This poses a problem. On one hand, we want to use continuous-time random processes with nonzero variances during dt. So we use positive numbers for the average values of $(dS_t)^2$ and $(dr_t)^2$. But under these conditions it would be inconsistent to call $(dS_t)^2$ and $(dr_t)^2$ "small" with respect to dt, and then equate them to zero; a step that can be taken if the variables in question are deterministic, as in the case of standard calculus.

Hence, in a stochastic environment with a continuous flow of randomness we have to write the relevant total differentials as:

$$dF(t) = F_s\, dS_t + F_r\, dr_t + F_t\, dt + \frac{1}{2}F_{ss}\, dS_t^2 + \frac{1}{2}F_{rr}\, dr_t^2 + F_{sr}\, dS_t\, dr_t. \quad (24)$$

This is an example of why we need to study "stochastic calculus." We want to learn how to exploit the chain rule in a stochastic environment and understand what a *differential* means in such a setting. The example above shows that the resulting expressions would be different from the ones obtained in deterministic calculus.

Note that if the notion of differential needs to be changed, then the notion of integral should also be reformulated. In fact, in such a stochastic environment we define *differentials* by using a new definition of integral. Otherwise, in continuous-time stochastic environments a formal definition of *derivative* does not exist.

4.2 Conclusions

One approach used to find the "fair market value" of derivative securities may at this point be summarized informally as follows.

Using arbitrage, determine an equation that ties various partial derivatives of an (unknown) function $F(S_t, t)$ into each other. Then, solve this (partial differential) equation for the form of $F(.)$. Using the boundary conditions determine the parameters of this function.

This chapter also introduced the fundamental mathematical problem faced in continuous-time finance. Standard formulas from calculus are not applicable when the variables under consideration are continuous-time stochastic processes. Increments of these processes have nonzero variances. This will make the average "size" of the second-order terms such as dS_t^2 nonnegligible.

---

[13]In *infinitesimal* intervals, we will see that the mean square *limits* of these terms are deterministic and proportional to dt.

5 References

Duffie (1996) is an excellent source on dynamic asset valuation. Ingersoll (1987) also provides a very good treatment. There are, however, several simpler books that one can consider for an understanding of simple asset valuation formulas. Cox and Rubinstein (1985) is a very good example. Finally, most of the valuation theory can be found in the excellent collection of papers in Merton (1990).

CHAPTER 5

Tools in Probability Theory

1 Introduction

In this chapter we review some basic notions in probability theory. The first purpose of this chapter is to prepare the groundwork for a discussion of martingales and martingale-related tools. In doing this, we discuss properties of random variables and stochastic processes. A reader with a good background in probability theory may want to skip these sections.

The second purpose of this chapter is to introduce the binomial process which plays an important role in derivative asset valuation. Pricing models for derivative assets are formulated in continuous time, but will be applied in discrete, "small" time intervals. Practical methods of asset pricing using "finite difference methods" or lattice methods fall within this category. Prices of underlying assets are assumed to be observed at time periods separated by small finite intervals of length Δ. In such small intervals, it is further assumed, prices can have only a limited number of possible movements.[1] These methods all rely on the idea that a continuous-time stochastic process representing the price of the underlying asset can be approximated arbitrarily well by a binomial process. This chapter introduces the mechanics of justifying such approximations.

2 Probability

Derivative products are contracts written on underlying assets whose prices fluctuate randomly. A mathematical model of randomness is thus needed.

[1]For example, prices can move up and down by some preset amounts.

Some elementary models of probability theory are especially well suited to pricing derivative assets.

This can be a bit surprising, given that many investors appear to be driven by "intuitive" notions of probabilities rather than by an axiomatic and formal probabilistic model. However, the discussion in Chapter 2 indicated that no matter what the "true" probabilities are, if there are no arbitrage opportunities, one can *represent* the fair market value of financial assets using *probability measures* constructed "synthetically." Hence, regardless of any subjective chances perceived by market participants, mathematical probability models have a natural use in pricing derivative products.

In working with random variables, one first defines a *probability space*. That is, one lays out explicitly the framework where the notion of chance and the resulting probability can be defined without falling into some inconsistencies.

To define probability models formally, one needs a set of basic states of the world. A particular state of the world is denoted by the symbol ω. The symbol Ω represents all possible states of the world. The outcome of an experiment is determined by the choice of an ω.

The intuitive notion of an *event* corresponds to a set of elementary ω's. The set of all possible events is represented by the symbol $\Im$. To each event $A \in \Im$, one assigns a probability $P(A)$.

These probabilities must be consistently defined. Two conditions of consistency are the following:

$$P(A) \geq 0, \qquad \text{any } A \in \Im, \tag{1}$$

$$\int_{A \in \Im} dP(A) = 1. \tag{2}$$

The first of these conditions implies that probabilities of events are either zero or positive. The second says that the probabilities should sum to one. Here, note the notation $dP(A)$. This is a measure theoretic notation and may be read as the incremental probability associated with an event A.

The triplet $\{\Omega, \Im, P\}$ is called a *probability space*. According to this, a point ω of Ω is chosen randomly. $P(A)$, where $A \in \Im$, represents the probability that the chosen point belongs to the set A.

2.1 Example

Suppose the price of an exchange-traded commodity future during a given day depends only on a harvest report the U.S. Department of Agriculture (USDA) will make public during that day.

The specifics of the report written by the USDA are equivalent to an ω.

Depending on what is in the report, we can call it either favorable or unfavorable. This constitutes an example of an *event*. Note that there are *several* ω's that may lead us to call the harvest report "favorable." It is in this sense that events are collections of ω's.

Hence, we may want to know the probability of a "favorable report." This is given by

$$P(\text{harvest report} = \text{favorable}). \qquad (3)$$

Finally, note that in this particular example the Ω is the set of *all* possible reports that the USDA may make public.

2.2 Random Variable

In general there is no reason for a probability to be representable by a *simple* mathematical formula. However, some convenient and simple mathematical models are found to be acceptable approximations for representing probabilities associated with financial data.[2]

A *random variable* X is a function, a mapping, defined on the set $\Im$. Given an event $A \in \Im$, a random variable will assume a particular numerical value. Thus, we have

$$X: \Im \to B, \qquad (4)$$

where B is the set made of all possible subsets of the real numbers R.

In terms of the example just discussed, note that a "favorable harvest report" may contain several judgmental statements besides some accompanying numbers. Let X be the value of the numerical estimate provided by the USDA and let 100 be some minimum desirable harvest. Then mappings such as

$$\text{favorable report} \Rightarrow 100 < X \qquad (5)$$

define the random variable X. Clearly, the values assumed by X are real numbers.

A mathematical model for the probabilities associated with a random variable X is given by the *distribution function* $G(x)$:

$$G(x) = P(X \le x). \qquad (6)$$

Note that $G(\cdot)$ is a function of x.[3]

---

[2]The sense in which a formula becomes a good approximation to a probability is an important question that we will discuss below.

[3]Here, X represents a random variable, whereas the lower-case x represents a certain "threshold."

When the function $G(x)$ is smooth and has a derivative, we can define the *density function* of X. This function is denoted by $g(x)$ and is obtained by

$$g(x) = \frac{dG(x)}{dx}. \tag{7}$$

It can be shown that under some technical conditions there always exists a distribution function $G(x)$. However, whether this function $G(x)$ can be written as a convenient formula is a different question. It turns out that there are some "well-known" models where this is possible. We review three basic probability models that are frequently used in pricing derivative products.

These examples are specially constructed so as to facilitate understanding of more complicated asset pricing methods to be discussed later. But first we need to review the notions of expectations and conditional expectations.

3 Moments

There are different ways one can classify models of distribution functions. One classification uses the notion of "moments." Some random variables can be fully characterized by their *first two* moments. Others need *higher-order* moments for a full characterization.

3.1 First Two Moments

The expected value $E[X]$ of a random variable X, with density $f(x)$, is called the *first* moment. It is defined by

$$E[X] = \int_{-\infty}^{\infty} x f(x)\, dx,$$

where $f(x)$ is the corresponding probability density function.[4] The variance $E[X - EX]^2$ is the *second* moment around the mean. The first moment of a random variable is the "center of gravity" of the distribution, while the second moment gives information about the way the distribution is spread out. The square root of the second moment is the standard deviation. It is a measure of the *average deviation of observations from the mean*. In financial markets, the standard deviation of a price change is called the *volatility*.

For example, in the case of a normally distributed random variable X, the density function is given by the well-known formula

$$f(x) = \frac{1}{\sqrt{2\pi\sigma^2}} e^{-\frac{1}{2\sigma^2}(x-\mu)^2}, \tag{8}$$

[4]If the density does not exist, we replace $f(x)\,dx$ by $dF(x)$.

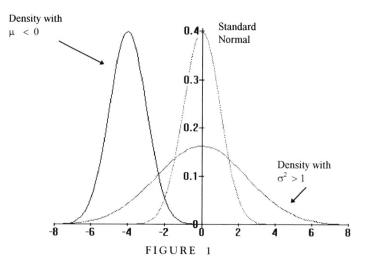

Density with
μ < 0

FIGURE   1

where the variance parameter σ^2 is the second moment around the mean and the parameter μ is the first moment. Figure 1 shows examples of normal distributions.

Integrals of this formula determine the probabilities associated with various values the random variable x can assume. Note that $f(x)$ depends on only two parameters, σ^2 and μ. Hence, the probabilities associated with a normally distributed random variable can be inferred if one has the sample estimates of these two moments.

A normally distributed random variable X would also have higher-order moments. For example, the centered third moment of any normally distributed random variable X will be given by

$$E\left[X - E[X]\right]^3 = 0.$$

In fact, all higher-order moments of normally distributed random variables can be expressed as a function of μ and σ^2. In other words, given the first two moments, higher-order moments of normally distributed variables do not provide any additional information.

3.2 Higher-Order Moments

Consider the nonsymmetric density shown in Figure 2. If the mean is the center of gravity and the variance is the width of the distribution, then one would need another parameter to characterize the skewness of the distribution. *Third moments* are indeed informative about such asymmetries.

In financial markets a more important notion is the phenomenon of *heavy tails*. Figure 2 displays a symmetric density which has another char-

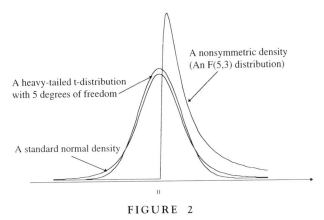

FIGURE 2

acteristic that differentiates it from normal distributions. The tails of this distribution are heavier *relative* to the middle part of the tails. Such densities are called heavy-tailed and are fairly common with financial data. Again, one would need a parameter other than variance and the mean to characterize the heavy-tailed distributions. *Fourth moments* are used for that end.

3.2.1 Heavy Tails

What is the meaning of heavy tails?

A distribution that has heavier tails than the normal curve means a higher probability of extreme observations. But, this point should be carefully made. Note that the normal density also has tails that extend to plus and minus infinities. Thus, a normally distributed random variable could also assume extreme values from time to time. However, in the case of a heavy-tailed distribution, these extreme observations have, relatively speaking, a higher frequency.

But there is more to heavy-tailed distributions than that. In a normal distribution, most of the observations would naturally be occurring around the center. More importantly, the occurrence of extremes is gradual, in the sense that the passage from ordinary, to large, and then to extreme observations occurs in a gradual fashion. In case of a heavy-tailed distribution, on the other hand, the passage from "ordinary" to extreme observations is more sudden. The middle tail region of the distribution contains relatively less weight than in the normal density. Compared to the normal density, one is likely to get "too many extreme observations."

In other words, a casual observer is more likely to be "surprised" by extreme observations in the case of heavy-tailed random variables.

4 Conditional Expectations

The operation of taking expectations of random variables is the formal equivalent of the heuristic notion of "forecasting." To forecast a random variable one utilizes some information denoted by the symbol I_t. Expectations calculated using such information are called *conditional* expectations. The corresponding mathematical operation is the "conditional expectation operator."[5] Since the information utilized could be, and in general is, different from one time to another, the conditional expectation operator is itself indexed by the time index.

In general, the information used by decision makers will increase as time passes. If we also assume that the decision maker never "forgets" past data, the information sets must be increasing over time:

$$I_{t_0} \subseteq I_{t_1} \subseteq \ldots \subseteq I_{t_k} \subseteq I_{t_{k+1}} \subseteq \ldots, \tag{9}$$

where t_i, $i = 0, 1, \ldots$ are times when the information set becomes available.

In the mathematical analysis, such information sets are called an increasing sequence of *sigma fields*. When such information sets become available *continuously*, a different term is used, and the family I_t satisfying (9) is called a *filtration*.

The conditional expectation operator can then be defined in several steps.

4.1 Conditional Probability

First, the probability density function needs to be discussed further.

If X is a random variable with density functions $f(x)$, and if x_0 is one possible value of this random variable, then for *small dx*, we have

$$P\left(|x - x_0| \leq \frac{dx}{2}\right) \approx f(x_0)\, dx. \tag{10}$$

This is the probability that the x will fall in a small neighborhood of x_0. The neighborhood is characterized by the "distance" dx.

These quantities are shown in Figure 3. Note that although $f(x)$ is a nonlinear curve in this figure, for small dx it can be approximated reasonably well by a straight line. Then, the rectangle in Figure 3 would be close to the probability that x will fall within a small neighborhood of x_0 represented by the quantity dx. If these probabilities are based on some

---

[5]An operator is a function that maps functions into functions. That is, it takes as input a function and produces as output another function.

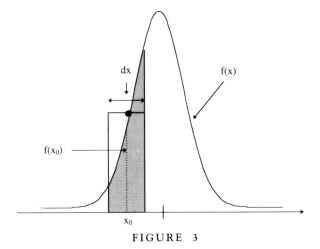

FIGURE 3

information set I_t, then $f(x)$ is called a *conditional density*. The dependence on the information I_t is formally denoted by $f(x|I_t)$.

If the $f(x)$ is not based on any particular information, the I_t term is dropped and the density is written as $f(x)$.

Consider a simple example. The odds of a stock market crash will be an example of unconditional probability. The odds of a crash given that one has entered a severe recession can be represented by a conditional probability. In this particular case the "information" is the knowledge that a severe recession has begun. The use of such information may certainly lead to a revision of the (unconditional) probability of a crash.

4.1.1 Conditional Expectation Operator

The second step in defining a conditional expectation is the "averaging" operator. In fact, every forecast is an average of possible future values. The values that the random variable can assume in the future are weighted by the probabilities associated with these values, and an average is obtained. The information contained in the conditional probabilities determines the conditioning information for this average as well.

Hence, the operation of conditional expectation involves calculating a weighted sum. Since the possible outcomes are likely to be not only infinite, but also uncountably many, this "sum" is represented by an integral.

The conditional expectation (forecast) of some random variable S_t given the information available at time u is given by

$$E[S_t|I_u] = \int_{-\infty}^{\infty} S_t f(S_t|I_u)\, dS_t, \qquad u < t. \tag{11}$$

In this expression the right-hand side should be read as follows: for a given t, the sum of all possible values that S_t might assume are weighted by the corresponding probabilities $[f(S_t|I_u)\,dS_t]$ and then summed. The averaging is done by using probabilities conditional on I_u. This way, any information that one has, gets incorporated in the forecast.

4.2 Properties of Conditional Expectations

It might be useful to list some properties of the conditional expectation operator. First note a convenient notation.

Often, the expectation conditional on an information set I_t is written compactly as

$$E[\cdot|I_t] = E_t. \tag{12}$$

The t subscript in E_t indicates that in the averaging operation one uses all information available up to time t.

The conditional expectation operator E_t has the following properties.

1. The conditional expectation of the sum of two random variables is the sum of conditional expectations:

$$E_u[S_t + F(t)] = E_u[S_t] + E_u[F(t)], \qquad u < t. \tag{13}$$

According to this, one can form separate forecasts of random variables and then add these forecasts to get a forecast of the *total*.

2. Suppose the most recent information set is I_t, but one is interested in forecasting the expectation $E_{t+T}[S_{t+T+u}]$, $T > 0, u > 0$. That is, one would like to say something about the forecast of a possible forecast. Since the information set I_{t+T} is unavailable at time t, the conditional expectation $E_{t+T}[S_{t+T+u}]$ is unknown. In other words, $E_{t+T}[S_{t+T+u}]$ is itself a random variable. A property of conditional expectations is that the expectation of this future expectation equals the present forecast of S_{t+T+u}:

$$E_t[E_{t+T}(S_{t+T+u})] = E_t[S_{t+T+u}]. \tag{14}$$

According to this, recursive application of conditional expectation operators always equals the conditional expectation with respect to the smaller information set:

$$E[E[\cdot|I_t]|I_o] = E[\cdot|I_0\cdot], \tag{15}$$

where I_0 is contained in I_t.

Finally, if the conditioning information set I_t is empty, then one obtains the "unconditional" expectation operator E. This means that E also has similar properties.

5 Some Important Models

This section discusses some important models for random variables. These models are useful not only in theory, but also in practical applications of asset pricing.

In this section we also extend the notion of a random variable to a random process.

5.1 Binomial Distribution in Financial Markets

Consider a trader who follows the price of an exchange-traded derivative asset $F(t)$ in real time, using a service such as Reuters, Telerate, or Bloomberg.

The price $F(t)$ changes continuously over time, but the trader is assumed to have limited scope of attention and checks the market price every Δ seconds. We assume that Δ is a small time interval.

More importantly, we assume that at any time t there are two possibilities:

1. There is either an *uptick* and prices increase according to

$$\Delta F(t) = +a\sqrt{\Delta}, \qquad a > 0. \tag{16}$$

2. Or, there is a *downtick* and prices decrease by

$$\Delta F(t) = -a\sqrt{\Delta}, \tag{17}$$

where $\Delta F(t)$ represents the *change* in the observed price during the "small" time interval Δ.

All other outcomes that may very well occur in reality are assumed *for the time being* to have negligible probability.

Then for fixed t, Δ, the $\Delta F(t)$ becomes a *binomial random variable*. In particular, $\Delta F(t)$ can assume only two possible values with the probabilities

$$P(\Delta F(t) = +a\sqrt{\Delta}) = p, \tag{18}$$

$$P(\Delta F(t) = -a\sqrt{\Delta}) = (1 - p). \tag{19}$$

The time index t starts from t_0 and increases by multiples of Δ:

$$t = t_0, t_0 + \Delta, \ldots, t_0 + n\Delta, \ldots. \tag{20}$$

At each time point a new $F(t)$ is observed. Each new increment $\Delta F(t)$ will equal either $+a\sqrt{\Delta}$ or $-a\sqrt{\Delta}$. If the $\Delta F(t)$'s are *independent* of each other, the *sequence* of increments $\Delta F(t)$, will be called a *binomial stochastic process*, or simply a *binomial process*.[6]

---

[6]Remember that a stochastic process is a sequence of random variables indexed by time.

Note that these assumptions are somewhat artificial for actual markets. In a given trading day, even in markets with very high turnover, there are many time periods where $\Delta F(t)$ does not change. Or, in some special circumstances it may change by more than an up or downtick. However, such complications will be dealt with later. For the time being we consider the simpler case of binomial processes.

5.2 Limiting Properties

An important element of the discussion involving the binomial process $\Delta F(t)$ is that the two possible values assumed by each $\Delta F(t)$ depend on the parameter Δ. This dependence permits a discussion of the *limiting behavior* of the binomial process. We can ask a number of questions that will eventually relate to pricing derivative products.

One important question is the following: what does a typical path followed by the $\Delta F(t)$'s look like? Clearly, such a trajectory will be made of a sequence of $+a\sqrt{\Delta}$ and $-a\sqrt{\Delta}$'s. If the probability of these outcomes is exactly equal to $1/2$, then a realization of $\{\Delta F(t), t = t_o, t_0 + \Delta, \ldots\}$ will, as Δ gets smaller, converge to an extremely erratic trajectory that fluctuates between $+a\sqrt{\Delta}$ and $-a\sqrt{\Delta}$.

In fact, as Δ gets smaller two things happen. First, the observation points come nearer, and second, $|a\sqrt{\Delta}|$ gets smaller.

The $\Delta F(t)$ was the *increment* in the price process. What kind of a path is followed by $F(t)$ itself? First note that if $F(t)$ represents the price of a derivative product at time t, then it will equal the *sum* of all up- and downticks since t_0. As $\Delta \to 0$, $F(t)$ will be given by

$$F(t) = F(t_0) + \int_{t_0}^{t} dF(s). \tag{21}$$

That is, beginning from an *initial price* $F(t_0)$, we obtain the price at time t by simply adding all subsequent *infinitesimal* changes. Clearly, in continuous time there are an uncountable number of such infinitesimal changes. Hence the use of integral notation. Also, at the limit, the notation for "small" incremental changes $\Delta F(t)$ is replaced by $dF(t)$, which represents infinitesimal changes.

Finally, consider the following question. At the limit the infinitesimal changes $dF(t)$ are still very erratic. Would the trajectories of $F(t)$ be of *bounded variation*?[7] The question is important, because if not, the

---

[7]See Chapter 3.

Riemann–Stieltjes way of constructing integrals cannot be exploited and a new definition of integral would be needed.

Another important point is the following: the integral in (21) is taken with respect to a *random process*, and not with respect to a deterministic variable as is the case in standard calculus. Clearly, this integral is *itself* a random variable. Can such an integral be successfully defined? Can we use the Riemann–Stieltjes procedure of approximations by appropriate rectangles to construct an integral with respect to a random process? These questions lead to the Ito integral and will be answered in Chapter 9.

5.3 Moments

One question that we would like to answer here concerns the moments of a binomial process.

Fix t. The expected value and the variance of $\Delta F(t)$ are defined as follows:

$$E[\Delta F(t)] = p(a\sqrt{\Delta}) + (1 - p)(-a\sqrt{\Delta}), \tag{22}$$

$$\mathrm{Var}(\Delta F(t)) = p(a\sqrt{\Delta})^2 + (1 - p)(-a\sqrt{\Delta})^2 - [E\Delta F(t)]^2. \tag{23}$$

If we have a 50–50 chance of an uptick at any time t, then

$$p = \frac{1}{2} \tag{24}$$

and the expected value will equal 0 while the variance is given by $a^2\Delta$.

It is important to realize that the variance of the binomial process is proportional to Δ. As Δ approaches zero, a variance that is proportional to Δ will go toward zero with the *same speed*. This means that if we think of Δ as a small but *nonnegligible* quantity, then the variance will also be nonnegligible.

In contrast, if $\Delta F(t)$ had instead fluctuated between, say, $+a\Delta$ and $-a\Delta$ the variance would be proportional to Δ^2. For "small" Δ, the value of Δ^2 would be much smaller. When $\Delta \to 0$, the variance would go to zero significantly faster. Under such conditions, it can be maintained without any contradiction that the variance of $\Delta F(t)$ is negligible, while Δ itself is not.

Heuristically speaking, a random variable with a variance proportional to Δ^2 will be *approximately constant* in infinitesimal time intervals.

Figure 4 illustrates the difference between a variance proportional to Δ (the 45° line) and one proportional to Δ^2. The latter becomes negligible for small Δ.

This last point is also relevant for higher-order moments of the binomial process. Again assume that $p = .5$ for simplicity. Then the expected value

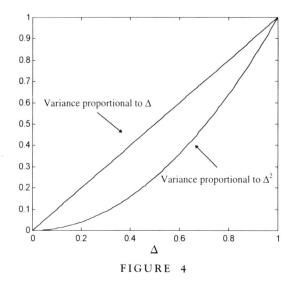

FIGURE 4

is zero and the third moment will be given by

$$E[\Delta F(t)]^3 = p(+a\sqrt{\Delta})^3 + (1 - p)(-a\sqrt{\Delta})^3. \qquad (25)$$

With $p = .5$, the third moment equals zero.
   The fourth-order moment is obtained as

$$E[\Delta F(t)]^4 = (+a\sqrt{\Delta})^4 = a^4\Delta^2. \qquad (26)$$

As $\Delta \to 0$, the fourth-order moment will become negligible. It is, proportional to a power of Δ that goes to zero faster than the time interval itself.
   These observations imply that for small intervals Δ, higher-order moments of a binomial random variable that assumes values proportional to $\sqrt{\Delta}$ can be ignored.

5.4 The Normal Distribution

Now consider the following experiment with the random variable $F(t)$ discussed in the previous section. We ask the computer to calculate *many* realizations of $F(t)$. Then, beginning from the same initial point $F(0)$ we plot these trajectories.

Beginning from $t_0 = 0$, in the *immediate* future, $F(t)$ had only two possible values:[8]

$$F(0 + \Delta) = \begin{cases} F(0) + a\sqrt{\Delta} & \text{with probability } p \\ F(0) - a\sqrt{\Delta} & \text{with probability } 1 - p \end{cases} \quad . \quad (27)$$

Hence, $F(t)$ *itself* is binomial at $t = 0 + \Delta$.

But, if we let some more time pass, and then look at $F(t)$ at, say, $t = 2\Delta$, $F(t)$ will assume one of *three* possible values. More precisely, we have the following possibilities:

$$F(2\Delta) = \begin{cases} F(0) + a\sqrt{\Delta} + a\sqrt{\Delta} & \text{with probability } p^2 \\ F(0) - a\sqrt{\Delta} + a\sqrt{\Delta} & \text{with probability } 2p(1 - p) \\ F(0) - a\sqrt{\Delta} - a\sqrt{\Delta} & \text{with probability } (1 - p)^2 \end{cases} \quad (28)$$

That is to say, $F(2\Delta)$ may equal $F(0) + 2a\sqrt{\Delta}$, $F(0) - 2a\sqrt{\Delta}$, or $F(0)$. Of these, the last outcome is most likely if there is a 50–50 chance of an uptick.

Now consider possible values of $F(t)$ once some more time elapses. Several more combinations of upticks and downticks become possible. For example, by the time $t = 5\Delta$, one possible but "extreme" outcome may be

$$F(5\Delta) = F(0) + a\sqrt{\Delta} + a\sqrt{\Delta} + a\sqrt{\Delta} + a\sqrt{\Delta} + a\sqrt{\Delta} \quad (29)$$

$$= F(0) + 5a\sqrt{\Delta}. \quad (30)$$

Another "extreme" may be to get five downticks in a row:

$$F(5\Delta) = F(0) - a\sqrt{\Delta} - a\sqrt{\Delta} - a\sqrt{\Delta} - a\sqrt{\Delta} - a\sqrt{\Delta}. \quad (31)$$

More likely are *combinations* of upticks and downticks. For example,

$$F(5\Delta) = F(0) - a\sqrt{\Delta} + a\sqrt{\Delta} - a\sqrt{\Delta} + a\sqrt{\Delta} + a\sqrt{\Delta} \quad (32)$$

or

$$F(5\Delta) = F(0) - a\sqrt{\Delta} + a\sqrt{\Delta} + a\sqrt{\Delta} - a\sqrt{\Delta} + a\sqrt{\Delta} \quad (33)$$

are two different sequences of price changes, each resulting in the same price at time $t = 5\Delta$.

There are several other possibilities. In fact, we can consider the general case and try to find the total number of possible values $F(n\Delta)$ can take. Obviously, as $n \to \infty$, $F(n\Delta)$ may take any of a possibly infinite number

---

[8]Note that $F(t)$ is the price and not the incremental change.

of values. A similar conclusion can be reached if $\Delta \to 0$ and $n \to \infty$ while the product Δn remains constant. In this case, we are considering a *fixed* time interval and subdividing it into finer and finer partitions.[9] For the case in which Δ was constant and $n \to \infty$, the time period under consideration increased indefinitely, and we looked at a limiting $F(t)$ projected towards a "distant" future.

One question is what happens to the *distribution* of the random variable $F(n\Delta)$ as $n \to \infty$ and Δ remains fixed?

A somewhat different question is what happens to the *distribution* of $F(n\Delta)$ as $\Delta \to 0$ while $n\Delta$ is fixed.[10]

Now, remember that at the *origin* $F(t)$ was binomial, but a little farther away the number of possible outcomes grew and it became *multinomial*. The probability distribution also changed accordingly. How does the *form* of the distribution change as $n \to \infty$? What would it look like at the limit?

Questions such as these fall in the domain of "convergence of random variables." There are two different ways one can investigate this issue. The first approach is that of the central limit theorem. The second is called *weak convergence*.

According to the central limit theorem, the distribution of $F(n\Delta)$ approaches the normal distribution as $n\Delta \to \infty$.

Assume that $p = .5$ and that

$$F(0) = 0. \tag{34}$$

Then, for fixed Δ and "large" n, the distribution of $F(n\Delta)$ can be approximated by a normal distribution with mean 0 and variance $a^2 n\Delta$. The approximating *density* function will be given by

$$g(F(n\Delta) = x) = \frac{1}{\sqrt{2\pi a^2 n\Delta}} e^{-\frac{1}{2a^2 n\Delta}(x)^2}. \tag{35}$$

The corresponding *distribution* function does not have a *closed-form* formula. It can only be represented as an integral.

The convergence in distribution is illustrated in Figure 5. It is important for practical asset pricing to realize the meaning of this convergence in distribution. We observe a sequence of random variables, indexed by n.[11]

---

[9]In fact, this latter type of convergence is of interest to us. These types of experiments fall in the domain of *weak convergence* and give us an approximate distribution for a *whole* sequence of random variables observed during an interval.

[10]Note that here, also, $n \to \infty$.

[11]That is, we have a stochastic process.

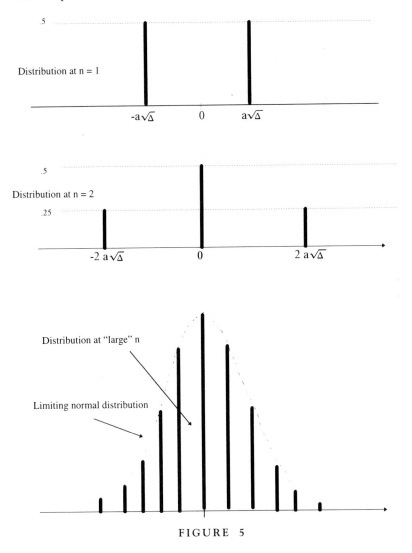

FIGURE 5

As n increases, the distribution function of the nth random variable starts to resemble normal distribution.[12]

It is the notion of *weak convergence* that describes the way distribution of *whole* sequences of random variables converge.

---

[12]Again, we emphasize that we are dealing with the distribution of $F(n\Delta)$, and *not* with the whole *sequence* $\{F(0), F(\Delta), F(2\Delta), \ldots F(n\Delta)\ldots\}$.

5.5 The Poisson Distribution

In dealing with continuous-time stochastic processes, we need *two* building blocks. One is the continuous-time equivalent of the normal distribution known as Brownian motion or, equivalently, as the Wiener process. As the discussion in the previous section indicates, trajectories of normally distributed random variables are likely to be continuous.

This implies that Gaussian model is useful when new information arriving during infinitesimal periods is itself infinitesimal. As illustrated for the binomial approximation, with $\Delta \to 0$, the values assumed by $\Delta F(t)$ become smaller and smaller and the variance of new information given by

$$\text{Var}(\Delta F(t)) = a^2 \Delta \qquad (36)$$

goes to zero.

That is, in infinitesimal intervals, the $F(t)$ cannot "jump." Changes are incremental, and at the limit they converge to zero.

Continuous-time versions of the Normal distribution are very useful in asset pricing. Under some conditions, however, they may not be sufficient to approximate trajectories of asset prices observed in some financial markets. We may need a model for prices that show "jumps" as well. Examples of such "jumps" were many during the October 1987 crash of stock markets around the world.

How can we represent such phenomena?

The Poisson distribution is the second building block. A Poisson-distributed random process consists of jumps at unpredictable *occurrence times* $t_i, i = 1, 2, \dots$. The jump times are assumed to be independent of each other, and each jump is assumed to be of the same size.[13] Further, during a small time interval Δ the probability of observing *more than* one jump is negligible. The total number of jumps observed up to time t is called a *Poisson counting process* and is denoted N_t.

For a Poisson process, the probability of a jump during a *small* interval Δ will be given approximately by

$$P(\Delta N_t = 1) \cong \lambda \Delta, \qquad (37)$$

where λ is a positive constant called the *intensity*.

Note the contrast with normal distribution. For a normally distributed normal variable, the probability of obtaining a value exactly equal to zero was nil. Yet with Poisson distribution, if Δ is "small" this probability is approximately

$$P(\Delta N_t = 0) \cong 1 - \lambda \Delta. \qquad (38)$$

---

[13]Both of these assumptions can be altered. However, to keep the Poisson characteristic, the jump times need to be independent.

Hence, during a small interval there is a "high" probability that no jump will occur. Thus, the trajectory of a Poisson process will consist of a continuous path broken by occasional jumps.

The probability that during a finite interval Δ there will be n jumps is given by

$$P(\Delta N_t = n) = \frac{e^{-\lambda\Delta}(\lambda\Delta)^n}{n!}, \tag{39}$$

which is the corresponding distribution.

6 Convergence of Random Variables

The notion of *convergence* has several uses in asset pricing. Some of these are theoretical, others practical. The binomial example of the previous section introduced the notion of convergence as a way of approximating a complicated random variable with a simpler model. As $\Delta \to 0$, the approximation improved. In this section we provide a more systematic treatment of these issues. Again, the discussion here should be considered as a brief and heuristic introduction.

6.1 Types of Convergence and Their Uses

In pricing financial securities, a minimum of *three* different convergence criteria are used.

The first is *mean square convergence*. This is a criterion utilized to define the Ito integral. This latter, on the other hand, is utilized in characterizing stochastic differential equations (SDEs). As a result, mean square convergence plays a fundamental role in numerical calculations involving SDEs.

DEFINITION: Let $X_0, X_1, \ldots, X_n, \ldots$ be a sequence of random variables. Then X_n is said to converge to X in *mean square* if

$$\lim_{n\to\infty} E\,[X_n - X]^2 = 0. \tag{40}$$

According to this definition, the random approximation error ϵ_n defined by

$$X_n = X + \epsilon_n \tag{41}$$

will have a smaller and smaller variance as n goes to infinity.

Note that for finite n, the variance of ϵ_n may be small, but not necessarily zero. This has an important implication. In doing numerical calculations, one may have to take such approximation errors into account explicitly. One way of doing this is to use the standard deviation of ϵ_n as an estimate.

6.1.1 Relevance of Mean Square Convergence

Mean square (m.s.) convergence is important because the Ito integral is defined as the mean square limit of a certain sum. In particular, if one uses other definitions of convergence this limit may not exist.

We would like to discuss this important point further.

Consider a more "natural" extension of the notion of limit used in standard calculus.

DEFINITION: A random variable X_n converges to X *almost surely* (a.s.) if, for arbitrary $\delta > 0$,

$$P\left(\left|\lim_{n \to \infty} X_n - X\right| > \delta\right) = 0. \tag{42}$$

This definition is a natural extension of the limiting operation used in standard calculus. It says that as n goes to infinity, the difference between the two random variables becomes negligibly small. In the case of mean square convergence, it was the variance that converged to zero. Now, it is the difference between X_n and X. In the limit, the two random variables are almost the same.

6.1.2 Example

Let S_t be an asset price observed at equidistant time points:

$$t_0 < t_0 + \Delta < t_0 + 2\Delta < \cdots < t_0 + n\Delta = T. \tag{43}$$

Define the random variable X_n, indexed by n:

$$X_n = \sum_{i=0}^{n} S_{t_0+i\Delta}[S_{t_0+(i+1)\Delta} - S_{t_0+i\Delta}]. \tag{44}$$

Here $[S_{t_0+(i+1)\Delta} - S_{t_0+i\Delta}]$ represents the *increment* in the asset price at time $t_0 + i\Delta$. The observations begin at time t_0 and are recorded every Δ minutes.

Note that X_n is similar to a Riemann–Stieltjes sum. It is as if an interval $[t_0, T]$ is partitioned into n subintervals and the X_n is defined as an approximation to

$$\int_{t_0}^{T} S_t \, dS_t. \tag{45}$$

But there is a fundamental difference. The sum X_n now involves random processes. Hence, in taking a limit of (44), a new type of convergence criterion should be used. The standard definition of limit from calculus is not applicable.

Which (random) convergence criterion should be used?

It turns out that if S_t is a Wiener process, then X_n will *not* converge almost surely,[14] but a mean square limit will exist. Hence, the type of approximation one uses *will* make a difference. This important point is taken up during the discussion of the Ito integral, in later chapters.

6.2 Weak Convergence

The notion of m.s. convergence is used to find approximations to *values* assumed by random variables. As some parameter n goes to infinity, values assumed by some random variable X_n can be approximated by values of some limiting random variable X.

In the case of *weak convergence*, what is being approximated is not the value of a random variable X_n, but the *probability* associated with a sequence $X_0, \dots, X_n$. Weak convergence is used in approximating the *distribution function* of families of random variables.

DEFINITION: Let X_n be a random variable indexed by n with probability distribution P_n. We say that X_n converges to X weakly and

$$\lim_{n \to \infty} P_n = P, \tag{46}$$

where P is the probability distribution of X if

$$E^{P_n} f(X_n) \to E^P f(X), \tag{47}$$

where $f(\cdot)$ is any bounded, continuous, real-valued function.

According to this definition, a random variable X_n converges to X *weakly* if functions of the two random variables have *expectations* that are close enough. Thus, X_n and X do not necessarily assume values that are very close, yet they are governed by arbitrarily close probabilities as $n \to \infty$.

6.2.1 Relevance of Weak Convergence

We are often interested in values assumed by a random *variable* as some parameter n goes to infinity. For example, to define an Ito integral, a random variable with a simple structure is first constructed. This random variable will depend on some parameter n. In the second step, one shows that as $n \to \infty$ this simple variable converges to the Ito integral in the m.s. sense.

Hence, in defining an Ito integral, *values* assumed by a random variable are of fundamental interest, and mean square convergence needs to be used.

---

[14]The same result applies if in addition S_t displays occasional jumps.

At other times, such specific values may not be relevant. Instead, one may be concerned only with *expectations*—i.e., some sort of average—of random *processes*.

For example, $F(S_T, T)$ may denote the random price of a derivative product at expiration time T. The derivative is written on the underlying asset S_T. We know that if there are no arbitrage opportunities, then there exists a "risk-neutral" probability $\tilde{P}$, such that, under some simplifying assumptions, the value of the derivative at time t is given by

$$F(t) = e^{-r(T-t)} E_t^{\tilde{P}} [F(S_T, T)] \qquad (48)$$

Thus, instead of being concerned with the exact future value of S_T, we need to calculate the *expectation* of some function $F(\cdot)$ of S_T. Using the concept of *weak convergence*, an approximation S_T^n of S_T can be utilized. This may be desirable if S_T^n is more convenient to work with than the actual random variable S_T. For example, S_T may be a continuous-time random process, whereas S_T^n may be a random *sequence* defined over small intervals that depend on some parameter n. If the work is done on computers, S_T^n will be easier to work with than S_T. This idea was utilized earlier in obtaining a binomial approximation to a continuous normally distributed process.

6.2.2 An Example

Consider a time interval $[0, 1]$ and let $t \in [0, 1]$ represent a particular *time*.[15] Suppose we are given n observations ϵ_i, $i = 1, 2, \ldots, n$ drawn independently from the uniform distribution $U(0, 1)$.[16]

Next define the random variables $X_i(t)$, $i = 1, \ldots, n$ by

$$X_i(t) = \begin{cases} 1 & \text{if } \epsilon_i \leq t \\ 0 & \text{otherwise} \end{cases} . \qquad (50)$$

According to this, $X_i(t)$ is either 0 or 1, depending on the t and on the value assumed by ϵ_i.

Using $X_i(t)$, $i = 1, \ldots, n$, we define the random variable $S_n(t)$:

$$S_n(t) = \frac{1}{\sqrt{n}} \sum_{i=1}^{n} (X_i(t) - t) \qquad (51)$$

---

[15] We may, for example, let the expiration time of some derivative contract be 1, while 0 represents the *present*.

[16] This means that

$$\text{Prob}(\epsilon_i \leq t) = t \qquad (49)$$

for any $0 \leq t \leq 1$.

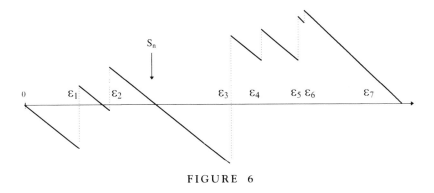

FIGURE 6

Figure 6 displays this construction for $n = 7$. Note that $S_n(t)$ is a *piece-wise continuous function* with jumps at ϵ_i.

As $n \to \infty$, the jump points become more frequent and the "oscillations" of $S_n(t)$ more pronounced. The sizes of the jumps, however, will diminish. At the limit $n \to \infty$, $S_n(t)$ will be very close to a normally distributed random variable for each t. Interestingly, the process will be continuous at the limit, the initial and the end points being identically equal to zero.[17]

Clearly, what happens here is that as $n \to \infty$, the $S_n(t)$ starts to behave more and more like a normally distributed process. For large n, we may find a limiting Gaussian process more convenient to work with than $S_n(t)$.

It should also be emphasized that in this example, as n increases, the number of points at which $S_n(t)$ changes will increase. In applications where we go from small discrete intervals towards continuous-time analysis, this would often be the case.

7 Conclusions

This chapter briefly reviewed some basic concepts of probability theory to be needed later.

We spent a minimum of time on the standard definitions of probability. However, we made a number of important points.

First, we characterized normally distributed random variables and Poisson processes as two basic building blocks.

Second, we discussed an important binomial process. This example was used to introduce the important notion of convergence of stochastic processes.

---

[17]Such a process is called a Brownian bridge.

The binomial example discussed here also happens to have practical implications, since it is very similar to the *binomial tree-models* routinely used in pricing financial assets.

8 References

In the remainder of this book, we don't really need any further results on probability than what is reviewed here. However, a financial market participant or a finance student will always benefit from a good understanding of the theory of stochastic processes. An excellent introduction is Ross (1994). Liptser and Shiryayev (1977) is an excellent advanced introduction. Cinlar (1978) provides another source at the intermediate level.

CHAPTER 6

Martingales and Martingale Representations

1 Introduction

Martingales are one of the central tools in the modern theory of finance. In this chapter we introduce the basics of martingale theory. However, this theory is vast, and we only emphasize those aspects that are directly relevant to pricing financial derivatives.

We begin with a comment on notation. In this chapter we use the notation ΔW_t or ΔS_t to represent "small" changes in W_t or S_t. Occasionally, we may also use their incremental versions dW_t, dS_t, which represent stochastic changes during infinitesimal intervals. For the time being, the reader can interpret these differentials as "infinitesimal" stochastic changes observed over a continuous time axis. These concepts will be formally defined in Chapter 9.

To denote a small interval, in this book we use the symbols h or Δ. An infinitesimal interval, on the other hand, is denoted by dt. In later chapters we show that these notations are not equivalent. An operation such as

$$E[S_{t+\Delta} - S_t] = 0,$$

where Δ is a "small" interval, is well defined. Yet, writing

$$E[dS_t] = 0$$

is informal, since dS_t is only a symbolic expression, as we will see in the definition of the Ito integral.

Salih N. Neftci, *An Introduction to the Mathematics of Financial Derivatives*
Copyright 1996 by Academic Press   0-12-515390-2

Martingales and Martingale Representations

1 Introduction

Martingales are one of the central tools in the modern theory of finance. In this chapter we introduce the basics of martingale theory. However, this theory is vast, and we only emphasize those aspects that are directly relevant to pricing financial derivatives.

We begin with a comment on notation. In this chapter we use the notation ΔW_t or ΔS_t to represent "small" changes in W_t or S_t. Occasionally, we may also use their incremental versions dW_t, dS_t, which represent stochastic changes during infinitesimal intervals. For the time being, the reader can interpret these differentials as "infinitesimal" stochastic changes observed over a continuous time axis. These concepts will be formally defined in Chapter 9.

To denote a small interval, in this book we use the symbols h or Δ. An infinitesimal interval, on the other hand, is denoted by dt. In later chapters we show that these notations are not equivalent. An operation as

$$E[S_{t+\Delta} - S_t] = 0,$$

where Δ is a "small" interval, is well defined. Yet, writing

$$E[dS_t] = 0$$

is informal, since dS_t is only a symbolic expression, as we will see in the definition of the Ito integral.

2 Definitions

Martingale theory classifies observed time series according to the way they "trend." A stochastic process behaves like a *martingale* if its trajectories display no discernible trends or periodicities. A process that, on the average, increases is called a *submartingale.* The term *supermartingale* represents processes that, on the average, decline. This section gives formal definitions of these concepts. First some notation.

2.1 Notation

Suppose we observe a family of random variables indexed by time index t. We assume that time is continuous and deal with continuous-time stochastic processes. Let the observed process be denoted by $\{S_t, t \in [0, \infty]\}$. Let $\{I_t, t \in [0, \infty]\}$ represent a family of information sets that become continuously available to the decision maker as time passes.[1] With $s < t < T$, this family of information sets will satisfy

$$I_s \subseteq I_t \subseteq I_T \ldots. \tag{1}$$

The set $\{I_t, t \in [0, T]\}$ is called a *filtration.*

In discussing martingale theory (and throughout the rest of this book), we occasionally need to consider values assumed by some stochastic process at some particular points in time. This is often accomplished by selecting a sequence $\{t_i\}$ such that

$$0 = t_0 < t_1 < \ldots < t_{k-1} < t_k = T \tag{2}$$

represent various time periods over a continuous time interval $[0, T]$. Note the way the initial value and the endpoint of the interval are handled in this notation. The symbol t_0 is assigned to the initial point, whereas t_k is the "new" symbol for T. In this notation, as $k \to \infty$, and $(t_i - t_{i-1}) \to 0$, the interval $[0, T]$ would be partitioned into finer and finer pieces.

Now consider the random price process S_t during the finite interval $[0, T]$. At some particular time t_i, the value of the price process will be S_{t_i}. If the value of S_t is included in the information set I_t at each $t \geq 0$, then it is said that $\{S_t, t \in [0, T]\}$ is *adapted* to $\{I_t, t \in [0, T]\}$. That is, the value S_t will be known, given the information set I_t.

We can now define continuous-time martingales.

---

[1]Depending on the problem at hand, the I_t will represent different types of information. The most natural use of I_t will be to represent the information one can obtain from the realized prices in financial markets up to time t.

2.2 Continuous-Time Martingales

Using different information sets one can conceivably generate different "forecasts" of a process $\{S_t\}$. These forecasts are expressed using conditional expectations. In particular,

$$E_t[S_T] = E[S_T|I_t], \qquad t < T, \tag{3}$$

is the formal way of denoting the forecast of a future value, S_T of S_t, using the information available as of time t. $E_u S_T, u < t$, would denote the forecast of the same variable using a smaller information set, namely the one available earlier, as of time u.

The defining property of a martingale relates to these conditional expectations.

DEFINITION: We say that a process $\{S_t, t \in [0, \infty]\}$ is a *martingale* with respect to the family of information sets I_t and with respect to the probability P, if, for all $t > 0$,

1. S_t is known, given I_t. (S_t is I_t-adapted.)
2. Unconditional "forecasts" are finite:

$$E|S_t| < \infty. \tag{4}$$

3. And if

$$E_t[S_T] = S_t, \qquad \text{for all } t < T, \tag{5}$$

with probability 1.

That is, the best forecast of unobserved future values is the last observation on S_t.

Here, all expectations $E[\cdot]$, $E_t[\cdot]$ are assumed to be taken with respect to the probability P.

According to this definition, martingales are random variables whose future *variations* are completely unpredictable given the current information set. For example, suppose S_t is a martingale and consider the forecast of the *change* in S_t over an interval of length $u > 0$:

$$E_t[S_{t+u} - S_t] = E_t S_{t+u} - E_t S_t. \tag{6}$$

But $E_t S_t$ is a forecast of a random variable whose value is already "revealed" (since $S(t)$ is by definition I_t-adapted). Hence, it equals S_t. If S_t is a martingale, $E_t S_{t+u}$ would also equal S_t. This gives

$$E_t[S_{t+u} - S_t] = 0, \tag{7}$$

i.e., the best forecast of the *change* in S_t over an arbitrary interval $u > 0$ is zero. In other words, the directions of the future movements in martingales are impossible to forecast. This is the fundamental characteristic of processes that behave as martingales. If the trajectories of a process display clearly recognizable long- or short-run "trends," then the process is not a martingale.[2]

Before closing this section, we reemphasize a *very* important property of the definition of martingales. A martingale is always defined *with respect to* some information set, *and* with respect to some probability measure. If we change the information content and/or the probabilities associated with the process, the process under consideration may cease to be a martingale.

The opposite is also true. Given a process X_t which does not behave like a martingale, we may be able to modify the relevant probability measure P and convert X_t into a martingale.

3 The Use of Martingales in Asset Pricing

According to the definition above, a process S_t is a martingale if its future movements are completely unpredictable given a family of information sets. Now, we know that stock prices or bond prices are *not* completely unpredictable. The price of a discount bond is expected to *increase* over time. In general, the same is true for stock prices. They are expected to increase on the average. Hence, if B_t represents the price of a discount bond maturing at time $T, t < T$,

$$B_t < E_t[B_u], \qquad t < u < T. \tag{8}$$

Clearly, the price of a discount bond does not move like a martingale.

Similarly, in general a risky stock S_t will have a positive expected return and will not be a martingale. For a small interval Δ, we can write approximately

$$E_t[S_{t+\Delta} - S_t] \cong \mu\Delta, \tag{9}$$

where μ is a positive rate of expected return.[3]

---

[2] A sample path of a martingale may still contain patterns that "look like" short-lived trends. However, these up or down trends are completely random and do not have any systematic character.

[3] The approximation here is in the sense of dropping higher-order terms involving Δ in a Taylor series expansion of $E_t[S_{t+\Delta} - S_t]$,

$$E_t[S_{t+\Delta} - S_t] = \mu\Delta + o(\Delta),$$

where $o(\Delta)$ represents all higher-order terms of the corresponding Taylor series expansion.

A similar statement can be made about futures or options. For example, options have "time value," and as time passes the price of European-style options will decline ceteris paribus. Such a process is a *supermartingale*.[4]

If asset prices are more likely to be sub- or supermartingales, then why such an interest in martingales?

It turns out that although most financial assets are not martingales, one can *convert* them into martingales. For example one can find a probability distribution $\tilde{P}$ such that bond or stock prices discounted by the risk-free rate become martingales. If this is done, equalities such as

$$E_t^{\tilde{P}}\left[e^{-ru}B_{t+u}\right] = B_t, \qquad 0 < u < T - t, \tag{10}$$

for bonds, or

$$E_t^{\tilde{P}}\left[e^{-ru}S_{t+u}\right] = S_t, \qquad 0 < u, \tag{11}$$

for stock prices, can be very useful in pricing derivative securities.

One important question that we study in later chapters is how to obtain this conversion. There are in fact *two* ways of converting submartingales into martingales.

The first method should be obvious. We can subtract an *expected trend* from $e^{-rt}S_t$ or $e^{-rt}B_t$. This would make the *deviations* around the trend completely unpredictable. Hence, the "transformed" variables would be martingales.

This methodology is equivalent to using the so-called representation results for martingales. In fact, Doob–Meyer decomposition implies that, under some general conditions, an arbitrary continuous-time process can be decomposed into a martingale and an increasing (or decreasing) process. Elimination of the latter leaves the martingale to work with. Doob–Meyer decomposition is handled in this chapter.

The second method is more complex and, surprisingly, more useful. Instead of transforming the submartingale directly, we can transform its *probability distribution*. That is, if one had

$$E_t^{P}\left[e^{-ru}S_{t+u}\right] > S_t \qquad 0 < u, \tag{12}$$

where $E_t^{P}[.]$ is the conditional expectation calculated using a probability distribution P, we may try to find an "equivalent" probability $\tilde{P}$, such that the new expectations satisfy

$$E_t^{\tilde{P}}\left[e^{-ru}S_{t+u}\right] = S_t, \qquad 0 < u, \tag{13}$$

and the $e^{-rt}S_t$ becomes a martingale.

---

[4]Deep in the money, *American* puts may have *negative* time value.

Probability distributions that convert equations such as (12) into equalities such as (13) are called *equivalent martingale measures*. They will be treated in Chapter 14.

If this second methodology is selected to convert arbitrary processes into martingales, then the transformation is done using the *Girsanov theorem*. In financial asset pricing, this method is more promising than the Doob–Meyer decompositions.

4 Relevance of Martingales in Stochastic Modeling

In the absence of arbitrage possibilities, market equilibrium suggests that we can find a synthetic probability distribution $\tilde{P}$ such that all properly discounted asset prices S_t, behave as martingales:

$$E^{\tilde{P}}\left[e^{-ru}S_{t+u}|I_t\right] = S_t, \qquad u > 0. \tag{14}$$

Because of this, martingales have a fundamental role to play in practical asset pricing.

But this is not the only reason why martingales are useful tools. Martingale theory is very rich and provides a very fertile environment for discussing stochastic variables in continuous time. In this section we discuss these useful technical aspects of martingale theory.

Let X_t represent an asset price that has the martingale property with respect to the filtration $\{I_t\}$ and with respect to the probability $\tilde{P}$

$$E^{\tilde{P}}\left[X_{t+\Delta}|I_t\right] = X_t, \tag{15}$$

where $\Delta > 0$ represents a small time interval.

What type of trajectories would such an X_t have in continuous time?

To answer this question, first define the *martingale difference* ΔX_t,

$$\Delta X_t = X_{t+\Delta} - X_t, \tag{16}$$

and then note that since X_t is a martingale,

$$E^{\tilde{P}}[\Delta X_t|I_t] = 0. \tag{17}$$

As mentioned earlier, this equality implies that increments of a martingale should be totally unpredictable, no matter how small the time interval Δ is. But, since we are working with continuous time, we can indeed consider *very* small Δ's. Martingales should then display very irregular trajectories. In fact, X_t should not display any trends discernible by eye examination, even during infinitesimally small time intervals Δ. If it did, it would become predictable.

FIGURE 1

Such irregular trajectories can occur in two different ways. They can be *continuous*, or they can display *jumps*. The former leads to *continuous martingales*, whereas the latter are called *right continuous martingales*.

Figure 1 displays an example of a continuous martingale. Note that the trajectories are continuous, in the sense that for $\Delta \to 0$,

$$P(\Delta X_t > \epsilon) \to 0, \qquad \text{for all } \epsilon > 0. \tag{18}$$

Figure 2 displays an example of a right continuous martingale. Here, the trajectory is interrupted with occasional jumps.[5] What makes the trajectory *right* continuous is the way jumps are modeled. At jump times t_0, t_1, t_2, the martingale is continuous rightwards (but not leftwards.)

This irregular behavior and the possibility of incorporating jumps in the trajectories is certainly desirable as a theoretical tool for representing asset prices, especially given the arbitrage theorem.

But martingales have significance beyond this. In fact, suppose one is dealing with a continuous martingale X_t that also has a finite second moment

$$E\left[X_t^2\right] < \infty \tag{19}$$

for all $t > 0$.

Such a process has finite variance and is called a *continuous square integrable martingale*. It is significant that one can represent all such martingales by running the Brownian motion at a modified time clock. (See Karatzas and Shreve (1991). In other words, the class of continuous square integrable

---

[5]Note that the process still does not have a trend.

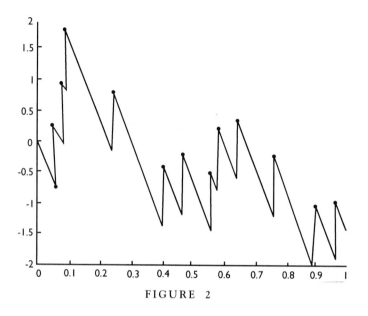

FIGURE   2

martingales is very close to the Brownian motion. This suggests that the un-predictability of the changes and the absence of jumps are two properties of Brownian motion in continuous time.

Note what this essentially means. If the continuous square integrable martingale is appropriate for modeling an asset price, one may as well assume normality for small increments of the price process.

4.1 An Example

We will construct a martingale using two independent Poisson processes observed during "small intervals" Δ.

Suppose financial markets are influenced by "good" and "bad" news. We ignore the content of the news, but retain the information on whether it is "good" or "bad."

The N_t^G denotes the total *number* of instances of "good" news until time t. The process N_t^B denotes the total *number* of instances of "bad" news. We assume further that the way news arrives in financial markets is totally unrelated to past data, and that the "good" and "bad" news is independent.

Finally, during a small interval Δ at most *one* instance of good news or one instance of bad news can occur, and the probability of this occurrence is the *same* for both types of news. Thus, the probabilities of incremental changes $\Delta N^G, \Delta N^B$ during Δ is assumed to be given approximately by

$$P(\Delta N^G_t = 1) = P(\Delta N^B_t = 1) \cong \lambda \Delta. \tag{20}$$

Then the variable M_t, defined by

$$M_t = N^G_t - N^B_t, \tag{21}$$

will be a martingale.

To see this, note that the increments of M_t over small intervals Δ will be given by

$$\Delta M_t = \Delta N^G_t - \Delta N^B_t. \tag{22}$$

Apply the conditional expectation operator:

$$E_t[\Delta M_t] = E_t[\Delta N^G_t] - E_t[\Delta N^B_t]. \tag{23}$$

But, approximately,

$$E_t[\Delta N^G_t] \cong 0 \cdot (1 - \lambda \Delta) + 1 \cdot \lambda \Delta \tag{24}$$

$$\cong \lambda \Delta, \tag{25}$$

and similarly for $E_t[\Delta N^B_t]$. This means that

$$E_t[\Delta M_t] \cong \lambda \Delta - \lambda \Delta = 0. \tag{26}$$

Hence, increments in M_t are unpredictable given the family I_t. It can be shown that M_t satisfies other (technical) requirements of martingales. For example, at time t, we know the "good" or "bad" news that has already happened. Hence, M_t is I_t-adapted.

Thus, as long as the probability of "good" and "bad" news during Δ is given by the same expression $\lambda \Delta$ for both N^G_t and N^B_t, the process M_t will be a martingale with respect to I_t and with respect to these probabilities.

However, if we assume that "good" news can occur with a slightly greater probability than "bad" news,

$$P(\Delta N^G_t = 1) \cong \lambda^G \Delta > P(\Delta N^B_t = 1) \cong \lambda^B \Delta, \tag{27}$$

then M_t will cease to be martingale with respect to I_t, since

$$E_t[\Delta M_t] \cong \lambda^G \Delta - \lambda^B \Delta > 0. \tag{28}$$

(In fact, M_t will be a submartingale.) Hence, changing the underlying probabilities or the information set may change martingale characteristics of a process.

5 Properties of Martingale Trajectories

The properties of the trajectories of continuous square integrable martingales can be made more precise.

Assume that $\{X_t\}$ represents a trajectory of a continuous square integrable martingale. Pick a time interval $[0, T]$ and consider the times $\{t_i\}$:

$$t_0 = 0 < t_1 < t_2 < \ldots < t_{n-1} < t_n = T. \tag{29}$$

We define the *variation* of the trajectory as

$$V^1 = \sum_{i=1}^{n} |X_{t_i} - X_{t_{i-1}}|. \tag{30}$$

The *quadratic* variation is given by

$$V^2 = \sum_{i=1}^{n} |X_{t_i} - X_{t_{i-1}}|^2. \tag{31}$$

One can similarly define *higher-order* variations. For example, the fourth-order variation is defined as

$$V^4 = \sum_{i=1}^{n} |X_{t_i} - X_{t_{i-1}}|^4. \tag{32}$$

Obviously, the V^1 or V^2 are different measures of how much X_t varies over time. The V^1 represents the sum of absolute changes in X_t observed during the subintervals $t_i - t_{i-1}$. The V^2 represents the sums of squared changes.

When X_t is a continuous martingale, the V^1, V^2, V^3, V^4 happen to have some very important properties.

First we recall some relevant points. Remember that we want X_t to be continuous and to have a nonzero variance. As mentioned earlier, this means two things. First, as the partitioning of the interval $[0, T]$ gets finer and finer, "consecutive" X_t's get nearer and nearer, for any $\epsilon > 0$

$$P(|X_{t_i} - X_{t_{i-1}}| > \epsilon) \to 0, \tag{33}$$

if $t_i \to t_{i-1}$, for all i. Second, as the partitions get finer and finer we still want

$$P\left(\sum_{i=1}^{n} |X_{t_i} - X_{t_{i-1}}|^2 > 0 \right) = 1. \tag{34}$$

This is true because X_t is after all a random process with nonzero variance.

Now consider some properties of V^1 and V^2.

First of all, note that even though X_t is a continuous martingale and X_{t_i} approaches $X_{t_{i-1}}$ as the subinterval $[t_i, t_{i-1}]$ becomes smaller and smaller, this does not mean that V^1 also approaches zero. The reader may find this surprising. After all, V^1 is made of the sum of such incremental changes:

$$V^1 = \sum_{i=1}^{n} |X_{t_i} - X_{t_{i-1}}|. \tag{35}$$

As X_{t_i} approaches $X_{t_{i-1}}$, wouldn't V^1 go toward zero as well?

Surprisingly, the opposite is true. As $[0, T]$ is partitioned into finer and finer subintervals, changes in X_t get smaller. But at the same time, the *number* of terms in the sum defining V^1 increases. It turns out that in the case of a continuous-time martingale, the second effect dominates and the V^1 goes toward infinity. The trajectory of continuous martingales have *infinite* variation, except for the case when the martingale is a constant.

This can be shown heuristically as follows. We have

$$\sum_{i=1}^{n} |X_{t_i} - X_{t_{i-1}}|^2 < \left[\max_i |X_{t_i} - X_{t_{i-1}}|\right] \sum_{i=1}^{n} |X_{t_i} - X_{t_{i-1}}|, \tag{36}$$

since the right-hand side is obtained by factoring out the "largest" $X_{t_i} - X_{t_{i-1}}$.[6] This means that

$$V^2 < \max_i |X_{t_i} - X_{t_{i-1}}| V^1. \tag{37}$$

As $t_i \to t_{i-1}$, for all i, the continuity of the martingale implies that "consecutive" X_{t_i}'s will get very near each other. At the limit,

$$\max_i |X_{t_i} - X_{t_{i-1}}| \to 0 \tag{38}$$

This, according to Equation (37), means that unless V^1 get very large, V^2 will go towards zero in some probabilistic sense. But this is not allowed, because, X_t is a stochastic process with a nonzero variance and consequently $V^2 > 0$ even for very fine partitions of $[0, T]$. This implies that we must have $V^1 \to \infty$.

Now consider the same property for higher-order variations. For example, consider V^4 and apply the same "trick" as in (37):

$$V^4 < \left[\max_i |X_{t_i} - X_{t_{i-1}}|^2\right] V^2. \tag{39}$$

---

[6]The notation $\max_i |X_{t_i} - X_{t_{i-1}}|$ should be read as choosing the largest observed increment out of all incremental changes in X_{t_i}.

As long as V^2 converges to a well-defined random variable,[7] the right-hand side of (39) will go to zero. The reason is the same as above. The X_t is a continuous martingale and its increments get smaller as the partition of the interval $[0, T]$ becomes finer. Hence, as $t_i \to t_{i-1}$ for all i:

$$\max_i |X_{t_i} - X_{t_{i-1}}|^2 \to 0. \tag{40}$$

This means that V^4 will tend to zero. The same argument can be applied to all variations greater than two.

For formal proofs of such arguments the reader can consult, Karatzas and Shreve (1991). Here we summarize the three properties of the trajectories:

• The variation V^1 will converge to infinity in some probabilistic sense and the continuous martingale will be very irregular.

• The quadratic variation V^2 will converge to some well-defined random variable. This means that regardless of how irregular the trajectories are, the martingale is square integrable and the sums of *square* of the increments over small subperiods converge. This is possible because the square of a small number is even smaller. Hence, even though the sum of increments is "too large" in some probabilistic sense, the sum of *squared* increments is not.

• All higher-order variations will vanish in some probabilistic sense. A heuristic way of interpreting this is to say that higher-order variations do not contain much information beyond those in V^1 and V^2.

These properties have important implications. First of all, we see that V^1 is not a very useful quantity to use in the calculus of continuous square integrable martingales, while the V^2 can be used in a meaningful way. Second, higher-order variations can be ignored, if one is certain that the underlying process is a *continuous* martingale.

These themes will reappear when we deal with the differentiation and integration operations in stochastic environments. A reader who remembers the definition of the Riemann–Stieltjes integral can already see that the same methodology cannot be used for integrals taken with respect to continuous square integrable martingales. This is the case since Riemann–Stieltjes integral uses the equivalent of V^1 in deterministic calculus and considers finer and finer partitions of the interval under consideration. In stochastic environments such limits do not converge.

Instead, stochastic calculus is forced to use V^2.

---

[7]And does not converge to infinity.

6 Examples of Martingales

In this section we consider some examples of continuous-time martingales.

6.1 Example 1: Brownian Motion

Suppose X_t represents a continuous process whose increments are normally distributed. Such a process is called a (generalized) Brownian motion. We observe a value of X_t for each t. At every instant the infinitesimal *change* in X_t is denoted by dX_t. Incremental changes in X_t are assumed to be independent across time.

Under these conditions, if Δ is a small interval, the increments ΔX_t during Δ will have a normal distribution with mean $\mu\Delta$ and variance $\sigma^2\Delta$. This means

$$\Delta X_t \sim N(\mu\Delta, \sigma^2\Delta). \tag{41}$$

The fact that increments are uncorrelated can be expressed as[8]

$$E\big[(\Delta X_u - \mu\Delta)(\Delta X_t - \mu\Delta)\big] = 0. \tag{43}$$

Leaving aside formal aspects of defining such a process X_t, here we ask a simple question:

Is X_t a martingale?

The process X_t is the "accumulation" of infinitesimal increments over time, that is,

$$X_{t+T} = X_0 + \int_0^{t+T} dX_u. \tag{44}$$

Assuming that the integral is well defined, we can calculate the relevant expectations.[9]

Consider the expectation taken with respect to the probability distribution given in (41), and given the information on X_t observed up to time t:

$$E_t[X_{t+T}] = E_t\left[X_t + \int_t^{t+T} dX_u\right]. \tag{45}$$

---

[8]It is not clear why the variance of ΔX_t should be proportional to Δ. For example, is it possible that

$$\mathrm{Var}(\Delta X_t) = \sigma^2(\Delta)^2? \tag{42}$$

This question is more complicated to answer than it looks. It will be at the core of the next chapter.

[9]Note that we have not yet defined integrals of random incremental changes.

But at time t, future values of ΔX_{t+T} are predictable because all changes during small intervals Δ have expectation equal to $\mu\Delta$. This means

$$E_t\left[\int_t^{t+T} dX_u\right] = \mu T. \qquad (46)$$

So,

$$E_t\left[X_{t+T}\right] = X_t + \mu T. \qquad (47)$$

Clearly, $\{X_t\}$ is not a martingale with respect to the distribution in (41) and with respect to the information on current and past X_t.

But, this last result gives a clue on how to generate a martingale with $\{X_t\}$. Consider the new process:

$$Z_t = X_t - \mu t. \qquad (48)$$

It is easy to show that Z_t is a martingale

$$E_t[Z_{t+T}] = E[X_{t+T} - \mu(t+T)] \qquad (49)$$

$$= E[X_t + (X_{t+T} - X_t)] - \mu(t+T), \qquad (50)$$

which means

$$E_t[Z_{t+T}] = X_t + E[X_{t+T} - X_t] - \mu(t+T). \qquad (51)$$

But the expectation on the right-hand side is equal to μT, as shown in (47). This means

$$E_t[Z_{t+T}] = X_t - \mu t \qquad (52)$$

$$= Z_t. \qquad (53)$$

That is, Z_t is a martingale.

Hence, we were able to transform X_t into a martingale by subtracting a deterministic function. Also note that this deterministic function was *increasing* over time. This result holds in more general settings as well.

6.2 Example 2: A Squared Process

Now consider a process S_t with uncorrelated increments during small intervals Δ

$$\Delta S_t \sim N(0, \sigma^2\Delta), \qquad (54)$$

where the initial point is given by

$$S_0 = 0. \qquad (55)$$

Define a new random variable:

$$Z_t = S_t^2. \qquad (56)$$

According to this, Z_t is a nonnegative random variable equaling the square of S_t. Is Z_t a martingale?

The answer is no because the squares of the increments of Z_t are predictable. Using a "small" interval Δ, consider the expectation of the increment in Z_t:

$$E_t[S_{t+\Delta}^2 - S_t^2] = E_t[[S_t - (S_t - S_{t+\Delta})]^2 - S_t^2]$$
$$= E_t[S_{t+\Delta} - S_t]^2.$$

The last equality follows because increments in S_t are uncorrelated with current and past S_t's. As a result, the cross product terms drop. But this means that

$$E[\Delta Z_t] = \sigma^2 \Delta, \tag{57}$$

which proves that increments in Z_t are predictable. The Z_t cannot be a martingale.

But, using the same approach as in Example 1, we can "transform" the Z_t with a mean change and obtain a martingale. In fact, the following equality is easy to prove:

$$E_t[Z_{t+T} - \sigma^2(T+t)] = Z_t - \sigma^2 t. \tag{58}$$

By subtracting $\sigma^2 t$ from Z_t we obtain a martingale.

This example again illustrates the same principle. If somehow a stochastic process is not a martingale, then by subtracting a proper "mean"[10] it can be transformed into a martingale.

This brings us to the point made earlier. In financial markets one cannot expect the observed market value of a risky security to equal its expected value discounted by the risk-free rate. There is a risk premium. Hence, any risky asset price, when discounted by the risk-free rate, will not be a martingale. But the previous discussion suggests that such securities prices can perhaps be transformed into one. Such a transformation would be very convenient for pricing financial assets.

6.3 Example 3: An Exponential Process

The third example is more complicated and will only be partially dealt with here.

Again assume that X_t is as defined in Example 1 and consider the transformation

$$S_t = e^{\{\alpha X_t - \frac{\alpha^2}{2} t\}}, \tag{59}$$

where α is any real number. Suppose the mean of X_t is zero.

---

[10]That is, by subtracting from it a function of time, say, $g(t)$.

Does this transformation result in a martingale?

The answer to this question is yes. We shall prove it in later chapters.[11] However, notice something odd. The X_t itself is a martingale. Why is it that one still has to subtract the function of time $g(t)$,

$$g(t) = \frac{\alpha^2}{2}t, \tag{60}$$

in order make sure that S_t is a martingale? Were not the increments of X_t impossible to forecast anyway?

The answers to these questions have to do with the way one takes derivatives in stochastic environments. This is treated in later chapters.

6.4 Example 4: Right Continuous Martingales

We consider again the Poisson counting process N_t discussed in this chapter. Clearly, N_t will increase over time, since it is a counting process and the number of jumps will grow as time passes.

Hence, N_t cannot be a martingale. It has a clear upward trend.

Yet, the *compensated Poisson process* denoted by N_t^*,

$$N_t^* = N_t - \lambda t, \tag{61}$$

will be a martingale. Clearly, the N_t^* also has increments that are unpredictable. It is a right continuous martingale. Its variance is finite, and it is square integrable.

7 Martingale Representations

The previous examples showed that it is possible to transform a wide variety of continuous-time processes into martingales by subtracting appropriate means.

In this section we formalize these special cases and discuss the so-called Doob–Meyer decomposition.

First, a fundamental example will be introduced. The example is important for (at least) three reasons.

The first reason is practical. By working with a partition of a continuous time interval, we illustrate a practical method used to price securities in financial markets.

Second, it is easier to understand the complexities of the Ito integral if one begins with such a framework.

---

[11] Once we learn about Ito's lemma.

And finally, the example provides a concrete discussion of a probability space and how one can assign probabilities to various trajectories associated with asset prices.

7.1 An Example

Suppose a trader observes at times t_i,

$$t_0 < t_1 < \ldots < t_{k-1} < t_k = T, \tag{62}$$

the price of a financial asset S_t.

If the intervals between the times t_{i-1} and t_i are very small, and if the market is "liquid," the price of the asset is likely to exhibit at most one uptick or one downtick during a typical $t_i - t_{i-1}$. We formalize this by saying that at each instant t_i, there are only two possibilities for the way S_{t_i} can change:

$$\Delta S_{t_i} = \begin{cases} 1 & \text{with probability } p \\ -1 & \text{with probability } (1-p) \end{cases} . \tag{63}$$

It is assumed that these changes are independent of each other. Further, if $p = 1/2$, then the expected value of ΔS_{t_i} will equal zero. Otherwise the mean of price changes is nonzero.

Given these conditions, we first show how to construct the underlying *probability space*.

We observe ΔS_t at k distinct time points.[12] We begin with the notion of probability. The $\{p, (1-p)\}$ refers to the probability of a change in S_{t_i} and is only a (marginal) probability distribution. What is of interest to us is the probability of a *sequence* of price changes. In other words, we would like to discuss probabilities associated with various "trajectories."[13] Doing this requires constructing a probability space.

Given that a typical object of interest is a *sample path*, or trajectory, of price changes, we first need to construct a *set* made of all possible paths. This space is called a *sample space*. Its elements are made of sequences of $+1$'s and -1's. For example, a typical sample path can be

$$\{\Delta S_{t_1} = -1, \ldots, \Delta S_{t_k} = +1\}. \tag{64}$$

Since k is finite, given an initial point S_{t_0} we can easily determine the trajectory followed by the asset price by adding incremental changes. This way we can construct the set of all possible trajectories, i.e., the *sample space*.

---

[12] Note the important assumption that k is finite.

[13] For example, the trader may be interested in the length of the current uptrend or downtrend in asset prices.

Next we define a *probability* associated with these trajectories. When the price changes are independent (and when k is finite), doing this is easy. The probability of a certain sequence is found by simply multiplying the probabilities of each price change.

For example, the particular sequence ΔS^* that begins with $+1$ at time t_0 and alternates until time t_k,

$$\Delta S^* = \{\Delta S_{t_1} = +1, \ \Delta S_{t_2} = -1, \ldots, \Delta S_{t_k} = -1\}, \tag{65}$$

will have the probability (assuming k even)

$$P(\Delta S^*) = p^{k/2}(1 - p)^{k/2}. \tag{66}$$

The probability of a trajectory that continuously declines during the first $k/2$ periods, then continuously increases until time t_k, will also be the same.

Since k is finite, there are a finite number of possible trajectories in the sample space, and we can *assign* a probability to every one of these trajectories.

It is worth repeating what enables us to do this. The finiteness of k plays a role here, since with a finite number of possible trajectories this assignment of probabilities can be made one by one. Pricing derivative products in financial markets often makes the assumption that k is finite and exploits this property of generating probabilities.

Another assumption that simplified this task was the *independence* of successive price changes. This way, the probability of the whole trajectory can be obtained by simply multiplying the probabilities associated with each incremental change.

Up to this point we dealt with the sequence of *changes* in the asset price. Derivative securities are (in general) written on the price itself. For example, in the case of an option written on the S&P500, our interest lies with the *level* of the index, not the *change*.

One can easily obtain the level of the asset price from subsequent changes, given the opening price S_{t_0}:

$$S_{t_k} = S_{t_0} + \sum_{i=1}^{k}(S_{t_i} - S_{t_{i-1}}). \tag{67}$$

Note that since a typical S_{t_k} is made of the *sum* of ΔS_{t_i}'s, probabilities such as (66) can be used to obtain the probability distribution of the S_{t_k} as well. In doing this we would simply add the probabilities of different trajectories that lead to the same S_{t_k}.[14]

---

[14]Addition of probabilities is permitted if the underlying events are mutually exclusive. In this particular case, different trajectories satisfy this condition by definition.

To be more precise, the highest possible value for S_{t_k} is $S_{t_0} + k$. This value will result if all incremental changes ΔS_{t_i}, $i = 1, \ldots, k$ were made of $+1$'s. The probability of this outcome is

$$P(S_{t_k} = S_{t_0} + k) = p^k. \tag{68}$$

Similarly, the lowest possible value of S_{t_k} is $S_{t_0} - k$. The probability of this is given by

$$P(S_{t_k} = S_{t_0} - k) = (1 - p)^k. \tag{69}$$

In these extreme cases, there is only *one* trajectory that gives $S_{t_k} = S_{t_0} + k$ or $S_{t_k} = S_{t_0} + k$.

In general, the price would be somewhere between these two extremes. Of the k incremental changes observed, m would be made of $+1$'s and $k - m$ made of -1's, with $m \leq k$. The S_{t_k} will assume the value

$$S_{t_k} = S_{t_0} + m - (k - m). \tag{70}$$

Note that there are several possible trajectories that eventually result in the same value for S_{t_k}. Adding the probabilities associated with all these combinations, we obtain

$$P(S_{t_k} = S_{t_0} + 2m - k) = C_k^{(k-m)} p^m (1 - p)^{k-m}, \tag{71}$$

where

$$C_k^{(k-m)} = \frac{k!}{m!(k-m)!}.$$

This probability is given by the *binomial distribution*. As $k \to \infty$, this distribution converges to normal distribution.[15]

7.1.1 Is S_{t_k} a Martingale?

Is the $\{S_{t_k}\}$ defined in Equation (67) a martingale with respect to the information set consisting of the increments of "past" price changes ΔS_{t_k}?

Consider the expectations under the probabilities given in (71)

$$E^P\left[S_{t_k} | S_{t_0}, \Delta S_{t_1}, \ldots, \Delta S_{t_{k-1}}\right] = S_{t_{k-1}} + [(+1)p + (-1)(1 - p)], \tag{72}$$

where the second term on the right hand side is the expectation of ΔS_{t_k}, the unknown increment given the information at time $I_{t_{k-1}}$. Clearly, if $p = 1/2$, this term is zero, and we have

$$E^P[S_{t_k} | S_{t_0}, \Delta S_{t_1}, \ldots, \Delta S_{t_{k-1}}] = S_{t_{k-1}}, \tag{73}$$

[15]This is an example of weak convergence.

which means that $\{S_{t_k}\}$ will be a martingale with respect to the information set generated by past price changes *and* with respect to this particular probability distribution.

If $p \neq 1/2$, the $\{S_{t_k}\}$ will cease to be a martingale with respect to $\{I_{t_k}\}$. However, the centered process Z_{t_k}, defined by

$$Z_{t_k} = \left[S_{t_0} + (1 - 2p)\right] + \sum_{i=1}^{k} \left[\Delta S_{t_i} + (1 - 2p)\right] \tag{74}$$

or

$$Z_{t_k} = S_{t_k} + (1 - 2p)(k + 1), \tag{75}$$

will again be a martingale with respect to I_{t_k}.[16]

7.2 Doob–Meyer Decomposition

Consider the case where the probability of an uptick at any time t_i is somewhat greater than the probability of downtick for a particular asset, so that we expect a general upward trend in observed trajectories:

$$1 > p > 1/2. \tag{76}$$

Then, as shown earlier,

$$E^p[S_{t_k} | S_{t_0}, S_{t_1}, \ldots, S_{t_{k-1}}] = S_{t_{k-1}} + (1 - 2p), \tag{77}$$

which means,

$$E^p[S_{t_k} | S_{t_0}, S_{t_1}, \ldots, S_{t_{k-1}}] > S_{t_{k-1}}, \tag{78}$$

since $2p > 1$ according to (76).

This implies that $\{S_{t_k}\}$ is a *submartingale*.

Now, as shown earlier, we can write

$$S_{t_k} = -(1 - 2p)(k + 1) + Z_{t_k}, \tag{79}$$

where Z_{t_k} is a martingale. Hence, we *decomposed* a submartingale into two components. The first term on the right-hand side is an increasing deterministic variable. The second term is a martingale that has a value of $S_{t_0} + (1 - 2p)$ at time t_0. The expression in (79) is a simple case of Doob–Meyer decomposition.[17]

---

[16]It can be checked that the expectation of $\{Z_{t_k}\}$ conditional on past $\{Z_{t_k}\}$'s will equal $\{Z_{t_{k-1}}\}$.

[17]This term is often used for martingales in continuous time. Here we are working with a discrete partition of a continuous-time interval.

7.2.1 The General Case

The decomposition of an upward-trending submartingale into a deterministic trend and a martingale component was done for a process observed at a finite number of points during a continuous interval. Can a similar decomposition be accomplished when we work with *continuously* observed processes?

The Doob–Meyer theorem provides the answer to this question. We provide the theorem without proof.

Let $\{I_t\}$ be the family of information sets discussed above.

THEOREM: If $X_t, 0 \le t \le \infty$ is a right continuous *sub*martingale with respect to the family $\{I_t\}$, and if $E[X_t] < \infty$ for all t, then X_t admits the decomposition

$$X_t = M_t + A_t, \tag{80}$$

where M_t is a right continuous martingale, and A_t is an increasing process measurable with respect to I_t.

This theorem shows that even if continuously observed asset prices contain occasional jumps and trend upwards at the same time, then we can convert them into martingales by subtracting a process observed as of time t.

If the original continuous-time process does not display any jumps, but is continuous, then the resulting martingale will also be continuous.

7.2.2 The Use of Doob Decomposition

The fact that we can take a process that is not a martingale and convert it into one may be quite useful in pricing financial assets. In this section we consider a simple example.

We assume again that time $t \in [0, T]$ is continuous. The value of a call option C_t written on the underlying asset S_t will be given by the function

$$C_T = \max[S_T - K, 0] \tag{81}$$

at expiration date T.

According to this, if the underlying asset price is above the strike price K, the option will be worth as much as this spread. If the underlying asset price is below K, the option has zero value.

At an earlier time t, $t < T$, the exact value of C_T is unknown. But we can calculate a forecast of it using the information I_t available at time t,

$$E^P[C_T|I_t] = E^P[\max[S_T - K, 0] \mid I_t], \tag{82}$$

where the expectation is taken with respect to the distribution function that governs the price movements.

122   CHAPTER · 6   Martingales and Martingale Representations

Given this forecast, one may be tempted to ask if the fair market value C_t will equal a properly discounted value of $E^P[\max[S_T - K, 0]|I_t]$?

For example, suppose we use the (constant) risk-free interest rate r to discount $E^P[\max[S_T - K, 0]|I_t]$, to write

$$C_t = e^{-r(T-t)}E^P[\max[S_T - K, 0] \mid I_t]. \tag{83}$$

Would this equation indeed give the fair market value C_t of the call option?

The answer to this question depends on whether $e^{-r(t)}C_t$ is a martingale with respect to the pair I_t, P or not. If it is, we have

$$E^P[e^{-rT}C_T|C_t] = e^{-rt}C_t, \qquad t < T, \tag{84}$$

or, after multiplying both sides of the equation by e^{-rt},

$$E^P\left[e^{-r(T-t)}C_T|C_t\right] = C_t, \qquad t < T. \tag{85}$$

Then $e^{-rt}C_t$ will be a martingale.

But can we expect $e^{-rt}S_t$ to be a martingale under the true probability P?

As discussed in Chapter 2, under the assumption that investors are risk-averse, for a typical risky security we have

$$E^P\left[e^{-r(T-t)}S_T|S_t\right] > S_t. \tag{86}$$

That is,

$$e^{-rt}S_t \tag{87}$$

will be a submartingale.

But, according to Doob–Meyer decomposition, we can decompose the

$$e^{-rt}S_t \tag{88}$$

to obtain

$$e^{-rt}S_t = A_t + Z_t, \tag{89}$$

where A_t is an increasing I_t measurable random variable, and Z_t is a martingale with respect to the information I_t.

If the function A_t can be obtained explicitly, we can use the decomposition in (89) along with (86) to obtain the fair market value of a call option at time t.

However, this method of asset pricing is rarely pursued in practice. It is more convenient and significantly easier to convert asset prices into martingales, not by subtracting their drift, but instead by changing the underlying probability distribution P.

8 The First Stochastic Integral

We can use the results thus far to define a new martingale M_{t_i}.

Let $H_{t_{i-1}}$ be any random variable adapted to $I_{t_{i-1}}$.[18] Let Z_t be any martingale with respect to I_t and with respect to some probability measure P.

Then the process defined by

$$M_{t_k} = M_{t_0} + \sum_{i=1}^{k} H_{t_{i-1}}[Z_{t_i} - Z_{t_{i-1}}] \tag{90}$$

will also be a martingale with respect to I_t.

The idea behind this representation is not difficult to describe. Z_t is a martingale and has unpredictable increments. The fact that $H_{t_{i-1}}$ is $I_{t_{i-1}}$-adapted means $H_{t_{i-1}}$ are "constants" given $I_{t_{i-1}}$. Then, increments in Z_{t_i} will be uncorrelated with $H_{t_{i-1}}$ as well. Using these observations, we can calculate

$$E_{t_0}[M_{t_k}] = M_{t_0} + E_{t_0}\left[\sum_{i=1}^{k} E_{t_{i-1}}[H_{t_{i-1}}[Z_{t_i} - Z_{t_{i-1}}]]\right]. \tag{91}$$

But increments in Z_{t_i} are unpredictable as of time t_{i-1}.[19] Also, $H_{t_{i-1}}$ is I_t-adapted. This means, we can move the $E_{t_{i-1}}[\cdot]$ operator "inside" to get

$$H_{t_{i-1}} E_{t_{i-1}}\left[Z_{t_i} - Z_{t_{i-1}}\right] = 0.$$

This implies

$$E_{t_0}\left[M_{t_k}\right] = M_{t_0}. \tag{92}$$

M_t has the martingale property.

It turns out that M_t defined this way is the first example of a *stochastic integral*. The question is whether we can obtain a similar result when $\sup_i[t_i - t_{i-1}]$ goes to zero. Using some analogy, can we obtain an expression such as

$$M_t = M_0 + \int_0^t H_u dZ_u, \tag{93}$$

where dZ_u represents an infinitesimal stochastic increment with zero mean given the information at time t?

The question that we will investigate in the next few chapters is whether such an integral can be defined meaningfully. For example, can the Riemann–Stieltjes approximation scheme be used to define the stochastic integral in (93)?

---

[18]We remind the reader that this means, given the information in $I_{t_{i-1}}$, that the value of $H_{t_{i-1}}$ will be known exactly.

[19]Remember that $E_{t_0}[E_{t_{i-1}}[\cdot]] = E_{t_0}[\cdot]$.

8.1 *Application to Finance: Trading Gains*

Stochastic integrals have interesting applications in financial theory. One of these applications is discussed in this section.

We consider a decision maker who invests in a riskless and a risky security at *trading times* t_i:

$$0 = t_o < \ldots t_i < \ldots, t_n = T.$$

Let $\alpha_{t_{i-1}}$ and $\beta_{t_{i-1}}$ be the *number* of shares of riskless and risky securities held by the investor right before time t_i trading begins. Clearly, these random variables will be I_{t_i}-adapted.[20] α_{t_0} and β_{t_0} are the nonrandom initial holdings. Let B_{t_i} and S_{t_i} denote the prices of the riskless and risky securities at time t_i.

Suppose we now consider trading strategies that are *self-financing*. These are strategies where time t_i investments are financed solely from the proceeds of time t_{i-1} holdings. That is, they satisfy

$$\alpha_{t_{i-1}} B_{t_i} + \beta_{t_{i-1}} S_{t_i} = \alpha_{t_i} B_{t_i} + \beta_{t_i} S_{t_i}, \tag{94}$$

where $i = 1, 2, \ldots, n$.

According to this strategy, the investor can sell his holdings at time t_i for an amount equal to the left-hand side of the equation, and with all of these proceeds purchase $\alpha_{t_i}, \beta_{t_i}$ units of riskless and risky securities. In this sense his investment today is completely financed by his investment in the previous period.

We can now substitute recursively for the left-hand side using Equation (94) for $t_{i-1}, t_{i-2}, \ldots$ and using the definitions

$$B_{t_i} = B_{t_{i-1}} + \left[B_{t_i} - B_{t_{i-1}} \right]$$

$$S_{t_i} = S_{t_{i-1}} + \left[S_{t_i} - S_{t_{i-1}} \right].$$

We obtain

$$\alpha_{t_0} B_{t_0} + \beta_{t_0} S_{t_0} + \sum_{j=1}^{i-1} [\alpha_{t_j} [B_{t_{j+1}} - B_{t_j}] + \beta_{t_j} [S_{t_{j+1}} - S_{t_j}]] \tag{95}$$

$$= \alpha_{t_i} B_{t_i} + \beta_{t_i} S_{t_i},$$

where the right-hand side is the wealth of the decision maker *after* time t_i trading.

A close look at the expression (95) indicates that the left-hand side has exactly the same setup as the *stochastic integral* discussed in the previous

---

[20] At time t_i, the investor knows his holdings of riskless and risky securities.

section. Indeed, the α_{t_j} and β_{t_j} are $I_{t_{j+1}}$-adapted, and they are multiplied by increments in securities prices.

Hence, stochastic integrals are natural models for formulating intertemporal budget constraints of investors.

9 Conclusions

This chapter dealt with martingale tools. Martingales were introduced as processes with no recognizable time trends. We discussed several examples that will be useful in later chapters.

This chapter also introduced ways of obtaining martingales from processes that had positive (or negative) time trends.

We close this chapter with a discussion that illustrates why theoretical concepts introduced here are relevant to a practitioner.

Let S_t be the price of an asset observed by a trader at time t. During infinitesimal periods, the trader receives new unpredictable information on S_t. These are denoted by

$$dS_t = \sigma_t \, dW_t,$$

where σ_t is the volatility and dW_t is an increment of Brownian motion. Note that volatility has a time subscript, and consequently changes over time. Also note that dS_t has no predictable drift component.

Over a longer period, such unpredictable information will accumulate. After an interval T, the asset price becomes

$$S_{t+T} = S_t + \int_t^{t+T} \sigma_u \, dW_u.$$

This equation has the same form as (93). If every incremental news is unpredictable, then the sum of incremental news should also be unpredictable (as of time t). But this means that S_t should be a martingale, and we must have

$$E_t \left[\int_t^{t+T} \sigma_u dW_u \right] = 0.$$

This is an important property of stochastic integrals. But it is also a restriction imposed on financial market participants by the way information flows in markets. Martingale methods were central in discussing such equalities. They are also essential for practitioners.

10 References

A reader willing to learn more about martingale arithmetic should consult the introductory book by Williams (1991). The book is very readable and provides details on the mechanics of all major martingale results using simple models. Revuz and Yor (1994) is an excellent advanced text on martingales. The survey by Shiryayev (1984) is an intermediate-level treatment that contains most of the recent results. For trading gains and stochastic integrals, the reader may consult Cox and Huang (1989). Dellacherie and Meyer (1980) is a comprehensive source on martingales.

CHAPTER 7

Differentiation in Stochastic Environments

1 Introduction

Differentiation in deterministic environments was reviewed in Chapter 3. The derivative of a function $f(x)$ with respect to x gave us information about the rate at which $f(\cdot)$ would respond to a small change in x, denoted by dx. This response was calculated as

$$df = f_x \, dx, \tag{1}$$

where f_x is the derivative of $f(x)$ with respect to x.

We need similar concepts in stochastic environments as well. For example, given the variations in the price of an underlying asset S_t, how would the price of, say, a call option written on S_t react? In deterministic environments one would use "standard" rules of differentiation to investigate such questions. But in pricing financial assets we deal with *stochastic* variables, and the notion of risk plays a central role. Can similar formulas be used when the underlying variables are continuous-time stochastic processes?

The notion of differentiation is closely linked to models of *ordinary differential equations* (ODE), where the effect of a change in a variable on another set of variables can be modeled explicitly. In fact, (vector) differential equations are formal ways of modeling the dynamics of deterministic processes, and the existence of the derivative is necessary for doing this.

Can differential equations be used in modeling the dynamics of asset prices as well?

The first difficulty in doing this has to do with the randomness of asset prices. The way heat is transferred in a metal rod may be approximated reasonably well by a *deterministic* model. But, in the case of pricing *derivative* assets, the randomness of the underlying instrument is essential. After all, it is the desire to eliminate, or to take, risk that leads to the existence of derivative assets. In deterministic environments, where everything can be fully predicted, there will be no risk. Consequently, there will be no need for financial derivative products. But if randomness is essential, how would one define differentiation in a stochastic environment?

Can one simply attach random error terms to ordinary differential equations and use them in pricing financial derivatives? Or are there new difficulties in defining *stochastic differential equations* (SDE) as well?

This chapter treats differentiation in stochastic environments using the stochastic differential equations as the underlying model. We first "construct" the SDE from scratch, and then show the difficulties of importing the differentiation formulas directly from deterministic calculus.

More precisely, we first show under what conditions the behavior of a continuous-time process, S_t, can be approximated using the dynamics described by the *stochastic differential equation*

$$dS_t = a(S_t, t)\, dt + b(S_t, t)\, dW_t, \tag{2}$$

where dW_t is an *innovation term* representing unpredictable events that occur during the infinitesimal interval dt. The $a(S_t, t)$ and the $b(S_t, t)$ are the *drift* and the *diffusion* coefficients, respectively. They are I_t-adapted.

Second, we study the properties of the innovation term dW_t, which drives the system and is the source of the underlying randomness. We show that W_t is a very irregular process and that its derivative does not exist in the sense of deterministic calculus. Hence, increments such as dS_t or dW_t have to be justified by some other means.

Constructing the SDE from scratch has a side benefit. This is one way we can get familiar with methods of continuous-time stochastic calculus. It may provide a bridge between discrete-time and continuous-time calculations, and several misconceptions may be eliminated this way.

2 Motivation

This section gives a heuristic comparison of differentiation in deterministic and stochastic environments.

Let S_t be the price of a security, and let $F(S_t, t)$ denote the price of a derivative instrument written on S_t. A stockbroker will be interested in knowing dS_t, the next instant's incremental change in the security price. On the other hand, a derivatives desk needs dF_t, the incremental change in the price of the derivative instrument written on S_t. How can one calculate the dF_t departing from some estimate of dS_t?

Note that what is of interest here is not how the underlying instrument changes, but instead, how the financial derivative *responds* to change in the price of the underlying asset. In other words, a "chain rule" needs to be utilized. If the rules of standard calculus are applicable, a market participant can use the formula

$$dF_t = \frac{\partial F}{\partial S} dS_t, \tag{3}$$

or, in the partial derivative notation,

$$dF_t = F_s \, dS_t. \tag{4}$$

But are the rules of deterministic calculus really applicable? Can this chain rule be used in stochastic environments as well?

Below we show that the rules of differentiation are indeed different in stochastic environments. We proceed with the discussion by utilizing a function $f(x)$ of x.

As discussed in Chapter 3, standard differentiation is the limiting operation defined as

$$\lim_{h \to 0} \frac{f(x+h) - f(x)}{h} = f_x, \tag{5}$$

where the limit satisfies

$$f_x < \infty.$$

Here, $f(x+h) - f(x)$ represents the change in the function as x changes by h. Hence, if x represents time, then the derivative is the *rate* at which $f(x)$ is changing during an infinitesimal interval.[1] In this case, time is a deterministic variable, and one can use "standard" calculus.

But what if the x in $f(x)$ is a random variable moving along a continuous time axis? Can one define the derivative in a similar fashion and use standard rules?

The answer to this question is, in general, no. We begin with a heuristic discussion of this important issue.

---

[1]Note that by dividing $f(x+h) - f(x)$ by h, we obtain a ratio. This ratio tells us how much $f(x)$ changes per h. Hence, it is a *rate*.

Suppose $f(x)$ is a function of a *random* process x.[2] Now suppose we want to expand $f(x)$ around a known value of x, say x_0.[3] A Taylor series expansion will yield

$$f(x) = f(x_0) + f_x(x_0)[x - x_0] + \frac{1}{2}f_{xx}(x_0)[x - x_0]^2 \tag{6}$$

$$+ \frac{1}{3!}f_{xxx}(x_0)[x - x_0]^3 + R(x, x_0), \tag{7}$$

where $R(x, x_0)$ represents all the remaining terms of the Taylor series expansion. Note that this remainder is made of three types of terms: partial derivatives of $f(x)$ of order higher than 3, factorials of order higher than 3, and powers of $(x - x_0)$ higher than 3.

Now switch to a Taylor series approximation and consider the terms on the right-hand side other than $R(x, x_0)$.

The $f(x)$ can be rewritten as $f(x_0 + \Delta x)$, if we let

$$\Delta x = x - x_0. \tag{8}$$

Then the Taylor series approximation will have the form[4]

$$f(x_0 + \Delta x) - f(x_0) \cong f_x(\Delta x) + \frac{1}{2}f_{xx}(\Delta x)^2 + \frac{1}{3!}f_{xxx}(\Delta x)^3. \tag{9}$$

On the right-hand side of this representation, Δx represents a "small" *change* in the random variable x. Note that although this change is considered to be small, we do not want it to be so small that it becomes negligible. After all, our purpose is to evaluate the effect of a change in x on the $f(x)$, and this cannot be done by considering "negligible" changes in x. Hence, in a potential approximation of the right-hand side, we would like to *keep* the term $f_x \Delta x$.

Consider the second term $\frac{1}{2}f_{xx}(\Delta x)^2$. If the variable x was deterministic, one could have said that the term $(\Delta x)^2$ is small. This could have been justified by keeping the size of Δx nonnegligible, yet small enough that its square $(\Delta x)^2$ *is* negligible. In fact, if Δx was small, the square of it would be even smaller *and at some point* would become negligible. However, in the present case x is a random variable. So, changes in x will also be random.

---

[2] For the sake of notational simplicity, we omit the time subscript on x.

[3] The interested reader is referred back to Chapter 3 for a review of Taylor series expansions.

[4] In the following, for the sake of notational simplicity, we omit the arguments of $f_x(x_0), f_{xx}(x_0), f_{xxx}(x_0)$.

Suppose these changes have zero mean. Then a random variable is *random*, because it has a positive variance:

$$E[\Delta x]^2 > 0. \tag{10}$$

But read literally, this equality means that, "on the average" the size of $(\Delta x)^2$ is nonzero. In other words, as soon as x becomes a random variable, treating $(\Delta x)^2$ as if it were zero will be equivalent to equating its variance to zero. This amounts to approximating the random variable x by a non-random quantity and will defeat our purpose. After all, we are trying to find the effect of a *random* change in x on $f(x)$.

Hence, as long as x is random, the right-hand side of the Taylor series approximation must keep the second-order term.

On the other hand, note that while keeping the first- and second-order terms in Δx on the right-hand side is required, one can still make a reasonable argument to drop the term that contains the third- and higher-order powers of Δx. This would not cause any inconsistency if higher-order moments are "negligible."[5]

As a result, one candidate for a Taylor-style approximation can be written as

$$f(x_0 + \Delta x) - f(x_0) \sim f_x \Delta x + \frac{1}{2} f_{xx} E[(\Delta x)^2], \tag{11}$$

where the $(\Delta x)^2$ is replaced with its expectation. This is equivalent to replacing the term $\frac{1}{2} f_{xx}(\Delta x)^2$ with its "average" value as a method of approximation. In Chapter 16, we introduce tools that take exactly this direction.

A second possibility is to use, instead of $E[(\Delta x)^2]$, some appropriate limit of the random variable $(\Delta x)^2$ as the time interval under consideration goes to zero. Such approximation were discussed in Chapter 4. It turns out that under some conditions, these two procedures would result in the same expression. In fact, if h represents the time period during which the change Δx is observed, and if h is "small," under some conditions $\sigma^2 h$ may be close enough to $(\Delta x)^2$ in the mean square sense.

Thus, we have *two* possible approximating equations, depending on whether x is random or not.

---

[5]Some readers may remember the discussion involving *variations* of continuous-time martingales in Chapter 6. There, we showed that for continuous square integrable martingales, the first variation was infinite and the quadratic variation converged to a meaningful random variable, while the higher-order variations all vanished. Hence, if the x is a continuous square integrable martingale, the higher-order terms in Δx can be set equal to zero in some approximate sense.

- If x is random, we can write

$$f(x_0 + \Delta x) - f(x_0) \sim f_x \Delta x + \frac{1}{2} f_{xx} E[(\Delta x)^2] \qquad (12)$$

or

$$f(x_0 + \Delta x) - f(x_0) \sim f_x \Delta x + \frac{1}{2} f_{xx} [x^*], \qquad (13)$$

where x^* is the mean square limit of $(\Delta x)^2$.
- Once x becomes deterministic, we can assume that $(\Delta x)^2$ is negligible for small Δx, and use

$$f(x_0 + \Delta x) - f(x_0) \sim f_x \Delta x. \qquad (14)$$

One result of all this is the way differentiation is handled in deterministic and stochastic environments.

For example, in the case of Equation (14), we can try to divide both sides by Δx and obtain the approximation

$$\frac{f(x_0 + \Delta x) - f(x_0)}{\Delta x} \sim f_x. \qquad (15)$$

But with stochastic Δx, it is not clear whether we can let $\Delta x \to 0$ in (9),

$$\lim_{\Delta x \to 0} \frac{f(x_0 + \Delta x) - f(x_0)}{\Delta x} \sim f_x + \frac{1}{2} f_{xx} \lim_{\Delta x \to 0} \frac{(\Delta x)^2}{\Delta x}, \qquad (16)$$

and define a derivative. This is discussed next.

3 A Framework for Discussing Differentiation

The concept of differentiation deals with incremental changes in infinitesimal intervals. In applications to financial markets, what is of interest are the changes in asset prices over incremental *time* periods. In addition, these changes are assumed to be random. Thus, in stochastic calculus, the concept of derivative has to use some type of probabilistic convergence.[6]

The natural framework to utilize for discussing differentiation is the stochastic differential equation (SDE):

$$dS(t) = a(S(t), t) \, dt + b(S(t), t) \, dW_t. \qquad (17)$$

---

[6]Remember that in probabilistic convergence we are interested in finding a random variable X^*, to which a sequence or family of random variables X_n converges. For "large" n, the limiting random variable X^* can then be used as an approximation for X_n, since often the limiting variable would be easier to handle than X_n itself.

In order to understand the way differentiation can proceed in stochastic environments, the SDE will be "constructed" from scratch. The construction will proceed from discrete time to continuous time.

We will consider a time interval $t \in [0, T]$.

Consider Figure 1. The x axis, $[0, T]$, is partitioned into n intervals of equal length h. In terms of the notation used in the previous chapters, we consider intervals given by the partition

$$0 = t_0 < t_1 < \ldots < t_k < \ldots t_n = T. \tag{18}$$

One major difference in this chapter is that we have for all k

$$t_k - t_{k-1} = h, \tag{19}$$

which means that

$$t_k = kh. \tag{20}$$

Thus, we have the relation

$$n = \frac{T}{h}. \tag{21}$$

We define the following quantities observed during these finite intervals:

$$S_k = S(kh) \tag{22}$$

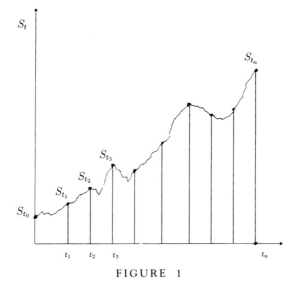

FIGURE 1

and

$$\Delta S_k = S(kh) - S((k-1)h). \tag{23}$$

The latter represents the change in the security price $S(t)$ during a finite interval h.

Now pick a particular interval k. As long as the corresponding expectations exist, we can *always* define a random variable ΔW_k in the following fashion:

$$\Delta W_k = [S_k - S_{k-1}] - E_{k-1}[S_k - S_{k-1}]. \tag{24}$$

Here, the symbol $E_{k-1}[.]$ represents the expectation conditional on information available at the end of interval $k - 1$. The ΔW_k is the part in $[S_k - S_{k-1}]$ that is totally unpredictable given the information available at the end of the $(k-1)$th interval. The first term on the right-hand side represents actual change in the asset price $S(t)$ during the kth interval. The second term is the change that a market participant would have predicted given the information set I_{k-1}.[7] We call unpredictable components of new information "innovations."

Note the following properties of the innovation terms.

· ΔW_k is unknown at the end of the interval $(k - 1)$. It is observed at the end of interval k. In the terminology of measure theory, ΔW_k is said to be *measurable with respect to* I_k. That is, given the set I_k, one can tell the exact value of ΔW_k.

· values of ΔW_k are unpredictable given the information set of time $k-1$:

$$E_{k-1}[\Delta W_k] = 0, \qquad \text{for all } k. \tag{25}$$

They are known given I_k:

$$E_k[\Delta W_k] = \Delta W_k. \tag{26}$$

· ΔW_k represents changes in a martingale process and is called a *martingale difference*. The accumulated error process W_k will be given by

$$W_k = \Delta W_1 + \ldots + \Delta W_k \tag{27}$$

$$= \sum_{i=1}^{k} \Delta W_i, \tag{28}$$

where we assume that the initial point W_0 is zero.

---

[7]If the information set is completely uninformative about the future movements in $S(t)$, then this prediction will be zero. Under these conditions, $[S_k - S_{k-1}]$ will itself be the unpredictable component.

We can show that W_k is a martingale:

$$E_{k-1}W_k = E_{k-1}[\Delta W_1 + \ldots + \Delta W_k] \qquad (29)$$

$$E_{k-1}W_k = [\Delta W_1 + \ldots + \Delta W_{k-1}] = W_{k-1}. \qquad (30)$$

The latter is true because $E_{k-1}[\Delta W_k]$ equals zero and the $\Delta W_i, i = 1, \ldots, k-1$ are known given I_{k-1}.

What is the importance of ΔW_k?

Consider a financial markets participant. For this decision maker, the important information contained in asset prices is indeed ΔW_k. These un-predictable "news" occur continuously and can be observed "on line" in all major networks such as Reuters or Bloomberg. Hence, "on line" move-ments in asset prices will be dominated by ΔW_k. This implies that in order to discuss differentiation in stochastic environments, one needs to study the properties of ΔW_k. In particular, we intend to show that under some fairly acceptable assumptions, ΔW_k^2 and its infinitesimal equivalent dW_t^2 cannot be considered as "negligible" in Taylor-style approximations.

4 The "Size" of Incremental Errors

The innovation term ΔW_k represents an unpredictable change. $(\Delta W_k)^2$ is its square. In deterministic environments, the concept of differentiation deals with terms such as ΔW_k, and squared changes are considered as negligible. Indeed, in *deterministic* calculus, terms such as $(\Delta W_k)^2$ do not show up in derivatives.[8] On the other hand, in stochastic calculus, one in general has to take into account the variation in the *second-order* terms. This section deals with a formal approximation of these terms.

There are two ways of doing this. One is the method used in courses on stochastic processes. The second is the one discussed in Merton (1990). We use Merton's approach because it permits a better understanding of the economics behind the assumptions that will be made along the way. Merton's approach is to study the characteristics of the information flow in financial markets and to try to model this information flow in some precise way.

We first need to define some notation.

Let the (unconditional) variance of ΔW_k be denoted by V_k:

$$V_k = E_0[\Delta W_k^2]. \qquad (31)$$

---

[8]They are confined to higher-order derivatives.

The variance of cumulative errors is defined as:

$$V = E_0 \left[\sum_{k=1}^{n} \Delta W_k \right]^2 = \sum_{k=1}^{n} V_k, \tag{32}$$

where the property that ΔW_k are uncorrelated across k is used and the expectation of cross product terms are set equal to zero.

We now introduce some assumptions, following Merton (1990).

ASSUMPTION 1:

$$V > A_1 > 0, \tag{33}$$

where A_1 is independent of n.

This assumption imposes a lower bound on the volatility of security prices. It says that when the period $[0, T]$ is divided into finer and finer sub-intervals,[9]

$$n \to \infty, \tag{34}$$

the variance of cumulative errors V will be positive. That is, more and more frequent observations of securities prices will not eliminate *all* the "risk." Clearly, most financial market participants will accept such an assumption. Uncertainty of asset prices never vanishes even when one observes the markets during finer and finer time intervals.

ASSUMPTION 2:

$$V < A_2 < \infty, \tag{35}$$

where A_2 is independent of n.

This assumption imposes an upper bound on the variance of cumulative errors and makes the *volatility* bounded from above. As the time axis is chopped into smaller and smaller intervals, more frequent trading is allowed. Such trading does not bring unbounded instability to the system. A large majority of market participants will agree with this assumption as well. After all, allowing for more frequent trading and having access to on-line screens does not lead to infinite volatility.

For the third assumption, define

$$V_{max} = \max_k [V_k, k = 1, \ldots, n]. \tag{36}$$

That is, V_{max} is the variance of the asset price during the most volatile subinterval.

---

[9]Remember that the subintervals have the same length h.

Finally, we have a third assumption:

ASSUMPTION 3:

$$\frac{V_k}{V_{max}} > A_3, \quad 0 < A_3 < 1, \tag{37}$$

with A_3 independent of n.

According to this assumption, uncertainty of financial markets is not *concentrated* in some special periods. Whenever markets are open, there exists at least *some* volatility. This assumption rules out lotterylike uncertainty in financial markets.

Now we are ready to discuss a very important property of $(\Delta W_k)^2$. The following proposition is at the center of stochastic calculus.

PROPOSITION: Under assumptions 1, 2, and 3, the variance of ΔW_k is proportional to h,

$$E[\Delta W_k]^2 = \sigma_k^2 h, \tag{38}$$

where σ_k is a finite constant that does not depend on h. It may depend on the information at time $k - 1$.

According to this proposition, asset prices become less volatile as h gets smaller.

Since this is a central result, we provide a proof of the proposition.

PROOF: Use assumption 3:

$$V_k > A_3 V_{max}. \tag{39}$$

Sum both sides over all intervals:

$$\sum_{k=1}^{n} V_k > n A_3 V_{max}. \tag{40}$$

Assumption 2 says that the right-hand side of this is bounded from above:

$$A_2 > \sum_{k=1}^{n} (V_k) > n A_3 V_{max}. \tag{41}$$

Now divide both sides by $n A_3$:

$$\frac{1}{n} \frac{A_2}{A_3} > V_{max}. \tag{42}$$

Note that $n = \frac{T}{h}$. Then,

$$\frac{1}{n}\frac{A_2}{A_3} > V_{max} > V_k \tag{43}$$

$$\frac{h}{T}\frac{A_2}{A_3} > V_k. \tag{44}$$

This gives an upper bound on V_k that depends only on h. We now obtain a lower bound that depends only on h also. We know that

$$\sum_{k=1}^{n} V_k > A_1 \tag{45}$$

is true. Then,

$$nV_{max} > \sum_{k=1}^{n} V_k > A_1. \tag{46}$$

Use Assumption 3:

$$V_k > A_3 V_{max}. \tag{47}$$

Divide (46) by n:

$$V_{max} > \frac{A_1}{n}. \tag{48}$$

Then,

$$V_{max} > \frac{A_1}{T} h \tag{49}$$

$$V_k > A_3 V_{max} > \frac{A_3 A_1}{T} h. \tag{50}$$

This means that

$$V_k > \frac{A_1 A_3}{T} h. \tag{51}$$

Therefore,

$$\frac{h}{T}\frac{A_2}{A_3} > V_k > \frac{A_3 A_1}{T} h. \tag{52}$$

Clearly the variance term V_k has upper and lower bounds that are *linear* functions of h, regardless of what n is. This means that we should be able to find a constant σ_k *depending* on k, such that V_k is proportional to h:

$$V_k = E[\Delta W_k]^2 = \sigma_k^2 h. \tag{53}$$

This proves the proposition.

5 One Implication

This proposition has several implications. An immediate one is the following. First, remember that if the corresponding expectations exist, one can always write

$$S_k - S_{k-1} = E_{k-1}[S_k - S_{k-1}] + \sigma_k \Delta W_k, \tag{54}$$

where ΔW_k now has variance h.[10] After dividing both sides by h:

$$\frac{S_k - S_{k-1}}{h} = \frac{E_{k-1}[S_k - S_{k-1}]}{h} + \frac{\sigma_k \Delta W_k}{h}. \tag{55}$$

But according to the proposition:

$$E[\Delta W_k^2] = h. \tag{56}$$

Suppose we use this to justify the approximation:

$$\Delta W_k^2 \cong h. \tag{57}$$

(In Chapter 9 we show that this approximation is valid in the sense of mean square convergence.)

In Chapter 3, when we defined the standard notion of derivative, we let h go to zero. Suppose we do the same here and *pretend* we can take the "limit" of the random variable:

$$\lim_{h \to 0} \frac{W_{(k-1)h+h} - W_{(k-1)h}}{h}. \tag{58}$$

Then, this could be interpreted as a time derivative of W_t. The approximation in (57) indicates that this derivative may not be well defined:

$$\lim_{h \to 0} \frac{|W_{(k-1)h+h} - W_{(k-1)h}|}{h} \to \infty.$$

---

[10]In this equation, the parameter σ_k is explicitly made a coefficient of the ΔW_k term. This is a trivial transformation, since the term $\sigma_k \Delta W_k$ will now have a variance equal to $\sigma^2 h$.

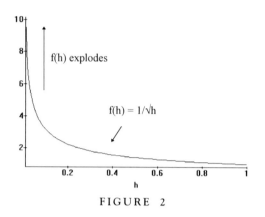

FIGURE 2

Figure 2 shows this graphically. We plot the function $f(h)$:

$$f(h) = \frac{h^{1/2}}{h}.$$

Clearly, as h gets smaller $f(h)$ goes to infinity. A well-defined limit does not exist.

Of course, the argument presented here is heuristic. The limiting operation was applied to random variables rather than deterministic functions, and it is not clear how one can formalize this. But the argument is still quite instructive, because it shows that the fundamental characteristic of unpredictable "news" in infinitesimal intervals, namely, that

$$E[\sigma_k \Delta W_k]^2 = \sigma_k^2 h,$$

may lead to insurmountable difficulties in defining a stochastic equivalent of time derivative.

6 Putting the Results Together

Up to this point we have accomplished two things. First, we saw that one can take any stochastic process S_t and write its variation during some finite interval h as

$$S_k - S_{k-1} = E_{k-1}[S_k - S_{k-1}] + \sigma_k \Delta W_k, \tag{59}$$

where the term ΔW_k is unpredictable given the information at the beginning of the time interval.[11]

---

[11] Assuming that the corresponding expectations exist.

Second, we showed that the unpredictable innovation term has a variance that is proportional to the length of the time interval, h:

$$\text{Var}(\Delta W_k) = h. \tag{60}$$

In order to obtain a stochastic difference equation defined over finite intervals, we need a third and last step. We need to approximate the first term on the right-hand side of (59),

$$E_{k-1}[S_k - S_{k-1}]. \tag{61}$$

This term is a conditional expectation, or a forecast of a change in asset prices. The magnitude of this change depends on the latest information set and on the length of the time interval one is considering. Hence, $E_{k-1}[S_k - S_{k-1}]$ can be written as

$$E_{k-1}[S_k - S_{k-1}] = A(I_{k-1}, h), \tag{62}$$

where $A(.)$ represents some function. Viewed this way, it is clear that *if* $A(.)$ is a *smooth* function of h, it will have a Taylor series expansion around $h = 0$

$$A(I_{k-1}, h) = A(I_{k-1}, 0) + a(I_{k-1})h + R(I_{k-1}, h), \tag{63}$$

where $a(I_{k-1})$ is the first derivative of $A(I_{k-1}, h)$ with respect to h evaluated at $h = 0$. The $R(I_{k-1}, h)$ is the remainder of the Taylor series expansion.[12]

Now if $h = 0$, time will not pass, and the predicted change in asset prices will be zero. In other words,

$$A(I_{k-1}, 0) = 0. \tag{64}$$

Also, the convention in the literature dealing with *ordinary* stochastic differential equations is that any deterministic terms having powers of h greater than 1 are small enough to be ignored.[13]

Thus, as in standard calculus, we can let

$$R(I_{k-1}, h) \cong 0 \tag{65}$$

and obtain the first-order Taylor series approximation:

$$E_{k-1}[S_k - S_{k-1}] \cong a(I_{k-1}, kh)h. \tag{66}$$

---

[12]Note that, given I_{k-1}, we are dealing with nonrandom quantities, and the derivatives in the Taylor series expansion can be taken in a "standard" fashion.

[13]Since h^2 is a deterministic function, this is consistent with the standard calculus, which ignores all second-order terms in differentiation.

Utilizing these results together, we can rewrite (59) as a stochastic difference equation:[14].

$$S_{kh} - S_{(k-1)h} = a(I_{k-1}, kh)h + \sigma_k[W_{kh} - W_{(k-1)h}].\qquad(67)$$

In later chapters we let $h \to 0$ and obtain the infinitesimal version of (59), which is the stochastic differential equation (SDE):

$$dS(t) = a(I_t, t)\,dt + \sigma_t\,dW(t).\qquad(68)$$

This stochastic differential equation is said to have a *drift* $a(I_t, t)$ and a *diffusion* σ_t component.

6.1 Stochastic Differentials

At several points in this chapter we had to discuss limits of random increments. Clearly, the need to obtain formal definitions for incremental changes such as dS_t, dW_t is evident.

How can these terms be made more explicit?

It turns out that to do this we need to define the fundamental concept of the Ito integral. Only with the Ito integral can we formalize the notion of *stochastic differentials* such as dS_t, dW_t, and hence give a solid interpretation of the tool of stochastic differential equations. This, however, has to wait until Chapter 9.

7 Conclusions

We can summarize the main points of this chapter.

Differentiation in standard calculus cannot be extended in a straightforward fashion to stochastic derivatives, because in infinitesimal intervals the variance of random processes does not equal zero. Further, when the flow of new information obeys some fairly mild assumptions, continuous-time random processes become very erratic, and time derivatives may not exist. In small intervals, ΔW_k dominates h. As the latter becomes smaller, the ratio of ΔW_k to h is likely to get larger in absolute value. A well-defined limit cannot be found.

On the other hand, the difficulty of defining the differentials notwithstanding, we needed few assumptions to construct a SDE. In this sense, a stochastic differential equation is a fairly general representation that can be written down for a large class of stochastic processes. It is basically

---

[14]Here, we are reintroducing the h in the notation for S_k and W_k. This shows the dependence of these terms on h explicitly.

constructed by decomposing the change in a stochastic process into a predictable and an unpredictable part, and then making some assumptions about the smoothness of the predictable part.

8 References

The proof that, under the three assumptions, unpredictable errors will have a variance proportional to h, is from Merton (1990). The chapter in Merton (1990) on the mathematics of continuous-time finance could at this point be useful to the reader.

CHAPTER 8

The Wiener Process and Rare Events in Financial Markets

1 Introduction

At every instant of an *ordinary* trading day, there are three states of the world: prices may go up by one tick, may decrease by one tick, or may show no change. In fact, the price of a liquid instrument rarely changes by more than a minimum tick. Hence, pricing financial assets in continuous time may proceed quite realistically with just three states of the world, as long as one ignores "rare" events. Unfortunately, most markets for financial assets and derivative products may from time to time exhibit "extreme" behavior. These periods are exactly when we have the greatest need for accurate pricing.

What makes an event "extreme" or "rare"? Is turbulence in financial markets the same as "rare events"? In this chapter we intend to clarify the probabilistic structure of rare events and contrast them with the behavior of Wiener processes. In particular, we discuss the types of events that a Wiener process is capable of characterizing. This discussion naturally leads to the characterization of rare events.

We show that "rare events" have to do with the discontinuity of observed price processes. This is not the same as turbulence. Increased variance or volatility can be accounted for by continuous-time stochastic processes.

What distinguishes "rare events" is the way their size and their probability of occurrence changes (or does not change) with the observation

144

interval. In particular, as the interval of observation, h, gets smaller, the *size* of normal events also gets smaller. This is, after all, what makes them "ordinary." In one month, several large price changes may be observed. In a week, fewer are encountered. Observing a number of large price jumps during a period of a few minutes is even less likely. Often, the events that occur during an "ordinary" minute are not worth much attention. This is the main characteristic of "normal" events. They become unimportant as $h \to 0$.

On the other hand, because they are ordinary, even in a very small time interval h, their probability of occurrence is *not* zero. During small time intervals, there is always a nonzero probability that some "nonnoticeable" news will arrive.

A *rare event* is different. By definition, they are supposed to occur infrequently. In continuous time, this means that as $h \to 0$, their probability of occurrence goes to zero. Yet, their *size* may not shrink. A market crash such as the one in 1987 is "rare." On a given day, during a very short period, there is negligible probability that one will observe such a crash. But when such crashes occur, their size may not be very different whether one looks at an interval of 10 minutes or a full trading day.

The previous chapter established one important result. Under some very mild assumptions, the surprise component, $\sigma_t \Delta W_t$ of asset prices had a variance

$$E[\sigma_t \Delta W_t]^2 = \sigma_t^2 h \tag{1}$$

during a small interval.

In heuristic terms, this means that unpredictable changes in the asset price will have the expected size $\sigma_t \sqrt{h}$.[1]

But remember how a "standard deviation" is obtained: one multiplies possible sizes, with the corresponding probabilities. It is made of products of *two* terms, the probability *times* the "size" of the event. A variance proportional to h can be obtained either by probabilities that depend on h while the size is independent, or by probabilities that are independent of h while the size is dependent.[2]

The first case corresponds to "rare events," the second to "normal" events.

1.1 Relevance of the Discussion

This chapter is focused on the distinction between rare and normal events. The reader may be easily convinced that, from a technical point,

---

[1]Note that "the expected size" refers only to the absolute value of the change. Since surprises are, by definition, unpredictable, one knows nothing about the *sign* of these changes.

[2]Or by a combination of the two.

such a distinction is important—especially if the existence of rare events implies discontinuous paths for asset prices. But are there *practical* applications of such discontinuities? Would pricing financial assets proceed differently if rare events exist?

The answers to these questions are in general affirmative. One has to use *different* formulas if asset prices exhibit jump discontinuities. This will indeed affect the pricing of financial assets.

As an example, consider recent issues in risk management. One issue is capital requirements. How much capital should a financial institution put aside to cover losses due to adverse movements in the market?

The answer depends on how much "value" is at risk. There are several ways of calculating such *value-at-risk measures*, but they all try to measure changes in a portfolio's value when some underlying asset price moves in some *extreme* fashion.

Clearly, during such an exercise it is very important to know if there exist rare events that cause prices to jump discontinuously. If such jumps are not likely, value-at-risk calculations can proceed using normal distribution. Price changes can be modeled as outcomes of normally distributed random processes, and under appropriate conditions, the value-at-risk will also be normally distributed. It would then be straightforward to attach a probability to the amount one can lose under some extreme price movement.

On the other hand, if sporadic jumps are a systematic part of asset price changes, then value-at-risk calculations become more complicated. Attaching a probability to the amount one is likely to lose in extreme circumstances requires modeling the "rare event" process as well.

2 Two Generic Models

There are two basic building blocks in modeling continuous time asset prices. One is the Wiener process, or Brownian motion. This is a *continuous* stochastic process and can be used if markets are dominated by "ordinary" events while "extremes" occur only infrequently, according to the probabilities in the tail areas of a normal distribution. The second is the Poisson process which can be used for modeling systematic jumps caused by rare events. The Poisson process is discontinuous.

By combining these two building blocks appropriately, one can generate a model that is suitable for a particular application.

Before discussing rare and normal events, this section reviews these two building blocks.

2.1 The Wiener Process

In continuous time, "normal" events can be modeled using the Wiener process, or Brownian motion. A Wiener process is appropriate if the underlying random variable, say W_t, can only change continuously. With a Wiener process, during a small time interval h, one in general observes "small" changes in W_t, and this is consistent with the events being "ordinary."

There are several ways one can discuss a Wiener process.

One approach was introduced earlier. Consider a random variable ΔW_{t_i} that takes one of the two possible values $\sqrt{h}$ or $-\sqrt{h}$ at instants

$$0 = t_0 < t_1 < \ldots < t_i < \ldots t_n = T, \tag{2}$$

where for all i,

$$t_i - t_{i-1} = h. \tag{3}$$

Suppose ΔW_{t_i} is independent of ΔW_{t_j} for $i \neq j$. Then the sum

$$W_{t_n} = \sum_{i=1}^{n} \Delta W_{t_i} \tag{4}$$

will converge weakly to a Wiener process as n goes to infinity. Heuristically, this means that the Wiener process will be a good approximating model for the sum on the right-hand side.[3]

In this definition, a Wiener process is obtained as the limit, in some probabilistic sense, of a sum of independent identically distributed random variables. The important point to note is that possible outcomes for these increments are *functions of* h, the length of subintervals. As $h \to 0$, changes in W_t become smaller.

With this approach, we see that the Wiener process will have a Gaussian (normal) distribution.

One can also approach the Wiener process as a continuous square integrable martingale. In fact, suppose W_t is a process that is continuous, has finite variance,[4] and has increments that are unpredictable given the family of information sets $\{I_t\}$.[5] Then, according to a famous theorem by Lévy,

---

[3] As n goes to infinity, the expression on the right-hand side will be a sum of a very large number of random variables that are independent of each other and that are all of infinitesimal size. Under some conditions the distribution of the sum will be approximately normal. This is typical of central limit theorems, or, in continuous time, of weak convergence.

[4] That is, it is square integrable.

[5] This also means that the increments are uncorrelated over time.

these properties are sufficient to guarantee that the increments in W_t are normally distributed with mean zero and variance $\sigma^2 \, dt$.

The formal definition of Wiener processes approached as martingales is as follows:

DEFINITION: A Wiener process W_t, relative to a family of information sets $\{I_t\}$, is a stochastic process such that

1. The pair I_t, W_t is a square integrable martingale with $W_0 = 0$ and

$$E\left[(W_t - W_s)^2\right] = t - s, \qquad s \le t. \tag{5}$$

2. The trajectories of W_t are continuous over t.

This definition indicates the following properties of a Wiener process:

• W_t has uncorrelated increments because it is a martingale, and because every martingale has unpredictable increments.

• W_t has zero mean because it starts at zero, and the mean of every increment equals zero.

• W_t has variance t.

• Finally, the process is continuous in the sense that in infinitesimal intervals, the movements of W_t are infinitesimal.

Note that in this definition nothing is said about increments being normally distributed. When martingale approach is used, the normality follows from the assumptions stated in the definition.[6]

The Wiener process is the natural model for an asset price that has unpredictable increments but nevertheless moves over time continuously. Before we discuss this point, however, we need to clarify a possible confusion.

2.1.1 Wiener Process or Brownian Motion?

The reader may have noticed the use of the term *Brownian motion* to describe processes such as W_t. Do the terms Brownian motion and Wiener process refer to the same concept, or are there any differences?

The definition of Wiener process given earlier used the fact that W_t was a square integrable martingale. But nothing was said about the *distribution* of W_t.

We now give the definition of Brownian motion:

DEFINITION: A random process $B_t, t \in [0, T]$ is a (standard) Brownian motion if:

---

[6] This is the famous Lévy theorem.

1. The process begins at zero, $B_0 = 0$.
2. B_t has stationary, independent increments.
3. The B_t is continuous in t.
4. The increments $B_t - B_s$, have a normal distribution with mean zero and variance $|t - s|$:

$$(B_t - B_s) \sim N(0, |t - s|). \tag{6}$$

This definition is, in many ways, similar to that of the Wiener process. There is, however, a crucial difference. W_t was assumed to be a martingale, while no such statement is made about B_t. Instead, it is posited that B_t has a normal distribution.

These appear to be very important differences. In fact, the reader may think that W_t is much more general than the Brownian motion, since no assumption is made about its distribution.

This first impression is not correct. The well known Lévy theorem states that there are no differences between the two processes.

THEOREM: Any Wiener process W_t relative to a family I_t is a Brownian motion process.

This theorem is very explicit. We can use the terms Wiener process and Brownian motion interchangeably. Hence, no distinction will be made between these two concepts in the remaining chapters.

2.2 The Poisson Process

Now consider a quite different type of random environment. Suppose N_t represents the total number of extreme shocks that occur in a financial market until time t. Suppose these major events occur in an unpredictable fashion.

The increments in N_t can have only one of two possible values. Either they will equal zero, meaning that no new major event has occurred, or they will equal one, implying that some major event has occurred. Given that major events are "rare," increments in N_t that have size 1 should also occur "rarely."

We use the symbol dN_t to represent incremental changes in N_t during an *infinitesimal* time period of length dt. Consider the following characterization of the incremental changes in N_t:[7]

$$dN_t = \begin{cases} 1 & \text{with probability } \lambda \, dt \\ 0 & \text{with probability } 1 - \lambda \, dt \end{cases}. \tag{7}$$

---

[7]At this point, the use of dN_t and dt instead of ΔN_t and h should be considered symbolic. In later chapters, it is hoped that the meaning of the notation dN_t and dt will become more clear.

Note that here we have increments in N_t which can assume two possible values during an infinitesimal interval dt. The critical difference with the case of Brownian motion is that, this time, the size of Poisson outcomes does *not* depend on dt. Instead, the *probabilities* associated with the outcomes *are* functions of dt. As the observation period goes towards zero, the increments of Brownian motion become smaller[8] while the movements in N_t remain of the same size.

The reader would recognize N_t as the Poisson counting process. Assuming that the rate of occurrence of these events during dt is λ, the process defined as

$$M_t = N_t - \lambda t \tag{8}$$

will be a discontinuous square integrable martingale.[9]

It is interesting to note that

$$E[M_t] = 0 \tag{9}$$

and

$$E[M_t]^2 = \lambda t. \tag{10}$$

Thus, although the trajectories of M_t are discontinuous, the first and second moments of M_t and W_t have the same characterization. In particular, over small time intervals of length h, both processes have increments with variance proportional to h.[10]

We emphasize the following points.

The trajectories followed by the two processes are very different. One is continuous, the other is of pure jump type.

Secondly, the probability that M_t will show a jump during a very small interval goes to zero. Heuristically, this means that the trajectories of M_t are *less* irregular than the trajectories of W_t, since the Poisson counting process is constant "most of the time." Although M_t displays discrete jumps, it will

---

[8]At a speed proportional to $\sqrt{h}$.

[9]M_t is called a *compensated* Poisson process. The term λt is referred to as the *compensatory*. It "compensates" for the positive trend in N_t and converts it into a "trendless" process M_t.

[10]A heuristic way of calculating the variance of dM_t is as follows:

$$E[dM_t]^2 = [1]^2 \lambda \, dt + [0]^2 [1 - \lambda \, dt], \tag{11}$$

which gives

$$E[dM_t]^2 = \lambda \, dt. \tag{12}$$

This is heuristic because we do not know whether we can treat increments such as dM_t as "objects" similar to standard random variables. To make the discussion precise, one must begin with a finite subdivision of the time interval, and then present some type of limiting argument.

not have unbounded variation. W_t, on the other hand, displays infinitesimal changes, but these changes are uncountably many. As a result, the variation becomes unbounded. Hence, it may be more difficult to define integrals such as

$$\int_{t_0}^{T} f(W_t)\, dW_t$$

than integrals with respect to M_t:

$$\int_{t_0}^{T} f(M_t)\, dM_t.$$

Indeed, it is true that, in general, the Riemann–Stieltjes definition may be applied to this latter integral.

2.3 Examples

Some examples may be useful.

Figure 1 displays a Poisson process generated by a computer. First, a $\lambda = 13.4$ was selected. Next, the size of h was determined as $h = .001$.

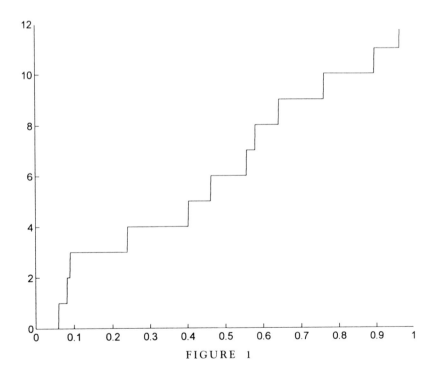

FIGURE 1

The computer was asked to generate a trajectory for the Poisson counting process N_t, $t \in [0, 1]$. This trajectory is displayed in Figure 1. We note the following characteristics of the Poisson paths:

- The trajectory has a positive slope. (Hence, N_t is not a martingale.)
- Changes occur in equal jumps of size 1.
- The trajectory is constant between these jumps.
- In this particular example there are 14 jumps, which is very close to the mean.

Figure 2 displays a mixture. First a trajectory was drawn from the Poisson process. Next, the computer was asked to generate a trajectory from a standard Wiener process with variance $h = .001$. The two trajectories were added to each other.

We see the following characteristics of this sample path:

- The path shows occasional jumps, due to the Poisson component.
- Between jumps, the process is not constant; it fluctuates randomly. This is due to the Wiener component.

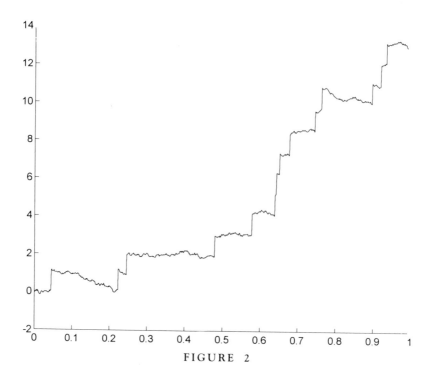

FIGURE 2

• The noise introduced by the Wiener process is much smaller than the jumps due to the Poisson process. This may change if we select a Wiener process with higher variance. Then, it could be very difficult to distinguish between jumps and noise caused by the Wiener component.

2.4 Back to Rare Events

Compared to events that occur in a routine fashion, a rare event is by definition something that has a "large" size. This classification seems obvious, but at a closer look, is not very easy to justify. Consider the Wiener process. A stochastic differential equation that is driven by a Wiener process amounts to assuming that in small intervals of length h, unexpected price changes occur with a variance of $\sigma^2 h$, where the σ may depend on the available information as well. Further, the distribution of these unexpected price changes is normal.

Now, a normal distribution has tails that extend to infinity. With *small* but nonzero h, there is a *positive* probability that a very large, unexpected price change will occur. Hence, with a nonzero h, the Wiener process seems to be perfectly capable of introducing "large" events in the stochastic differential equations.

Why would we then need another discussion of "rare" or large events?

The problem with characterizing rare events using a Wiener process is the following. As h goes to zero, the tails of the normal distribution carry less and less weight. At the limit, $h = 0$, these tails have completely vanished. In fact, the whole distribution has concentrated on zero. This is to be expected because the Wiener process is continuous with probability one. As $h \rightarrow 0$, the *size* of price changes represented by the Wiener process *has* to become smaller and smaller. In this sense, the Wiener process is not suitable for representing situations where, in an extremely short interval, prices can move in some extreme fashion.

What we need is a disturbance term that is capable of generating large events in extremely small intervals. In other words, we need a process that may exhibit jumps. Such a process will have outcomes that do not depend on h, and as h gets small, the size of the outcomes will not shrink.

Thus, "rare" events correspond to occasional jumps in the sample paths of the process.

Several markets in derivatives exhibit jumps in prices. This is more often the case in commodities, where a single news item is more likely to carry important information for the underlying commodity. Reports on crops, for example, are likely to cause jumps in futures on the same commodity. In the case of financial derivatives, this will be less likely. The weight of a

single news item in determining the price of interest rate or currency derivatives is significantly smaller, although present.

In the following sections we characterize normal and rare events, and
learn ways of modeling price series that are likely to exhibit occasional
jumps.

3 SDE in Discrete Intervals, Again

A deeper analysis of normal vs. rare events is best done by considering a
stochastic differential equation in finite intervals.[11]

Consider again the SDE that was introduced for discrete intervals of
equal size h in Chapter 7:

$$S_k - S_{k-1} = a(S_{k-1}, k)h + \sigma(S_{k-1}, k)\Delta W_k, \qquad k = 1, 2, \ldots, n, \quad (13)$$

where the $a(S_{k-1}, k)h$ is the drift component which determines how, on
the average, the increment $S_k - S_{k-1}$ is expected to behave during the next
interval. ΔW_k is the innovation term, determining the "surprise" component
of asset prices. It was shown that under some assumptions, the variance of
the innovation term was proportional to h, the length of the interval. The
term $\sigma(S_{k-1}, k)^2$ was the factor of proportionality.

In order to study "normal" and "rare" events in more detail, we make a
further simplifying assumption.[12]

ASSUMPTION 4: ΔW_k can assume only a *finite* number of possible values. The possible outcomes of ΔW_k and the corresponding probabilities
are[13]

$$\sigma_k \Delta W_k = \begin{cases} w_1 & \text{with probability} & p_1 \\ w_2 & \text{with probability} & p_2 \\ \vdots & \vdots & \\ w_m & \text{with probability} & p_m \end{cases} . \quad (14)$$

---

[11] Remember from Chapter 7 that in order to obtain the SDE in discrete intervals, we
used several approximations. For small but noninfinitesimal h, such equations hold in an
approximate sense only.

[12] Here also we follow Merton (1990).

[13] There are two reasons why we introduce this assumption. First, the distinction between
rare and normal events will be much easier to introduce if the possibilities are *finite*.

Second, actual asset pricing in financial markets often proceeds with either binomial or
trinomial *trees*. In the case of binomial trees, the market participant assumes that, at any
instant, there are only two possible moves for the price. With trinomial trees, possible moves
are raised to three. Hence, in practical situations, the total number of possible states is selected
as finite anyway.

4 Characterizing Rare and Normal Events

Although it is not clear *which* event will occur, the set of possible events is known by all agents. A typical w_i represents a possible outcome of the innovation term $\sigma_k \Delta W_k$, while p_i denotes the associated probability. The parameter m is the total number of possible outcomes. It is an integer.[14]

There are two types of w_i's. The first three represent "normal" outcomes. For example, w_1 may represent an uptick, w_2 may be a downtick, and the w_3 may represent "no change" in asset prices. In real time, these are certainly routine developments in financial markets.

The remaining possibilities, $w_4, w_5, \ldots$ are reserved for various types of special events that may occur rarely. For example, if the underlying security is a derivative written on grain futures, w_4 may be the effect of a major drought, the w_5 may be the effect of an unusually positive crop forecast, and so on. Clearly, if such possibilities refer to extreme price changes, and if they are rare, then they must lead to price changes greater than one tick. Otherwise, price changes are caused by normal events w_1, w_2, w_3.

This setup will be used in the next section to determine the probabilistic structure of rare events.

4 Characterizing Rare and Normal Events

Under assumptions 1–3 of the previous chapter, an important result was proven. It was shown that the variance of $\sigma_k \Delta W_k$,

$$E[\sigma_k \Delta W_k]^2 = \sigma_k^2 h, \tag{15}$$

was proportional to the observation interval h where σ_k was a known parameter given the information set I_{k-1}.

This result can be exploited further if we use assumption 4. In fact, a very explicit characterization of rare and normal events can be given this way, although the reader may find the notation a bit unpleasant. However, this is a small price to pay if a useful characterization of rare and normal events is eventually obtained.

According to assumption 4, ΔW_k can assume only a finite number of values. In terms of w_i and the corresponding probabilities, p_i, we can explicitly write the variance as

$$\text{Var}[\sigma_k \Delta W_k] = \sum_{i=1}^{m} p_i w_i^2. \tag{16}$$

[14]Both w_i and p_i can very well be made to depend on the information set I_k. However, this would add a k subscript to these variables and would make the notation more cumbersome. To avoid this, we make w_i and p_i independent of k.

Using the important proposition of the previous chapter, this means

$$\sum_{i=1}^{m} p_i w_i^2 = \sigma_k^2 h, \tag{17}$$

where the parameter m is the number of possible states. The left-hand side of Equation (17) is simply the weighted average of squared deviations from the mean, which in this case is zero. The "weights" are probabilities associated with possible outcomes.[15]

Now, the left-hand side of (17) is a sum of m finite, nonnegative numbers. If the sum of such numbers is proportional to h, and if each element is positive (or zero), then *each* term in the sum should also be proportional to h or should equal zero. In other words, *each* $p_i w_i^2$ will be given by

$$p_i w_i^2 = c_i h, \tag{18}$$

where $0 < c_i$ is some factor of proportionality.[16]

Equation (18) says that all terms such as $p_i w_i^2$ are linear functions of h. Then, one can visualize the p_i and the w_i as two *functions* of h, whose product is proportional to h. That is,

$$p_i = p_i(h) \tag{19}$$

$$w_i = w_i(h), \tag{20}$$

such that

$$p_i(h)w_i(h)^2 = c_i h. \tag{21}$$

We follow Merton (1990) and assume specific exponential forms for these functions $p_i(h)$ and $w_i(h)$:

$$w_i(h) = \bar{w}_i h^{r_i} \tag{22}$$

and

$$p_i(h) = \bar{p}_i h^{q_i}, \tag{23}$$

where r_i and q_i are *nonnegative* constants. $\bar{w}_i$ and $\bar{p}_i$ are constants that may depend on i or k, but are independent of h, the size of the observation interval.

Figure 3 displays some choices for h^{r_i}. Three examples are shown: the case when $r_i = 1$ (not allowed in this particular discussion), the case when

[15] We show the potential dependence of w_i, p_i on the information that becomes available as time passes, by adding the k subscript to σ_k.

[16] In general, c_i will depend on k as well. To keep notation simple, we eliminate the k subscript.

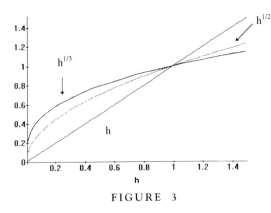

FIGURE 3

$r_i = .5$, and the case when $r_i = .1/3$. In particular, we see that for small h, $h^{r_i} > h$.

According to Equations (22) and (23), both the *size* and the *probability* of the event may depend on the interval length, h. As h gets larger, then the (absolute) magnitude of the observed price change and its probability will get larger, except when r_i or q_i are zero.

To characterize rare and normal events we use the parameters r_i and q_i.

Both of these parameters are nonnegative. r_i governs how fast the *size* of the event goes to zero as the observation interval gets smaller. q_i governs how fast the *probability* goes to zero as the observation interval decreases. It is, of course, possible that r_i or q_i vanish, although they cannot do so at the same time.[17]

We now show explicitly how restrictions on the parameters r_i, q_i can distinguish between rare and normal events.

The variance of ΔW_k in (18) is made of terms such as

$$p_i w_i^2 = \bar{w}_i^2 \bar{p}_i h^{2r_i} h^{q_i}. \tag{24}$$

But we know that *each* $p_i w_i^2$ is proportional to h as well:

$$p_i w_i^2 = c_i h. \tag{25}$$

Hence,

$$\bar{w}_i^2 \bar{p}_i h^{(q_i + 2r_i)} = c_i h. \tag{26}$$

But this implies that

$$q_i + 2r_i = 1 \tag{27}$$

---

[17]Remember that the product of w_i^2 and p_i must be proportional to h. If both r_i and q_i equal zero, these products will not depend on h, and this is not allowed.

and

$$c_i = \bar{w}_i^{\,2}\,\bar{p}_i. \tag{28}$$

Thus, the parameters q_i, r_i must satisfy the restrictions

$$0 \le r_i \le \frac{1}{2} \tag{29}$$

and

$$0 \le q_i \le 1. \tag{30}$$

We find that there are, in fact, only two cases of interest—namely,

$$r_i = 1/2, \qquad q_i = 0, \tag{31}$$

and

$$r_i = 0, \qquad q_i = 1. \tag{32}$$

The first case leads to events that we call "normal." The second is the case of "rare" events. We discuss these in turn.

4.1 Normal Events

The condition for "normal" events is

$$\frac{1}{2} \ge r_i > 0. \tag{33}$$

To interpret this, consider what happens when we select $r_i = 1/2$.

First, we know that the q_i *must* equal zero.[18] As a result, the functions that govern the size and the probability of the outcome w_i become, respectively,

$$w_i = \bar{w}_i h^{1/2} = \bar{w}_i \sqrt{h} \tag{35}$$

$$p_i = \bar{p}_i. \tag{36}$$

According to this, the sizes of events having $r_i = .5$ will get smaller as the interval length h gets smaller. On the other hand, their probability does not depend on h. These outcomes are "small" but have a constant probability of occurrence as observation intervals get smaller. They are "ordinary."

Now suppose all possible outcomes for ΔW_k are of this type and have $r_i = .5$. Then the sample paths of the resulting $W(t)$ process will have a number of interesting properties.

---

[18]Remember that

$$2r_i + q_i = 1 \tag{34}$$

and that q_i cannot be negative.

4.1.1 Continuous Paths

If there are no rare events, then all w_i will have $r_i = .5$, and their size

$$w_i = \bar{w}_i \sqrt{h} \tag{37}$$

will shrink as h gets smaller. At the same time, as h goes to zero, the values of w_i approach each other. This means that the process W_k will, in the limit, be continuous. The steps taken by ΔW_k will approach zero:

$$\lim_{h \to 0} w_i = \lim_{h \to 0} \bar{w}_i h^{1/2} = 0. \tag{38}$$

This will be true for every "normal" event w_i. In the limit, the trajectories of W_t will be such that one *could* plot the data without lifting one's hand. Each incremental value will have infinitesimal size.

On the other hand, since $q_i = 0$ for "normal" events, the probabilities of these w_i will *not* tend to zero as $h \to 0$. In fact, the probability of these events will be independent of h:

$$p_i = \bar{p}_i. \tag{39}$$

It is in this sense that normal events can generate continuous time paths.

4.1.2 Smoothness of Sample Paths

The sample paths of an innovation term that has outcomes with $r_i = 1/2$ are continuous. But they are not *smooth*.

First remember what smoothness means within the context of a deterministic function. Heuristically, a function will be "smooth" if it does not change abruptly. In other words, suppose we select a point x_0 where the function $f(x)$ is evaluated. $f(x)$ will be smooth at x_0 if for small h, the ratio

$$\frac{f(x_0 + h) - f(x_0)}{h} \tag{40}$$

stays finite as h get smaller and smaller. That is, the function is smooth if it has a derivative at that point.

Is the same definition of smoothness valid for nondeterministic functions such as W_t as well?

In the particular case discussed here, there are a finite number m of possible values that ΔW_k can assume. The sizes of these events are all proportional to $h^{1/2}$. In other words, as time passes, the new events that affect prices will cause changes of the order $\sqrt{h}$.

At any time t, the unexpected *rate* of change of prices can be written as

$$\frac{W_{t+h} - W_t}{h} = \frac{w_i}{h} \tag{41}$$

for some i. Taking limits,

$$\lim_{h \to 0} \frac{W_{t+h} - W_t}{h} = \lim_{h \to 0} \frac{w_i}{h}, \tag{42}$$

or, after substituting for w_i,

$$= \lim_{h \to 0} \bar{w}_i \frac{h^{\frac{1}{2}}}{h} \tag{43}$$

$$= \bar{w}_i \lim_{h \to 0} \frac{1}{h^{\frac{1}{2}}} \to \infty. \tag{44}$$

This means that as the interval h gets smaller, the W_t starts to change at an infinite *rate*. Asset prices will behave continuously but erratically. (Here we assumed without any loss of generality, that $\bar{w}_i$ was positive.)

Note the advantage of working with an error term ΔW_k that has a finite number of possible outcomes. The discussion could proceed with individual events w_i and by using the standard notion of limit. When one considers continuous events, and the number of possible outcomes becomes uncountably infinite, similar arguments cannot be used. One has to work with probabilistic limits.

This concludes the discussion of trajectories that are generated by events of normal size. We now consider paths generated by rare events.

4.2 Rare Events

Assume that for some event w_i, the parameter r_i equals zero. Then, the corresponding q_i equals 1, and the probability of this particular outcome will by definition be given by

$$p_i = \bar{p}_i h. \tag{45}$$

The events w_i that have a $r_i = 0$, $q_i = 1$ are "rare" events, since, according to this equation, their probability vanishes as $h \to 0$.

On the other hand, the size of the events will be given by

$$w_i = \bar{w}_i \tag{46}$$

i.e., they will *not* depend on the length of the interval h.

We make the following observations concerning rare events.

4.2.1 Sample Paths
Sample paths of an innovation term that contains rare events will be discontinuous. In fact, the sizes of those w_i with $q_i = 1$ do not depend on h. As h goes to zero, ΔW_k will from time to time assume values that do not get any smaller. The size of unexpected price changes will be independent of h.

When such rare outcomes occur, W_t will have a jump.

On the other hand, if $q_i = 1$, the probability of these jumps *will* depend on h, and as the latter gets smaller, the probability of observing a jump will also go down. Hence, although the trajectory contains jumps, these jumps are not common.

Clearly, if the random variable ΔW_k contains jumps, its sample paths will not be continuous. One would need a model other than the Wiener process to capture the behavior of such random shocks.

4.2.2 Further Comments
What can be said of the remaining values for r_i and q_i? In other words, consider the ranges

$$0 < r_i < \frac{1}{2} \tag{47}$$

and

$$0 < q_i < 1. \tag{48}$$

What types of sample paths would the W_t possess if the possible outcomes have r_i and q_i within these ranges?

It turns out that for all r_i, q_i within these ranges, the sample paths will be continuous but nonsmooth, just as in the case of a Wiener process.

This is easy to see. As long as $0 < r_i < .5$ is satisfied, the size of w_i's will be a function of h. As $h \to 0$, w_i will go to zero. In terms of *size*, they are not rare events.

Note that for such outcomes the corresponding probabilities also go to zero. Thus, these outcomes are not observed frequently. But given that their size will get smaller, they are not qualified as rare events.

5 A Model for Rare Events

What type of models can one use to represent asset prices if there are rare events?

Consider what is needed. Our approach tries to represent asset prices by an equation that decomposes observed changes into two components: one that is predictable given the information at that time, and another that is unpredictable. In small intervals of length h, we write

$$S_k - S_{k-1} = a(S_{k-1}, k)h + \sigma(S_{k-1}, k)\Delta W_k, \qquad k = 1, 2, \ldots, n. \quad (49)$$

As h gets smaller, we obtain the continuous-time version valid for infinitesimal intervals:

$$dS_t = a(S_t, t)\,dt + \sigma(S_t, t)\,dW_t. \quad (50)$$

In later chapters we study the SDEs more precisely and show what the differentials such as dS_t or dW_t really mean.

There is no need to adopt a different representation in order to take into account rare events. These also occur unexpectedly, and their variance is also proportional to h, the time interval. In fact, the only difference from the case of a Wiener process occurs in the continuity of sample paths. Hence, the same SDE representation can be used with a simple modification.

What is needed is a new *model* for the random, unpredictable errors dW_t.

In the case of rare events, the defining factors are that the size of the event is not infinitesimal even when h is, while its probability does become negligible with $h \to 0$. Accordingly, the new innovation term should be able to represent (random) jumps in asset prices that occur rarely. Further, the model should be flexible enough to capture any potential variation of the probability of occurrence of such jumps.

One can be more specific. First, split the error term into two. It is clear from the previous discussion that changes in asset prices will be a mixture of normal events that occur in a continuous fashion, and jumps that occur sporadically. We denote the first component by ΔW_k. The second component is denoted by the symbol ΔN_k. To make this more precise, assume that the event is a jump in asset prices of size 1. At any instant $k - 1$, one has

$$N_k - N_{k-1} = \begin{cases} 1 & \text{with probability } \lambda h \\ 0 & \text{with probability } 1 - \lambda h \end{cases}, \quad (51)$$

where λ does *not* depend on the information set available at time $k - 1$. We let

$$\Delta N_k = N_k - N_{k-1}. \quad (52)$$

Such ΔN_k represent jumps of size 1 that occur with a constant rate λ.[19]

---

[19] Note that the rate of occurrence of the jump during an interval h can be calculated by dividing the corresponding probability λh by h.

It is clear that N_k can be modeled using a Poisson counting process. In fact, a Poisson process has the following properties:

1. During a small interval h, at most one event can occur with probability very close to 1.[20]
2. The information up to time t does not help to predict the occurrence (or the nonoccurrence) of the event in the next instant h.
3. The events occur at a constant rate λ.

In fact, the Poisson process is the only process that satisfies all these conditions simultaneously. It seems to be a good candidate for modeling jump discontinuities. We may, however, need two modifications.

First, the rate of occurrence of jumps in a certain asset price may change over time. The Poisson process has a *constant* rate of occurrence and cannot accommodate such behavior. Some adjustment is needed.

Second, the increments in N_t have nonzero mean. The SDE approach deals with innovation terms with zero mean only. Another modification is needed to eliminate the mean of dN_t's.

Consider the modified variable

$$J_t = (N_t - \lambda t). \tag{53}$$

The increments ΔJ_k will have zero mean and will be unpredictable. Further, if we multiply the J_t by a (time-dependent) constant, say, $\sigma_2(S_{k-1}, k)$, the size of the jumps will be time-dependent. Hence, $\sigma_2(S_{k-1}, k)\Delta J_k$ is an appropriate candidate to represent unexpected jumps in asset prices.

This means that, if the market for a financial instrument is affected by sporadic rare events, the stochastic differential equations can be written as

$$S_k - S_{k-1} = a(S_{k-1}, k)h + \sigma_1(S_{k-1}, k)\Delta W_k$$
$$+ \sigma_2(S_{k-1}, k)\Delta J_k, \qquad k = 1, 2, \ldots, n. \tag{54}$$

This, as h gets small, becomes

$$dS_t = a(S_t, t)\,dt + \sigma_1(S_t, t)\,dW_t + \sigma_2(S_t, t)\,dJ_t. \tag{55}$$

This stochastic differential equation will be able to handle "normal" and "rare" events simultaneously.

Finally, note that the jump component $dJ(t)$ and the Wiener component $dW(t)$ have to be statistically independent at every instant t. As h gets smaller, the size of "normal" events has to get smaller, while the size of rare events remains the same. Under these conditions the two types of events cannot be "related" to each other. Their instantaneous correlation must be zero.

---

[20] As $h \to 0$, this probability will become 1.

6 Moments That Matter

The distinction between "normal" and "rare" events is important for another reason as well.

Practical work with observed data proceeds either directly or indirectly by using appropriate "moments" of the underlying processes. In Chapter 5, we defined the term "moment" as representing various expectations of the underlying process. For example, the simple expected value $E[X_t]$ is the first moment. The variance

$$\text{Var}(X_t) = E[X_t - E[X_t]]^2 \tag{56}$$

is the second (centered) moment. Higher-order (centered) moments are obtained by

$$E[X_t - E[X_t]]^k, \tag{57}$$

where $k > 2$.

As mentioned earlier, moments give information about the process under consideration. For example, variance is a measure of how volatile the prices are. The third moment is a measure of the skewness of the distribution of price changes. The fourth moment is a measure of heavy tails.

In this section we show that when dealing with changes over infinitesimal intervals, in the case of normal events only the first *two* moments matter. Higher-order moments are of marginal significance. However, for rare events all moments need to be taken into consideration.

Consider again the case where the unpredictable surprise components are made of m possible events denoted by w_i.

The first two moments of such an unpredictable error term will be given by[21]

$$E[\sigma_1 \Delta W_k + \sigma_2 \Delta J_k] = [p_1 w_1 + \cdots + p_m w_w] = 0 \tag{58}$$

$$\text{Var}[\sigma_1 \Delta W_k + \sigma_2 \Delta J_k] = [p_1 w_1^2 + \cdots + p_m w_m^2], \tag{59}$$

where the independence of ΔW_k and ΔJ_k is implicitly used.

Now consider the magnitude of these moments when all events are of the "normal" type, having a size proportional to $h^{1/2}$. That is, consider the case when all $q_i = 0$.

The first moment is a weighted sum of m such values. Unless it is zero, it will be proportional to $h^{1/2}$:

$$E[\sigma_1 \Delta W_k] = h^{1/2}[p_1 \bar{w}_1 + \cdots + p_m \bar{w}_m]. \tag{60}$$

---

[21] In the remaining part of this section, $\sigma_i(S_t, t), i = 1, 2$ will be abbreviated as σ_i.

As we divide this by h, we obtain the average *rate* of unexpected changes in prices. Clearly, for small h the $\sqrt{h}$ is *larger* than h, and the expression

$$\frac{E[\Delta W_k]}{h} \tag{61}$$

gets larger as h gets smaller. We conclude that when the first moment is not equal to zero, it is "large" and cannot be ignored even in small intervals h.

The same is true for the second moment. The variance of an unpredictable change in prices contains terms such as w_i^2. When the w_i are of normal type, their size is proportional to $h^{1/2}$. Hence, the variance will be proportional to h:

$$\mathrm{Var}(\sigma_1 \Delta W_k) = h\left[\sum_{i=1}^{m} p_i \bar{w}_i^2\right]. \tag{62}$$

As we divide this by h, we obtain the average *rate* of variance. Clearly, the h's will cancel out and the rate of variance remains *constant* as h gets smaller.

This means that the variance does not become negligible as $h \to 0$. In the case of "normal" events, the variance provides significant information about the underlying randomness even during an infinitesimal interval h.

Now consider what happens with higher-order moments:

$$E[\sigma_1 \Delta W_k]^n = [p_1 w_1^n + \cdots + p_m w_m^n] \tag{63}$$

with $n > 2$.

Here, when the events under consideration are of the normal type, raising the w_i to a power of n will result in terms such as

$$w_i^n = \bar{w}_i^n (h^{1/2})^n. \tag{64}$$

But when $n > 2$, for small h we have

$$h^{n/2} < h. \tag{65}$$

Consequently, as we divide higher-order moments by h, we obtain the corresponding rate:

$$\frac{E[\sigma_1 \Delta W_k]^n}{h} = h^{(n-2)/2} \sum_{i=1}^{m} \bar{w}_i^n. \tag{66}$$

And this rate will depend on h positively. As h gets smaller, $h^{(n-2)/2}$ will converge to zero.[22]

Consequently, for small h, higher-order moments of unpredictable price changes will not carry any useful information if the underlying events are

[22]Note that when n is greater than 2, the exponent of h will be positive.

all of the "normal" type. A probabilistic model that depends only on *two* parameters, one representing the first moment and the second representing the variance, will be *sufficient* to capture all the relevant information in price data. The Wiener process, is then a very natural choice if there are no rare events.

If there are rare events, the situation is different.

Suppose all events are rare. By definition, rare events assume values w_i that do not depend on h. For the second moment we obtain

$$E\left[\sigma_2 \Delta J_k\right]^2 = h\left[\sum_{i=1}^{m} w_i^2 \bar{p}_i\right], \tag{67}$$

where the w_i *do not depend on* h. As we divide the right-hand side of the last equation by h, it will become independent of h. Hence, variance cannot be considered negligible. Here, there is no difference from Wiener processes.

However, the higher-order moments will be given by

$$E[\sigma_2 \Delta J_k]^n = h\left[\sum_{i=1}^{m} w_i^n \bar{p}_i\right]. \tag{68}$$

This is the case because with rare events, the probabilities are proportional to h, and the latter can be factored out. With $n > 2$, higher-order moments are *also* of order h. As we divide higher-order moments of ΔJ_k by h, they will *not* get any smaller as $h \to 0$. Unlike Wiener processes, higher-order moments of ΔJ_t cannot be ignored over infinitesimal time intervals.

This means that if prices are affected by rare events, higher-order moments may provide useful information to market participants.

This discussion illustrates when it is appropriate to limit the innovation terms of SDEs to Wiener processes. If one has enough conviction that the events at the roots of the volatility in financial markets are of the "normal" type, then a distribution function that depends on the first two moments only will be a reasonable approximation. The assumption of normality of dW_t will be acceptable in the sense of making little difference for the end results, since in small intervals the data will depend on the first two moments anyway.

However, if rare events are a systematic part of the data, the use of a Wiener process may not be appropriate.

7 Conclusions

In the next two chapters we formalize the notion of stochastic differential equations. This chapter and the previous one laid out the groundwork for SDEs. We showed that the dynamics of an asset price can always be captured by a stochastic differential equation,

$$dS_t = a(S_t, t) \, dt + [\sigma_1(S_t, t) \, dW_t + \sigma_2(S_t, t) \, dJ(t)], \qquad (69)$$

where the first term on the right-hand side is the expected change in S_t, and the second term in brackets is the surprise component, unpredictable given the information at time t. The stochastic differentials were not defined formally, so the discussion proceeded using "small" increments, ΔS_k and ΔW_k.

The unpredictable components of SDEs were made of two parts. dW_t captures events of insignificant size that happen regularly. $dJ(t)$ captures "large" events that occur rarely.

In small intervals, the random variable W_t is described fully by the first- and second-order moments. Higher-order moments do not provide any additional information. Hence, assuming normality and letting W_t be the Wiener process provides a good approximation for such events.

Rare events cannot be captured by normal distribution. If they are likely to affect the financial market under consideration, the unexpected components should be complemented by the dJ_t process. The Poisson process would represent the properties of such a term reasonably well.

Given that the market participant can pick the parameters $\sigma_1(S_t, t)$ and $\sigma_2(S_t, t)$ at will, the combination of the Wiener and Poisson processes can represent all types of disturbances that may affect financial markets.

8 References

The discussion characterizing rare events is covered in Merton (1990). The assumption that innovation terms have a finite number of possible values simplified the discussion significantly. A reader interested in the formal arguments justifying the statements made in this chapter can consider Bremaud (1979). Bremaud adopts a martingale approach to discuss the dynamics of point processes, which can be labeled as generalizations of Poisson processes.

CHAPTER 9

Integration in Stochastic Environments

The Ito Integral

1 Introduction

One source of practical interest in differentiation and integration operations is the need to obtain *differential equations*. Differential equations are
used to describe the dynamics of physical phenomena. A simple linear differential equation will be of the form

$$\frac{dX_t}{dt} = AX_t + By_t, \qquad t \geq 0, \tag{1}$$

where dX_t/dt is the derivative of X_t with respect to t and where y_t is an
exogenous variable. A and B are parameters.[1]

Ordinary differential equations are necessary tools for practical modeling. For example, an engineer may think that there is some variable y_t that
together with the "past" of X_t, determines future changes in X_t. This relationship is approximated by the differential equation, which can be utilized
in various applications.[2]

The following agenda is used to obtain the ordinary differential equation.
First, a notion of derivative is defined. It is shown that for most functions
of interest denoted by X_t, this derivative *exists*. Once existence is established, the agenda proceeds with approximating dX_t/dt using Taylor series

---

[1] If $B = 0$, the equation is said to be homogenous. When y_t is independent of t, the system
becomes *autonomous*. Otherwise, it is nonautonomous.

[2] For example, the engineer may have in mind some desired future path for X_t. Then, the
issue is to find the proper $\{y_t\}$ which will ensure that X_t follows this path.

expansions. After taking into consideration any restrictions imposed by the theory under consideration, one gets the differential equation.

At the end of the agenda, the *fundamental theorem of calculus* is proved to show that there is a close correspondence between the notions of integral and derivative. In fact, integral denotes a *sum* of increments, while derivative denotes a rate of *change*. It seems natural to expect that if one adds changes dX_t in a variable X_t, with initial value $X_0 = 0$, one would obtain the latest value of the variable:

$$\int_0^t dX_u = X_t. \tag{2}$$

This suggests that for every differential equation we can devise a corresponding *integral equation*.

In stochastic calculus, application of the same agenda is *not* possible. If unpredictable "news" arrives continuously, and if equations representing the dynamics of the phenomena under consideration are a function of such noise, a meaningful notion of derivative cannot be defined.

Yet, under some conditions, an *integral* can be obtained successfully. This permits replacing *ordinary* differential equations by *stochastic* differential equations

$$dX_t = a_t\,dt + \sigma_t\,dW_t, \quad t \in [0, \infty), \tag{3}$$

where future movements are expressed in terms of differentials dX_t, dt, and dW_t instead of derivatives such as dX_t/dt. These differentials are defined using a new concept of integral. For example, as h gets smaller, the increments

$$X_{t+h} - X_t = \int_t^{t+h} dX_u \tag{4}$$

can be used to give meaning to dX_t. In fact, at various earlier points, we made use of differentials such as dS_t or dW_t but never really discussed them in any precise fashion. The definition of the Ito integral will permit doing so.

Now, consider the SDE which represents dynamic behavior of some asset price S_t:

$$dS_t = a(S_t, t)\,dt + \sigma(S_t, t)\,dW_t, \quad t \in [0, \infty). \tag{5}$$

After we take integrals on both sides, this equation implies that

$$\int_0^t dS_u = \int_0^t a(S_u, u)\,du + \int_0^t \sigma(S_u, u)\,dW_u, \tag{6}$$

where the last term on the right-hand side is an integral with respect to increments in the Wiener process W_t.

The interpretation of the integrals on the right-hand side of (6) is not immediate. As discussed in Chapters 5 through 7, increments in W_t are "too" erratic during small intervals h. The *rate* of change of the W_t was, on the average, equal to $h^{-1/2}$, and this became larger as h became smaller.[3] If these increments are too erratic, would not their sum be infinite?

This chapter intends to show how this seemingly difficult problem can be solved.

1.1 The Ito Integral and SDEs

Obtaining a formal definition of the Ito integral will make the notion of a stochastic differential equation more precise. Once the integral

$$\int_0^t \sigma(S_u, u) \, dW_u \tag{7}$$

is defined in some precise way, then one could integrate both sides of the SDE in (5):

$$S_{t+h} - S_t = \int_t^{t+h} a(S_u, u) \, du + \int_t^{t+h} \sigma(S_u, u) \, dW_u, \tag{8}$$

where h is some finite time interval.

From here, one can obtain the *finite difference approximation* that we used several times in Chapters 7 and 8. Indeed, if h is small, $a(S_u, u)$ and $\sigma(S_u, u)$ may not change very much during $u \in [t, t + h]$, especially if they are smooth functions S_u and u. Then, we could rewrite this equation as:

$$S_{t+h} - S_t \cong a(S_t, t) \int_t^{t+h} du + \sigma(S_t, t) \int_t^{t+h} dW_u. \tag{9}$$

Taking the integrals in a straightforward way, we would obtain the finite difference approximation:

$$S_{t+h} - S_t \cong a(S_t, t)h + \sigma(S_t, t)[W_{t+h} - W_t]. \tag{10}$$

Rewriting:

$$\Delta S_t \cong a(S_t, t)h + \sigma(S_t, t)\Delta W_t. \tag{11}$$

This is the SDE representation in finite intervals that we often used in previous chapters. The representation is an *approximation* for at least two

---

[3]By the average *rate* of change we mean the standard deviation of $W_{t+h} - W_t$ divided by h. In Chapter 6 it was shown that under fairly general assumptions, the standard deviations of unpredictable shocks were proportional to $h^{1/2}$.

reasons. First, the $E_t[S_{t+h} - S_t]$ was set equal to a *first-order* Taylor series approximation with respect to h:

$$E_t[S_{t+h} - S_t] = a(S_t, t)h.$$

Second, the $a(S_u, u), \sigma(S_u, u), u \in [t, t + h]$ were approximated by their value at $u = t$. Both of these approximations require some smoothness conditions on $a(S_u, u)$ and $\sigma(S_u, u)$. All of this implies that when we write

$$dS_t = a(S_t, t) dt + \sigma(S_t, t) dW_t, \qquad (12)$$

we in fact mean that in the *integral equation*,

$$\int_t^{t+h} dS_u = \int_t^{t+h} a(S_u, u) du + \int_t^{t+h} \sigma(S_u, u) dW_u, \qquad (13)$$

the second integral on the right-hand side is defined in the Ito sense and that as $h \to 0$,

$$\int_t^{t+h} \sigma(S_u, u) dW_u \simeq \sigma(S_t, t) dW_t. \qquad (14)$$

That is, the diffusion terms of the SDEs are in fact Ito integrals approximated during infinitesimal time intervals.

For these approximations to make sense, an integral with respect to W_t should first be defined formally. Second, we must impose conditions on the way $a(S_t, t)$ and $\sigma(S_t, t)$ move over time. In particular, we cannot allow these I_t-measurable parameters to be too erratic.

1.2 The Practical Relevance of the Ito Integral

In practice, the Ito integral is used less frequently than stochastic differential equations. Practitioners almost never use the Ito integral *directly* to calculate derivative asset prices. As will be discussed later, arbitrage-free prices are calculated either by using partial differential equation methods or by using martingale transformations. In neither of these cases is there a need to calculate any Ito integrals directly.

Hence, it may be difficult at this point to see the practical relevance of this concept from the point of view of, say, a trader. It may appear that defining the Ito integral is essentially a theoretical exercise, with no practical implications. A practitioner may be willing to accept that the Ito integral exists, and may prefer to proceed directly into using SDEs.

The reader is cautioned against this. Understanding the definition of the Ito integral is important (at least) for two reasons. First, as mentioned earlier, a stochastic differential equation can be defined only in terms of the Ito integral. To understand the real meaning behind the SDEs, one has to have some understanding of the Ito integral. Otherwise, errors can be made in applying SDEs to practical problems.

This brings us to the second reason why the Ito integral is relevant. Given that SDEs are defined for infinitesimal intervals, their use in finite intervals may require some *approximations*. In fact, the approximation shown in (14) may not be valid if h is not "small." Then, a new approximation will have to be defined using the definition of the Ito integral.

This point is important from the point of view of pricing financial derivatives, since in practice one always does calculations using finite intervals. For example, "one day" is clearly not an infinitesimal interval, and the utilization of SDEs for such periods may require approximations. The precise form of these approximations will be obtained by taking into consideration the definition of Ito integral.

To summarize, the ability to go from the stochastic difference equation during the finite interval,

$$\Delta S_k = a_k h + \sigma_k \Delta W_k \quad k = 1, 2, \dots, n, \tag{15}$$

to the stochastic differential equation,

$$dS_t = a(S_t, t)\, dt + \sigma(S_t, t)\, dW_t, \quad t \in [0, \infty), \tag{16}$$

and vice versa, is the ability to interpret dW_t by defining $\int_t^{t+h} \sigma(S_u, u)\, dW_u$, in a meaningful manner. This can only be done by constructing a stochastic integral.

2 The Ito Integral

The Ito integral is one way of defining sums of uncountable and unpredictable random increments over time. Such an integral cannot be obtained by utilizing the method used in the Riemann–Stieltjes integral. It is useful to see why this is so.

As was seen earlier, increments in a Wiener process, dW_t, represent random variables that are unpredictable, even in the immediate future. The value of the Wiener process at time t, written as W_t, is then a sum of an uncountable number of independent increments:

$$W_t = \int_0^t dW_u. \tag{17}$$

(Remember that at time zero, the Wiener process has a value of zero. Hence, $W_0 = 0$.) This is the simplest *stochastic integral* one can write down.

A more relevant stochastic integral is obtained by integrating the inno-vation term in the SDE:

$$\int_0^t \sigma(S_u, u) \, dW_u. \tag{18}$$

The integrals in (17) and (18) are summations of *very* erratic random variables, since two shocks that are $\epsilon > 0$ apart from each other, dW_t and $dW_{t+\epsilon}$, are still uncorrelated. The question that arises is whether the sum of such erratic terms can be meaningfully defined. After all, the sum of so many (uncountably many) erratic elements can very well be unbounded.

Consider again the way standard calculus defines integral.

2.1 The Riemann–Stieltjes Integral

Suppose we have a nonrandom function $F(x_t)$ where x_t is a deterministic variable of time, and where $F(\cdot)$ is continuous and differentiable, with the derivative:

$$\frac{dF(x_t)}{dx_t} = f(x_t). \tag{19}$$

In this particular case, where the derivative $f(\cdot)$ exists, the Riemann–Stieltjes integral can be written in two ways:

$$\int_0^T f(x_t) \, dx_t = \int_0^T dF(x_t). \tag{20}$$

The integral on the left-hand side is taken *with respect* to x_t, where t varies from 0 to T. Then, the value of $f(\cdot)$ at each x_t is multiplied by the infinitesimal increment dx_t. These (uncountably many) values are added to obtain the integral. This notation is in general preserved for the Riemann integral.

In the notation on the right-hand side, the integral is taken *with respect to $F(\cdot)$*. Increments in $F(\cdot)$ are added to obtain the integral. We can complicate the latter notation further. For example, we may be interested in calculating the integral

$$\int_0^T g(x_t) \, dF(x_t). \tag{21}$$

Here, we have an integral of a function $g(x_t)$ taken with respect to $F(\cdot)$.

Similar notation occurs when we deal with expectations of random variables. For example, $F(\cdot)$ may represent the distribution function of a random variable x_t, and we may want to calculate the expected value of some

$g(x_t)$ for *fixed* t:[4]

$$E[g(x_t)] = \int_{-\infty}^{\infty} g(x_t)\, dF(x_t). \qquad (22)$$

Heuristically, in this integral, x_t is varied from minus to plus infinity and the corresponding values of $g(\cdot)$ are averaged using the increments in $dF(\cdot)$, which in this case represents the probability associated with those values.

Note the important difference between the integral in (21) and the one in (22). In the first case it is the t that moves from 0 to T. The value of x_t for a particular t is left unspecified. It could very well be a random variable. This would make the integral itself a random variable.

The integral in (22) is quite different. The t is constant, and it is x_t that goes from minus to plus infinity. The integral is not a random variable.

For the case when there are no random variables in the picture, Riemann–Stieltjes integral was defined as a limit of some infinite sum. The integral would exist as long as this limit was well defined. To highlight differences with Ito integral, we review Riemann-Stieltjes methodology once again.

Suppose we would like to calculate

$$\int_0^T g(x_t)\, dF(x_t).$$

The formal calculation using Riemann–Stieltjes methodology is based upon the familiar construction where the interval $[0, T]$ is *partitioned* into n smaller intervals using the times

$$t_0 = 0 < t_1 < \cdots < t_{n-1} < t_n = T. \qquad (23)$$

Then, the finite *Riemann sum* V_n is defined:

$$V_n = \sum_{i=0}^{n-1} g(x_{t_{i+1}})[F(x_{t_{i+1}}) - F(x_{t_i})]. \qquad (24)$$

The right-hand side of this equation is a sum of elements such as

$$g(x_{t_{i+1}})[F(x_{t_{i+1}}) - F(x_{t_i})], \qquad (25)$$

which is a product of $g(x_{t_{i+1}})$ with $[F(x_{t_{i+1}}) - F(x_{t_i})]$. The first term represents $g(\cdot)$ evaluated at a point $x_{t_{i+1}}$. The second term resembles the increments $dF(x_t)$. These quantities are shown geometrically in Figure 1. Each element $g(x_{t_{i+1}})[F(x_{t_{i+1}}) - F(x_{t_i})]$ is a rectangle with base $[F(x_{t_{i+1}}) - F(x_{t_i})]$ and height $g(x_{t_{i+1}})$.

---

[4]When the function $g(\cdot)$ is the square or the cube of x_t, this integral will simply be the second or third moment.

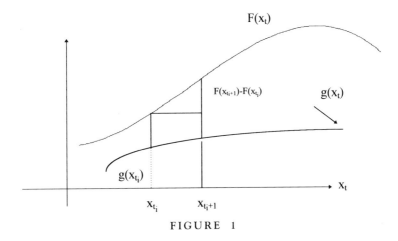

FIGURE 1

The V_n is the sum of all such rectangles. If the consecutive t_i, $i = 0, \ldots, n$ are not very distant from each other—that is, if we have a *fine* partition of $[0, T]$—this approximation may work reasonably well. In other words, if the function $g(\cdot)$ is integrable, then the limit

$$\lim_{\sup_i |t_i - t_{i-1}| \to 0} \sum_{i=0}^{n-1} g(x_{t_{i+1}})[F(x_{t_{i+1}}) - F(x_{t_i})] = \int_0^T g(x_t)\, dF(x_t) \qquad (26)$$

will exist and will be called the Riemann–Stieltjes integral. The reader should read this equality as a definition. The integral is defined as the limit of the sums on the right-hand side.[5] The sums V_n were called Riemann sums.[6]

2.2 Stochastic Integration and Riemann Sums

Hence, the value of the Riemann–Stieltjes integral can be approximated using rectangles with a "small" base and varying heights. Can we adopt similar reasoning in the case of stochastic integration?

---

[5] That is, if this limit converges.

[6] Note that there are many different ways rectangles can approximate the area under a curve. One can pick the base of the rectangle the same way, but change the height of the rectangle to either $g(x_{t_i})$ or to $g(\frac{x_{t_{i+1}} + x_{t_i}}{2})$.

We can ask this question more precisely by considering the SDE written over finite intervals of *equal* length h:[7]

$$S_k - S_{k-1} = a(S_{k-1}, k)h + \sigma(S_{k-1}, k)\Delta W_k, \quad k = 1, 2, \ldots, n. \quad (27)$$

Suppose we sum the increments ΔS_k on the left-hand side of (27):

$$\sum_{k=1}^{n-1}[S_k - S_{k-1}] = \sum_{k=1}^{n-1}[a(S_{k-1}, k)h] + \sum_{k=1}^{n-1}\sigma(S_{k-1}, k)[\Delta W_k]. \quad (28)$$

Can we use a methodology similar to the Riemann–Stieltjes approach and define an integral with respect to the random variable S_t as (some type of) a limit

$$\int_0^T dS_u = \lim_{n\to\infty}\left\{\sum_{k=1}^{n}[a(S_{k-1}, k)h] + \sum_{k=1}^{n}\sigma(S_{k-1}, k)[\Delta W_k]\right\}, \quad (29)$$

where as usual, it is assumed that $T = nh$?

The first term on the right-hand side of (29) does not contain any random terms once the information of time k becomes available. More importantly, the integral is taken with respect to increments in time h. By definition, time is a smooth function and has "finite variation." This means that the same procedure used for the Riemann–Stieltjes case can be applied to define an integral such as[8]

$$\int_0^T a(S_u, u)du = \lim_{n\to\infty}\sum_{k=1}^{n}[a(S_{k-1}, k)h]. \quad (31)$$

However, the second term on the right-hand side of (28) contains random variables even after I_{k-1} is revealed. In fact, as of time $k - 1$, the term

$$[W_k - W_{k-1}] \quad (32)$$

is a random variable, and the sum

$$\sum_{k=1}^{n}\sigma(S_{k-1}, k)[W_k - W_{k-1}] \quad (33)$$

is an integral with respect to a *random variable.*

---

[7]By considering intervals of *equal* length, the partition of $[0, T]$ can be made finer with $n \to 0$. Otherwise, the condition $\sup_i |t_i - t_{i-1}| \to 0$ has to be used.

[8]The sum on the right-hand side can be written in a more detailed form as

$$\lim_{n\to\infty}\sum_{k=1}^{n}[a(S_{(k-1)h}, kh)][(k)h - (k - 1)h], \quad (30)$$

with $kh = t_k$.

We can ask several questions:

- Which notion of limit should be used? The question is relevant because the sum in (33) is random and, in the limit, should converge to a random variable. The deterministic notion of limit utilized by Riemann–Stieltjes methodology cannot be used here.
- Under what conditions would such a limit converge (i.e., do the sums in (33) really have a meaningful limit)?
- What are the properties of the limiting random variable?

We limit our attention to a particular integral determined by the error terms in the SDEs. It turns out that, under some conditions, it is possible to define a stochastic integral as the limit *in mean square* of the random sum:

$$\sum_{k=1}^{n} \sigma(S_{k-1}, k)[W_k - W_{k-1}]. \tag{34}$$

This integral would be a *random variable.*

The use of *mean square convergence* implies that the difference between the sum

$$\sum_{k=1}^{n} \sigma(S_{k-1}, k)[W_k - W_{k-1}] \tag{35}$$

and the random variable called the *Ito integral,*

$$\int_0^T \sigma(S_u, u)\, dW_u, \tag{36}$$

has a variance that goes to zero as n increases toward infinity. Formally:

$$\lim_{n \to \infty} E \left[\sum_{k=1}^{n} \sigma(S_{k-1}, k) \left[W_k - W_{k-1} \right] - \int_0^T \sigma(S_u, u)\, dW_u \right]^2 = 0. \tag{37}$$

2.3 Definition: The Ito Integral

We can now provide a definition of the Ito integral within the context of stochastic differential equations.

DEFINITION: Consider the finite interval approximation of the stochastic differential equation

$$S_k - S_{k-1} = a(S_{k-1}, k)h + \sigma(S_{k-1}, k)[W_k - W_{k-1}], \qquad k = 1, 2, \dots, n, \tag{38}$$

where $[W_k - W_{k-1}]$ is a standard Wiener process with zero mean and variance h. Let

1. The $\sigma(S_t, t)$ be *non-anticipative*, in the sense that they are independent of the future.
2. The random variables $\sigma(S_t, t)$ be "non-explosive":

$$E\left[\int_0^T \sigma(S_t, t)^2 \, dt\right] < \infty. \tag{39}$$

Then, the Ito integral,

$$\int_0^T \sigma(S_t, t) \, dW_t, \tag{40}$$

is the mean square limit

$$\sum_{k=1}^n \sigma(S_{k-1}, k)[W_k - W_{k-1}] \rightarrow \int_0^T \sigma(S_t, t) \, dW_t \tag{41}$$

as $n \rightarrow \infty$ $(h \rightarrow 0.)$[9]

According to this definition, as the number of intervals goes to infinity and the length of each interval becomes infinitesimal, the finite sum will approach the random variable represented by the Ito integral. Clearly, the definition makes sense only if such a limiting random variable exists. The assumption that $\sigma(S_{k-1}, k)$ is nonanticipating turns out to be a fundamental condition for the existence of such a limit.[10]

To summarize, we see three major differences between deterministic and stochastic integrations. First, the notion of limit used in stochastic integra- tion is different. Second, the Ito integral is defined for nonanticipative func- tions only. And third, while integrals in standard calculus are defined using the actual "paths" followed by functions, stochastic integrals are defined within *stochastic equivalence*. It is essentially these differences that make some rules of stochastic calculus different from standard calculus.

The following example illustrates the utilization of mean square conver- gence in defining the Ito integral. In a second example, we show why the Ito integral cannot be defined "pathwise."

---

[9]Remember that $[0, T]$ is partitioned into n *equal* intervals, with $T = nh$.

[10]One technical point is whether the limiting random variable, that is, the Ito integral, depends on the choice of how one partitions the $[0, T]$. It can be shown that the choice of partition does not influence the value of the Ito integral.

2.4 An Expository Example

The Ito integral is a limit. It is the mean square limit of a certain finite sum. Thus, in order for the Ito integral to exist, some appropriate sums must converge.

Given proper conditions, one can show that Ito sums converge and that the corresponding Ito integral exists. Yet it is, in general, not possible to calculate *explicitly* the mean square limit. This can be done only in some special cases. In this section we consider an example where the mean square limit can be evaluated explicitly.[11]

Suppose one has to evaluate the integral

$$\int_0^T x_t \, dx_t, \tag{42}$$

where it is known that $x_0 = 0$.

If x_t was a deterministic variable, one could calculate this integral using the finite sums defined in (24). To do this, one would first partition the interval $[0, T]$ into n smaller subintervals all of size h using

$$t_0 = 0 < t_1 < \cdots < t_n = T, \tag{43}$$

where, as usual, $T = nh$ and for any i, $t_{i+1} - t_i = h$.[12] Second, one would define the sums

$$V_n = \sum_{i=0}^{n-1} x_{t_{i+1}} [x_{t_{i+1}} - x_{t_i}] \tag{44}$$

and let n go to infinity. The result is well known. The Riemann–Stieltjes integral of (42) with $x_0 = 0$ will be given by

$$\int_0^T x_t \, dx_t = \frac{1}{2} x_T^2. \tag{45}$$

This situation can easily be seen in Figure 2, where we consider an arbitrary function of time x_t and use a *single* rectangle to obtain the area under the curve.[13]

Now, if x_t is a Wiener process, the same approach cannot be used.

---

[11] This is in contrast to a proof where it is shown that the limit "exists."

[12] Equal-sized subintervals is a convenience. The same result can be shown with unequal $t_{i+1} - t_i$ as well.

[13] A single rectangle works because the function being integrated, $f(x_t)$, is just the 45-degree line, $f(x_t) = x_t$.

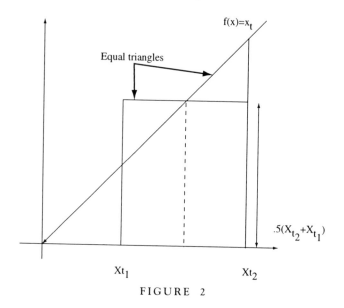

FIGURE 2

First of all, the V_n must be modified to

$$V_n = \sum_{i=0}^{n-1} x_{t_i}[x_{t_{i+1}} - x_{t_i}].$$ (46)

In other words, the first x_t has to be evaluated at time t_i instead of at t_{i+1}, because otherwise these terms will fail to be *nonanticipating*. The $x_{t_{i+1}}$ will be *unknown* as of time t_i, and will be correlated with the increments $[x_{t_{i+1}} - x_{t_i}]$. In the case of the Riemann–Stieltjes integral, one could use either type of sum and still get the same answer in the end. In the case of stochastic integration, results will change depending on whether one used $x_{t_{i+1}}$ or x_{t_i}. As will be seen later, it is a fundamental condition of the Ito integral that the integrands be nonanticipating.

Second, V_n is now a random variable and simple limits cannot be taken. In taking the limit of V_n one has to use a probabilistic approach. As mentioned earlier, the Ito integral uses the mean square limit.

Thus, we have to determine a limiting random variable V such that

$$\lim_{n \to \infty} E[V_n - V]^2 = 0.$$ (47)

Or, equivalently,

$$\lim_{n \to \infty} E\left[\sum_{i=0}^{n-1} x_{t_i} \Delta x_{t_{i+1}} - V\right]^2 = 0,$$ (48)

where for simplicity we let

$$\Delta x_{t_{i+1}} = x_{t_{i+1}} - x_{t_i}. \tag{49}$$

Below we calculate this limit explicitly.

2.4.1 Explicit Calculation of Mean Square Limit

We intend to calculate the limiting random variable V step by step in order to clarify the meaning of Ito integral as a mean square limit of a random sum. The first step is to manipulate the terms inside the V_n.

We begin by noting that for any a and b we have

$$(a+b)^2 = a^2 + b^2 + 2ab, \tag{50}$$

or

$$ab = \frac{1}{2}[(a+b)^2 - a^2 - b^2]. \tag{51}$$

Applying this transformation to $a = x_{t_i}$ and $b = \Delta x_{t_{i+1}}$ gives

$$V_n = \frac{1}{2} \sum_{i=0}^{n-1} [(x_{t_i} + \Delta x_{t_{i+1}})^2 - x_{t_i}^2 - \Delta x_{t_{i+1}}^2]. \tag{52}$$

But:

$$x_{t_i} + \Delta x_{t_{i+1}} = x_{t_{i+1}}, \tag{53}$$

which gives:

$$V_n = \frac{1}{2} \left[\sum_{i=0}^{n-1} x_{t_{i+1}}^2 - \sum_{i=0}^{n-1} x_{t_i}^2 - \sum_{i=0}^{n-1} \Delta x_{t_{i+1}}^2 \right]. \tag{54}$$

Now the first and second summations in (54) are the same except for the very first and last elements. Canceling similar terms and noting that $x_0 = 0$ by definition:[14]

$$V_n = \frac{1}{2} \left[x_T^2 - \sum_{i=0}^{n-1} \Delta x_{t_{i+1}}^2 \right]. \tag{55}$$

Note that x_T is independent of n, and consequently the mean square limit of V_n will be determined by the mean square limit of the term $\sum_{i=0}^{n-1} \Delta x_{t_{i+1}}^2$.

In other words, we now have to find the Z in

$$\lim_{n \to \infty} E \left[\sum_{i=0}^{n-1} \Delta x_{t_{i+1}}^2 - Z \right]^2 = 0. \tag{56}$$

In this expression there are two "squares" on the right-hand side. One is due to the random variable itself, and the other to the type of limit we are using. Hence, the limit will involve fourth powers of $\Delta x_{t_{i+1}}$.

---

[14]Note that by construction $t_n = T$.

First, we calculate the expectation:

$$E\left[\sum_{i=0}^{n-1} \Delta x_{t_{i+1}}^2\right]. \tag{57}$$

This will be a good candidate for Z. Taking expectations in a straightforward way:

$$E\left[\sum_{i=0}^{n-1} \Delta x_{t_{i+1}}^2\right] = \sum_{i=0}^{n-1} E[\Delta x_{t_{i+1}}^2] = \sum_{i=0}^{n-1}(t_{i+1} - t_i), \tag{58}$$

which simplifies to

$$\sum_{i=0}^{n-1}(t_{i+1} - t_i) = T. \tag{59}$$

Now using this as a candidate for Z, we can evaluate the expectation:

$$E\left[\sum_{i=0}^{n-1} \Delta x_{t_{i+1}}^2 - T\right]^2$$

$$= E\left\{\sum_{i=0}^{n-1} \Delta x_{t_{i+1}}^4 + 2\sum_{i=0}^{n-1}\sum_{j<i}^{n-1}[\Delta x_{t_{i+1}}^2][\Delta x_{t_{j+1}}^2] + T^2 - 2T\sum_{i=0}^{n-1} \Delta x_{t_{i+1}}^2\right\}. \tag{60}$$

We consider the components of the right-hand side of (60) individually. Realizing that Wiener process increments are independent,

$$E[\Delta x_{t_{i+1}}^2 \cdot \Delta x_{t_{j+1}}^2] = (t_{i+1} - t_i)(t_{j+1} - t_j) \tag{61}$$

and

$$E[\Delta x_{t_{i+1}}^4] = 3(t_{i+1} - t_i)^2, \tag{62}$$

we obtain

$$E\left[\sum_{i=0}^{n-1} \Delta x_{t_{i+1}}^2 - T\right]^2 = \sum_{i=0}^{n-1} 3(t_{i+1} - t_i)^2$$

$$+ 2\sum_{i=0}^{n-1}\sum_{j<i}^{n-1}(t_{i+1} - t_i)(t_{j+1} - t_j) \tag{63}$$

$$+ T^2 - 2T\sum_{i=0}^{n-1}(t_{i+1} - t_i).$$

Now we use the fact that $t_{i+1} - t_i = h$, for all i, since all intervals are the same size. We have the following:

$$\sum_{i=0}^{n-1} 3(t_{i+1} - t_i)^2 = 3nh^2 \tag{64}$$

$$2 \sum_{i=0}^{n-1} \sum_{j<i}^{n-1} (t_{i+1} - t_i)(t_{j+1} - t_j) = n(n-1)h^2 \tag{65}$$

and

$$T^2 - 2T \sum_{i=0}^{n-1} (t_{i+1} - t_i) = -T^2 = -n^2 h^2. \tag{66}$$

Put all these together

$$E\left[\sum_{i=0}^{n-1} \Delta x_{t_{i+1}}^2 - T\right]^2 = 3nh^2 + n(n-1)h^2 - n^2 h^2, \tag{67}$$

which means that

$$E\left[\sum_{i=0}^{n-1} \Delta x_{t_{i+1}}^2 - T\right]^2 = 2nh^2 = 2Th. \tag{68}$$

This implies that as $n \to \infty$, the size of the intervals will go to zero, and

$$\lim_{h \to 0} E\left[\sum_{i=0}^{n-1} \Delta x_{t_{i+1}}^2 - T\right]^2 = \lim_{h \to 0} 2hT = 0. \tag{69}$$

Thus, the mean square limit of $\sum_{i=0}^{n-1} \Delta x_{t_{i+1}}^2$ is T.

Going back to V_n,

$$V_n = \frac{1}{2}\left[x_T^2 - \sum_{i=0}^{n-1} \Delta x_{t_{i+1}}^2\right], \tag{70}$$

we find the mean square limit of V_n by using the mean square limit of $\sum_{i=0}^{n-1} \Delta x_{t_{i+1}}^2$ just obtained:

$$\lim_{n \to \infty} E[V_n]^2 = \frac{1}{2}\left[x_T^2 - T\right]. \tag{71}$$

The term on the right-hand side is the Ito integral:

$$\int_0^T x_t \, dx_t. \tag{72}$$

We see that the Ito integral results in a different expression than in the case of standard calculus. The Ito integral is given by

$$\int_0^T x_t dx_t = \frac{1}{2}\left[x_T^2 - T\right]. \tag{73}$$

In the case of the Riemann integral, there was no additional term T.

This is one example where the Ito integral can be calculated explicitly using mean square limits. We find that the Ito integral is the *limiting* random variable $\frac{1}{2}[x_T^2 - T]$.

2.4.2 An Important Remark

In the previous section it was shown that

$$\lim_{n\to\infty} E\left[\sum_{i=0}^{n-1} \Delta x_{t_{i+1}}^2 - T\right]^2 = 0. \tag{74}$$

It is interesting to convert this into integral notation.

Assume that x_t is a Wiener process and consider the integral

$$\int_0^T (dx_t)^2, \tag{75}$$

which can be interpreted as the sum of squared increments in x_t.

If this integral exists in the Ito sense, then by definition,

$$\lim_{n\to\infty} E\left[\sum_{i=0}^{n-1} \Delta x_{t_{i+1}}^2 - \int_0^T (dx_t)^2\right]^2 = 0. \tag{76}$$

But we know that

$$\int_0^T dt = T. \tag{77}$$

Putting the equalities (74), (76), and (77) together we obtain a result that may seem a bit "unusual" to one who is used to working with standard calculus

$$\int_0^T (dx_t)^2 = \int_0^T dt, \tag{78}$$

where the equality holds in the mean square sense. It is in this sense that, if W_t represents a Wiener process, for infinitesimal dt, one can write:

$$(dW_t)^2 = dt. \tag{79}$$

In fact, in all practical calculations dealing with stochastic calculus, it is a common practice to replace the terms involving dW_t^2 by dt. The preceding discussion traces the logic behind this procedure. The equality should be interpreted in the sense of mean square convergence.

3 Properties of the Ito Integral

Consider the stochastic differential equation

$$dS_t = a(S_t, t)\, dt + \sigma(S_t, t)\, dW_t. \tag{80}$$

Integrating this equation over an interval $[0, T]$, we obtain

$$\int_0^T dS_t = \int_0^T a(S_t, t)\, dt + \int_0^T \sigma(S_t, t)\, dW_t, \tag{81}$$

where the second integral on the right-hand side is defined in the sense of Ito. What can we say about the properties of this integral?

3.1 The Ito Integral Is a Martingale

It turns out that the Ito integral is a martingale. This property is useful in modeling the innovation terms of asset prices in financial theory. The property is also important for practical calculations of asset prices.

Models that describe the dynamic behavior of asset prices contain innovation terms that represent unpredictable news. As a result, an integral of the form[15]

$$\int_t^{t+\Delta} \sigma_u\, dW_u \tag{82}$$

is a sum of unpredictable disturbances that affect asset prices during an interval of length Δ. Now, if each increment is unpredictable given the information set at time t, the sum of these increments should also be unpredictable. This makes the integral shown in (82) a *martingale difference*:

$$E_t\left[\int_t^{t+\Delta} \sigma_u\, dW_u\right] = 0. \tag{83}$$

Then, the integral

$$\int_0^t \sigma_u\, dW_u \tag{84}$$

becomes a martingale:

$$E_s\left[\int_0^t \sigma_u\, dW_u\right] = \int_0^s \sigma_u\, dW_u, \quad 0 < s < t. \tag{85}$$

Hence, the existence of unpredictable innovation terms in equations describing the dynamics of asset prices coincides well with the martingale property of the Ito integral.

---

[15] We are simplifying the notation by letting $\sigma(S_u, u) = \sigma_u$.

The condition that ensures this martingale property is the one that requires σ_t be nonanticipative given the information set I_t.

We consider two cases of interest.

3.1.1 Case 1

Assume that the volatility parameter $\sigma(S_t, t)$ is a constant independent of the level of asset price S_t, and of time t:

$$\sigma(S_t, t) = \sigma. \tag{86}$$

Then the Ito integral will be identical to the Riemann integral and will be given by

$$\int_t^{t+\Delta} \sigma dW_u = \sigma[W_{t+\Delta} - W_t]. \tag{87}$$

Consider a forecast of the integral

$$E\left\{\int_0^{t+\Delta} \sigma \, dW_u \,\middle|\, \int_0^t \sigma \, dW_u\right\} = \int_0^t \sigma \, dW_u \tag{88}$$

$$= \sigma(W_t - W_0), \tag{89}$$

where $\Delta > 0$. This is the case because increments in the Wiener process have zero mean and are uncorrelated:

$$E[\sigma(W_{t+\Delta} - W_0)|(W_t - W_0)]$$

$$= E[\sigma(W_{t+\Delta} - W_t) + \sigma(W_t - W_0)|(W_t - W_0)] \tag{90}$$

$$= \sigma(W_t - W_0). \tag{91}$$

We see again that the Ito integral has the martingale property.[16]

Thus, when σ is constant, the Riemann and Ito integrals will coincide and both will be martingales.

3.1.2 Case 2

On the other hand, if σ depends on S_t, which in turn depends on W_t, the Ito integral diverges from the Riemann integral and remains a martingale, whereas the Riemann integral ceases to be one.

For example, if the price of the underlying asset has a geometric distribution with the diffusion term

$$\sigma(S_t, t) = \sigma S_t, \tag{92}$$

---

[16]Remember that $W_0 = 0$.

then the Ito integral will be different from the Riemann integral, and using Riemann sums to approximate the Ito integral may lead to self-contradiction.

This is illustrated by the following example.

3.1.3 An Example
Suppose asset prices follow the SDE

$$dS_t = a(S_t, t)\, dt + \sigma(S_t, t)\, dW_t, \qquad 0 \le t, \tag{93}$$

where the drift and diffusion parameters are given as

$$a(S_t, t) = \mu S_t \tag{94}$$

and

$$\sigma(S_t, t) = \sigma S_t. \tag{95}$$

That is, both parameters are proportional to the last observed asset price S_t.

Consider again a small interval of length Δ and integrate this SDE:

$$\int_t^{t+\Delta} dS_u = \int_t^{t+\Delta} \mu S_u\, du + \int_t^{t+\Delta} \sigma S_u\, dW_u. \tag{96}$$

Note that the term $\sigma S(W_t)$ depends on W_t indirectly, through S_t.[17]

Now consider what happens when we try to approximate the second integral on the right-hand side using Riemann sums.

One approximation used by Riemann sums uses the values of the Wiener process observed at "midpoints" of subintervals. This amounts to calculating first the terms

$$\sigma S\left(\frac{W_{t+\Delta} + W_t}{2}\right) \tag{97}$$

and then multiplying these by the "base" of the rectangle, $W_{t+\Delta} - W_t$.

Riemann sums would then involve terms such as

$$S\left(\frac{W_{t+\Delta} + W_t}{2}\right)[W_{t+\Delta} - W_t]. \tag{98}$$

Clearly, the expectation of such terms is not zero, since the argument of $S(\cdot)$ and the base of the rectangle contains terms that are correlated.

We consider the simple case where the SDE is given by

$$dS_t = \sigma W_t\, dW_t.$$

---

[17]Here we abuse the notation in writing $S(W_t) = S_t$. But it simplifies the exposition.

The innovation terms in this equation will be of the form

$$\int_t^{t+\Delta} \sigma W_u \, dW_u.$$

To approximate such an integral with a Riemann sum, a rectangle with base $W_{t+\Delta} - W_t$ and height $\sigma\left[\frac{W_{t+\Delta}+W_t}{2}\right]$ may be used:[18]

$$\int_t^{t+\Delta} \sigma W_u \, dW_u \cong \sigma\left[\frac{W_{t+\Delta} + W_t}{2}\right](W_{t+\Delta} - W_t).$$

But, applying the conditional expectation operator $E_t[.]$ to the right-hand side,

$$E\left[\left(\frac{W_{t+\Delta} + W_t}{2}\right)(W_{t+\Delta} - W_t)|W_t\right] = E\left[\frac{1}{2}(W_{t+\Delta}^2 - W_t^2)|W_t\right] \quad (99)$$

$$= \frac{1}{2}\Delta, \quad (100)$$

and $\Delta \neq 0$. This means that the approximating sum has a conditional expectation that is *not* equal to zero. It is *predictable*. Clearly this contradicts the claim that the integral on the left-hand side represents an innovation term.

If such correlations are not zero, evaluating the Ito integral using Riemann sums will imply innovation disturbance terms with nonzero expectations:

$$E_t\left[\int_t^{t+\Delta} \sigma_s \, dW_s\right] \neq 0, \qquad 0 < \Delta. \quad (101)$$

In order to preserve the *nonanticipating* property of $\sigma(S_t, t)$, approximation of the Ito integral must use rectangles such as

$$\sigma(S_t, t)(W_{t+\Delta} - W_t), \quad (102)$$

where the terms $\sigma(S_t, t)$ will, by definition, be uncorrelated with the increments ΔW_t.

The proceding discussion shows that the Riemann integral is not consistent with assumptions made in asset pricing models, except in the very special case when

$$\sigma(S_t, t) = \sigma(t). \quad (103)$$

There is an additional comment that relates to the same point. If the functions being integrated are not nonanticipating, then there will be no

[18]Here, for simplicity we use *one* rectangle. In fact, much finer partitions of the interval $[t, t + \Delta]$ can be used.

guarantee that the partial sums used to construct the Ito integral will converge in mean square to a meaningful random variable. Hence, there is an even more fundamental problem than losing the martingale property. The integral may not exist.

The next section discusses this point briefly.

3.2 Pathwise Integrals

In stochastic calculus, one occasionally encounters the statement that stochastic integrals cannot be defined *pathwise*. What does this mean?

Consider the binomial process $S_{t_{i+1}} - S_{t_i}$, $i = 1, 2, \ldots, n$, measured over discrete intervals of length Δ during a period $[0, T]$:

$$S_{t_{i+1}} - S_{t_i} = \begin{cases} \sqrt{\Delta} & \text{with probability } p \\ -\sqrt{\Delta} & \text{with probability } 1 - p \end{cases}, \qquad (104)$$

where, as usual $T = n\Delta$.

A typical *path* of this process will be a sequence of $+\sqrt{\Delta}$ and $-\sqrt{\Delta}$ following each other. For example, a typical realization may look like

$$\{\sqrt{\Delta}, \sqrt{\Delta}, -\sqrt{\Delta}, \sqrt{\Delta} \ldots\}. \qquad (105)$$

Suppose a financial analyst has to approximate an integral of the form

$$\int_0^T f(S_t)\, dS_t$$

using a finite sum such as:

$$V_n = \sum_{i=0}^{n-1} f(S_{t_{i+1}})[S_{t_{i+1}} - S_{t_i}]. \qquad (106)$$

Suppose V_n is calculated using a particular *path* for S_t. For example, consider the path where plus and minus $\sqrt{\Delta}$'s alternate:

$$\{\sqrt{\Delta}, -\sqrt{\Delta}, \sqrt{\Delta}, -\sqrt{\Delta}, \ldots, \sqrt{\Delta}\}. \qquad (107)$$

Replacing the $S_{t_{i+1}} - S_{t_i}$ in V_n with these observed values, we get

$$V_n = \left[f(-\sqrt{\Delta})(-\sqrt{\Delta}) + f(\sqrt{\Delta})\sqrt{\Delta} + f(-\sqrt{\Delta})(-\sqrt{\Delta}) + \cdots + f(\sqrt{\Delta})\sqrt{\Delta} \right].$$
$$(108)$$

Clearly, the value of V_n depends on a *particular* trajectory of S_t. If V_n converges, it can be called a *pathwise* integral.

It turns out that there is no guarantee that such pathwise integrals converge in stochastic environments. We consider a simple example.

Let the functions $f(\cdot)$ in V_n be given by

$$f(S_{t_{i+1}}) = \text{sign}(S_{t_{i+1}} - S_{t_i}). \tag{109}$$

In other words, $f(\cdot)$ assumes the value of plus or minus one, depending on the sign of $S_{t_{i+1}} - S_{t_i}$.

This means that all elements in V_n are positive, so

$$V_n = \sum_{i=0}^{n-1} \sqrt{\Delta} = n\sqrt{\Delta}. \tag{110}$$

Using $T = n\Delta$,

$$V_n = \frac{T}{\sqrt{\Delta}}. \tag{111}$$

Clearly, as $\Delta \to 0$, V_n will go to infinity.

If such paths have a positive probability of occurrence, then the *pathwise* sum V_n cannot converge in any probabilistic sense.

This example is important for two reasons.

First, we see the meaning of a pathwise integral. In calculating the integral pathwise, we did not use the *probabilities* associated with $\Delta S_{t_{i+1}}$. The integral was calculated using the actual realization of the process. The Ito integral, on the other hand, is calculated using mean square convergence, and the integral is determined within stochastic equivalence.

Second, we see the importance of using nonanticipative functions as $f(\cdot)$. In fact, because $f(\cdot)$ was able to "see the future," it anticipated the sign of $S_{t_{i+1}} - S_{t_i}$. That made all the elements in the summation sign positive and led to an exploding V_n as n increased.

4 Other Properties of the Ito Integral

The Ito intgral has some other properties.

4.1 Existence

One can ask the question: when does the Ito integral of a general random function $f(S_t, t)$, where $\{S_t\}$ is given by (6),

$$\int_0^t f(S_u, u)\, dS_u, \tag{112}$$

exist?

It turns out that if the function $f(\cdot)$ is continuous, and if it is *nonanticipating*, this integral exists. In other words, the finite sums

$$\sum_{i=0}^{n-1} f(S_{t_i}, t_i)[S_{t_{i+1}} - S_{t_i}] \tag{113}$$

converge in mean square to "some" random variable that we call the Ito integral.[19]

4.2 Correlation Properties

It should not be forgotten that the Ito integral is a random variable. (More precisely, it is a random process.) Therefore, it will have various moments.

The martingale property gives the first moment of the integral of a nonanticipating $f(\cdot)$ with respect to a Wiener process

$$E\left[\int_0^T f(W_t, t)\, dW_t\right] = 0, \tag{114}$$

where W_t is a Wiener process. The second moments are given by the variance and covariances

$$E\left[\int_0^t f(W_u, u)\, dW_u \int_0^t g(W_u, u)\, dW_u\right]$$
$$= \int_0^t E[f(W_u, u)g(W_u, u)]\, du \tag{115}$$

and

$$E\left[\int_0^t f(W_u, u)\, dW_u\right]^2 = E\left[\int_0^t f(W_u, u)^2\, du\right]. \tag{116}$$

Note the recurring use of the equivalence $dW_t^2 = dt$ discussed earlier.

4.3 Addition

The Ito integral also has some properties that are similar to those of the Riemann–Stieltjes integral.

In particular, the integral of the sum of two (random) functions of S_t in (6) is equal to the sum of their integrals:

$$\int_0^T [f(S_t, t) + g(S_t, t)]\, dS_t = \int_0^T f(S_t, t)\, dS_t + \int_0^T g(S_t, t)\, dS_t. \tag{117}$$

---

[19] Although it may exist, determining such a limit explicitly is not guaranteed.

5 Integrals with Respect to Jump Processes

What complicated the definition of a stochastic integral was the extreme irregularity both of continuous-time martingales and of the Wiener process. This made a pathwise definition of the integral impossible.

Do we have the same problem if we have a stochastic integral with respect to some jump process? Could one use the Riemann–Stieltjes integral when dealing with, say, Poisson processes?

Surprisingly, the answer to this question is affirmative under some conditions.

Suppose a process M_t is a martingale that exhibits finite jumps only and has no Wiener component. Trajectories of such an M_t will exhibit occasional jumps, but otherwise will be very smooth. Then, one could define a V_n,

$$V_n = \sum_{i=0}^{n-1} f(M_{t_i})[M_{t_{i+1}} - M_{t_i}], \qquad (118)$$

pathwise.

This V_n will converge, and the variation of the process M_t will be finite with probability one. Under these conditions, we say that V_n converges *pathwise*.

6 Conclusions

This chapter dealt with the definition of the Ito integral.

From the point of view of a practitioner, there are two important points to keep in mind. First, the error terms in stochastic differential equations are defined in the sense of the Ito integral. Numerical calculations must obey the conditions set by this definition. Second, the stochastic differential equations routinely used in asset pricing are also defined in the sense of the Ito integral.

Above all, we saw that the Ito integral is the mean square limit of some random sums.

These random sums are carefully put together so that the resulting integral is a martingale.

We also discussed several examples and showed that the rules of integration are in general very different in stochastic environments, when compared with the deterministic case. This was the result of using mean square convergence.

Fortunately, in evaluating Ito integrals, the direct route of obtaining the mean square limit will rarely be used. Instead, Ito integrals can be evaluated in a more straightforward fashion using a result called Ito's lemma. This will be discussed in the next chapter, where we will also discuss further examples of evaluating the Ito integral.

7 References

There are several excellent sources on the derivation of the Ito integral. Karatzas and Shreve (1991) and Revuz and Yor (1994) were already mentioned. Two additional sources that the reader may find a bit easier to read are Oksendal (1992) and Protter (1990). The former source could be a very good manual for quantitatively oriented practitioners and for beginning graduate students. It is well written and easy to understand. Technicalities are avoided as much as possible.

CHAPTER 10

Ito's Lemma

1 Introduction

As discussed earlier, in stochastic environments a formal notion of derivative does not exist. Shocks to asset prices are assumed to be unpredictable, and in continuous time they become "too erratic." The resulting asset prices may be continuous, but they are not smooth. Stochastic differentials need to be used in place of derivatives.

Ito's rule provides an analytical formula that simplifies handling stochastic differentials and leads to explicit computations. Ito's rule is the main topic of this chapter.

We begin by discussing various types of derivatives.

2 Types of Derivatives

Suppose we have a function $F(S_t, t)$ depending on *two* variables S_t and t, where S_t itself varies with time t. Further, assume that S_t is a random process.

In standard calculus, where all variables are deterministic, there are three sorts of derivatives that one can talk about.

The first are the *partial derivatives* of $F(S_t, t)$, denoted by

$$F_s = \frac{\partial F(S_t, t)}{\partial S_t}, \qquad F_t = \frac{\partial F(S_t, t)}{\partial t}. \tag{1}$$

The second is the *total derivative* dealing with differentials:

$$dF_t = F_s \, dS_t + F_t \, dt. \tag{2}$$

194

In (2) dF_t is used as a shorthand notation for $dF(S_t, t)$. This should not be confused with F_t, the partial of $F(\cdot)$ with respect to t.

The third is the *chain rule*:

$$\frac{dF(S_t, t)}{dt} = F_s \frac{dS_t}{dt} + F_t. \tag{3}$$

A financial market participant may be interested in these derivatives for various reasons.

The partial derivative has no direct real-life counterpart, but gives "multipliers" that can be used in evaluating responses of asset prices to observed changes in risk factors. For example, F_s measures the response of $F(S_t, t)$ to a small change in S_t only. As such, F_s is a hypothetical concept, since the only way a continuous random variable S_t can change is if some time passes. Hence, in reality, t has to change as well. Partial derivatives abstract from such questions. Because they are simple multipliers, there is no difference between the way stochastic and deterministic environments define partial derivatives.

A classical example of the use of partial derivatives occurs in *delta hedging*. Suppose a market participant knows the functional form of $F(S_t, t)$. Then, this mathematical formula can be differentiated with respect to S_t only, in order to find the partial derivative F_s. This F_s is a measure of how much the derivative asset price will change *per* unit change in S_t. In this sense, one does not have any of the difficulties encountered in defining a time derivative for Wiener processes. What is under investigation is not how $F(S_t, t)$ moves over time, but how $F(\cdot)$ responds to a "small" hypothetical change in S_t, with time fixed.

The total derivative is a more "realistic" notion. It is assumed that both time t and the underlying security price S_t change, and then the total response of $F(S_t, t)$ is calculated. The result is the (stochastic) differential dF_t. This is clearly a very useful quantity to the market participant. It represents the observed change in the price of the derivative asset during an interval dt.

The chain rule is quite similar to the total derivative. In classical calculus, the chain rule expresses the *rate* of change in a variable as a chain effect of some initial variation. In stochastic calculus, we know that operations such as dF_t/dt, dS_t/dt cannot be defined for continuous-time square integrable martingales, or Brownian motion. But, a stochastic equivalent of the chain rule can be formulated in terms of absolute changes such as dF_t, dS_t, dt, and the Ito integral can be used to justify these terms. Thus, in stochastic calculus, the term "chain rule" will refer to the way *stochastic differentials* relate to each other. In other words, a stochastic version of total differentiation is developed.

2.1 Example

We discuss a simple example before going into Ito's formula. The example will help to clarify the mechanics of taking various derivatives. Let $F(r_t, t)$ be the price of a T-bill that matures at time T, and let r_t be a fixed continuously compounding risk-free rate. Then

$$F(r_t, t) = e^{-r_t(T-t)}100. \tag{4}$$

Let us calculate the partial derivatives F_r, F_t:

$$F_r = \frac{\partial F}{\partial r_t} = -(T-t)[e^{-r_t(T-t)}100] \tag{5}$$

and

$$F_t = \frac{\partial F}{\partial t} = r_t[e^{-r_t(T-t)}100]. \tag{6}$$

Note that these partials will be the same regardless of whether r_t is deterministic or random. By taking these partial derivatives, we are simply calculating the rate of change of $F(\cdot)$ with respect to small hypothetical changes in r_t or in t.

On the other hand, the total derivative clearly relates to the actual occurrence of random events. In standard calculus, with *nonrandom* r_t, the total derivative of this particular $F(\cdot)$ will be given by

$$dF(r_t, t) = -(T-t)[e^{-r_t(T-t)}100]\, dr_t + r_t[e^{-r_t(T-t)}100]\, dt. \tag{7}$$

This example suggests that when r_t is random, we may be able to define the counterpart of total derivative, using the Ito integral, which gives a meaning to stochastic differentials such as dr_t. This intuition is correct, and the result is Ito's formula. However, with stochastic r_t not only does the interpretation of dr_t change,[1] but the formula will also be different.

3 Ito's Lemma

The stochastic version of the chain rule is known as Ito's lemma. Let S_t be a continuous time process which depends on the Wiener process W_t. Suppose we are given a function of S_t, denoted by $F(S_t, t)$, and suppose we would like to calculate the change in $F(\cdot)$ when dt amount of time passes. Clearly, passing time would influence the $F(S_t, t)$ in two different ways. First, there is a *direct* influence through the t variable in $F(S_t, t)$. Second,

---

[1]Remember that such quantities are defined in terms of mean square convergence and within stochastic equivalence.

as time passes, one obtains new information about W_t and observes a new increment, dS_t. This will also make $F(\cdot)$ change. The sum of these two effects is represented by the stochastic differential $dF(S_t, t)$ and is given by the stochastic equivalent of the chain rule.

Let the random process S_t be observed in continuous time. We again partition the time interval $[0, T]$ into n equal pieces, each with length h, and use the finite difference approximation. However, we write this as an equality

$$\Delta S_k = a_k h + \sigma_k \Delta W_k, \qquad k = 1, 2, \ldots, n, \qquad (8)$$

using the mean square equivalence between the left- and right-hand side as $h \to 0$. This notation will be preserved throughout this chapter. Also, note that we shortened the notation for $a(S_{k-1}, k)$ to a_k and for $\sigma(S_{k-1}, k)$ to σ_k.

We calculate Ito's formula in this setting. To do this, we use Taylor series.

Remember the Taylor series expansion of a smooth (i.e., infinitely differentiable) function $f(x)$ around some arbitrary point x_0,

$$f(x) = f(x_0) + f'(x_0)(x - x_0) + \frac{1}{2} f''(x_0)(x - x_0)^2 + R, \qquad (9)$$

where R denotes the *remainder*.

We apply this formula to $F(S_t, t)$. That means, at the outset, that $F(\cdot)$ has to be a smooth function of S_t.[2] But there are two additional complications. The Taylor series formula in (9) is valid for a $f(x)$ which is a function of a single variable x, while $F(S_t, t)$ depends on *two* variables, S_t and t. Secondly, the formula in (9) is valid for deterministic variables, while S_t is a random process. Before using Taylor series, these complications must be addressed.

The extension of a univariate Taylor series formula to two variables is straightforward. One adds the partials with respect to the second variable. With two variables, cross partials should be included as well.

The applicability of the Taylor series formula to a random environment is a deeper issue. First, it should be remembered that some of the terms in Taylor series are *partial* derivatives. Also, with respect to partial derivatives, one does not have any difficulty with differentiation in stochastic environments. Second, we have differentials such as dS_t. Here, we do need an adjustment. However, the adjustment is in terms of the interpretation of the equality and not in the Taylor series expansion itself. The formula for

---

[2]Incidentally, some readers may wonder if this "smoothness" does not contradict the extreme irregularity of S_t. Note that $F(\cdot)$ can be a smooth function of S_t while still being a very irregular stochastic process. Irregularity is used here in the sense of how $F(\cdot)$ changes over *time*. It is not a statement about how S_t relates to $F(\cdot)$.

Taylor series expansion will remain the same, but the meaning of the equality sign would change. The equality would have to be interpreted in the sense of mean square convergence.

We apply the Taylor series formula to $F(S_k, k)$, $k = 1, 2, \ldots$, where the S_k is assumed to obey

$$\Delta S_k = a_k h + \sigma_k \Delta W_k. \tag{10}$$

First fix k. Given the information set I_{k-1}, S_{k-1} is a known number. Next, apply Taylor's formula to expand the $F(S_k, k)$ around S_{k-1} and $k - 1$,

$$F(S_k, k) = F(S_{k-1}, k - 1) + F_s[S_k - S_{k-1}] + F_t[h] + \frac{1}{2}F_{ss}[S_k - S_{k-1}]^2$$

$$+ \frac{1}{2}F_{tt}[h]^2 + F_{st}[h(S_k - S_{k-1})] + R, \tag{11}$$

where the partials $F_s, F_{ss}, F_t, F_{tt}, F_{st}$ are all evaluated at $S_{k-1}, k - 1$. R represents the remaining terms of the Taylor series expansion. Here we are keeping the F_t, F_{st}, F_{tt} notation for convenience, although these partials are with respect to k.

Transfer $F(S_{k-1}, k - 1)$ on the right-hand side of (11) to the left, and relabel the increments in (11) as follows:

$$F(S_k, k) - F(S_{k-1}, k - 1) = \Delta F(k) \tag{12}$$

$$S_k - S_{k-1} = \Delta S_k. \tag{13}$$

Also note that Equation (11) already uses the increment for the time variable:

$$kh - (k - 1)h = h. \tag{14}$$

Now substitute these into (11):

$$\Delta F(k) = F_s \Delta S_k + F_t[h] + \frac{1}{2}F_{ss}[\Delta S_k]^2$$

$$+ \frac{1}{2}F_{tt}[h]^2 + F_{st}[h \Delta S_k] + R. \tag{15}$$

But we know that the dynamics of S_t is governed by Equation (10), and that we have

$$\Delta S_k = a_k h + \sigma_k \Delta W_k. \tag{16}$$

We can substitute the right-hand side of this for ΔS_k in the Taylor series expansion (11):

$$\Delta F(k) = F_s[a_k h + \sigma_k \Delta W_k] + F_t[h] + \frac{1}{2}F_{ss}[a_k h + \sigma_k \Delta W_k]^2$$

$$+ \frac{1}{2}F_{tt}[h^2] + F_{st}(h)[a_k h + \Delta W_k] + R. \tag{17}$$

What does this equation mean? We give a brief heuristic discussion. On the left-hand side, $\Delta F(k)$ indicates the total change in $F(S_k, k)$ due to changing k and changing S_k. Hence, if this term is the price of a derivative security, on the left-hand side we have the change in the derivative asset's price during a short interval. This change is explained by the terms on the right-hand side.

The *first-order* effects are the effects of time, represented by $F_t[h]$, and the effects of change in underlying securities price, $[a_k h + \sigma_k \Delta W_k]$. In the latter we again see that changes in security prices have a predictable and an unpredictable component. *Second-order* effects are those changes that are represented, for the time being, by squared terms and by cross products. Higher-order terms are grouped in the remainder R.

In order to obtain a chain rule in stochastic environments, the terms on the right-hand side will be classified as negligible and nonnegligible. Then, it will be shown that in "small" time intervals, negligible terms can be dropped from the right-hand side and a chain rule formula can be obtained. In addition, as $h \to 0$, a limiting argument can be used and a precise formula can be obtained in mean square sense. This formula is known as Ito's lemma.

The first step of this derivation is to separate the terms on the right-hand side. This requires an explicit criterion for deciding which terms are negligible. After this, one can consider the size of the terms on the right-hand side of (11) one by one and decide which ones are to be dropped.

3.1 The Notion of "Size" in Stochastic Calculus

This section discusses the convention used in determining which variables can be classified as "negligible" in stochastic calculus.

In standard calculus, the Taylor series expansion of some function $f(S)$ around S_0 will be given by

$$\Delta f = f_s(S_0)\,\Delta S + \frac{1}{2}f_{ss}(S_0)(\Delta S)^2 + \frac{1}{3!}f_{sss}(S_0)(\Delta S)^3 + R. \qquad (18)$$

But the formula for total derivatives is only

$$df = f_s\,dS. \qquad (19)$$

This is equivalent to assuming that in the Taylor series expansion (18), while ΔS is small, yet nonnegligible, the terms involving $(\Delta S)^2, (\Delta S)^3, \ldots$ are smaller and can be ignored as $\Delta S \to 0$. consequently, in the limit the term $f_s\,dS$ is preserved, while all other terms are dropped. The result is the (total) differentiation formula (19).

To see why such a convention makes sense, note that as ΔS gets smaller, terms such as $(\Delta S)^2, (\Delta S)^3, \ldots$ get small *faster*. This is shown in Figure 1, where the functions

$$g_1(\Delta S) = \Delta S \tag{20}$$

$$g_2(\Delta S) = [\Delta S]^2 \tag{21}$$

are graphed. Note that the function $g_2(\Delta S)$ approaches zero much faster than the function $g_1(\Delta S)$ as ΔS gets smaller and smaller.

Thus, in standard calculus, all terms involving powers of dS higher than 1 are assumed to be negligible and are dropped from total derivatives. The question is whether we can do the same in stochastic calculus.

The answer to this important question is no. In stochastic settings, the time variable t is still deterministic. So, with respect to the *time* variable, the same criterion of smallness as in deterministic calculus can be applied. Any terms involving powers of dt higher than one, may be considered negligible.

On the other hand, the same rationale cannot be used for a stochastic differential such as dS_t^2. Chapter 9 already showed that, in the mean square sense, we have

$$dW_t^2 = dt. \tag{22}$$

Hence, terms involving dS_t^2 are likely to have sizes of order dt, which was considered as nonnegligible. If terms involving dt are preserved in Taylor approximations, the same must apply to squares of stochastic differentials.

We can give another discussion of this important point.

If ΔS_t is a random increment with mean zero, then $E[\Delta S_t]^2$ will be the variance of this increment. Since ΔS_t is random, its variance will be

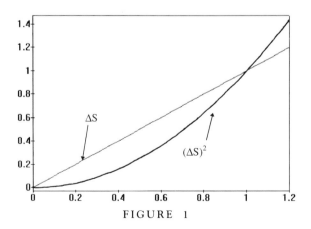

FIGURE 1

positive. But variance is the "size" of a *typical* $[\Delta S_t]^2$. Hence, on the average, assuming that $[\Delta S_t]^2$ is negligible will be equivalent to assuming that its variance is approximately zero—that S_t is, approximately, not random. This is a contradiction, and it defeats the purpose of using SDEs in markets for derivative products. After all, the objective is to price *risk*, and risk is generated by unexpected news.

Hence, in contrast to deterministic environments, terms such as ΔS_k^2 cannot be ignored in stochastic differentiation.

Given that the terms of size h are of first order, and that these are by convention not small, the following rule will be used to distinguish negligible terms from nonnegligible ones.

CONVENTION: Given a function $g(\Delta W_k, h)$ depending on the increments of the Wiener process W_t, and on the time increment, consider the ratio

$$\frac{g(\Delta W_k, h)}{h}. \tag{23}$$

If this ratio vanishes (in m.s. sense) as $h \rightarrow 0$, then we consider $g(\Delta W_k, h)$ as negligible in small intervals. Otherwise, $g(\Delta W_k, h)$ is nonnegligible.

This convention amounts to comparing various terms with h. In particular, if the mean square limit of the function $g(\Delta W_k, h)$ is proportional to h^r with $r > 1$, it will go toward zero faster than h (e.g., the square of a small number is smaller than the number itself.) On the other hand, if $r < 1$, then the mean square limit of $g(\Delta W_k, h)$ will be proportional to a larger power of h than h itself.[3]

The following discussion uses this convention in deciding which terms of a stochastic Taylor series expansion can be considered small.

3.2 First-Order Terms

Now consider equation (11) again:

$$\Delta F(k) = F_s[a_k h + \sigma_k \Delta W_k] + F_t[h]$$

$$+ \frac{1}{2} F_{ss}[a_k h + \sigma_k \Delta W_k]^2 \tag{24}$$

$$+ \frac{1}{2} F_{tt}[h]^2 + F_{st}[h][a_k h + \sigma_k \Delta W_k] + R.$$

---

[3]Here, it should not be forgotten that the function $g(\Delta W_k, h)$ depends on powers of ΔW_k, and that these also determine whether the ratio in (23) becomes negligible as h gets smaller. Such is the case when we deal with cross-product terms of Taylor series expansions.

Here, the terms that contain h or ΔS_k are clearly first-order increments that cannot be considered negligible. As $F_s[a_k h + \Delta W_k]$ or $F_t[h]$ are divided by h, and h is made smaller and smaller, these terms do not vanish. For example, the ratios

$$\lim_{h \to 0} \frac{F_s a_k h}{h} = F_s a_k \qquad (25)$$

and

$$\lim_{h \to 0} \frac{F_t h}{h} = F_t \qquad (26)$$

are clearly independent of h, and do not vanish as h gets smaller.

On the other hand, we already know that the ratio

$$\frac{F_s \Delta W_k}{h} \qquad (27)$$

gets larger (in a probabilistic sense) as h becomes smaller, since the term ΔW_k is of the order $h^{1/2}$.

Hence, all first-order terms in (24) are nonnegligible.

3.3 Second-Order Terms

Now divide the second-order terms on the right-hand side of (24) by h, and consider the ratio

$$\frac{F_{tt}[h]^2}{2h}. \qquad (28)$$

Clearly this term remains proportional to h, since in the numerator we have an increment that depends on h^2, a power of h higher than one, and the increment is *not* random. Hence, this term is negligible:

$$\lim_{h \to 0} F_{tt}[h] = 0. \qquad (29)$$

Next, consider the second-order term that depends on $[\Delta S_k]^2$:

$$\frac{1}{2} F_{ss}[\Delta S_k]^2.$$

Substituting for ΔS_k, expanding the square, and dividing by h:

$$\frac{1}{2} F_{ss} \left[\frac{a_k^2 h^2}{h} + \frac{(\sigma_k \Delta W_k)^2}{h} + \frac{2 a_k \sigma_k h \Delta W_k}{h} \right]. \qquad (30)$$

In this equation, the first term is "small." The numerator contains a power of h greater than one, and the term is not random. The third term is also "small." It involves a cross product (see next section). The second term, on the other hand, contains the *random* variable $(\Delta W_k)^2$. This is the square of a random variable with mean zero that is unpredictable from the past. Its variance was shown to be

$$\text{Var}(\sigma_k \Delta W_k) = \sigma_k^2 h. \tag{31}$$

It was also shown that in the mean square sense discussed earlier,

$$dW_t^2 = dt. \tag{32}$$

Thus, ΔW_k^2 is a term that cannot be considered negligible, since by definition, we are dealing with stochastic S_k, and the nonzero variance of ΔS_k implies:

$$\sigma_k > 0. \tag{33}$$

Consequently, using the criterion of negligibility, we write for small h:

$$\frac{1}{2} F_{ss} \left[\frac{a_k^2 h^2}{h} + \frac{(\sigma_k \Delta W_k)^2}{h} + \frac{2a_k \sigma_k h \Delta W_k}{h} \right] \cong \frac{1}{2} F_{ss} \sigma_k^2. \tag{34}$$

Again, this approximation should be interpreted in the m.s. sense. That is, in small intervals, the difference between the two sides of equality (34) has a variance that will tend to zero as $h \to 0$.

Before one can write the Ito formula, the remaining terms of the Taylor series expansion in (24) must also be discussed.

3.4 Terms Involving Cross Products

The terms in (24) involving cross products are also negligible in small intervals under the assumption that the unpredictable components do not contain any "jumps." The argument rests on the continuity of the sample paths for S_t.

Consider the following cross-product term in (24) and divide it by h:

$$\frac{F_{st}[h][a_k \sigma_k \Delta W_k]}{h} = F_{st}[a_k \sigma_k \Delta W_k]. \tag{35}$$

The right-hand side of (35) depends on ΔW_k. As $h \to 0$, ΔW_k goes to zero. In particular, ΔW_k becomes negligible, because as $h \to 0$ its variance $\sigma_k^2 h$ goes to zero. That is, W_k does not change at the limit $h = 0$. This is another way of saying that the Wiener process has continuous sample paths.

As long as the processes under consideration are continuous and do not display any jumps, terms involving cross products of ΔW_k and h would be negligible according to the convention adopted earlier.

3.5 Terms in the Remainder

All the remaining terms in the remainder R contain powers of h and of ΔW_k *greater* than 2. According to the convention adopted earlier, *if* the unpredictable shocks are of "normal" type—i.e., there are no "rare events"—powers of ΔW_k greater than two will be negligible. In fact, it was shown in Chapter 8 that continuous martingales and Wiener processes have higher-order moments that are negligible as $h \to 0$.

4 The Ito Formula

We can now summarize the discussion involving the terms in (24). As $h \to 0$ and we drop all negligible terms, we obtain the following result:

ITO'S LEMMA: Let $F(S_t, t)$ be a twice-differentiable function of t and of the random process S_t

$$dS_t = a_t \, dt + \sigma_t \, dW_t, \qquad t \geq 0,$$

with well-behaved drift and diffusion parameters, a_t, σ_t.[4] Then we have

$$dF_t = \frac{\partial F}{\partial S_t} \, dS_t + \frac{\partial F}{\partial t} \, dt + \frac{1}{2} \frac{\partial^2 F}{\partial S_t^2} \sigma_t^2 \, dt, \tag{36}$$

or, after substituting for dS_t using the relevant SDE,

$$dF_t = \left[\frac{\partial F}{\partial S_t} a_t + \frac{\partial F}{\partial t} + \frac{1}{2} \frac{\partial^2 F}{\partial S_t^2} \sigma_t^2 \right] dt + \frac{\partial F}{\partial S_t} \sigma_t \, dW_t, \tag{37}$$

where the equality holds in the mean square sense.

In situations where one has to apply the Ito formula, one will in general be given an SDE that drives the process S_t:

$$dS_t = a(S_t, t) \, dt + \sigma(S_t, t) \, dW_t. \tag{38}$$

Thus, the Ito formula can be seen as a vehicle that takes the SDE for S_t and determines the SDE that corresponds to $F(S_t, t)$. In fact, Equation (37) is a stochastic differential equation for $F(S_t, t)$.

Ito's formula is clearly a very useful tool to have in dealing with financial derivatives. The latter are contracts written on underlying assets. Using the Ito formula we can determine the SDE for financial derivatives once we are given the SDE for the underlying asset. For a market participant who wants to price a derivative asset, but who is willing to take the behavior of the underlying as exogenous, Ito's formula is a necessary tool.

---

[4]With this we mean that the drift and diffusion parameters are not too irregular. Square integrability would satisfy this condition. Also note that for notational simplicity we write $a(S_t, t)$ as a_t and $\sigma(S_t, t)$ as σ_t.

5 Uses of Ito's Lemma

The first use of Ito's lemma was just mentioned. The formula provides a tool for obtaining stochastic differentials for functions of random processes.

For example, we may want to know what happens to the price of an option if the underlying asset's price changes. Letting $F(S_t, t)$ be the option price, and S_t the underlying asset's price, we can write

$$dF(S_t, t) = F_s\, dS_t + F_t dt + \frac{1}{2} F_{ss} \sigma_t^2\, dt. \tag{39}$$

If one has an exact formula for $F(S_t, t)$, one can then take the partial derivatives explicitly and replace them in the foregoing formula to get the stochastic differential, $dF(S_t, t)$. Later in this section we give some examples of this use of Ito's lemma.

The second use of Ito's lemma is quite different. Ito's lemma is useful in evaluating Ito integrals. This may be unexpected, because Ito's formula was introduced as a tool to deal with stochastic differentials. Under normal circumstances, one would not expect such a formula to be of much use in "taking" Ito integrals. Yet stochastic calculus is different. It is not like ordinary calculus, where integral and derivative are separately defined and then related by the fundamental theorem of calculus. As we pointed out earlier, the differential notation of stochastic calculus is a *shorthand* for stochastic integrals. Thus, it is not surprising that Ito's lemma is useful for evaluating stochastic integrals.

We give some simple examples of these uses of Ito's lemma. More substantial examples will be seen in later chapters when derivative asset pricing is discussed.

5.1 Ito's Formula as a Chain Rule

A discussion of some simple examples may be useful in getting familiar with the new terms in Ito's formula.

We first discuss two examples to practice the way Ito's formula works.

5.1.1 Example 1
Consider a function of the *standard* Wiener process W_t given by

$$F(W_t, t) = W_t^2. \tag{40}$$

Remember that W_t has a drift parameter 0 and a diffusion parameter 1. Applying the Ito formula to this function:

$$dF_t = \frac{1}{2}[2\, dt] + 2W_t\, dW_t \tag{41}$$

or

$$dF_t = dt + 2W_t\, dW_t. \tag{42}$$

Note that Ito's formula results, in this particular case, in an SDE that has

$$a(I_t, t) = 1 \tag{43}$$

and

$$\sigma(I_t, t) = 2W_t. \tag{44}$$

Hence, the drift is constant and the diffusion depends on the information set I_t.

5.1.2 Example 2
Next, we apply Ito's formula to the function

$$F(W_t, t) = 3 + t + e^{W_t}. \tag{45}$$

We obtain

$$dF_t = dt + e^{W_t}\, dW_t + \frac{1}{2}e^{W_t}\, dt. \tag{46}$$

Grouping:

$$dF_t = \left[1 + \frac{1}{2}e^{W_t}\right] dt + e^{W_t}\, dW_t. \tag{47}$$

In this case we obtain an SDE for $F(S_t, t)$ with I_t-dependent drift and diffusion terms:

$$a(I_t, t) = \left[1 + \frac{1}{2}e^{W_t}\right] \tag{48}$$

and

$$\sigma(I_t, t) = e^{W_t}. \tag{49}$$

5.2 Ito's Formula as an Integration Tool

Suppose one needs to evaluate the following Ito integral, which was discussed in Chapter 9:

$$\int_0^t W_s\, dW_s. \tag{50}$$

In Chapter 9, this integral was evaluated directly by taking the mean square limit of some approximating sums. That evaluation used straightforward but lengthy calculations. We now exploit Ito's lemma in evaluating the same integral in a few steps.

Define

$$F(W_t, t) = \frac{1}{2} W_t^2 \tag{51}$$

and apply the Ito formula to $F(W_t, t)$:

$$dF_t = 0 + W_t \, dW_t + \frac{1}{2} \, dt. \tag{52}$$

This is an SDE with drift 1/2 and diffusion W_t. Writing the corresponding integral equation

$$F(W_t, t) = \int_0^t W_s \, dW_s + \frac{1}{2} \int_0^t ds, \tag{53}$$

or, after taking the second integral on the right-hand side, and using the definition of $F(W_t, t)$,

$$\frac{1}{2} W_t^2 = \int_0^t W_s \, dW_s + \frac{1}{2} t. \tag{54}$$

Rearranging terms, we obtain the desired result

$$\int_0^t W_s dW_s = \frac{1}{2} W_t^2 - \frac{1}{2} t, \tag{55}$$

which is the same result that was obtained in Chapter 9 using mean square convergence.

It is important to summarize how Ito's formula was exploited to evaluate Ito integrals.

1. We "guessed" a form for the function $F(W_t, t)$.
2. Then, Ito's lemma was used to obtain the SDE for $F(W_t, t)$.
3. We applied the integral operator to both side of this new SDE and obtained an integral equation.[5] This equation contained integrals that were simpler to evaluate than the original integral.
4. Rearranging the integral equation gave us the desired result.

---

[5]In fact, SDE notation is simply a shorthand for integral equations. Hence, this step amounts to writing the SDE in full detail.

The technique is indirect but straightforward. The only difficulty is in guessing an exact form of the function $F(W_t, t)$.

This technique of using Ito's lemma in evaluating integrals will be exploited in the next chapter.

5.2.1 Another Example
Suppose we need to evaluate

$$\int_0^t s\, dW_s \tag{56}$$

where W_t is again a Wiener process.

We use Ito's lemma.

First we define a function $F(W_t, t)$:

$$F(W_t, t) = tW_t. \tag{57}$$

Applying Ito's lemma to $F(\cdot)$:

$$dF_t = W_t\, dt + t\, dW_t + 0. \tag{58}$$

Using the definition of dF_t in the corresponding integral equation:

$$\int_0^t d[sW_s] = \int_0^t W_s\, ds + \int_0^t s\, dW_s. \tag{59}$$

Rearranging, we obtain the desired integral:

$$\int_0^t s\, dW_s = tW_t - \int_0^t W_s\, ds. \tag{60}$$

Here the first term on the right-hand side is obtained from

$$\int_0^t d[sW_s] = tW_t - 0. \tag{61}$$

Again, the use of Ito's lemma yields the desired integral in an indirect but straightforward series of operations.

6 Integral Form of Ito's Lemma

As mentioned several times, stochastic differentials are simply shorthand for Ito integrals over "small" time intervals. Thus, it is not surprising that one can write the Ito formula in integral form.

Integrating both sides of (37), we obtain

$$F(S_t, t) = F(S_0, 0) + \int_0^t \left[F_u + \frac{1}{2}F_{ss}\sigma_u^2 \right] du + \int_0^t F_s\, dS_u, \tag{62}$$

where use has been made of the equality

$$\int_0^t dF_u = F(S_t, t) - F(S_0, 0). \tag{63}$$

We can use the version of the Ito formula shown in (62) in order to obtain another characterization. Rearranging (62):

$$-\int_0^t F_s \, dS_u = -\left[F(S_t, t) - F(S_0, 0)\right] + \int_0^t \left[F_u + \frac{1}{2} F_{ss} \sigma_u^2\right] du. \tag{64}$$

This equality provides an expression where integrals with respect to Wiener processes or other continuous-time stochastic processes are expressed as a function of integrals with respect to time. It should be kept in mind that in (62) and (64) F_s and F_{ss} depend on u as well.

7 Ito's Formula in More Complex Settings

Ito's formula is seen to be a way of obtaining the SDE for a function $F(S_t, t)$, given the SDE for the underlying process S_t. Such a tool is clearly very useful when $F(S_t, t)$ is the price of a financial derivative and S_t is the underlying asset. But the Ito formula introduced thus far may end up not being sufficiently general under some plausible circumstances that a practitioner may face in financial markets.

The discussion thus far established Ito's formula in a univariate case, and under the assumption that unanticipated news can be characterized using Wiener process increments.

We can visualize two quite plausible circumstances where this model may not apply. Under some conditions, the function $F(\cdot)$ may depend on more than a single *stochastic* variable S_t. Then, a multivariate version of the Ito formula needs to be used. The extension is straightforward, but it is best to discuss it briefly.

The second generalization is more complex. One may argue that financial markets are affected by rare events, and that it is inappropriate to consider error terms made of Wiener processes only. One may want to add jump processes to the SDEs that drive asset prices. The corresponding Ito formula would clearly change. This is the second generalization that we discuss in this section.

7.1 Multivariate Case

In this section we extend the Ito formula to a multivariate framework and give an example. For simplicity, we pick the bivariate case and hope that the reader can readily extend the formula to higher-order systems.

Suppose S_t is a 2×1 vector of stochastic processes obeying the following stochastic differential equation:[6]

$$\begin{pmatrix} dS_1(t) \\ dS_2(t) \end{pmatrix} = \begin{pmatrix} a_1(t) \\ a_2(t) \end{pmatrix} dt + \begin{pmatrix} \sigma_{11}(t) & \sigma_{12}(t) \\ \sigma_{21}(t) & \sigma_{22}(t) \end{pmatrix} \begin{pmatrix} dW_1(t) \\ dW_2(t) \end{pmatrix}. \tag{65}$$

This means that we have two equations of the following form

$$dS_1(t) = a_1(t) \, dt + [\sigma_{11}(t) \, dW_1(t) + \sigma_{12}(t) \, dW_2(t)] \tag{66}$$

and

$$dS_2(t) = a_2(t) \, dt + [\sigma_{21}(t) \, dW_1(t) + \sigma_{22}(t) \, dW_2(t)], \tag{67}$$

where $a_i(t)$, $\sigma_{ij}(t)$, $i = 1, 2$, $j = 1, 2$ are the drift and diffusion parameters possibly depending on $S_i(t)$, and where $W_1(t)$, $W_2(t)$ are two *independent* Wiener processes.

In this bivariate framework, $S_1(t), S_2(t)$ represent two stochastic processes that are influenced by the same Wiener components. Because the parameters $\sigma_{ij}(t)$ may be different across equations, error terms affecting the two equations may end up being quite different.

Yet, because the $S_1(t), S_2(t)$ have common error components, they will in general be correlated, except for the special case when

$$\sigma_{12}(t) = 0, \qquad \sigma_{21}(t) = 0, \tag{68}$$

for all t.

Suppose now we have a continuous, twice-differentiable function of $S_1(t)$ and $S_2(t)$ that we denote by $F(S_1(t), S_2(t), t)$. How can we write the stochastic differential dF_t?

The answer is provided by the multivariate form of Ito's lemma,[7]

$$dF_t = F_t \, dt + F_{s_1} \, dS_1 + F_{s_2} \, dS_2$$
$$+ \frac{1}{2}[F_{s_1 s_1} \, dS_1^2 + F_{s_2 s_2} \, dS_2^2 + 2F_{s_1 s_2} \, dS_1 \, dS_2], \tag{69}$$

where the squared differentials $[dS_1]^2, [dS_2]^2$ and the cross-product term $dS_1 dS_2$ need to be equated to their mean square limits.

We already know that dt^2 and cross products such as $dt dW_1(t)$ and $dt dW_2(t)$ are equal to zero in the mean square sense. This point was discussed in obtaining the univariate Ito's lemma. The only novelty now is the

---

[6]Note that there is a slight change in the notation dealing with the time variable t.

[7]In the following equation we write the stochastic differentials without showing their dependence on t.

existence of cross products such as $dW_1(t)dW_2(t)$.[8] Here we have the product of the increments of two independent Wiener processes. Over a finite interval Δ we expect

$$E[\Delta W_1(t)\Delta W_2(t)] = 0. \qquad (70)$$

Hence, a limiting argument can be constructed so that in the mean square sense,

$$dW_1(t)dW_2(t) = 0. \qquad (71)$$

This gives the following mean square approximations for $dS_1(t)^2$ and $dS_2(t)^2$:

$$dS_1(t)^2 = [\sigma_{11}^2(t) + \sigma_{12}^2(t)]\,dt \qquad (72)$$

and

$$dS_2(t)^2 = [\sigma_{21}^2(t) + \sigma_{22}^2(t)]\,dt. \qquad (73)$$

The cross-product term is given by

$$dS_1(t)dS_2(t) = [\sigma_{11}(t)\sigma_{21}(t) + \sigma_{12}(t)\sigma_{22}(t)]\,dt. \qquad (74)$$

These expressions can be substituted into the bivariate Ito formula in (69) to eliminate $dS_1(t)^2$, $dS_2(t)^2$, and $dS_1(t)dS_1(t)$.

7.1.1 An Example from Financial Derivatives

Options written on bonds are among the most popular interest rate derivatives. In valuing these derivatives, the *yield curve* plays a fundamental role. One class of models of interest rate options assumes that the yield curve depends on *two* state variables, r_t representing a short rate and R_t representing a long rate. The price of the interest rate derivative will then be denoted by $F(r_t, R_t, t)$, $t \in [0, T]$.

These interest rates are assumed to follow the following SDEs:

$$dr_t = a_1(t)\,dt + [\sigma_{11}(t)dW_1(t) + \sigma_{12}(t)dW_2(t)] \qquad (75)$$

and

$$dR_t = a_2(t)\,dt + [\sigma_{21}(t)\,dW_1(t) + \sigma_{22}(t)\,dW_2(t)]. \qquad (76)$$

Thus, the short and the long rate have correlated errors. Over a finite interval of length h, this correlation is given by

$$\mathrm{Corr}(\Delta r_t, \Delta R_t) = [\sigma_{11}(t)\sigma_{21}(t) + \sigma_{12}(t)\sigma_{22}(t)]h. \qquad (77)$$

[8] Terms such as $dS_1(t)dS_2(t)$ will depend on $dW_1(t)dW_2(t)$.

The market participant can select the parameters $\sigma_{ij}(t)$ so that the equations capture the correlation and volatility properties of the observed short and long rates.

In valuing these interest rate options, one may want to know how the option price reacts to small changes in the yield curve, that is, to dr_t and dR_t. In other words, one needs the stochastic differential dF_t. Here the multivariate form of the Ito formula must be used:[9]

$$dF_t = F_t\, dt + [F_r dr_t + F_R dR_t] + \frac{1}{2}[F_{rr}(\sigma_{11}^2 + \sigma_{12}^2)$$

$$+ F_{RR}(\sigma_{21}^2 + \sigma_{22}^2) + 2F_{rR}(\sigma_{11}\sigma_{21} + \sigma_{12}\sigma_{22})]\, dt. \tag{78}$$

The stochastic differential dF_t would measure how the price of an interest rate derivative will change during a small interval dt, and given a small variation in the yield curve, the latter being caused by dr_t and dR_t.

7.1.2 Wealth

An investor buys $N_i(t)$ units of the ith asset at a price $P_i(t)$. There are n assets, and both the $N_i(t)$ and $P_i(t)$ are continuous-time stochastic processes, potentially a function of the same random shocks.

The total value of the investment is given by the wealth $W(t)$ at time t:

$$W(t) = \sum_{i=1}^{n} N_i(t)P_i(t). \tag{79}$$

Suppose, now, we would like to calculate the increments in wealth as time passes. We use Ito's lemma:

$$dW(t) = \sum_{i=1}^{n} N_i(t)dP_i(t) + \sum_{i=1}^{n} dN_i(t)P_i(t) + \sum_{i=1}^{n} dN_i(t)dP_i(t). \tag{80}$$

It is clear that if one used the formulas in standard calculus, the last term of the equation would not be present.

7.2 Ito's Formula and Jumps

Thus far, the underlying process S_t was always assumed to be a function of random shocks representable by Wiener processes. This assumption may be too restrictive. There may be a jump component to random errors as well. In this section, we provide this extension of the Ito formula.

---

[9]Again, for notational simplicity we write $\sigma_{ij}(t)$ as σ_{ij}.

Suppose we observe a process S_t, which is believed to follow the SDE

$$dS_t = a_t \, dt + \sigma_t \, dW_t + dJ_t, \qquad t \geq 0 \tag{81}$$

where dW_t is a standard Wiener process. The new term dJ_t represents possible unanticipated jumps. This jump component has zero mean during a finite interval h:

$$E[\Delta J_t] = 0. \tag{82}$$

We need to make this assumption, since this term is part of the unpredictable innovation terms. This assumption is not restrictive, as any predictable part of the jumps may be included in the drift component a_t.

We assume the following structure for the jumps.

Between jumps, J_t remains constant. At jump times τ_j, $j = 1, 2, \ldots$, it varies by some discrete and random amount. We assume that there are k possible types of jumps, with sizes $\{a_i, i = 1, \ldots, k\}$. The jumps occur at a rate λ_t that may depend on the latest observed S_t. Once a jump occurs, the jump type is selected randomly and independently. The probability that a jump of size a_i will occur is given by p_i.[10]

Thus, during a finite but small interval h, the increment ΔJ_t will be given (approximately) by

$$\Delta J_t = \Delta N_t - \left[\lambda_t h \left(\sum_{i=1}^{k} a_i p_i \right) \right], \tag{83}$$

where N_t is a process that represents the sum of all jumps up to time t. More precisely, ΔN_t will have a value of a_i if there was a jump during the h, *and* if the value of the jump was given by a_i. The term $(\sum_{i=1}^{k} a_i p_i)$ is the expected size of a jump, whereas $\lambda_t h$ represents, loosely speaking, the probability that a jump will occur. These are subtracted from ΔN_t to make ΔJ_t unpredictable.

Under these conditions, the drift coefficient a_t can be seen as representing the sum of two separate drifts, one belonging to the Wiener continuous component, the other to the pure jumps in S_t,

$$a_t = \alpha_t + \lambda_t \left(\sum_{i=1}^{k} a_i p_i \right), \tag{84}$$

where α_t is a drift coefficient of the continuous movements in S_t.

It is worth discussing one aspect of the jump process again. The process has *two* sources of randomness. The occurrence of a jump is a random

---

[10]In the case of the standard Poisson process, all jumps have size 1. Hence, this step is redundant.

event. But once the jump occurs, the size of the jump is also random. More-over, the structure just given assumes that these two sources of randomness are independent of each other.

Under these conditions, the Ito formula is given by

$$dF(S_t, t) = \left[F_t + \lambda_t \sum_{i=1}^{k} (F(S_t + a_i, t) - F(S_t, t)) p_i + \frac{1}{2} F_{ss} \sigma^2 \right] dt + F_s dS_t + dJ_F,$$

(85)

where dJ_F is given by

$$dJ_F = [F(S_t, t) - F(S_t^-, t)] - \lambda_t \left[\sum_{i=1}^{k} (F(S_t + a_i, t) - F(S_t, t)) p_i \right] dt. \quad (86)$$

Finally, S_t^- is defined as

$$S_t^- = \lim_{s \to t} S_s, \qquad s < t. \tag{87}$$

That is, it is the value of S at an infinitesimal time before t.

How would one calculate the dJ_F in practice? One would first evaluate the expected change due to possible random jumps. That is the second term on the right hand-side of Equation (86). Note that to do this one uses both the rate of possible jumps occurring during dt and the expected size of jump in $F(\cdot)$ caused by jumps in S_t. If during that particular time a jump is observed, then the first term on the right-hand side is also included. Otherwise, the term will equal zero.

8 Conclusions

Ito's lemma is the central differentiation tool in stochastic calculus. There are a few basic things to remember. First, the formula helps to determine stochastic differentials for financial derivatives given movements in the un-derlying asset. Second, the formula is completely dependent on the defini-tion of Ito integral. This means that equalities should be interpreted within stochastic equivalence.

Finally, from a practical point of view, the reader should remember that standard formulas used in deterministic calculus give significantly different results than the Ito formula. In particular, if one uses standard formulas, this would amount to assuming that all processes under observation have zero infinitesimal volatility. Clearly, this is not a pleasant assumption when one is trying to price risk using financial derivatives.

9 References

The sources recommended for Chapter 9 are also good here. Ito's lemma and the Ito integral are two topics that are always treated together. One additional source the reader may want to know about is the book by Kushner (1995). Kushner provides several examples of Ito's lemma with jump processes.

CHAPTER 11

The Dynamics of Derivative Prices

Stochastic Differential Equations

1 Introduction

The concept of a stochastic differential equation (SDE) was introduced in Chapter 7. In Chapter 9 we used the Ito integral to formalize this concept. The notation

$$dS_t = a(S_t, t)\, dt + \sigma(S_t, t)\, dW_t, \quad t \in [0, \infty), \tag{1}$$

was justified as a symbolic way of writing

$$\int_t^{t+h} dS_u = \int_t^{t+h} a(S_u, u)\, du + \int_t^{t+h} \sigma(S_u, u)\, dW_u \tag{2}$$

when h is infinitesimal.

We repeat some aspects of this derivation. First of all, no concept from financial markets or financial theory was used to obtain (1). The basic tools used were the Ito integral and the ability to split some increment in a random price into predictable and unpredictable components.

This brings us to another point. Given that the decomposition in Equation (1) is done using the information set available at time t, then to the extent different players may have access to different sets of information, the SDE in (1) may also be different. For example, consider the following extreme case. Suppose a market participant has "inside information" and learns *all* the random events that influence price changes in advance. Under these (unrealistic) conditions, the diffusion term in 1 would be zero. Since the participant knows how dS_t is going to change, he or she can predict this

216

variable perfectly, and $dW_t = 0$ for all t. Hence, if we were to write this participant's SDE we would get

$$dS_t = a^*(S_t, t)\, dt, \tag{3}$$

whereas for all other market participants,

$$dS_t = a(S_t, t)\, dt + \sigma(S_t, t)\, dW_t. \tag{4}$$

In these two equations the drift and the diffusion terms cannot be the same. Clearly, the error terms that drive the SDEs are different, which makes $a^*(S_t, t)$ different from $a(S_t, t)$. This example shows that the exact form of the SDE, and hence the definition of the error term dW_t, always depends on the family of information sets $\{I_t, t \in [0, T]\}$. If we had access to a different family of information sets, we would make different prediction errors, and the probabilistic behavior of the error terms would change. Given a different family of information sets I_t^*, we may have to denote the errors by dW_t^* instead of dW_t. It may be that dW_t^* has a smaller variance than dW_t.

In stochastic calculus, this property of W_t is formally summarized by saying that the Wiener process W_t is *adapted to* the family of information sets I_t.

The SDEs are utilized in pricing derivative assets because they give us a formal model of how an underlying asset's price changes over time. But it is also true that the formal derivation of SDEs is compatible with the way dealers behave in financial markets. In fact, in a given trading day a trader is continuously trying to forecast the price of an asset and record the realization of the "new events" as time passes. These events always contain some parts that are unpredictable until one observes the dS_t. After that, they become known and become part of the new information set the trader possesses.

This chapter considers some properties of stochastic differential equations.

1.1 Conditions on a_t and σ_t

The drift and diffusion parameters of the SDE

$$dS_t = a(S_t, t)\, dt + \sigma(S_t, t)\, dW_t, \quad t \in [0, \infty), \tag{5}$$

were allowed to depend on S_t and t. Hence, these parameters are themselves random variables. The point is that given the information at time t, they are observed by the market participant. Conditional on available information, they "become" constant. This is the consequence of the important assumption that these parameters are I_t-adapted.

At several points during the previous chapters, we made assumptions suggesting that these parameters should be well behaved.

It is customary to specify these "regularity conditions" each time an SDE is proposed as a model.

The $a(S_t, t)$ and $\sigma(S_t, t)$ parameters are assumed to satisfy the conditions

$$P\left(\int_0^t |a(S_u, u)|\, du < \infty\right) = 1$$

and

$$P\left(\int_0^t \sigma(S_u, u)^2\, du < \infty\right) = 1.$$

These conditions have similar meanings. They require that the drift and diffusion parameters do not vary "too much" over time.

Note that the integrals in these conditions are taken with respect to time. In this sense, they can be defined in the "usual" sense. According to this, the conditions imply that the drift and diffusion parameters are functions of bounded variation with probability one.

In the remainder of this book, we assume that these conditions are always satisfied and never repeat them.

2 A Geometric Description of Paths Implied by SDEs

Consider the stochastic differential equation

$$dS_t = a(S_t, t)\, dt + \sigma(S_t, t)\, dW_t, \quad t \in [0, \infty), \tag{6}$$

where the drift and diffusion parameters depend on the level of observed asset price S_t and (possibly) on t.

What type of geometric behavior would such an SDE imply for S_t?

An example of this is shown in Figure 1. We consider small but discrete intervals of length h. We see that over time, the behavior of S_t can be decomposed into two types of movements. First, there is an *expected* path during the interval. These are indicated by upward- or downward-sloping arrows. Then, at each $t_k = kh$, there is a second movement orthogonal to the predicted changes.[1] These are represented by vertical arrows. Sometimes they are negative; other times they are positive. The actual movement of S_t over time is determined by the sum of these two components and is indicated by the heavy line.

This geometric derivation emphasizes once again that the trajectories of S_t are likely to be very erratic when h becomes infinitesimal.

---

[1]"Orthogonal" is used here in the sense of "uncorrelated."

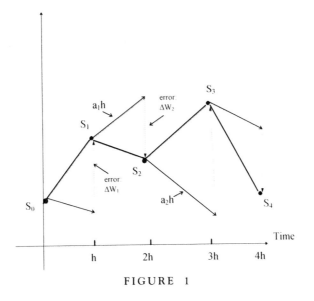

FIGURE 1

3 Solution of SDEs

A stochastic differential equation is by definition an *equation*. That is, it contains an *unknown*. This unknown is the stochastic process S_t. Hence, the notion of a solution to an SDE is more complicated than it may seem at the outset. What we are searching for is not a number or vector of numbers. It is a random process whose trajectories and the probabilities associated with those trajectories need to be determined exactly.

3.1 What Does a Solution Mean?

First, consider the finite difference approximation in small, discrete intervals:

$$S_k - S_{k-1} = a(S_{k-1}, k)h + \sigma(S_{k-1}, k)\Delta W_k, \quad k = 1, 2, \ldots, n. \quad (7)$$

The solution of this equation is a random process S_t. We are interested in finding a sequence of random variables indexed by k, such that the increments ΔS_k satisfy (7). In particular, we would like to know the moments and the distribution function of a process S_k that satisfies Equation (7). At the outset, it is not clear that, given a particular $a(\cdot)$ and $\sigma(\cdot)$, we could find a sequence of random numbers whose trajectories will satisfy the equality in (7) for all k.

More importantly, our purpose is to look for this solution when h, the interval length, goes to zero. If a continuous time process S_t satisfies the equation

$$\int_0^t dS_u = \int_0^t a(S_u, u)\, du + \int_0^t \sigma(S_u, u)\, dW_u, \tag{8}$$

for all $t > 0$, then we say that S_t is the solution of

$$dS_t = a(S_t, t)\, dt + \sigma(S_t, t)\, dW_t, \tag{9}$$

Because the solutions of SDEs are random processes, the nature of these solutions could be quite different when compared with ordinary differential equations. In fact, in stochastic calculus, there can be *two* types of solutions.

3.2 Types of Solutions

The first type of solution to an SDE is similar to the case of ordinary differential equations. Given the drift and diffusion parameters *and* given the random innovation term dW_t, we determine a random process S_t, paths of which satisfy the SDE:

$$dS_t = a(S_t, t)\, dt + \sigma(S_t, t)\, dW_t, \quad t \in [0, \infty). \tag{10}$$

Clearly, such a solution S_t will depend on time t, and on the past and contemporaneous values of the random variable W_t, as the underlying integral equation illustrates

$$S_t = S_0 + \int_0^t a(S_u, u)\, du + \int_0^t \sigma(S_u, u)\, dW_u, \tag{11}$$

for all $t > 0$. The *solution* determines the exact form of this dependence. When W_t on the right-hand side of (8) is given exogenously and then S_t is determined, we obtain the so called *strong solution* of the SDE. This is similar to solutions of ordinary differential equations.

The second solution concept is specific to stochastic differential equations. It is called the *weak solution*. In the *weak solution*, one determines the process $\tilde{S}_t$,

$$\tilde{S}_t = f(t, \tilde{W}_t), \tag{12}$$

where $\tilde{W}_t$ is a Wiener process whose distribution is determined *simultaneously* with $\tilde{S}_t$. According to this, for the weak solution of SDEs the "givens" of the problems are *only* the drift and diffusion parameters, $a(\cdot)$ and $\sigma(\cdot)$, respectively.

The idea of a weak solution can be explained as follows. Given that solving SDEs involves finding random variables that satisfy Equation (8), one can argue that finding an $\tilde{S}_t$ *and* a $\tilde{W}_t$ such that the pair $\{\tilde{S}_t, \tilde{W}_t\}$ satisfies this equation is also a type of solution to the stochastic differential equation.

In this type of solution we are given the drift parameter $a(S_t, t)$ and the diffusion parameter $\sigma(S_t, t)$. We then find the processes $\tilde{S}_t$ and $\tilde{W}_t$ such that the the Equation (8) is satisfied. This is in contrast to strong solutions where one does not *solve* for the W_t, but considers it another given of the problem.

Clearly, there are some potentially confusing points here. First of all, what is the difference between dW_t and $d\tilde{W}_t$ if both are Wiener processes with zero mean and variance dt? Are these not the same object?

If looked at in terms of the *form* of distribution functions, this is a valid question. The "density functions" of dW_t and $d\tilde{W}_t$ are both given by the same formula. In this sense, there is no difference between the two random errors. The difference will be in the sequence of information sets that define dW_t and $d\tilde{W}_t$.[2] Although the underlying densities may be the same, the two random processes could indeed represent very different real-life phenomena if they are measurable with respect to different information sets.

This has to be made more precise because it re-emphasizes an important point made earlier—a point that needs to be clarified in order for the reader to understand the structure of continuous-time stochastic models. Consider the following SDE, where the diffusion term contains the exogenously given dW_t:

$$dS_t = a(S_t, t)\, dt + \sigma(S_t, t)\, dW_t. \tag{13}$$

Heuristically, the error process dW_t symbolizes infinitesimal events that affect prices in a completely unpredictable fashion. The "history" generated by such infinitesimal events is the set of information that we have at time t. This we denoted by I_t.[3]

The strong solution then calculates an S_t that satisfies Equation (13) with dW_t given. That is, in order to obtain the strong solution S_t, we need to know the family I_t. This means that the strong solution S_t will be I_t-adapted.

The weak solution $\tilde{S}_t$, on the other hand, is not calculated using the process that generates the information set I_t. Instead, it is found along with *some* process $\tilde{W}_t$. The process $\tilde{W}_t$ could generate some other information

---

[2] Also, as we see in Chapter 14, the two Wiener processes may imply different probability measures on dS_t.

[3] As mentioned earlier, mathematicians call such information sets σ-field or σ-algebra.

set H_t. The corresponding $\tilde{S}_t$ will not necessarily be I_t-adapted. But $\tilde{W}_t$ will still be a martingale with respect to histories H_t.[4]

Hence, the weak solution will satisfy

$$d\tilde{S}_t = a(\tilde{S}_t, t)\,dt + \sigma(\tilde{S}_t, t)\,d\tilde{W}_t, \tag{14}$$

where the drift and the diffusion components are the same as in (8), and where $\tilde{W}_t$ is adapted to some family of information sets H_t.

3.3 Which Solution Is To Be Preferred?

Note that the strong and the weak solutions have the same drift and diffusion components. Hence, S_t and $\tilde{S}_t$ will have similar statistical properties. Given some means and variances, we will not be able to distinguish between the two solutions.

Yet the two solutions may also be different.[5]

The use of a strong solution implies knowledge of the error process W_t. If this is the case, the financial analyst may work with strong solutions.

Often when the price of a derivative is calculated using a solution to an SDE, one does not know the exact process W_t. One may use only the volatility and (sometimes) the drift component. Hence, in pricing derivative products under such conditions, one works with weak solutions.

3.4 A Discussion of Strong Solutions

The stochastic differential equation is, as mentioned earlier, an *equation*. This means that it contains an *unknown* that has to be solved for. In the case of SDEs, the "unknown" under consideration is a stochastic process. By solving an SDE, we mean determining a process S_t such that the integral equation

$$S_t = S_0 + \int_0^t a(S_u, u)\,du + \int_0^t \sigma_u(S_u, u)\,dW_u, \quad t \in [0, \infty), \tag{15}$$

is valid for all t. In other words, the evolution of S_t, starting from an initial point S_0, is determined by the two integrals on the right-hand side. The solution process S_t must be such that, when these integrals are added together, they should yield the increment $S_t - S_0$. This would *verify* the solution.

---

[4]Because of this martingale property, the Ito integrals that are in the background of SDEs can still be defined the same way.

[5]Clearly, any strong solution is also a weak solution. But the reverse is not true.

This approach verifies the solution using the corresponding integral equation rather than using the SDE directly. Why is this so? Note that according to the discussion up to this point, we do not have a theory of differentiation in stochastic environments. Hence, if we have a candidate for a solution of an SDE, we *cannot* take derivatives and see if the corresponding derivatives satisfy the SDE. Instead, two alternative routes exist.

The process of verifying solutions to SDEs can best be understood if we start with a deterministic example. Consider the simple ordinary differential equation

$$\frac{dX_t}{dt} = aX_t, \tag{16}$$

where a is a constant and where X_0 is given. Note that there is no random innovation term; hence, this is not a stochastic differential equation. A candidate for the solution can be verified directly. For example, suppose it is suspected that the function

$$X_t = X_0 e^{at} \tag{17}$$

is a solution of (16). Then, the solution must satisfy *two* conditions. First, if we take the derivative of X_t with respect to t, this derivative must equal a times the function itself. Second, when evaluated at $t = 0$, the function should give a value equal to X_0, the initial point, which is assumed to be known.

We proceed to verify the solution to Equation (16). Taking the straightforward derivative of X_t,

$$\frac{d}{dt}(X_0 e^{at}) = a[X_0 e^{at}], \tag{18}$$

which is indeed a times the function itself. The first condition is satisfied.

Letting $t = 0$, we get

$$(X_0 e^{a0}) = X_0. \tag{19}$$

Hence, the candidate solution satisfies the initial condition as well. We thus say that X_t solves the ODE in (16).

Notice that this method verified the solution using the notion of derivative.[6]

Clearly, if there is no differentiation theory of continuous stochastic processes, a similar approach cannot be utilized in verifying solutions of SDEs.

---

[6]Of course, the reader may wonder how the candidate solution was obtained to begin with. This topic belongs to texts on differential equations. Here, we just deal with models routinely used in finance.

In fact, if one uses the same differentiation methodology, assuming (mistakenly) that it holds in stochastic environments, and tries to "verify" solutions to SDEs by taking derivatives, one would get the *wrong* answer. As seen earlier, the rules of differentiation that hold for deterministic functions are not valid for functions of random variables.

Some further comments on this point might be useful.

Note that in an ordinary differential equation:

$$\frac{dX_t}{dt} = aX_t \tag{20}$$

with X_0 given, both sides of the equation contain terms in the unknown function X_t. That is why the ODE is an *equation*. The *solution* of the equation is then a specific *function* that depends on the remaining parameters and known variables in the ODE. The parameters are $\{a, X_0\}$, and the only known variable is the time t. Hence, the solution expresses the unknown function X_t as a function of the known quantities:

$$X_t = X_0 e^{at}. \tag{21}$$

Verifying the solution involves differentiating this function X_t with respect to the right-hand-side variable t, and then checking to see if the ODE is satisfied.

Now consider the special case of the SDE given by

$$dS_t = a\,dt + \sigma\,dW_t, \qquad t \geq 0 \tag{22}$$

with S_0 given.[7] When a strong solution of this SDE is obtained, it will be some function $f(\cdot)$ that depends on the time t, on the parameters $\{a, \sigma, S_0\}$, *and* on the W_t:

$$S_t = f(a, \sigma, S_0, t, W_t). \tag{23}$$

Hence, the solution will be a stochastic process because it depends on the random variable W_t.[8]

Using deterministic differentiation formulas to check whether this $f(\cdot)$ satisfies the SDE in (22) means taking the derivatives of S_t and W_t with respect to t. But these derivatives with respect to t are not well defined. Hence, the solution cannot be verified by using the same methodology as in the deterministic case.

---

[7]Note that the drift and diffusion parameters are constant and do not depend on the information available at time t.

[8]It is important to keep in mind that the SDE discussed above is a special case. In general, the strong solution S_t shown in (23) will depend on the *integrals* of $a(S_u, u)$, $\sigma(S_u, u)$, and dW_u. Hence, the dependence will be on the whole trajectory of W_t.

Instead, one should consider a candidate solution, and then, using Ito's lemma, try to see if this candidate satisfies the SDE or the corresponding integral equation. In the example below, we consider this point in detail.

3.5 Verification of Solutions to SDEs

Again consider the special SDE,

$$dS_t = \mu S_t \, dt + \sigma S_t \, dW_t, \quad t \in [0, \infty), \tag{24}$$

which was used by Black–Scholes (1973) in pricing call options. Here, S_t represents the price of a security that did not pay any dividends.

Dividing both sides by S_t we get

$$\frac{1}{S_t} dS_t = \mu \, dt + \sigma \, dW_t. \tag{25}$$

First we calculate the implied integral equation:

$$\int_0^t \frac{dS_u}{S_u} = \int_0^t \mu \, du + \int_0^t \sigma \, dW_u. \tag{26}$$

Since the first integral on the right-hand side does not contain any random terms, it can be calculated in the standard way:

$$\int_0^t \mu \, du = \mu t. \tag{27}$$

The second integral does contain a random term, but the coefficient of dW_u is a time-invariant constant. Hence, this integral can also be taken in the usual way

$$\int_0^t \sigma \, dW_u = \sigma[W_t - W_0], \tag{28}$$

where by definition $W_0 = 0$. Thus, we have

$$\int_0^t \frac{1}{S_u} dS_u = \mu t + \sigma W_t. \tag{29}$$

Any solutions of the SDE must satisfy this integral equation. In this particular case, we can show this simply by using Ito's lemma.

Consider the candidate

$$S_t = S_0 e^{\{(a - \frac{1}{2}\sigma^2)t + \sigma W_t\}}. \tag{30}$$

Note that this solution candidate is indeed a function of the parameters a and σ, of time t, and of the random variable W_t. Clearly, we are dealing with a *strong* solution, since S_t depends on W_t and is I_t-adapted.

How do we verify that this function is indeed a solution?

Consider calculating the stochastic differential dS_t using Ito's lemma,

$$dS_t = [S_0 e^{\{(a-\frac{1}{2}\sigma^2)t+\sigma W_t\}}]\left[\left(a - \frac{1}{2}\sigma^2\right)dt + \sigma\, dW_t + \frac{1}{2}\sigma^2\, dt\right], \qquad (31)$$

where the very last term on the right-hand side corresponds to the second-order term in Ito's lemma.

Canceling similar terms and replacing by S_t we obtain

$$dS_t = S_t[a\, dt + \sigma\, dW_t], \qquad (32)$$

which is the original SDE with a equal to μ. It is interesting to note that the terms $\frac{1}{2}\sigma^2 dt$ are eliminated by the application of Ito's lemma. If the rules of deterministic differentiation were used, these terms would not disappear in Equation (32), and the function in (30) would not verify the SDE.

In fact, if we had used ordinary calculus, the total differentiation would instead give

$$dS_t = S_t\left[\left(a - \frac{1}{2}\sigma^2\right)dt + \sigma\, dW_t\right], \qquad (33)$$

and this would not be the same as the original SDE if a equals μ. Hence, if we used ordinary calculus, we would have mistakenly concluded that the function in (30) is not a solution of the SDE in (24).

3.6 An Important Example

Suppose S_t is some asset price with a *random* rate of appreciation. In other words, we have

$$dS_t = rS_t\, dt + \sigma S_t\, dW_t, \quad t \in [0, \infty). \qquad (34)$$

The previous section discussed a candidate for the (strong) solution of this SDE:

$$S_t = S_0 e^{\{(r-\frac{1}{2}\sigma^2)t+\sigma W_t\}}. \qquad (35)$$

Now, suppose S_T is the price at some future time $T > t$. As of time t, this S_T is unknown. But it can be predicted, and the best prediction will be given by the conditional expectation:

$$E_t[S_T] = E[S_T|I_t]. \qquad (36)$$

In asset pricing theory, one is interested in whether the following equality will hold:

$$S_t = e^{-r(T-t)}E_t[S_T]. \qquad (37)$$

This would make the current price equal to the expected price at time T discounted at a rate r. This martingale property is of interest because it can be exploited to calculate the current price, S_t.

We now calculate $E_t[S_T]$. The first step is to realize the following:

$$S_T = [S_0 e^{(r-\frac{1}{2}\sigma^2)T}][e^{\sigma W_T}], \tag{38}$$

so that expectations of S_T depend on expectations of the term

$$e^{\sigma W_T}, \tag{39}$$

where, for future reference, the expression is a nonlinear function of W_T. Hence, the S_T is a *nonlinear* function of W_T as well. This means that in taking the expectation $E_t[S_T]$, we cannot "move" the $E_t[\cdot]$ operator in front of the random term W_T.

One can approach the expectation $E_t[e^{\sigma W_T}]$ in two different ways.

One method would be to use the density function for the Wiener process W_T and "take" the expectation directly by integrating

$$E_t[e^{\sigma W_T}] = \int_{-\infty}^{\infty} e^{\sigma W_T} [f(W_T \mid W_t)] dW_T, \tag{40}$$

where the term in brackets inside the integral is the (conditional) density function of W_T. The (conditional) mean is W_t, and the variance is $T - t$.

Calculating this integral is not difficult. But we prefer using a second method, which is specific to "stochastic calculus." This method will illustrate Ito's lemma once again, and will introduce an important integral equation that sees frequent use in stochastic calculus.

According to Equation (38), S_t is given by the function

$$S_T = [S_0 e^{(r-\frac{1}{2}\sigma^2)T}][e^{\sigma W_T}]. \tag{41}$$

The idea behind the second method is to transform this nonlinear expression in W_t into a *linear* one, and *then* take the expectations directly without having to use the density function of the Wiener process.

The method is indirect, but fairly simple. First, denote the nonlinear random term in Equation (35) by Z_t:[9]

$$Z_t = e^{\sigma W_t}. \tag{42}$$

Second, apply Ito's lemma:

$$dZ_t = \sigma e^{\sigma W_t} dW_t + \frac{1}{2}\sigma^2 e^{\sigma W_t} dt. \tag{43}$$

---

[9]The next few derivations use the t subscript instead of T. This does not cause any loss of generality. It simplifies exposition.

Third, consider the corresponding integral equation:

$$Z_t = Z_0 + \sigma \int_0^t e^{\sigma W_s} \, dW_s + \int_0^t \frac{1}{2} \sigma^2 e^{\sigma W_s} \, ds. \tag{44}$$

Finally, take expectations on both sides, and note the following

$$E[Z_0] = 1, \tag{45}$$

since, by definition, $W_0 = 0$. Also,

$$E\left[\int_0^t e^{\sigma W_s} \, dW_s\right] = 0, \tag{46}$$

since the increments in a Wiener process are independent from the observed past. Consequently,

$$EZ_t = 1 + \int_0^t \frac{1}{2} \sigma^2 E[Z_s] \, ds, \tag{47}$$

with the substitution $e^{\sigma W_s} = Z_s$, which is true by the definition of Z_s.

Note some interesting characteristics of Equation (47). First of all, this equation does not contain any integrals defined with respect to a random variable. Secondly, the equation is *linear* in $E[Z_t]$. Hence, it can be solved in a standard fashion. For example, we can treat $E[Z_t]$ as a deterministic variable, call it x_t, and then recognize that

$$x_t = 1 + \int_0^t \frac{1}{2} \sigma^2 x_s \, ds \tag{48}$$

is equivalent to the *ordinary* differential equation[10]

$$\frac{dx_t}{dt} = \frac{1}{2} \sigma^2 x_t \tag{49}$$

with initial condition $x_0 = 1$. The solution of this ordinary differential equation is known to be

$$x_t = E[Z_t] = e^{\frac{1}{2}\sigma^2 t}. \tag{50}$$

Going back to $E_t[S_T]$:

$$E_t[S_T] = [S_0 e^{(r - \frac{1}{2}\sigma^2)(T)}] E_t[Z_T]. \tag{51}$$

Using the result just derived for $E[Z_t]$:

$$E_t[S_T] = [S_0 e^{(r - \frac{1}{2}\sigma^2)(T)}][e^{\sigma W_t} e^{\frac{1}{2}\sigma^2(T-t)}]. \tag{52}$$

---

[10]By taking the derivatives, with respect to t, of (48).

Recognizing that

$$S_t = S_0 e^{(r - \frac{1}{2}\sigma^2)t + \sigma W_t}, \tag{53}$$

we obtain

$$E_t[S_T] = [S_t e^{r(T-t)}], \tag{54}$$

which implies that

$$S_0 = e^{-rT} E_0[S_T]. \tag{55}$$

That is, at time $t = 0$, the asset price equals the expected future price discounted at a rate r. For any time t we have, correspondingly,

$$S_t = e^{-r(T-t)} E_t[S_T]. \tag{56}$$

It is worthwhile to repeat the way Ito's lemma is used in these calculations. By using Ito's lemma we were able to obtain an integral equation (47) *linear* in Z_t. This way we could move the $E[\cdot]$ operator in front of Z_t and use the fact that increments in Wiener process have zero expectations. This eliminates the integral with respect to the *random* variable. The second integral was with respect to time, and could be handled using standard calculus.

At this point, note that if instead of Ito's lemma we used the rules of standard calculus, Equation (43) would become

$$dZ_t = \sigma e^{\sigma W_t} dW_t, \tag{57}$$

and the expected value of the stock price would be written as

$$E[S_T] = S_t e^{(r + \frac{1}{2}\sigma^2)(T-t)}. \tag{58}$$

The use of standard calculus implies that today's stock price is *not* equal to the expected future value discounted at a rate r. We lose the martingale equality.

4 Major Models of SDEs

There are some specific SDEs that are found to be quite useful in practice. In this section we discuss these cases and show what types of asset prices they could represent and how they could be useful.

4.1 Linear Constant Coefficient SDEs

The simplest case of stochastic differential equations is where the drift and diffusion coefficients are independent of the information received over time,

$$dS_t = \mu \, dt + \sigma \, dW_t, \quad t \in [0, \infty), \tag{59}$$

where W_t is a standard Wiener process with variance t.

In this SDE, the coefficients μ and σ do not have time subscripts t. This means that as time passes, they do not change. Hence, they do not depend on the information sets I_t. The mean of ΔS_t during a small interval of length h is given by

$$E_t[\Delta S_t] = \mu h. \tag{60}$$

The expected variation in ΔS_t will be

$$\text{Var}(\Delta S_t) = \sigma^2 h. \tag{61}$$

An example of the paths that can be described by this SDE is shown in Figure 2. Computer simulations were used to obtain this path. First some desired values for μ and σ were selected:

$$\mu = .01 \tag{62}$$

$$\sigma = .03. \tag{63}$$

Then, a small but finite interval size was decided upon:

$$h = .001. \tag{64}$$

This is assumed to be an approximation to the infinitesimal interval dt.

FIGURE   2

Finally, a random number generator was used to obtain 1000 independent normally distributed random variables with mean zero and variance .001. The fact that W_t in (59) is a martingale permits the use of independent (normally distributed) random variables.

A discrete approximation of Equation (59) was used to obtain the S_t plotted in Figure 2. The observations were determined from the iterations

$$S_k = S_{k-1} + .01(.001) + .03(\Delta W_k), \qquad k = 1, 2, \ldots, 1000.$$

With the initial point S_0 given, one substitutes randomly drawn normal random numbers for ΔW_k and obtains the S_k successively. The initial point was selected as $S_0 = 100$.

As can be seen from this figure, the behavior of S_t seems to fluctuate around a *straight line* with slope μ. The size of σ determines the extent of the fluctuations around this line. In particular, note that these fluctuations do not become larger and larger as "time" passes.

This suggests when such a stochastic differential equation is appropriate in practice. In particular, this SDE will be a good approximation if the behavior of the asset prices is stable over time, if the "trend" is linear and if the "variations" do not get any larger. Finally, it will be a good approximation if there do not appear to be systematic "jumps" in asset prices.

4.2 Geometric SDEs

The standard SDE used to model underlying asset prices is not the linear constant coefficient model, but is the geometric process. It is the model exploited by Black and Scholes:

$$dS_t = \mu S_t \, dt + \sigma S_t \, dW_t, \quad t \in [0, \infty). \tag{65}$$

This model implies that in terms of the formal notation

$$a(S_t, t) = \mu S_t \tag{66}$$

$$\sigma(S_t, t) = \sigma S_t. \tag{67}$$

Hence, the drift and the diffusion coefficients depend on the information that becomes available at time t. However this dependence is rather straightforward. The drift and the standard deviation change proportionally with S_t. In fact, dividing both sides by S_t, we obtain

$$\frac{dS_t}{S_t} = \mu \, dt + \sigma \, dW_t. \tag{68}$$

This means that although the drift and the diffusion part of the increment in asset price changes, the drift and diffusion of *percentage change* in S_t still has time invariant parameters.

Figure 3 shows one realization of the S_t obtained from a finite difference approximation of

$$dS_t = .15S_t\, dt + .30S_t\, dW_t \tag{69}$$

with the initial point of $S_0 = 100$. As can be seen from this graph, the S_t is made of two components. First, there is an *exponential* trend that grows with a 15% growth rate. Second, there are random fluctuations around this trend. These variations *increase* over time because of higher prices.

What is the empirical relevance of this model when compared with constant coefficient SDEs?

It turns out that the constant coefficient SDE described an asset price that fluctuated around a linear trend, while this model gives prices that fluctuate randomly around an exponential trend. For most asset prices the exponential trend is somewhat more realistic.

But, this says nothing about the assumption concerning the diffusion coefficient. Is a diffusion coefficient proportional to S_t more realistic as well?

To answer this question, note that the "variance" of an incremental change in S_t between times t_k and t_{k-1} could be approximated by

$$\text{Var}(S_k - S_{k-1}) = \sigma^2 S_{k-1}^2. \tag{70}$$

Hence, the variance increases in a way proportional to the square of S_t. In some practical cases this may add too much variation to S_t.

FIGURE 3

4.3 Square Root Process

A model close to the one just discussed is the square root process:

$$dS_t = \mu S_t \, dt + \sigma\sqrt{S_t}\, dW_t, \quad t \in [0, \infty). \tag{71}$$

Here the S_t is made to follow an exponential trend, while the standard deviation is made a function of the square root of S_t, rather than S_t itself. This makes the "variance" of the error term proportional to S_t.

Hence, if the asset price volatility does not increase "too much" when S_t increases, this model may be more appropriate. This will, of course, be the case if $S_t > 1$.

As an example we provide, in Figure 4, the sample path obtained from the same dW_t terms used to generate the example in Figure 3. We consider the equation

$$dS_t = .15 S_t \, dt + .30\sqrt{S_t}\, dW_t, \tag{72}$$

where the drift and diffusion coefficients are as in the case of Figure 3, but where the diffusion is now proportional to $\sqrt{S_t}$ instead of being proportional to S_t. We select the initial point as $S_0 = 100$.

Clearly, the fluctuations in Figure 4 are more subdued than the ones in Figure 3, yet the sample paths have "similar" trends.

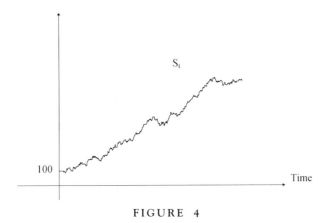

FIGURE 4

4.4 Mean Reverting Process

An SDE that has been found useful in modeling asset prices is the *mean reverting* model:[11]

$$dS_t = \lambda(\mu - S_t)\, dt + \sigma S_t\, dW_t. \tag{73}$$

According to this, as S_t falls below some "mean value" μ, the term in parentheses, $(\mu - S_t)$, will become positive. This makes dS_t more likely to be positive. Hence, S_t will eventually move towards the value μ. It reverts back to the mean μ.

A related SDE is the one where the drift is of the mean reverting type, but the diffusion is dependent on the square root of S_t:

$$dS_t = \lambda(\mu - S_t)\, dt + \sigma\sqrt{S_t}\, dW_t. \tag{74}$$

There is a significant difference between the mean reverting SDE and the two previous models.

The mean reverting process has a trend, but the deviations around this trend are not completely random. The process S_t can take an excursion away from the long-run trend. It eventually reverts back to that trend, but the excursion may take some time. The average length of these excursions is controlled by the parameter $\lambda > 0$. As this parameter becomes smaller, the excursions take longer. Thus, asset prices may exhibit some predictable periodicities. This usually makes the model inconsistent with market efficiency.

An example of a sample path of a mean reverting process is shown in Figure 5. We selected

$$\mu = .05, \qquad \lambda = .5, \qquad \sigma = .8. \tag{75}$$

This implies a long run mean of 5% and a percentage volatility of 80% during a time interval of length 1. The λ implies an adjustment of 50%.

We then selected the length of finite subintervals as $h = .001$. According to this, during a time interval of length 1, we will observe 1000 S_t's.

Random numbers with mean zero and variance .001 were obtained, and the sample path was generated by using the increments

$$\Delta S_k = .5(.05 - S_{k-1})(.001) + .8\Delta W_k, \qquad k = 1, 2, \ldots, 1000, \tag{76}$$

where the initial point was $S_0 = 100$.

The trajectory is shown in Figure 5. Note that because the diffusion term does not depend on S_t, in this particular case the process may become negative.

---

[11]This is often used to model interest rate dynamics.

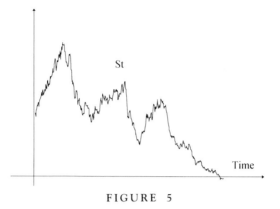

FIGURE 5

4.5 Ornstein–Uhlenbeck Process

Another useful SDE is the Ornstein–Uhlenbeck process,

$$dS_t = -\mu S_t \, dt + \sigma \, dW_t, \tag{77}$$

where $\mu > 0$. Here the drift depends on S_t negatively through the parameter μ, and the diffusion term is of the constant parameter type. Obviously, this is a special case of "mean reverting SDE."

This model can be used to represent asset prices that fluctuate around zero. The fluctuations can be in the form of excursions, which eventually revert back to the long-run mean of zero. The parameter μ controls how long excursions away from this mean will take. The larger the μ, the faster the S_t will go back toward the mean.

5 Stochastic Volatility

All previous examples of SDEs consisted of modeling the drift and diffusion parameters of SDEs, in some convenient fashion. The simplest case showed constant drift and diffusion. The most complicated case was the mean reverting process.

A much more general SDE can be obtained by making the drift and the diffusion parameters random. In the case of financial derivatives, this may have some interesting applications, because it implies that the volatility may be considered not only time-varying but also random given the S_t.

For example, consider the SDE for an asset price S_t,

$$dS_t = \mu \, dt + \sigma_t \, dW_{1t}, \tag{78}$$

where the drift parameter is constant, while the diffusion parameter is assumed to change over time. More specifically, σ_t is assumed to change according to another SDE,

$$d\sigma_t = \lambda(\sigma_0 - \sigma_t)\,dt + \alpha\sigma_t\,dW_{2t}, \tag{79}$$

where the Wiener processes W_{1t}, W_{2t} may very well be dependent.

Note what Equation (79) says about the volatility. The volatility of the asset has a long-run mean of σ_0. But at any time t, the actual volatility may deviate from this long-run mean, the adjustment parameter being λ. The increments dW_{2t} are unpredictable shocks to volatility that are independent of the shocks to asset prices S_t. The $\alpha > 0$ is a parameter.

The market participant has to calculate predictions for asset prices *and* for volatility.

Clearly, using such layers of SDEs one can obtain more and more complicated models for representing real-life, financial phenomena.

6 Conclusions

This chapter introduced the notion of solutions for SDEs. We distinguished between two types of solutions. The *strong* solution is similar to the case of ordinary differential equations. The *weak* solution is novel.

We did not discuss the *weak* solution in detail here. A major example will be discussed in later chapters.

This chapter also discussed major types of stochastic differential equations used to model asset prices.

7 References

In this chapter we followed the treatment of Oksendal (1992), which has several other examples of SDEs. An applications-minded reader will also benefit from having access to the literature on the numerical solution of SDEs. The book by Kloeden, Platen, and Schurz (1994) is both very accessible and comprehensive. It may very well be said that the best way to understand SDEs is to work with their numerical solutions.

CHAPTER 12

Pricing Derivative Products

Partial Differential Equations

1 Introduction

Thus far we have learned about major tools for modeling the dynamic behavior of a random process in continuous time, and the way one can (and cannot) take derivatives and integrals under these circumstances.

These tools were not discussed for their own sake. Rather, they were discussed because of their usefulness in pricing various derivative instruments in financial markets. Far from being mere theoretical developments, these tools are practical methods that can be used by market professionals. In fact, one can say that because of some special characteristics of derivative products, abstract theoretical models in this area are much more amenable to practical applications than in other areas of finance.

Modern finance has developed two major methods of pricing derivative products. The first of these leads to the utilization of partial differential equations, which are the subject of this chapter. The second requires transforming underlying processes into martingales. This necessitates utilization of equivalent martingale measures, which is the topic of Chapter 14. In principle, both methods should give the same answer. However, depending on the problem at hand, one method may be more convenient or cheaper to use than the other. The mathematical tools behind these two pricing methods are, however, very different.

First, we will briefly discuss the logic behind the method of pricing securities that leads to the use of PDEs. These results will be utilized in Chapter 13.

2 Forming Risk-Free Portfolios

Derivative instruments are contracts written on other securities, and these contracts have finite maturities. Hence, at the time of maturity denoted by T, the price F_T of the derivative contract should depend solely on the value of the underlying security S_T and the time T, and nothing else:

$$F_T = F(S_T, T). \tag{1}$$

This implies that at expiration, we know the *form* of the function $F(S_T, T)$ exactly. We assume that the same relationship is also true for times other than T, and that the price of the derivative product can be written as

$$F(S_t, t). \tag{2}$$

The increments in this price will be denoted by dF_t. At the outset, a market participant will not know the functional form of $F(S_t, t)$ at times other than expiration. This function needs to be found.

This suggests that if we have a law of motion for the S_t process—i.e., if we have an equation describing the way dS_t is determined—then we can use Ito's lemma to obtain dF_t. But this means that dF_t and dS_t would be increments that have the same source of underlying uncertainty, namely the innovation part in dS_t. In other words, at least in the present example, we have *two* increments, dF_t and dS_t, that depend on *one* innovation term. Such dependence makes it possible to form *risk-free portfolios* in continuous time.

Let P_t dollars be invested in a combination of $F(S_t, t)$ and S_t,

$$P_t = \theta_1 F(S_t, t) + \theta_2 S_t, \tag{3}$$

where θ_1, θ_2 are the quantities of the derivative instrument and the underlying security that are purchased. They represent portfolio weights.

The value of this portfolio would change as time t passes because of changes in $F(S_t, t)$ and S_t. Taking θ_1, θ_2 as constant, we can write this change as

$$dP_t = \theta_1 \, dF_t + \theta_2 \, dS_t. \tag{4}$$

In general, θ_1, θ_2 will vary over time and hence will carry a time subscript as well. At this point we ignore such dependence. In this equation, both dF_t and dS_t are increments that have an unpredictable component that comes from the innovation term dW_t in dS_t.

[An important remark about notation. dF_t should again be read as the total change in derivative price $F(S_t, t)$ during an interval dt. This should not be confused with F_t, which we reserve for the *partial* derivative of $F(S_t, t)$ with respect to t.]

Our main interest is in the price of the derivative product, and how this price changes. Thus, we begin by assuming a model that determines the dynamics of the underlying asset S_t, and from there we try to determine how $F(S_t, t)$ behaves. Accordingly, we assume that the stochastic differential dS_t obeys the SDE

$$dS_t = a(S_t, t)\, dt + \sigma(S_t, t)\, dW_t, \quad t \in [0, \infty). \tag{5}$$

Using this, we can apply Ito's lemma to find dF_t:

$$dF_t = F_t\, dt + \frac{1}{2}F_{ss}\sigma_t^2\, dt + F_s\, dS_t. \tag{6}$$

We substitute for dS_t using Equation (5), and obtain the SDE for the derivative asset price:

$$dF_t = \left[F_s a_t + \frac{1}{2}F_{ss}\sigma_t^2 + F_t \right] dt + F_s \sigma_t\, dW_t. \tag{7}$$

Note that we simplified the notation by writing a_t for the drift and σ_t for the diffusion parameter. If we knew the form of the function $F(S_t, t)$, we could calculate the corresponding partial derivatives, F_s, F_{ss}, F_t, and then obtain explicitly this SDE that governs the dynamics of the financial derivative. The functional form of $F(S_t, t)$, however, is not known. We can use the following steps to determine it.

We first see that the SDE in (7) describing the dynamics of dF_t is driven by the *same* Wiener increment dW_t that drives the S_t. One should, in principle, be able to use one of these SDEs to eliminate the randomness in the other. In forming risk-free portfolios, this is in fact what is done.

We now show how this is accomplished. First note that it is the market participant who selects the portfolio weights θ_1, θ_2.

Second, the latter can always be set such that the dP_t is independent of the innovation term dW_t and hence is *completely predictable*. The reason is as follows. Given that dF_t and dS_t have the same unpredictable component, and given that θ_1, θ_2 can be set as desired, one can always eliminate the dW_t component from Equation (4). To do this, consider again

$$dP_t = \theta_1\, dF_t + \theta_2\, dS_t \tag{8}$$

and substitute for dF_t using (6):

$$dP_t = \theta_1 \left[F_t\, dt + F_s\, dS_t + \frac{1}{2}F_{ss}\sigma_t^2\, dt \right] + \theta_2\, dS_t. \tag{9}$$

In this equation we are free to set θ_1, θ_2 the way we wish. We select

$$\theta_1 = 1 \tag{10}$$

$$\theta_2 = -F_s. \tag{11}$$

These particular values for portfolio weights lead to cancellation of the terms involving dS_t in (9) and reduces it to

$$dP_t = F_t\,dt + \frac{1}{2}F_{ss}\sigma_t^2\,dt. \tag{12}$$

Clearly, given the information set I_t, in this expression there is no random term. The dP_t is a completely *predictable*, deterministic increment for all times t. This means that the portfolio P_t is risk-free.[1]

Since there is no risk in P_t, its appreciation must equal the earnings of a risk-free investment during an interval dt in order to avoid arbitrage. Assuming that the (constant) risk-free interest rate is given by r, the expected capital gains must equal

$$rP_t\,dt \tag{13}$$

in the case where S_t pays no "dividends," and must equal

$$rP_t\,dt - \delta\,dt \tag{14}$$

in the case where S_t pays "dividends" of δ per time. In the latter case, the capital gains in (14) *plus* the dividends earned will equal the risk-free rate.[2]

Utilizing the case with no dividends, Equations (12) and (14) yield

$$rP_t\,dt = F_t\,dt + \frac{1}{2}F_{ss}\sigma_t\,dt. \tag{15}$$

Since the dt terms are common to all factors, they can be "eliminated" to obtain a partial differential equation:

$$r(F(S_t, t) - F_s S_t) = F_t + \frac{1}{2}F_{ss}\sigma_t. \tag{16}$$

---

[1]Note this important point: The value of θ_2 set at $-F_s$ will vary over time. For nonlinear products such as options, or structures containing options, the F_s will be a function of S_t. The latter, on the other hand, changes over time.

[2]Note this role played by the term dt. Some infinitesimal time must pass in order to earn some interest or receive some dividends. If no time passes at all, regardless of the level of interest rates r, the interest earnings will be zero. The same is true for dividend earnings.

[Note that we replaced $P(t)$ in (15) by its components.] We rewrite Equation (16) as

$$- rF + rF_s S_t + F_t + \frac{1}{2} F_{ss} \sigma_t = 0, \quad 0 \le S_t, \quad 0 \le t \le T, \qquad (17)$$

where the derivative asset price $F(S_t, t)$ is denoted simply by the letter F for notational convenience.

We have an additional piece of information. The derivative product will have an expiration date T, and the relationship between the price of the underlying asset and that of the derivative asset will, in general, be known exactly at expiration. That is, we know at expiration that the price of the derivative product is given by

$$F(S_T, T) = G(S_T, T), \qquad (18)$$

where $G(\cdot)$ is a *known* function of S_T and T. For example, in the case of a call option, $G(\cdot)$, the expiration price of the call with a strike price K is

$$G(S_T, T) = \max[S_T - K, 0]. \qquad (19)$$

According to this equation, if at expiration the stock price is below the strike price, $S_T - K$ will be negative and the call option will not be exercised. It will be worthless. Otherwise, the option will have a price equal to the differential between the stock and the strike prices.

Equation (17) is known as a *partial differential equation* (PDE). Equation (18) is an associated *boundary condition*.

The reason this method "works" and eliminates the innovation term from Equation (4) is that $F(\cdot)$ represents a price of a *derivative* instrument, and hence has the same inherent unpredictable component dW_t as S_t. Thus, by combining these two assets in a careful way, it becomes possible to eliminate their common unpredictable movements. As a result, P_t becomes a risk-free investment, since its future path will be known with certainty.

This construction of a risk-free portfolio is heuristic. In a formal approach one forms self-financing portfolios using completeness of markets with respect to a class of *trading strategies* and using the implied *"synthetic"* equivalents of the assets under consideration. Jarrow (1996) is an excellent source on these concepts.

3 Partial Differential Equations

We rewrite the partial differential equation (17) in a general form, using the shorthand notation $F(S_t, t) = F$,

$$a_0 F + a_1 F_s S_t + a_2 F_t + a_3 F_{ss} = 0, \quad 0 \le S_t, 0 \le t \le T, \qquad (20)$$

with the boundary condition

$$F(S_T, T) = G(S_T, T), \tag{21}$$

$G(\cdot)$ being a known function.[3]

The method of forming such risk-free portfolios in order to obtain arbitrage-free prices for derivative instruments will always lead to PDEs. Since derivative securities are always "derived" from some underlying asset(s), the formation of such arbitrage-free portfolios is in general quite straightforward. On the other hand, the boundary conditions as well as the implied PDEs may get more complicated depending on the derivative product one is working with. But, overall, the method will center on the solution of a PDE. Hence, this concept should be discussed in detail.

We discuss partial differential equations in several steps.

3.1 Why Is the PDE an "Equation"?

In what sense is the PDE in (20) an "equation"? With respect to which "unknown" is this equation to be solved?

Unlike the usual cases in algebra where equations are solved with respect to some *variable* or *vector* x, the unknown in Equation (20) is in the form of a *function*. In other words, it is not known what *type* of function $F(S_t, t)$ represents. What *is* known is that if one takes various partial derivatives of $F(S_t, t)$ and combines them by multiplying by coefficients a_i, the result will equal zero. Also, at time $t = T$ this function must equal the (known) $G(S_T, T)$—i.e., it must satisfy the boundary condition.

Hence, in solving PDEs one tries to find a function whose partial derivatives satisfy Equations (20) and (21).

3.2 What Is the Boundary Condition?

Partial differential equations are obtained by combining various partial derivatives of a function and then setting the combination equal to zero. The boundary conditions are an integral part of such equations. In physics,

---

[3]In the literature, the PDE notation is different than what is adopted in this section. For example, the PDE in (22) would be written as

$$a_0 F(X, t) + a_1 F_x(X, t)X + a_2 F_t(X, t) + a_3 F_{xx}(X, t) = 0, \quad 0 \le X, 0 \le t \le T, \tag{22}$$

with the boundary condition

$$F(X, T) = G(X, T).$$

In this section we keep using S_t instead of switching to a generic variable X, as is usually done.

boundary conditions are initial or terminal states of some physical phenomenon that evolves over time according to the PDE.

In finance, boundary conditions play a similar role. They represent some contractual clauses of various derivative products. Depending on the product and the problem at hand, boundary conditions would change. The most obvious boundary values are initial or terminal values of derivative contracts. Often, finance theory tells us some plausible conditions that prices of derivative contracts must satisfy at maturity. For example, futures prices and cash prices cannot be (very) different at the delivery date. In the case of options, option prices must satisfy an equation such as (19). In case of a discount bond, the asset price equals 100 at maturity.

If there are no boundary conditions, then finding price functions $F(S_t, t)$ that satisfy a given PDE will, in general, not be possible. Further, the fact that derivative products are known functions of the underlying asset at expiration will always yield a boundary condition to a market participant.

To see the role of boundary conditions and to consider some simple PDEs we look at some examples.

4 Classification of PDEs

One can classify PDEs in several different ways. First of all, PDEs can be *linear* or *nonlinear*. This refers to the coefficients applied to partial derivatives in the equation. If an equation is a linear combination of F and its partial derivatives, it is called a linear PDE.[4]

The second type of classification has to do with the *order* of differentiation. If all partial derivatives in the equation are first-order, then the PDE will also be first-order. If there are cross partials, or second partials, then the PDE becomes second-order. For nonlinear financial derivatives such as options, or instruments containing options, the resulting PDE will always be second-order.

Thus far, these classifications are similar to the case of ordinary differential equations. The third type of classification is specific to PDEs. The latter can also be classified as *elliptic, parabolic, or hyperbolic*. The PDE's we encounter in finance are similar to parabolic PDEs.

We first consider examples of linear first- and second-order PDEs. These examples have no direct relevance in finance. Yet they may help establish an intuitive understanding of what PDEs are, and why boundary conditions are important.

---

[4]In particular, this means that the coefficients of the partial derivatives are not functions of F.

4.1 Example 1: Linear, First-Order PDE

Consider the PDE for a function $F(S_t, t)$:

$$F_t + F_s = 0, \quad 0 \le S_t, \quad 0 \le t \le T. \tag{23}$$

According to this PDE, the negative of the partial of $F(\cdot)$ with respect to t is equal to its partial with respect to S_t. If t were to represent time, and S_t were to represent the price of the underlying security, then (23) would mean that the negative of the price change during a small time interval with S_t fixed, equals the price change due to a small movement in the price of the underlying asset when t is fixed.

Clearly, in a financial market there is no compelling reason why such a relationship should exist between the two partial derivatives. But suppose (23) is nevertheless written down and a solution $F(S_t, t)$ is sought. What would this function $F(S_t, t)$ look like?

We can immediately guess a solution:

$$F(S_t, t) = \alpha S_t - \alpha t + \beta, \quad \text{any } \alpha, \beta. \tag{24}$$

With such a function, the partials will be given by

$$\frac{\partial F}{\partial t} = -\alpha \tag{25}$$

and

$$\frac{\partial F}{\partial S_t} = \alpha. \tag{26}$$

Their sum will equal zero, and this is exactly what the PDE in (23) implies.

The solution suggested by the function (24) is a *plane* in a three-dimensional space. If no boundary conditions are given, this is all we know. We would not be able to determine exactly which plane $F(S_t, t)$ would represent, since we would not be able to pinpoint the values of α, β given the information in (24). All we can say is the following: at $t = 0, S_0 = 0$ the intercept will equal β. For a fixed S_t, the $F(S_t, t)$ has contours that are straight lines with slope $-\alpha$. For fixed t, the contours are straight lines with slope α.

Figures 1 and 2 show two examples of $F(S_t, t)$ that "solve" the PDE in (23). Figure 1 is the plot of the *plane*:

$$F(S_t, t) = 3S_t - 3t + 4, \quad -10 \le t \le 10, \; -10 \le S_t \le 10. \tag{27}$$

Note that in this case $F_s = 3$ and $F_t = -3$. Hence, this function satisfies the PDE in (23). This solution is a plane that increases with respect to S_t, but decreases with respect to t.

F(S$_t$,t)

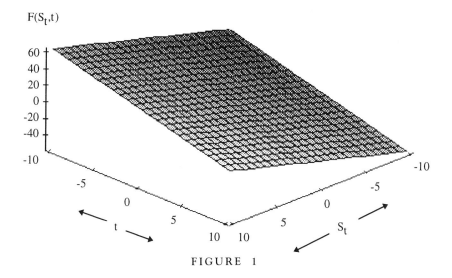

FIGURE 1

Figure 2 shows another example where

$$F(S_t, t) = -2S_t + 2t - 4, \quad -10 \le t \le 10, \quad -10 \le S_t \le 10. \quad (28)$$

We again see that $F(S_t, t)$ is a plane. But in this case it increases with respect to t, and decreases with respect to S_t.

Contours are again straight lines.

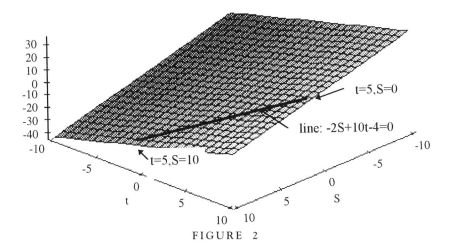

FIGURE 2

There is an important point to emphasize here. The examples of $F(S_t, t)$ given in (27) and (28) are clearly very different-looking functions. Yet they *both* solve the PDE in (23). This is because Equation (23) does not contain sufficient information to allow the function $F(S_t, t)$ to be determined precisely. There are uncountably many functions $F(S_t, t)$ whose first partials with respect to S_t and t are equal.

Now, if in addition to (24) we are given some boundary conditions as well, then we can determine the $F(S_t, t)$ precisely. For example, suppose we know that at expiration time $t = 5$ (the boundary for t) we have

$$F(S_5, 5) = 6 - 2S_5. \tag{29}$$

We can now determine the unknowns α and β in Equation (24):

$$\alpha = 2 \tag{30}$$

$$\beta = 4. \tag{31}$$

Clearly, this is the plane shown in Figure 2.

On the other hand, if we had a second boundary condition, say, at $S_t = 100$,

$$F(100, t) = 5 + .3t, \tag{32}$$

then there will be no meaningful solution because Equations (33) and (32) overdetermine the constants α and β.

Thus, in case the solution $F(S_t, t)$ is a plane, we need a single boundary condition to exactly pinpoint the function that solves the PDE.

This is easy to see geometrically, since a boundary condition corresponds to first selecting the "endpoint" for t (or S_t) and then obtaining the intersection of the plane with a surface orthogonal to time axis and passing from that t. In Figure 2, the boundary condition at $t = 5$,

$$F(S_5, 5) = 6 - 2S_5, \tag{33}$$

is shown explicitly. Note that the other candidate for $F(S_t, t)$ shown in Figure 1 will *not* pass from this line at $t = 5$. Hence, it cannot be a solution.

Also, when $F(S_t, t)$ is a plane, the terminal conditions with respect to t or S_t will be straight lines.

4.1.1 Remark

The solutions to the class of PDEs

$$F_t + F_s = 0 \tag{34}$$

are not restricted to planes. In fact, consider the function

$$F(S_t, t) = e^{\alpha S_t - \alpha t}. \tag{35}$$

This function will also satisfy the equality (34). It is the boundary condition that will determine the unique solution.

4.2 Example 2: Linear, Second-Order PDE

It was easy to guess the solution of the first-order PDE discussed in Example 1. Now consider a second-order PDE

$$\frac{\partial^2 F}{\partial t^2} = .3\frac{\partial^2 F}{\partial S_t^2},$$
(36)

or, more succinctly,

$$- .3F_{ss} + F_{tt} = 0.$$
(37)

First note that we are again dealing with a linear PDE, since the partials in question are combined by using constant coefficients.

Again, ignore the boundary conditions for the moment. We can try to guess a solution to (37). It is clear that the function $F(\cdot)$ has to be such that the second partials of $F(S_t, t)$ with respect to S_t and t are proportional with a factor of proportionality equal to .3. This relationship between F_{ss} and F_{tt} should be true at any S_t and t. What could this function be?

Consider the formula

$$F(S_t, t) = \frac{1}{2}\alpha(S_t - S_0)^2 + \frac{.3}{2}\alpha(t - t_0)^2 + \beta(S_t - S_0)(t - t_0),$$
(38)

where S_0, t_0 are unknown constants and where the parameters α and β are again unknown.

Now, if we take the second partials of $F(S_t, t)$:

$$\frac{\partial^2 F}{\partial t^2} = .3\alpha$$
(39)

$$\frac{\partial^2 F}{\partial S^2} = 1\alpha.$$
(40)

Hence the second partials F_{ss}, F_{tt} of the $F(S_t, t)$ in (40) will satisfy Equation (36). Thus, the $F(S_t, t)$ given in (36) is a solution of the partial differential equation (32).

Note that for fixed $F(S_t, t)$,

$$F(S_t, t) = F_o,$$
(41)

the contours of this function are ellipses.[5]

---

[5]See the next section.

Again, the solution of (36) is not unique, since the $F(S_t, t)$ with any α, β, S_0, t_0 could be a solution, as long as it is of the form (38). To obtain a unique solution we need boundary conditions.

One boundary condition could be at $S_t = 10$:

$$F(10, t) = 100 + t^2. \tag{42}$$

This is a function that traces a parabola in the F, t plane.

Yet such a boundary condition is not sufficient to determine all the parameters α, β, S_0, t_0. One would need a second boundary condition, say, at $t = 0$:

$$F(S_0, 0) = 50 + S_0^2. \tag{43}$$

This equation is another parabola. But the relevant plane is F, S_t.

We give an example of such an $F(S_t, t)$ in Figure 3. The figure displays the three-dimensional plot of the function

$$F(S_t, t) = -10(S_t - 4)^2 - 3(t - 2)^2, \qquad -10 \le t \le 10, \ -10 \le S_t \le 10. \tag{44}$$

The surface has contours as ellipses. In terms of boundary conditions, we can pick $t = 10$ as the terminal value for t and get a boundary condition that has the form of a parabola:

$$F(S_{10}, 10) = -10(S_{10} - 4)^2 - 192. \tag{45}$$

The boundary condition for $S_t = 0$ will be another parabola:

$$F(0, t) = -160 - 3(t - 2)^2. \tag{46}$$

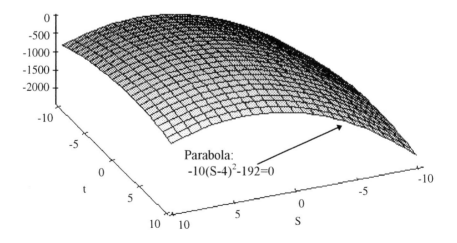

These two boundary conditions are satisfied for $\alpha = -20$, $\beta = 0$, $S_0 = 4$, $t_0 = 2$.

5 A Reminder: Bivariate, Second-Degree Equations

It turns out that frequently encountered graphs such as circles, ellipses, parabolas, or hyperbolas, can all be represented by a second-degree equation. In this section we briefly review this aspect of analytical geometry, since it relates to the terminology concerning PDEs.

For the time being, let x, y denote two deterministic variables. We can define an equation of the second degree as

$$Ax^2 + Bxy + Cy^2 + Dx + Ey + F = 0. \tag{47}$$

Here A, B, C, D, E, F represent various constants. The equation is of the *second* degree because the highest power of x or of y is a square.

By choosing different values for A, B, C, D, E, F, the locus of the equation can be in the form of an ellipse, a parabola, a hyperbola, or a circle.

It is worth discussing these briefly.

5.1 Circle

Consider the case where

$$A = C \quad \text{and} \quad B = 0. \tag{48}$$

The second-degree equation reduces to

$$Ax^2 + Ay^2 + Dx + Ey + F = 0. \tag{49}$$

After "completing the square," this can *always* be written as

$$(x - x_0)^2 + (y - y_0)^2 = R, \tag{50}$$

which most readers will recognize as the equation of a circle with radius R and center at (x_0, y_0). To see why this is so, expand (50):

$$(x)^2 + (y)^2 - 2x_0 x - 2y_0 y + x_0^2 + y_0^2 = R. \tag{51}$$

In this equation we can always let

$$\frac{1}{R} = A \tag{52}$$

$$-\frac{2x_0}{R} = D \tag{53}$$

$$-\frac{2y_0}{R} = E \tag{54}$$

and

$$\frac{x_0^2 + y_0^2}{R} = F. \tag{55}$$

Hence, with $A = C$, $B = 0$, the x and the y that satisfy the second-degree equation will always trace a circle in the x, y plane.

In the special case when $R = 0$, the circle reduces to a point. Another degenerate case can be obtained when $A = C = 0$. Then the circle has degenerated into a straight line, but the equation is not second-degree.

5.2 Ellipse

The second case of interest is when

$$B^2 - 4AC < 0. \tag{56}$$

This is similar to the case of a circle, except B is not zero, and the coefficients of x^2 and y^2 are different. We can again rewrite the second-degree equation in a different form,

$$\alpha(x - x_0)^2 + \beta(y - y_0)^2 + \gamma(x - x_0)(y - y_0) = R, \tag{57}$$

which will be recognized as the equation of an ellipse, where the *center* is at x_0, y_0.

Note that given values for A, B, C, D, E, F, we can always determine the values of the parameters $x_0, y_0, \alpha, \beta, \gamma, R$, since by equating the coefficients of the expanded form of (57) with those of (47), we will have six equations in six unknowns.

5.2.1 Example

The method of *completing the square* is useful for differentiating among ellipses, circles, parabolas, and hyperbolas. We illustrate this with a simple example.[6]

Consider the second-degree equation

$$9x^2 + 16y^2 - 54x - 64y + 3455 = 0. \tag{58}$$

Note that

$$B^2 - 4AC = -576, \tag{59}$$

so we must be dealing with an ellipse. We directly show this by "completing the squares":

$$9(x^2 - 6x + ?) + 16(y^2 - 4y + ?) = 3455. \tag{60}$$

---

[6]The method of "completing the square" is used frequently in calculations involving geometric SDEs.

By filling in for the question marks, we can make the two terms in parentheses become squares. We replace the first question mark with 9 for the first parenthesis. This requires adding 81 to the right-hand side. The second question mark needs to be replaced by 4. This requires adding 64 to the right-hand side. We obtain

$$9(x - 3)^2 + 16(y - 2)^2 = 3600 \tag{61}$$

or

$$\frac{(x - 3)^2}{400} + \frac{(y - 2)^2}{225} = 1. \tag{62}$$

This is the formula of an ellipse with center at $x = 3$, $y = 2$.

5.3 Parabola

The second-degree equation in (47) reduces to a parabola when we have

$$B^2 - 4AC = 0. \tag{63}$$

The easiest way to see this is to note that $B = 0$ and either $A = 0$ or $C = 0$ satisfies the required condition. But, when this happens the second-degree equation reduces to

$$Ax^2 + Dx + Ey + F = 0, \tag{64}$$

which is the general equation for a parabola.

5.4 Hyperbola

The general second-degree equation in (47) represents a hyperbola if the condition

$$B^2 - 4AC > 0 \tag{65}$$

is satisfied. This case will have limited use for us, so we will skip the details.

6 Types of PDEs

Example 2 suggests that the contours of $F(S_t, t)$ would in general be nonlinear equations. In case of Example 2, they were ellipses. In fact, partial differential equations of the form

$$a_0 + a_1 F_t + a_2 F_s + a_3 F_{ss} + a_4 F_{tt} + a_5 F_{st} = 0 \tag{66}$$

are called *elliptic* PDEs if we have

$$a_4^2 - 4a_3 a_5 < 0. \tag{67}$$

The PDE in (66) is called *parabolic* if

$$a_5^2 - 4a_3a_4 = 0. \tag{68}$$

Finally, the PDE is called *hyperbolic* if

$$a_5^2 - 4a_3a_4 > 0. \tag{69}$$

Clearly, $F(S_t, t)$ graphed in Figure 3 is a solution to a PDE that satisfies the condition of an elliptic PDE, since $a_4 = 0$ and both a_3 and a_4 are of the same sign. As a result, the condition

$$a_5^2 - 4a_3a_4 < 0 \tag{70}$$

is satisfied.

6.1 Example: Parabolic PDE

Figure 4 gives the graph of the function $F(S_t, t)$ defined as

$$F(S_t, t) = -10(S_t - 4)^2 - 3(t - 2). \tag{71}$$

Note that the contours of this function are parabolas. This $F(S_t, t)$ will have boundary conditions as parabolas with respect to t, and as straight lines with respect to S_t.

Such an $F(S_t, t)$ is one of the solutions of the PDE

$$-\frac{1}{4}F_{ss} + \frac{5}{3}F_t = 0. \tag{72}$$

The coefficients of the PDE are such that

$$a_5^2 - 4a_3a_4 = 0, \tag{73}$$

since $a_4 = 0$ and $a_5 = 0$. Hence, this PDE is parabolic.

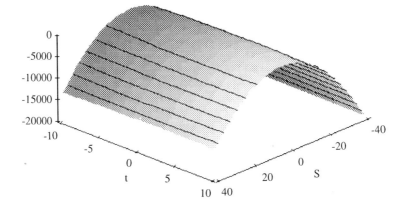

7 Conclusions

In this chapter we introduced the notion of a partial differential equation (PDE). These were *functional* equations, whose solutions were functions of the underlying variables. We discussed briefly various forms of PDEs and introduced the related terminology.

This chapter also showed that the relationship between financial derivatives and the underlying asset can be exploited to obtain PDEs that derivative asset prices must satisfy.

8 References

Most of our readers are interested in PDEs because at one point they will be applying them in practical derivative asset pricing. Thus, rather than books on the theory of PDEs, sources dealing with the numerical solution of PDEs will be more useful. In most cases, these sources contain a brief summary of the underlying theory as well. We recommend two books on PDEs. Smith (1985) is easy to read. Thomas (1995) is a more comprehensive and recent treatment.

CHAPTER 13

The Black–Scholes PDE

An Application

1 Introduction

In this chapter we provide some important examples of partial differential equation methods using derivative asset pricing.

One purpose of this chapter is to have a geometric look at the function that solves the PDE obtained by Black and Scholes (1973). The geometry of the Black–Scholes formula helps with the understanding of PDEs. In particular, we show geometrically the implications of having a *single* random factor in pricing call options.

Next, we complicate the original Black–Scholes framework by introducing a second factor. This leads to some major difficulties, which we will discuss briefly.

Finally, the third purpose of this chapter is to compare closed-form solutions for PDEs with numerical approaches. This chapter concludes with an example of a numerical asset price calculation.

2 The Black–Scholes PDE

In Chapter 12 we obtained the PDE that the price of a derivative written on the underlying asset S_t must satisfy under some conditions. The underlying security did not pay a dividend, and the risk-free interest rate was assumed to be constant at r.

Now, suppose we consider the special SDE where

$$a(S_t, t) = \mu S_t \tag{1}$$

254

and, more importantly,

$$\sigma(S_t, t) = \sigma S_t, \quad t \in [0, \infty). \tag{2}$$

In this chapter we occasionally write σ_t to denote σS_t. Under these conditions the fundamental PDE of Black and Scholes and the associated boundary condition are given by

$$-rF + rF_s S_t + F_t + \frac{1}{2} F_{ss} \sigma^2 S_t^2 = 0, \quad 0 \le S_t, \quad 0 \le t \le T \tag{3}$$

$$F(T) = \max[S_T - K, 0]. \tag{4}$$

Equations (3) and 4 were first used in finance by Black and Scholes (1973). Hence we call these equations "the fundamental PDE of Black and Scholes."[1]

Black and Scholes solve this PDE and obtain the form of the function $F(S_t, t)$ explicitly,

$$F(S_t, t) = S_t N(d_1) - Ke^{-r(T-t)} N(d_2), \tag{6}$$

where

$$d_1 = \frac{\ln(S_t/K) + (r + \frac{1}{2}\sigma^2)(T - t)}{\sigma\sqrt{T - t}} \tag{7}$$

$$d_2 = d_1 - \sigma\sqrt{T - t}. \tag{8}$$

$N(d_i), i = 1, 2$ are two integrals of the standard normal density:

$$N(d_i) = \int_{-\infty}^{d_i} \frac{1}{\sqrt{2\pi}} e^{-\frac{1}{2}x^2} \, dx. \tag{9}$$

To show that this function satisfies the Black–Scholes PDE and the corresponding boundary condition, we have to take the first and second partials of (6) with respect to S_t, and plug these in (3) with the $F(S_t, t)$ and its partial with respect to t. The result should equal zero. Also, as t approaches T the function should equal (4).

---

[1]Note that only one of the second partials, namely the one with respect to S_t, is present in this PDE. Also, note that there is no constant term. Under these conditions we can easily calculate the value of the expression from Chapter 12,

$$a_5^2 - 4a_3 a_4, \tag{5}$$

as zero. This means that leaving aside the presence of S_t and S_t^2, which are always positive, the Black–Scholes PDE is of the parabolic form.

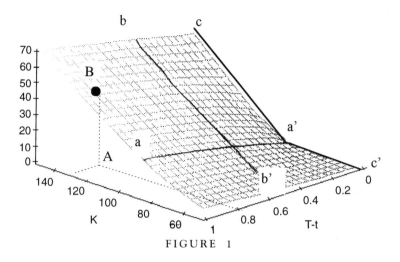

FIGURE 1

2.1 A Geometric Look at the Black–Scholes Formula

We saw in Chapter 12 that functions $F(S_t, t)$ satisfying various PDEs could be represented in three-dimensional space. We can do the same for the Black–Scholes PDE. The solution of this PDE was given by (6). We would like to pick numerical values for the parameters K, r, σ, T and represent this formula in the three-dimensional space $F \times S \times t$.

We pick

$$r = .065, \quad K = 100, \quad \sigma = .80, \quad T = 1 \tag{10}$$

and substitute these in the formula (6). These numbers imply a 6.5% risk-free borrowing cost, and an 80% volatility during the interval $t \in [0, 1]$. This type of volatility is high for most mature financial markets. But it makes the graphics easier to read. The life of the call option is normalized to be 1, with $T = 1$ implying one year, and the initial time is set at $t_0 = 0$. Finally, the strike price is set at 100.[2]

To plot the Black–Scholes formula with these particular parameters, we must select a range for the two variables S_t and t. We let S_t range from 50 to 140, and let t range from 0 to 1. The resulting surface is shown in Figures 1 and 2.

---

[2]If $T = 1$ means "one year," the interest rate and the volatility will be yearly rates. But $T = 1$ may very well mean six months, three months, or, for that matter, any time interval during which the financial instrument will exist. After all, we used $T = 1$ as a normalization. Under such conditions, the interest rate or the volatility numbers must be adjusted to the relevant time period.

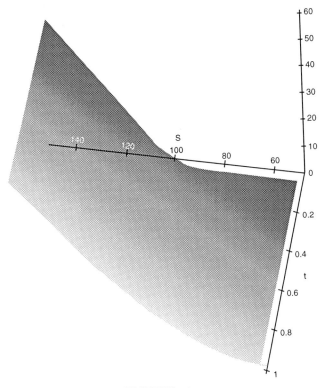

FIGURE 2

Figure 1 is easier to read; hence, we will comment on it.

In Figure 1, we have a "horizontal surface" defined by the axes labeled S_t and $1 - t$, where the latter represents "time to expiration." These two axes form a plane. For example, point A represents an underlying asset price of 130, and a "time to expiration" equal to .80. By going up vertically toward the surface we reach point B, which is in fact the value of the Black–Scholes formula evaluated at A:

$$B = F(130, .2). \tag{11}$$

We display two types of contours on the surface. First, we fix S_t at a particular level and vary t. This gives lines such as aa', which show how the call price will change as t goes from 1 to 0 when S_t is fixed at 100.

The second contour is shown as bb' and represents $F(S_t, t)$ when we fix t at .6 and move S_t from 60 to 140. It is interesting to see that as t goes toward 1, this contour goes toward the limit shown as cc'. The latter is the usual graph with a kink at K, which shows the option payoff at expiration.

In Figure 2, we show the same surface without the contours. We would like to emphasize a potentially confusing point using this graph. The Black–Scholes formula gives a surface, once we fix K, r, and σ. This surface will *not* move as random events occur and realized values of dW_t become known. Realization of the Wiener increments would only cause random movements *on* the surface. One such example is the trajectory denoted by C_0, C_T in Figure 8. Because the increments of the Wiener process are unpredictable, the movement of the stock price along the t direction will proceed in "random steps." Over infinitesimal intervals these steps are also infinitesimal, yet still unpredictable.

The trajectory C_0, C_T is interesting from another angle as well. As time passes, S_t will trace the trajectory shown on the $S_t \times t$ plane. Going vertically to the surface, we obtain the trajectory C_0, C_T. Note that there is a *deterministic* correspondence between the two trajectories. Given the trajectory of S_t on the horizontal plane, there is only one trajectory for $F(S_t, t)$ to follow on the surface. This is the consequence of having the same randomness in S_t and in $F(S_t, t)$.

Finally, we show in Figure 3 another look at the same surface from a different angle.

3   PDEs in Asset Pricing

The partial differential equation obtained by Black and Scholes is relevant under some specific assumptions. These are (1) the underlying asset is a stock, (2) the stock does not pay any dividends, (3) the derivative asset is a European-style call option that cannot be exercised before the expiration date, (4) the risk-free rate is constant, and (5) there are no indivisibilities or transaction costs such as commissions and bid–ask spreads.

In most applications of derivative asset pricing, one or more of these assumptions will be violated. If so, in general the Black–Scholes PDE will not apply, and a new PDE should be found. One exception is the violation of assumption 3. If the option is American-style, the PDE will remain the same. The boundary conditions will be different.

The relevant PDEs under these more complicated circumstances fall into one of a few general classes of applications. We discuss some examples next.

3.1 A Second Factor

If one is trying to price a call option, and if the option is written on a stock that pays dividends at a constant rate of δ units per time, the resulting

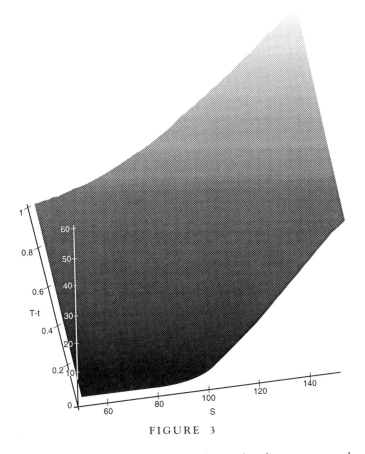

FIGURE 3

PDE will change only slightly. But if the change involves a new *random* factor, the arbitrage pricing methodology cannot be applied as before. In fact, one in general would need to consider *all* relevant equilibrium conditions simultaneously.

3.1.1 Constant Dividends

Suppose we change the Black–Scholes assumptions slightly and introduce a *constant* rate of dividends, δ, on the underlying asset S_t.

Again, we can try to form the same risk-free portfolio as in Chapter 12 by combining the underlying asset and the call option written on it:

$$P_t = \theta_1 F(S_t, t) + \theta_2 S_t, \quad t \in [0, T]. \tag{12}$$

The portfolio weights θ_1, θ_2 can be selected as

$$\theta_1 = 1, \quad \theta_2 = -F_s, \tag{13}$$

so that the "unpredictable" random component is eliminated and a perfect hedge is formed:

$$dP_t = F_t\, dt + \frac{1}{2} F_{ss} \sigma_t^2\, dt. \tag{14}$$

Up to this point there is no difference from the original Black–Scholes approach discussed in Chapter 12. The time path of the P_t will again be completely predictable.

The difference occurs in deciding how much this portfolio should appreciate in value. Before, the (completely predictable) capital gains were exactly equal to the earnings of a risk-free investment. But now, the underlying stock pays a known dividend at a rate of δ dollars per time that is predictable. Hence, the capital gains *plus* the dividends received must equal the earnings of a risk-free portfolio,

$$dP_t + \delta\, dt = rP_t\, dt, \tag{15}$$

or

$$dP_t = -\delta\, dt + rP_t\, dt. \tag{16}$$

Putting this together with (14), we get a slightly different PDE:

$$rF - rF_s S_t - \delta - F_t - \frac{1}{2} F_{ss} \sigma_t^2 = 0. \tag{17}$$

There is now a constant term δ. Hence, stocks paying dividends at a constant rate δ do not present a major problem.[3]

3.1.2 A Random Second Factor

The difficulty with a second factor begins if this factor contains "unpredictable" random components of its own. With a constant rate of dividends, the dividends earnings dD_t at time t are given by

$$dD_t = \delta\, dt. \tag{18}$$

If dividends depend on some Wiener process, we would instead have

$$dD_t = a^*\, dt + \sigma^*\, dW_t^*, \tag{19}$$

where a^*, σ^* are constants, and where dW_t^* represents increments in a Wiener process W_t^*.[4]

---

[3]Similarly, if a known dividend yield of δ per time unit is paid, then capital gains plus dividends will be given by $dP_t + \delta S_t\, dt$. The derivation of the PDE proceeds in an analogous fashion.

[4]With a constant diffusion parameter, this model may lead to negative D_t with positive probability. It is however notationally efficient to use this simple SDE in this particular section.

In this section we discuss this case with one minor modification. The second factor D_t will not represent dividends, but any factor that influences the call price other than time t and S_t. It could, for example, represent random interest rates, or random volatility. Our objective is to make the derivative price depend on an additional variable that introduces a *second* source of randomness in the pricing problem. Hence, we let this second factor follow the SDE

$$dD_t = a^* \, dt + \sigma^* \, dW_t^*, \tag{20}$$

with time-independent drift and diffusion parameters. In practical applications, the parameters a^* and σ^* will probably depend on some fundamental variables such as S_t.

How would the PDE obtained from the previous risk-free portfolio change?

First note that the derivative asset price $F(\cdot)$ could now depend on D_t directly and must be written as

$$F(t) = F(S_t, D_t, t), \quad t \in [0, T]. \tag{21}$$

Consider the stochastic differential

$$dF(t) = F_t \, dt + F_s \, dS_t + F_D \, dD_t + \frac{1}{2} F_{ss}(dS_t)^2 + \frac{1}{2} F_{DD}(dD_t)^2 \tag{22}$$
$$+ F_{Ds} \, dD_t \, dS_t.$$

The last term vanishes in infinitesimal intervals, in the mean square sense, if the unpredictable component of dS_t is uncorrelated with the unpredictable part of dD_t. For simplicity, we assume that it is so.[5] Replacing the squared increments with their limit in mean square:

$$dF(t) = F_t \, dt + F_s \, dS_t + F_D \, dD_t + \frac{1}{2} F_{ss}\sigma_t^2 \, dt + \frac{1}{2} F_{DD}\sigma^{*2} \, dt. \tag{23}$$

The increment in the value of the portfolio formed using S_t and the call option will be given by

$$dP_t = \theta_1 \, dS(t) + \theta_2 \left[F_t \, dt + F_s \, dS_t + F_D \, dD_t + \frac{1}{2} F_{ss}\sigma_t^2 \, dt + \frac{1}{2} F_{DD}\sigma^{*2} \, dt \right]. \tag{24}$$

As before, the parameters θ_1 and θ_2 are portfolio weights that can be picked freely by the decision maker.

What should the values of θ_1, θ_2 be in order for dP_t to be a nonrandom increment?

---

[5] In practice, this may not be true. Any small unpredictable event that affects S_t can potentially affect D_t.

Note that the problem is more difficult now. We have *two* sources of randomness in (24), namely the dS_t and the dD_t. If the choice

$$\theta_1 = -F_s \tag{25}$$

$$\theta_2 = 1 \tag{26}$$

is made, this would eliminate the random term involving dS_t from the right-hand side of (24), but dD_t would remain. As long as there is some unpredictable component in dD_t that is not in dS_t,[6] this particular choice of θ_1, θ_2 is not sufficient to make dP_t random.

Hence, the appreciation rate of the portfolio would be random and cannot be equated to a risk-free return. The method of the previous section would be inapplicable with the limited number of assets under consideration.

3.1.3 An Exception

There is a case similar to the previous example, where the method would work. Suppose D_t again represents a continuous *rate* of dividends paid by S_t. One can claim that all random shocks to the underlying asset price reflect instantaneously on D_t. This means that increments of D_t are random, but that this randomness is caused totally by the unpredictable movements that affect stock prices S_t. In other words, the D_t process is driven by the same Wiener term dW_t. That is, we have

$$dD_t = a_t^* \, dt + \sigma_t^* \, dW_t \tag{27}$$

$$dS_t = a_t \, dt + \sigma_t \, dW_t. \tag{28}$$

The underlying asset and the dividend process have different drift and diffusion coefficients, but the unexpected shocks are caused by the same Wiener process W_t.

Then, we can substitute the right-hand sides of (27) and (28) for the dS_t and dD_t in Equation (24) and obtain

$$
\begin{aligned}
dP_t = {} & \theta_1 (a_t \, dt + \sigma_t \, dW_t) \\
& + \theta_2 \Big[F_t \, dt + F_s(a_t \, dt + \sigma_t \, dW_t) + F_D(a_t^* \, dt + \sigma_t^* \, dW_t) \\
& \qquad + \tfrac{1}{2} F_{ss} \sigma_t^2 \, dt + \tfrac{1}{2} F_{DD} \sigma_t^{*2} \, dt + F_{sD} \sigma_t \sigma_t^* \, dt \Big].
\end{aligned}
\tag{29}
$$

---

[6] Or, more formally, if S_t and D_t are not perfectly correlated.

The last term involving F_{sD} is there because, with dW_t and dW_t^* being perfectly correlated, we have in the mean square sense

$$dS_t \, dD_t = \sigma_t \sigma_t^* \, dt. \tag{30}$$

We can group the terms involving dt and dW_t to get

$$dP_t = \theta_1 a_t \, dt + \theta_2 \left[F_t + F_s a_t + F_D a_t^* + \frac{1}{2} F_{ss} \sigma_t^2 + \frac{1}{2} F_{DD} \sigma_t^{*2} + F_{sD} \sigma_t \sigma_t^* \right] dt$$

$$+ \left[\sigma_t (\theta_1 + F_s \theta_2) + \theta_2 \sigma_t^* F_D \right] dW_t. \tag{31}$$

Letting

$$\theta_2 = 1 \tag{32}$$

and

$$\theta_1 = -\frac{(F_s \sigma_t + \sigma_t^* F_D)}{\sigma_t} \tag{33}$$

will again convert dP_t into a nonrandom increment, since these choices for θ_1, θ_2 will eliminate all terms involving the random dW_t from the right-hand side of (29).

4 Exotic Options

In the previous section, a complication to the Black–Scholes framework was discussed. The PDE satisfied by the arbitrage-free price of the derivative asset did change as the assumptions concerning dividend payments changed. This section discusses another complication.

Suppose the derivative asset is an option with possibly *random* expiration date. For example, there are some "down-and-out" and "up-and-out" options that are known as *barrier* derivatives.[7] Unlike "standard" options, the payoff of these instruments depends *also* on whether or not the spot price of the underlying asset crossed a certain barrier during the life of the option. If such a crossing has occurred, the payoff of the option changes. We briefly review some of these "exotic" options.

---

[7] These are also known as "knock-out" and "knock-in" options.

4.1 Lookback Options

In the standard Black–Scholes case, the call option payoff is equal to $S_T - K$, if the option expires in the money. In this payoff S_T is the price of the underlying asset *at expiration* and K is the constant strike price.

In the case of a *floating* lookback call option, the payoff is the difference $S_T - S_{min}$, where S_{min} is the minimum price of the underlying asset observed during the life of the option.[8]

A *fixed* lookback call option, on the other hand, pays the difference (if positive) between a fixed strike price K and S_{max}, where the latter is the maximum reached by the underlying asset price during the life of the option. These options have the characteristic that some positive payoff is guaranteed if the option is in the money during some time over its life. Hence, everything else being the same, they are more expensive.

4.2 Ladder Options

A ladder option has several *thresholds*, such that if the underlying price reaches these thresholds, the return of the option is "locked in."

4.3 Trigger or Knock-in Options

A down-and-in option gives its holder a European option if the spot price falls below a *barrier* during the life of the option. If the barrier is not reached, the option expires with some *rebate* as a payoff.[9]

4.4 Knock-out Options

Knock-out options are European options that expire immediately if, for example, the underlying asset price falls below a barrier during the life of the option. The option pays a rebate if the barrier is reached. Otherwise, it is a "standard" European option.[10] Such an option is called "down-and-out."

---

[8] The lookback option is *floating* because the strike price is not fixed.

[9] Similarly, there are up-and-in options that come into effect if the underlying asset price has an upcrossing of a certain barrier.

[10] The up-and-out option expires immediately if the underlying asset price has an upcrossing of a certain barrier.

4.5 Other Exotics

There are obviously many different ways one can structure an exotic option. Some common cases include the following:

- *Basket options*, which are derivatives where the underlying asset is a *basket* of various financial instruments. Such baskets dampen the volatility of the individual securities. Hence, basket options become more affordable in the case of *emerging market* derivatives.
- *Multi-asset options* have payoffs depending on the underlying price of more than one asset. For example, the payoff of such a call may be

$$F(S_{1T}, S_{2T}, T) = \max[0, \max(S_{1T}, S_{2T}) - K]. \qquad (34)$$

Another possibility is the *spread call*

$$F(S_{1T}, S_{2T}, T) = \max[0, (S_{1T} - S_{2T}) - K] \qquad (35)$$

or the *portfolio call*

$$F(S_{1T}, S_{2T}, T) = \max[0, (\theta_1 S_{1T} + \theta_2 S_{2T}) - K], \qquad (36)$$

where θ_1, θ_2 are known portfolio weights. As a final example, one may have a *dual strike call option*:

$$F(S_{1T}, S_{2T}, T) = \max[0, (S_{1T} - K_1), (S_{2T} - K_2)]. \qquad (37)$$

- Average or Asian options are quite common and have payoffs depending on the *average* price of the underlying asset over the lifetime of the option.[11]

4.6 The Relevant PDEs

It is clear from this brief list of exotic options that there are three major differences between exotics and the standard Black–Scholes case.

First, the *expiration value* of the option may depend on some event happening over the life of the option (e.g., it may be a function of the maximum of the underlying asset price). Clearly, these make the boundary conditions much more complicated than the Black–Scholes case.

Second, derivative instruments may have random expiration *dates*.

Third, the derivative may be written on more than one asset.

All these may lead to changes in the basic PDE that we derived in the Black–Scholes case. Not all examples can be discussed here. But consider the case of *knock-out options*. We discuss the case of a "down-and-out" call.

---

[11]Often arithmetic averages are used, and the average can be computed on a daily, weekly, or monthly basis.

Let the K_t be the *barrier* at time t. Let S_t and $F(S_t, t, K_t)$, respectively, be the price of the underlying asset and the price of the knock-out option. If the S_t reaches the K_t during the life of the option, the option holder receives a rebate R_t and the option suddenly expires. Otherwise, it is a standard European option.

In deriving the relevant PDE, the main difference from the standard case is in the boundary conditions. As long as the underlying asset price is *above* the barrier K_t during the life of the option, $t \in [0, T]$, the same PDE as in the standard case prevails:

$$\frac{1}{2}\sigma_t^2 F_{ss} + rF_s S_t - rF + F_t = 0 \quad \text{if} \quad S_t > K_t \tag{38}$$

and

$$F(S_T, T, K_T) = \max[S_T - K_T]. \tag{39}$$

But if the S_t falls below K_t during the life of the option, we have

$$F(S_t, t, K_t) = R_t, \quad \text{if } S_t \leq K_t. \tag{40}$$

Clearly, the form of the PDE is the same, but the boundary is different. This will result in a different solution for $F(S_t, t, K_t)$, as was discussed earlier.

5 Solving PDEs in Practice

Once a trader obtains a PDE representing the behavior over time of a derivative price $F(S_t, t)$ there will be two ways to proceed in calculating this value in practice.

5.1 Closed-Form Solutions

The first method is similar to the one used by Black and Scholes, which involves solving the PDE for a closed-form formula. It turns out that the PDEs describing the behavior of derivative prices cannot in every case be solved for closed forms. In general, either such PDEs are not easy to solve, or they do not have solutions that one can express as closed-form formulas.

First, let us discuss the difference between closed forms and numerical solutions of a PDE. The function $F(S_t, t)$ solves a PDE if the appropriate partial derivatives satisfy an equality such as

$$-rF + F_t + rF_s S_t + \frac{1}{2}F_{ss}\sigma^2 S_t^2 = 0, \quad 0 \leq S_t, \quad 0 \leq t \leq T. \tag{41}$$

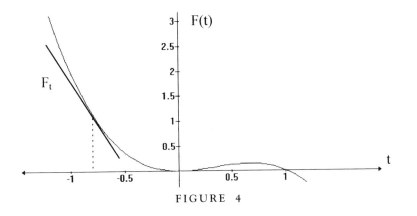

FIGURE 4

Now, it is possible that one can find a continuous surface such that the partial derivatives do indeed satisfy the PDE. But it may still be impossible to represent this surface in terms of an *easy* and convenient formula as in the case of Black–Scholes. In other words, although a solution may exist, this solution may not be representable as a convenient function of S_t and t.

We will discuss this by using an analogy. Consider the function of time $F(t)$ shown in Figure 4.

The way it is drawn, $F(t)$ is clearly continuous and smooth. So, in the region shown, $F(t)$ has derivatives with respect to time. But $F(t)$ was drawn in some *arbitrary* fashion, and there is no reason to expect that this curve can be represented by a compact formula involving a few terms in t. For example, it is obvious that an exponential formula

$$F = a_2 e^{a_1 t} + a_3, \tag{42}$$

where a_i, $i = 1, 2, 3$ are constants, cannot represent this curve. In fact, for a general continuous and smooth function, such closed-form formulas will not exist.[12,13]

The solutions of PDEs in the simple Black–Scholes case are surfaces in the three dimensional space generated by S_t, t and $F(S_t, t)$. Thus, the same argument as for Figures 5 and 6 can be made here as well. Given a smooth and continuous curve in three-dimensional space $F \times t \times S_t$, the

---

[12]On the other hand, if the curve is of a "special" type, one may be able to identify it as a simple polynomial and represent it with a formula. For example, the curve in Figure 5 looks like a parabola and has a simple closed-form representation as $a_0 + a_1 t + a_2 t^2$.

[13]If a curve is smooth and continuous, it may, however, be expanded as an infinite Taylor series expansion. Yet, Taylor series expansions are *not* closed form formulas. They are *representations* of such $F(\cdot)$.

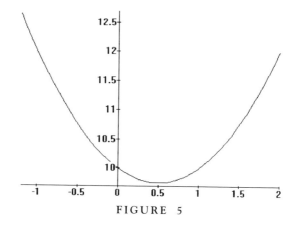

FIGURE 5

partial derivatives may be well defined and may satisfy a certain PDE, but the surface may not be representable by a compact formula.

Hence, a solution to a PDE may exist, but a closed-form expression for the formula may not. In fact, given that such formulas are very constrained in representing smooth surfaces in three (or higher) dimensions, this may often be the case rather than being the exception.

5.2 Numerical Solutions

When a closed-form solution does not exist, a market participant is forced to obtain *numerical solutions* to PDEs. A numerical solution is like calculating the surface represented by $F(S_t, t)$ *directly*, without first obtaining a closed-form formula for $F(S_t, t)$. Consider again the PDE obtained from the Black–Scholes framework:

$$-rF + F_t + rF_s S_t + \frac{1}{2}F_{ss}\sigma^2 S_t^2 = 0, \quad 0 \le S_t, \quad 0 \le t \le T. \quad (43)$$

To solve this PDE *numerically*, one assumes that the PDE is valid for finite increments in S_t and t. In particular, two "partitions" are needed.

1. A grid size for ΔS must be selected as a minimum increment in the price of the underlying security.
2. Time t is the second variable in $F(S_t, t)$. Hence, a grid size for Δt is needed as well. Needless to say, Δt, ΔS must be "small." How small is "small" can be decided by trial and error.
3. Next one has to decide on the range of possible values for S_t. To be more precise one selects, a priori, the minimum S_{min} and the maximum S_{max} as possible values of S_t. These extreme values should be

selected so that observed prices remain within the range

$$S_{min} \leq S_t \leq S_{max}. \tag{44}$$

4. The boundary conditions must be determined.
5. Assuming that for small but noninfinitesimal ΔS_t and Δt the same PDE is valid, the values of $F(S_t, t)$ at the grid points should be determined.

To illustrate the last step, let

$$F_{ij} = F(S_i, t_j), \tag{45}$$

where F_{ij} is the value at time t_i if the price of the underlying asset is at S_j. The limits of i, j will be determined by the choice of ΔS, Δt and of S_{min}, S_{max}.

We want to approximate $F(S_t, t)$ at a finite number of points F_{ij}. This is shown in Figure 6 for an arbitrary surface and in Figure 7 for the Black–Scholes surface. In either case, the dots represent the points at which $F(S_t, t)$ will be evaluated. The sizes of the grids ΔS and Δt determine how "close" these dots will be on the surface. Obviously, the closer these dots are, the better the approximation of the surface.

We let F_{ij} denote the "dot" that represents the ith value for S_t and the jth value for t. These values for S_t and t will be selected from their respective axes and then "plugged in" to $F(S_t, t)$. The result is written as F_{ij}.

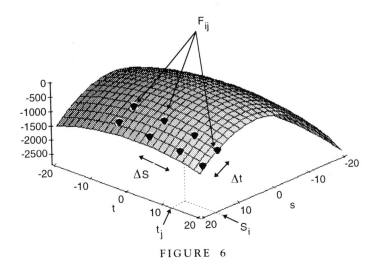

FIGURE 6

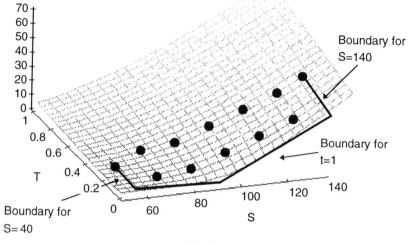

FIGURE 7

To carry on this calculation, we need to change the partial differential equation to a difference equation by replacing all differentials by appropriate differences. There are various methods of doing this, each with a different degree of accuracy. Here, we use the simplest method[14]

$$\frac{\Delta F}{\Delta t} + rS\frac{\Delta F}{\Delta S} + \frac{1}{2}\sigma^2 S^2 \frac{\Delta^2 F}{\Delta S^2} = rF, \qquad (46)$$

where the first-order partial derivatives are approximated by the corresponding differences. For first partials we can use the *backward* difference

$$\frac{\Delta F}{\Delta t} \simeq \frac{F_{ij} - F_{i,j-1}}{\Delta t} \qquad (47)$$

$$rS\frac{\Delta F}{\Delta S} \simeq rS_j\frac{F_{ij} - F_{i-1,j}}{\Delta S}, \qquad (48)$$

or we can use *forward* differences, an example of which is[15]

$$rS\frac{\Delta F}{\Delta S} \simeq rS_j\frac{F_{i+1,j} - F_{ij}}{\Delta S}. \qquad (49)$$

---

[14]We are ignoring i, j subscripts for notational convenience. As will be seen below, elements of this difference equation depend on i, j. For each i, j there exists one equation such as in (46).

[15]We can also use *centered* differences.

For the second-order partials we use the approximations

$$\frac{\Delta^2 F}{\Delta S^2} = \left[\frac{F_{i+1,j} - F_{ij}}{\Delta S} - \frac{F_{ij} - F_{i-1,j}}{\Delta S} \right] \frac{1}{\Delta S}, \tag{50}$$

where $i = 1, \ldots, n$ and $j = 1, \ldots, N$. The parameters N and n determine the number of points at which we decided to calculate the surface $F(S_t, t)$.

For example, in Figure 7 we can let $n = 5$ and $N = 22$. Hence, excluding the points on the boundary values, we have a total of 80 dots to calculate on the surface. These values can be calculated by solving *recursively* the (system of) equations in (46).

The recursive nature of the problem is due to the existence of boundary conditions. The next section deals with these.

5.2.1 Boundary Conditions

Now, some of the F_{ij} are known because of endpoint conditions. For example, we always know the value of the option as a function of S_t at expiration. Also, for extreme values of S_t we can use some approximations that are valid in the limit. In particular:

- For S_t that is very high, we let $S_t = S_{max}$ and

$$F(S_{max}, t) \cong S_{max} - Ke^{-r(T-t)}. \tag{51}$$

  Here S_{max} is a price chosen so that the call premium is very close to the expiration date payoff.
- For S_t that is very low, we let $S_t = S_{min}$ and

$$F(S_{min}, t) \cong 0. \tag{52}$$

  In this case, S_{min} is an extremely low price. There is almost no chance that the option will expire in the money. The resulting call premium is close to zero.
- For $t = T$, we know exactly that

$$F(S_T, T) = \max[S_T - K, 0]. \tag{53}$$

These give the boundary values for F_{ij}. In Figure 7, these boundary regions are shown explicitly.

Using these boundary values with Equation (46), we can solve for the remaining unknown F_{ij}.

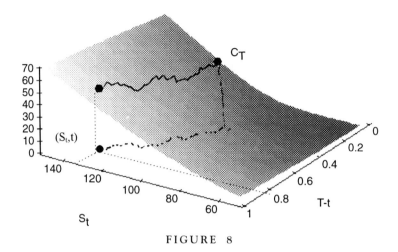

FIGURE 8

6 Conclusions

This chapter discussed some examples of PDEs that one faces in pricing derivative assets. In particular, we illustrated the difficulties of introducing a second random element in pricing call options. We also discussed some exotic derivatives and the way PDEs would change.

One important point was the geometry of the Black–Scholes surfaces. We saw that random trajectories for the underlying assets price led to random paths on this surface. This is shown in Figure 8.

7 References

Ingersoll (1987) provides several examples of PDEs from asset pricing. Our treatment of this topic is clearly intended to provide examples for a simple introduction to PDEs. An interested reader should consult these sources if information beyond a simple introduction is needed.

CHAPTER 14

Pricing Derivative Products

Equivalent Martingale Measures

1 Translations of Probabilities

Recent methods of derivative asset pricing do not necessarily exploit PDEs implied by arbitrage-free portfolios. They rest on converting prices of such assets into martingales. This is done through transforming the underlying probability distributions using the tools provided by the Girsanov theorem.

This approach is quite different from the method of PDEs. The tools involved exploit the existence of arbitrage-free portfolios indirectly, and hence are more difficult to visualize. A student of finance or economics is likely to be even less familiar with this new set of tools than with, say, the PDEs.

This chapter discusses these tools. We adopt a step-by-step approach. First we review some simple concepts and set the notation. Then, as motivation, we show some simple examples of the way the Girsanov theorem is used. The full theorem is stated next. We follow this with a section dealing with the intuitive explanation of various concepts utilized in the theorem. Finally, the theorem is applied in examples of increasing complexity. Overall, few examples are provided from financial markets. The next chapter deals with that. The purpose of the present chapter is to clarify the notion of transforming underlying probability distributions.

1.1 Probability as "Measure"

Consider a normally distributed random variable z_t at a fixed time t, with zero mean and unit variance. Formally:

$$z_t \sim N(0, 1). \tag{1}$$

The probability density $f(z_t)$ of this random variable is given by the well-known expression

$$f(z_t) = \frac{1}{\sqrt{2\pi}} e^{-\frac{1}{2} z_t^2}. \tag{2}$$

Suppose we are interested in the probability that z_t falls *near* a specific value $\bar{z}$. Then, this probability can be expressed by first choosing a small interval $\Delta > 0$, and next by calculating the integral of the normal density over the region in question:

$$P\left(\bar{z} - \frac{1}{2}\Delta < z_t < \bar{z} + \frac{1}{2}\Delta \right) = \int_{\bar{z} - \frac{1}{2}\Delta}^{\bar{z} + \frac{1}{2}\Delta} \frac{1}{\sqrt{2\pi}} e^{-\frac{1}{2} z_t^2} \, dz_t. \tag{3}$$

Now, if the region around $\bar{z}$ is small, then $f(z_t)$ will not change very much as z_t is varied from $\bar{z} - \frac{1}{2}\Delta$ to $\bar{z} + \frac{1}{2}\Delta$. This means we can approximate $f(z_t)$ by $f(\bar{z})$ during this interval and write the integral on the right-hand side of (3) as

$$\int_{\bar{z} - \frac{1}{2}\Delta}^{\bar{z} + \frac{1}{2}\Delta} \frac{1}{\sqrt{2\pi}} e^{-\frac{1}{2} z_t^2} \, dz_t \cong \frac{1}{\sqrt{2\pi}} e^{-\frac{1}{2} \bar{z}^2} \int_{\bar{z} - \frac{1}{2}\Delta}^{\bar{z} + \frac{1}{2}\Delta} dz_t \tag{4}$$

$$= \frac{1}{\sqrt{2\pi}} e^{-\frac{1}{2} \bar{z}^2} \Delta. \tag{5}$$

This construction is shown in Figure 1. The probability in (5) is a "mass" represented (approximately) by a rectangle with base Δ and height $f(\bar{z})$.

Visualized this way, probability corresponds to a "measure" that is associated with possible values of z_t in small intervals. Probabilities are called *measures* because they are mappings from arbitrary sets to nonnegative real

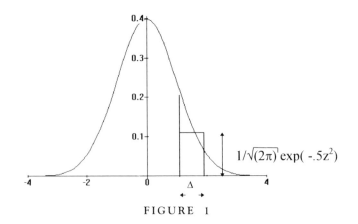

$$1/\sqrt{(2\pi)} \exp(-.5z^2)$$

FIGURE   1

numbers R^+. For infinitesimal Δ, which we write as dz_t, these measures are denoted by the symbol $dP(z_t)$, or simply dP when there is no confusion about the underlying random variable:

$$dP(\bar{z}) = P\left(\bar{z} - \frac{1}{2} dz_t < z_t < \bar{z} + \frac{1}{2} dz_t\right). \tag{6}$$

This can be read as the probability that the random variable z_t will fall within a small interval centered on $\bar{z}$ and of infinitesimal length dz_t. The sum of all such probabilities will then be given by adding these $dP(\bar{z})$ for various values of $\bar{z}$. Formally, this is expressed by the use of the integral

$$\int_{-\infty}^{\infty} dP(z_t) = 1. \tag{7}$$

A similar approach was used for calculating the expected value of z_t,

$$E[z_t] = \int_{-\infty}^{-\infty} z_t \, dP(z_t), \tag{8}$$

which can be seen as an "average" value of z_t. Geometrically, this determines the *center* of the probability mass. The variance was another weighted average:

$$E[z_t - Ez_t]^2 = \int_{-\infty}^{-\infty} [z_t - E[z_t]]^2 \, dP(z_t). \tag{9}$$

The variance had a geometric interpretation as well. It gives an indication of how the probability mass spreads around the center.

Accordingly, when we talk about a certain probability measure, dP, we always have in mind a *shape* and a *location* for the density of the random variable.[1]

Under these conditions, we can subject a probability distribution to two types of transformations:

- We can leave the shape of the distribution the same, but move the density to a different location. Figure 2 illustrates a case where the normal density that was centered at

$$\mu = -5 \tag{10}$$

is transformed into another normal density, this time centered at zero:

$$\mu = 0. \tag{11}$$

[1]In this book we always assume that this density exists. In other settings, the density function of the underlying random variables may not exist.

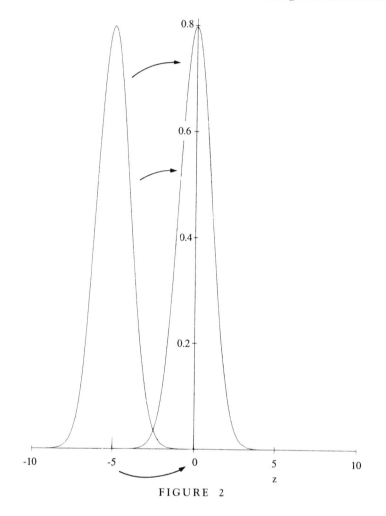

FIGURE 2

- We can also change the shape of the distribution. One way to do this is to increase or decrease the variance of the distribution. This can be accomplished by *scaling* the original random variable. Figure 3 displays a case where the variance of the random variable z_t is reduced from 4 to 1.

Modern methods for pricing derivative assets utilize a novel way of transforming the probability measure dP so that the mean of a random process z_t changes. The transformation permits treating an asset that carries a pos-

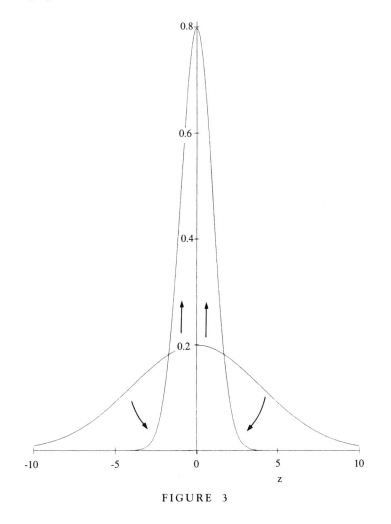

FIGURE 3

itive "risk premium" as if it were risk-free. This chapter deals with this complicated idea.

In the following section, we discuss two different methods of switching means of random variables.

2 Changing Means

Now, fix t and let z_t be a univariate random variable. There are two ways one can change the mean of z_t. In the first case, we operate on the *values* assumed by z_t. In the second, and counterintuitive, case, we leave the values assumed by z_t unchanged, but instead operate on the *probabilities* associated with z_t.

Both operations lead to a change in the original mean, while preserving other characteristics of the original random variable. However, while the first method cannot, in general, be used in asset pricing, the second method becomes a very useful tool.

We discuss these methods in detail next. The discussion proceeds within the context of a single random variable, rather than a stochastic process. The more complicated case of a continuous-time process is treated in the section on the Girsanov theorem.

2.1 Method 1: Operating on Possible Values

The first and standard method for changing the mean of a random variable is used routinely in econometrics and statistics. One simply adds a constant μ to z_t in order to obtain a new random variable $\tilde{z}_t = z_t + \mu$.[2] The $\tilde{z}_t$ defined this way will have a new mean.

For example, if originally

$$E[z_t] = 0, \tag{12}$$

then the new random variable $\tilde{z}_t$ will be such that

$$E[\tilde{z}_t] = E[z_t] + \mu = \mu. \tag{13}$$

2.1.1 Example 1

In spite of the simplicity of this transformation, it is important for later discussion to look at a precise example.

Suppose the random variable Z is defined as follows. A die is rolled and the values of Z are set according to the rule

$$Z = \begin{cases} 10 & \text{roll of 1 or 2} \\ -3 & \text{roll of 3 or 4} \\ -1 & \text{roll of 5 or 6} \end{cases} . \tag{14}$$

Assuming that the probability of getting a particular number is $1/6$, we can easily calculate the mean of Z as a weighted average of its possible values:

$$E[Z] = \frac{1}{3}[10] + \frac{1}{3}[-3] + \frac{1}{3}[-1] \tag{15}$$

$$= 2. \tag{16}$$

---

[2]Note that μ can be negative.

Now, suppose we would like to change the mean of Z using the method outlined earlier. More precisely, suppose we would like to calculate a new random variable with the same variance but with a mean of one. We call this new random variable $\tilde{Z}$ and let

$$\tilde{Z} = Z - 1. \tag{17}$$

Now using the formula for the mean, we calculate the $E[\tilde{Z}]$:

$$E[\tilde{Z}] = \frac{1}{3}[10 - 1] + \frac{1}{3}[-3 - 1] + \frac{1}{3}[-1 - 1] \tag{18}$$

$$= 1. \tag{19}$$

As can be seen from this transformation, in order to change the mean of Z, we operated on the *values* assumed by Z. Namely, we subtracted 1 from each possible value. The probabilities were not changed.

2.1.2 Example 2

We can illustrate this method for changing the means of random variables using a more relevant example from finance.

The yield of a triple-A-rated corporate bond R_t with fixed t will have the expected value

$$E[R_t] = r_t + E[\text{risk premium}], \tag{20}$$

where r_t is the known risk-free rate of treasury bonds with comparable maturity, and where $E[\cdot]$ expresses the expectation over possible states of the world. Let α be the (constant) expected risk premium:

$$E[R_t] = r_t + \alpha. \tag{21}$$

Then R_t is a random variable with mean $r_t + \alpha$.

The first method to change the mean of R_t is to add a constant and obtain a new random variable $\tilde{R}_t = R_t + \mu$. This random variable will have the mean

$$E[R_t + \mu] = r_t + \mu + \alpha. \tag{22}$$

In the case of normally distributed random variables, this is equivalent to preserving the shape of the density, while sliding the center of the distribution to a new location. Figure 2 displays an example.

If μ is selected as $-\alpha$, then such a transformation would eliminate the risk premium from R_t. Note that in order to use this method for changing means, we need to *know* the risk premium α. Only under these conditions could we arrive at subtracting the "right" quantity from R_t and obtain the equivalent risk-free yield.

This example is simple and does not illustrate *why* somebody might want to go through such a transformation of means to begin with. The next example is more illustrative in this respect.

2.1.3 Example 3

The example is discussed in discrete time first. Let S_t, $t = 1, 2, \ldots$ be the price of some financial asset that pays no dividends. The S_t is observed over discrete times $t, t+1, \ldots$.

Let r_t be the rate of risk-free return. A typical risky asset S_t must offer a rate of return R_t greater than r_t, since otherwise there will be no reason to hold it. This means that, using $E_t[\cdot]$, the expectation operator conditional on information available as of time t,

$$E_t[S_{t+1}] > (1 + r_t)S_t. \tag{23}$$

That is, on the average, the risky asset will appreciate faster than the growth of a risk-free investment. This equality can be rewritten as

$$\frac{1}{(1+r_t)} E_t[S_{t+1}] > S_t. \tag{24}$$

Here the left-hand side represents the expected future price discounted at the risk-free rate. For some $\mu > 0$,

$$\frac{1}{(1+r_t)} E_t[S_{t+1}] = S_t(1 + \mu). \tag{25}$$

Note that the positive constants μ or $\mu + \mu r_t$ can be interpreted as a risk premium. Transforming (25):

$$\frac{E_t[S_{t+1}]}{S_t} = (1 + r_t)(1 + \mu). \tag{26}$$

The term on the left-hand side of this equation, $E_t[S_{t+1}/S_t]$, represents expected gross return, $E_t[1 + R_t]$. This means that

$$E_t[1 + R_t] = (1 + r_t)(1 + \mu), \tag{27}$$

which says that the expected return of the risky asset must exceed the risk-free return approximately by μ

$$E_t[R_t] \cong r_t + \mu, \tag{28}$$

in the case where r_t and μ are small enough that the cross-product term can be ignored.

Under these conditions, μ is the risk premium for holding the asset for one period, and $\frac{1}{(1+r_t)}$ is the *risk-free discount* factor.

Now consider the problem of a financial analyst who wants to obtain the fair market value of this asset today. That is, the analyst would like to calculate S_t. One way to do this is to exploit the relation

$$E_t\left[\frac{1}{(1+R_t)}S_{t+1}\right] = S_t \qquad (29)$$

by calculating the expectation on the left-hand side.[3]

But doing this requires a knowledge of the distribution of R_t, which requires knowing the risk premium μ.[4] Yet it is rare that before knowing the fair market value S_t one can tell what the risk premium is. Hence, utilization of the relation in (29) will go nowhere in terms of calculating S_t.[5]

On the other hand, if one could "transform" the mean of R_t without having to use the μ, the method might work.[6] Hence, another way of transforming the distribution of R_t must be found.

If a new expectation using a different probability distribution $\tilde{P}$ yields an expression such as

$$E_t^{\tilde{P}}\left[\frac{1}{(1+r_t)}S_{t+1}\right] = S_t, \qquad (31)$$

this can be very useful for calculating S_t. In fact, one could exploit this equality by "forecasting" S_{t+1}, using a model that describes the dynamics of S_t, and then discounting the "average forecast" by the (known) r_t. This would provide an estimate of S_t.

What would $E_t^{\tilde{P}}[\cdot]$ and r_t represent in this particular case? r_t will be the risk-free rate. The expectation operator would be given by the risk-neutral probabilities. By making these transformations, we would be eliminating the risk premium from R_t:

$$R_t - \mu = r_t. \qquad (32)$$

The "trick" here is to accomplish this transformation in the mean without having to use the value of μ explicitly. Even though this seems an impossible

---

[3]This relation is just the definition of the yield R_t. If we discount the next period's price by $1 + R_t$, we naturally recover today's value.

[4]Because only by knowing μ can the mean of R_t be calculated, and the distribution of R_t be pinned down.

[5]There is an additional difficulty. The term on the left-hand side of (29) is a *nonlinear* function of R_t. Hence, we cannot simply move the expectation operator in front of R_t:

$$E_t\left[\frac{1}{(1+R_t)}S_{t+1}\right] \neq \left[\frac{1}{(1+E_tR_t)}S_{t+1}\right]. \qquad (30)$$

This further complicates the calculations.

[6]Because the mean of the distribution of R_t could be made equal to r_t.

task at the outset, the second method for changing means does precisely this.

2.2 Method 2: Operating on Probabilities

The second way of changing the mean of a random variable is to leave the random variable "intact," but transform the corresponding *probability measure* that governs z_t. We introduce this method using a series of examples that get more and more complicated. At the end we provide the Girsanov theorem, which extends the method to continuous-time stochastic processes. The idea may be counterintuitive, but is in fact quite simple, as Example 1 will show.

2.2.1 Example 1
Consider the first example of the previous section, with Z defined as a function of rolling a die:

$$Z = \begin{cases} 10 & \text{roll of 1 or 2} \\ -3 & \text{roll of 3 or 4} \\ -1 & \text{roll of 5 or 6} \end{cases}, \tag{33}$$

with a previously calculated mean of

$$E[Z] = 2 \tag{34}$$

and a variance

$$\text{Var}(Z) = E[Z - EZ]^2 = \frac{1}{3}[10 - 2]^2 + \frac{1}{3}[-3 - 2]^2 + \frac{1}{3}[-1 - 2]^2 = \frac{98}{3}. \tag{35}$$

Suppose we want to transform this random variable so that its mean becomes one, while leaving the variance unchanged.

Consider the following transformation of the original probabilities associated with rolling the die:

$$P(\text{getting 1 or 2}) = \frac{1}{3} \rightarrow \tilde{P}(\text{Getting a 1 or 2}) = \frac{122}{429} \tag{36}$$

$$P(\text{getting 3 or 4}) = \frac{1}{3} \rightarrow \tilde{P}(\text{Getting 3 or 4}) = \frac{22}{39} \tag{37}$$

$$P(\text{getting 5 or 6}) = \frac{1}{3} \rightarrow \tilde{P}(\text{Getting 5 or 6}) = \frac{5}{33}. \tag{38}$$

Note that the new probabilities are designated by $\tilde{P}$.

Now calculate the mean under these new probabilities:

$$E^{\tilde{P}}[Z] = \left[\frac{122}{429}\right][10] + \left[\frac{22}{39}\right][-3] + \left[\frac{5}{33}\right][-1] = 1. \tag{39}$$

The mean is indeed one. Calculate the variance:

$$E^{\tilde{P}}[Z]^2 = \frac{122}{429}[10 - 1]^2 + \frac{5}{33}[-1 - 1]^2 + \frac{22}{39}[-3 - 1]^2 = \frac{98}{3}. \qquad (40)$$

The variance has not changed. The transformation of probabilities shown in (38) accomplishes exactly what the first method did. Yet this second method operated on the probability measure $P(Z)$, rather than on the values of Z itself.

It is worth emphasizing that these new probabilities do not relate to the "true" odds of the experiment. The "true" probabilities associated with rolling the die are still given by the original numbers, P.

The reader may have noticed the notation we adopted. In fact, we need to write the new expectation operator as $E^{\tilde{P}}[\cdot]$, rather than $E[\cdot]$. The probabilities used in calculating the averages are no longer the same as P's, and the use of $E[\cdot]$ will be misleading. Clearly, when this method is used, special care should be given to designating the probability distribution utilized in calculating expectations under consideration.[7]

3 The Girsanov Theorem

The examples just discussed were clearly simplified. First, we dealt with random variables that were allowed to assume a finite number of values—the state space was finite. Second, we dealt with a single random variable instead of using a random process.

The Girsanov theorem provides the general framework for transforming one probability measure into another "equivalent" measure in more complicated cases. The theorem covers the case of Brownian motion. Hence, the state space is continuous, and the transformations are extended to continuous-time stochastic processes.

The probabilities so transformed are called "equivalent" because, as we will see in more detail later in this chapter, they assign positive probabilities to the same domains. Thus, although the two probability distributions are different, with appropriate transformations one can always recover one measure from the other. Since such recoveries are always possible, we may want to use the "convenient" distribution for our calculations, and then, if desired, switch back to the original distribution.

---

[7]Some readers may wonder how we found the new probabilities $\tilde{P}(Z)$. In this particular case, it was easy. We considered the probabilities as unknowns and used three conditions to solve for them. The first condition is that the probabilities sum to one. The second is that the new mean is one. The third is that the variance equals 98/3.

Accordingly, if we have to calculate an expectation and if this expectation is easier to calculate with an equivalent measure, then it may be worth switching probabilities, although the new measure may not be the one that governs the true states of nature. After all, the purpose is not to make a statement about the odds of various states of nature. The purpose is to calculate a quantity in a convenient fashion.

The general method can be summarized as follows: (1) We have an expectation to calculate. (2) We transform the original probability measure so that the expectation becomes easier to calculate. (3) We calculate the expectation under the new probability. (4) Once the result is calculated *and* if desired, we transform this probability back to the original distribution.

We now discuss such probability transformations in more complex settings. The Girsanov theorem will be introduced using special cases with growing complexity. Then we provide the general theorem and discuss its assumptions and implications.

3.1 A Normally Distributed Random Variable

Fix t and consider a normally distributed random variable z_t:

$$z_t \sim N(0, 1). \qquad (41)$$

Denote the density function of z_t by $f(z_t)$ and the implied probability measure by P such that

$$dP(z_t) = \frac{1}{\sqrt{2\pi}} e^{-\frac{1}{2}(z_t)^2} \, dz_t. \qquad (42)$$

Note that in this example the state space is continuous, although we are still working with a single random variable, instead of a random process.

Next, define the function

$$\xi(z_t) = e^{z_t \mu - \frac{1}{2}\mu^2}. \qquad (43)$$

When we multiply $\xi(z_t)$ by $dP(z_t)$, we obtain a new probability. This can be seen from the following:

$$[dP(z_t)][\xi(z_t)] = \frac{1}{\sqrt{2\pi}} e^{-\frac{1}{2}(z_t^2) + \mu z_t - \frac{1}{2}\mu^2} \, dz_t. \qquad (44)$$

After grouping the terms in the exponent, we obtain the expression

$$d\tilde{P}(z_t) = \frac{1}{\sqrt{2\pi}} e^{-\frac{1}{2}[z_t - \mu]^2} \, dz. \qquad (45)$$

Clearly $d\tilde{P}(z_t)$ is a *new* probability measure, defined by

$$d\tilde{P}(z_t) = dP(z_t)\xi(z_t). \qquad (46)$$

By simply reading from the density in (45), we see that $\tilde{P}(z_t)$ is the probability associated with a normally distributed random variable mean μ and variance 1.

It turns out that by multiplying $dP(z_t)$ by the function $\xi(z_t)$, and then switching to $\tilde{P}$, we succeeded in changing the mean of z_t. Note that in this particular case, the multiplication with $\xi(z_t)$ preserved the shape of the probability measure. In fact, (45) is still a bell-shaped, Gaussian curve with the same variance. But $P(z_t)$ and $\tilde{P}(z_t)$ *are* different measures. They have different *means* and they assign *different* weights to intervals on the z-axis.

Under the measure $P(z_t)$, the random variable z_t has mean zero, $E^P[z_t] = 0$ and variance, $E^P[z_t^2] = 1$. However, under the new probability measure $\tilde{P}(z_t)$, z_t has mean $E^{\tilde{P}}[z_t] = \mu$. The variance is unchanged.

What we have just shown is that there exists a function $\xi(z_t)$ such that if we multiply a probability measure by this function, we get a new probability. The resulting random variable is again normal but has a different mean.

Finally, the transformation of measures

$$d\tilde{P}(z_t) = \xi(z_t)\,dP(z_t) \tag{47}$$

that changed the mean of the random variable z_t is reversible:

$$\xi(z_t)^{-1}d\tilde{P}(z_t) = dP(z_t). \tag{48}$$

The transformation leaves the variance of z_t unchanged, and is unique, given μ and σ.

We can now summarize the two methods:[8]

- Method 1: Subtraction of means. Given a random variable

$$Z \sim N(\mu, 1), \tag{49}$$

define a new random variable $\tilde{Z}$ by transforming Z:

$$\tilde{Z} = \frac{Z - \mu}{1} \sim N(0, 1). \tag{50}$$

Then $\tilde{Z}$ will have a zero mean.
- Method 2: Using equivalent measures. Given a random variable Z with probability P,

$$Z \sim P = N(\mu, 1), \tag{51}$$

transform the probabilities dP through multiplication by $\xi(Z)$ and obtain a new probability $\tilde{P}$ such that

$$Z \sim \tilde{P} = N(0, 1). \tag{52}$$

[8]We simplify the notation slightly.

The next question is whether we can accomplish the same transformations if we are given a *sequence* of normally distributed random variables, $z_1, z_2, \ldots, z_t$.

3.2 A Normally Distributed Vector

The previous example showed how the mean of a normally distributed random variable could be changed by multiplying the corresponding probability measure by a function $\xi(z_t)$. The transformed measure was shown to be another probability that assigned a different mean to z_t, although the variance remained the same.

Can we proceed in a similar way if we are given a *vector* of normally distributed variables?

The answer is yes. For simplicity we show the bivariate case. Extension to an n-variate Gaussian vector is analogous.

With fixed t, suppose we are given the random variables z_{1t}, z_{2t}, *jointly* distributed as normal. The corresponding density will be

$$f(z_{1t}, z_{2t}) = \frac{1}{2\pi\sqrt{|\Omega|}} e^{-\frac{1}{2}[(z_{1t}-\mu_1) \quad (z_{2t}-\mu_2)]\begin{bmatrix}\sigma_1^2 & \sigma_{12}\\ \sigma_{12} & \sigma_2^2\end{bmatrix}^{-1}\begin{bmatrix}(z_{1t}-\mu_1)\\ (z_{2t}-\mu_2)\end{bmatrix}}, \quad (53)$$

where Ω is the variance covariance matrix of $[z_{1t}, z_{2t}]$,

$$\Omega = \begin{bmatrix} \sigma_1^2 & \sigma_{12}\\ \sigma_{12} & \sigma_2^2 \end{bmatrix}, \quad (54)$$

with σ_i^2, $i = 1, 2$ denoting the variances and σ_{12} the covariance between z_{1t}, z_{2t}. The $|\Omega|$ represents the determinant:

$$|\Omega| = \sigma_1^2\sigma_2^2 - \sigma_{12}^2. \quad (55)$$

Finally, μ_1, μ_2 are the means corresponding to z_{1t} and z_{2t}.

The joint probability measure can be defined using

$$dP(z_{1t}, z_{2t}) = f(z_{1t}, z_{2t})\, dz_{1t}\, dz_{2t}. \quad (56)$$

This expression is the probability mass associated with a small *rectangle* $dz_{1t}dz_{2t}$ centered at a particular value for the pair z_{1t}, z_{2t}. It gives the probability that z_{1t}, z_{2t} will fall in that particular rectangle *jointly*. Hence the name joint density function.

Suppose we want to change the means of z_{1t}, z_{2t} from μ_1, μ_2 to zero, while leaving the variances unchanged. Can we accomplish this by transforming the probability $dP(z_{1t}, z_{2t})$ just as in the previous example, namely, by multiplying by a function $\xi(z_{1t}, z_{2t})$?

The answer is yes. Consider the function defined by

$$\xi(z_{1t}, z_{2t}) = e^{-[z_{1t} \quad z_{2t}]\begin{bmatrix} \sigma_1^2 & \sigma_{12} \\ \sigma_{12} & \sigma_2^2 \end{bmatrix}^{-1}\begin{bmatrix} \mu_1 \\ \mu_2 \end{bmatrix} + \frac{1}{2}[\mu_1 \quad \mu_2]\begin{bmatrix} \sigma_1^2 & \sigma_{12} \\ \sigma_{12} & \sigma_2^2 \end{bmatrix}^{-1}\begin{bmatrix} \mu_1 \\ \mu_2 \end{bmatrix}}. \qquad (57)$$

Using this we can define a new probability measure $\tilde{P}(z_{1t}, z_{2t})$ by

$$d\tilde{P}(z_{1t}, z_{2t}) = \xi(z_{1t}, z_{2t})\, dP(z_{1t}, z_{2t}). \qquad (58)$$

$\tilde{P}(z_{1t}, z_{2t})$ can be obtained by multiplying expression (53) by $\xi(z_{1t}, z_{2t})$, shown in (57). The product of these two expressions gives

$$d\tilde{P}(z_{1t}, z_{2t}) = \left[\frac{1}{2\pi\sqrt{|\Omega|}} e^{-\frac{1}{2}[z_{1t} \quad z_{2t}]\begin{bmatrix} \sigma_1^2 & \sigma_{12} \\ \sigma_{12} & \sigma_2^2 \end{bmatrix}^{-1}\begin{bmatrix} z_{1t} \\ z_{2t} \end{bmatrix}}\right] dz_{1t}\, dz_{2t}. \qquad (59)$$

We recognize this as the bivariate normal probability for a random vector $[z_{1t}z_{2t}]$ with mean zero and variance–covariance matrix Ω. The multiplication by $\xi(z_{1t}, z_{2t})$ accomplished the stated objective. The nonzero mean of the bivariate vector was eliminated through a transformation of the underlying probabilities.

This example dealt with a bivariate random vector. Exactly the same transformation can be applied if instead we have a random sequence of k normally distributed random variables, $[z_{1t}, z_{2t}, \ldots, z_{kt}]$. Only the orders of the corresponding vectors and matrices in (53) need to be changed, with similar adjustments in (57).

3.2.1 A Note
With future discussion in mind, we would like to emphasize one regularity that the reader may already have observed.

Think of z_t as representing a vector of length k, or simply as a univariate random variable. In transforming the probability measures $P(z_t)$ into $\tilde{P}(z_t)$, the function $\xi(z_t)$ was utilized. This function had the following structure,

$$\xi(z_t) = e^{-z_t'\Omega^{-1}\mu + \frac{1}{2}\mu'\Omega^{-1}\mu}, \qquad (60)$$

which in the scalar case became

$$\xi(z_t) = e^{-\frac{z_t\mu}{\sigma^2} + \frac{1}{2}\frac{\mu^2}{\sigma^2}}. \qquad (61)$$

We will now discuss where this functional form comes from. In normal distributions, the parameter μ, which represents the mean, shows up only as an exponent of e. What is more, this exponent is in the form of a square:

$$-\frac{1}{2}\frac{(z_t - \mu)^2}{\sigma^2}. \qquad (62)$$

In order to convert this expression into

$$-\frac{1}{2}\frac{(z_t)^2}{\sigma^2},\qquad(63)$$

we need to add

$$\frac{-z_t\mu+1/2\mu^2}{\sigma^2}.\qquad(64)$$

This is what determines the functional form of $\xi(z_t)$. Multiplying the original probability measure by $\xi(z_t)$ accomplishes this transformation in the exponent of the e.

Given this, a reader may wonder if we could attach a deeper interpretation of what the $\xi(z_t)$ really represents. The next section discusses this point.

3.3 The Radon–Nikodym Derivative

Consider again the function $\xi(z_t)$ with $\sigma = 1$:[9]

$$\xi(z_t) = e^{-\mu z_t+\frac{1}{2}\mu^2}.\qquad(67)$$

We used the $\xi(z_t)$ in obtaining the new probability measure $\tilde{P}(z_t)$ from $dP(z_t)$:

$$d\tilde{P}(z_t) = \xi(z_t)dP(z_t).\qquad(68)$$

Or, dividing both sides by $dP(z_t)$:

$$\frac{d\tilde{P}(z_t)}{dP(z_t)} = \xi(z_t).\qquad(69)$$

This expression can be regarded as a derivative. It reads as if the "derivative" of the measure $\tilde{P}$ with respect to P is given by $\xi(z_t)$. Such derivatives are called Radon–Nikodym derivatives, and $\xi(z_t)$ can be regarded as the *density* of the probability measure $\tilde{P}$ with respect to the measure P.

According to this, if the Radon–Nikodym derivative of $\tilde{P}$ with respect to P exists, then we can use the resulting density $\xi(z_t)$ to transform the mean of z_t by leaving its variance structure unchanged.

[9]Incidentally, the function

$$\xi(z_t) = e^{-\mu z_t+\frac{1}{2}\mu^2}\qquad(65)$$

subtracts a mean from z_t, whereas the function

$$\xi(z_t)^{-1} = e^{\mu z_t-\frac{1}{2}\mu^2}\qquad(66)$$

would *add* a mean μ to a z with an original mean of zero.

Clearly, such a transformation is very useful for a financial market participant, since the risk premiums of asset prices can be "eliminated" while leaving the volatility structure intact. In the case of options, for example, the option price does not depend on the mean growth of the underlying asset price, whereas the volatility of the latter is a fundamental determinant. In such circumstances, transforming original probability distributions using $\xi(z_t)$ would be very convenient.

In Figure 4, we show one example of this function $\xi(z_t)$.

3.4 Equivalent Measures

When would the Radon–Nikodym derivative

$$\frac{d\tilde{P}(z_t)}{dP(z_t)} = \xi(z_t) \tag{70}$$

exist? That is, when would we be able to perform transformations such as

$$d\tilde{P}(z_t) = \xi(z_t)dP(z_t)? \tag{71}$$

In heuristic terms, note that in order to write the ratio

$$\frac{d\tilde{P}(z_t)}{dP(z_t)} \tag{72}$$

meaningfully, we need the probability mass in the denominator to be different from zero. To perform the inverse transformation, we need the numerator to be different from zero. But the numerator and the denominator are probabilities assigned to infinitesimal intervals dz. Hence, in order for the Radon–Nikodym derivative to exist, when $\tilde{P}$ assigns a nonzero probability to dz, so must P, and vice versa. In other words:

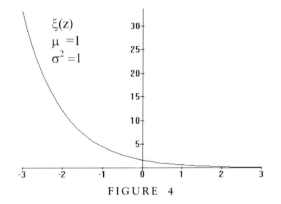

FIGURE 4

CONDITION: Given an interval dz_t, the probabilities P and $\tilde{P}$ satisfy

$$\tilde{P}(dz) > 0 \qquad \text{if and only if} \qquad P(dz) > 0. \qquad (73)$$

If this condition is satisfied, then $\xi(z_t)$ would exist, and we can always go back and forth between the two measures $\tilde{P}$ and P using the relations

$$d\tilde{P}(z_t) = \xi(z_t)\, dP(z_t) \qquad (74)$$

and

$$dP(z_t) = \xi(z_t)^{-1}\, d\tilde{P}(z_t). \qquad (75)$$

This means that, for all practical purposes, the two measures are *equivalent.* Hence, they are called *equivalent probability measures.*

4 Statement of the Girsanov Theorem

In applications of continuous-time finance, the examples provided thus far will be of limited use. Continuous-time finance deals with continuous or right continuous stochastic processes, whereas the transformations thus far involved only a *finite* sequence of random variables. The Girsanov theorem provides the conditions under which the Radon–Nikodym derivative $\xi(z_t)$ exists for cases where z_t is a continuous stochastic process. Transformations of probability measures in continuous finance use this theorem.

We first state the formal version of the Girsanov theorem. A motivating discussion follows afterwards.

The setting of the Girsanov theorem is the following. We are given a family of information sets $\{I_t\}$ over a period $[0, T]$. T is finite.[10]

Over this interval, we define a random process ξ_t:

$$\xi_t = e^{\left(\int_0^t X_u\, dW_u - \frac{1}{2}\int_0^t X_u^2\, du\right)}, \qquad t \in [0, T], \qquad (76)$$

where X_t is an I_t-measurable process.[11] The W_t is a Wiener process with probability distribution P.

We impose an additional condition on X_t. X_t should not vary "too much":

$$E\left[e^{\int_0^t X_u^2\, du}\right] < \infty, \qquad t \in [0, T]. \qquad (77)$$

---

[10]Note that this is not a very serious restriction in the case of financial derivatives. Almost all financial derivatives have finite expiration dates. Often, the maturity of the derivative instrument is less than one year.

[11]That is, given the information set I_t, the value of X_t is known exactly.

This means that X_t cannot increase (or decrease) "too fast" over time. Equation (77) is known as the Novikov condition.

In continuous time, the density ξ_t has a "new" property that turns out to be very important. It turns out that if the Novikov condition is satisfied, then ξ_t will be a square integrable martingale. We first show this explicitly.

Using Ito's lemma, calculate the differential

$$d\xi_t = \left[e^{(\int_0^t X_u\, dW_u - \frac{1}{2}\int_0^t X_u^2\, du)}\right][X_t\, dW_t], \tag{78}$$

which reduces to:

$$d\xi_t = \xi_t X_t\, dW_t. \tag{79}$$

Also, we see by simple substitution of $t = 0$ in (76):

$$\xi_0 = 1. \tag{80}$$

Thus, by taking the stochastic integral of (79):

$$\xi_t = 1 + \int_0^t \xi_s X_s\, dW_s. \tag{81}$$

But the term

$$\int_0^t \xi_s X_s\, dW_s \tag{82}$$

is a stochastic integral with respect to a Wiener process. Also, the term $\xi_s X_s$ is I_t-adapted and does not move "too fast." All these imply, as shown in Chapter 6, that the integral is a (square integrable) martingale,

$$E\left[\int_0^t \xi_s X_s\, dW_s | I_u\right] = \int_0^u \xi_s X_s\, dW_s, \tag{83}$$

where $u < t$.

Due to (81), this implies that ξ_t is a (square integrable) martingale. We are now ready to state the Girsanov theorem.

THEOREM: If the process ξ_t defined by (76) is a martingale with respect to information sets I_t, then $\tilde{W}_t$, defined by

$$\tilde{W}_t = W_t - \int_0^t X_u\, du, \qquad t \in [0, T], \tag{84}$$

is a Wiener process with respect to I_t and the probability measure $\tilde{P}_T$ given by

$$\tilde{P}_T(A) = E^P[1_A \xi_T], \tag{85}$$

with A being an event in I_T and 1_A being the indicator function of the event.

In heuristic terms, this theorem says the following. If we are given a Wiener process W_t, then multiplying the probability distribution of this process by ξ_t, we can obtain a *new* Wiener process $\tilde{W}_t$ with probability distribution $\tilde{P}$. The two processes are related to each other through

$$d\tilde{W}_t = dW_t - X_t\,dt. \tag{86}$$

That is, $\tilde{W}_t$ is obtained by subtracting an I_t-adapted drift from W_t.

The main condition for performing such transformations is that ξ_t is a martingale with $E[\xi_T] = 1$.

We now discuss the notation and the assumptions of the Girsanov theorem in detail. The proof of the theroem can be found in Liptser and Shiryayev (1977).

5 A Discussion of the Girsanov Theorem

In this section we go over the notation and the assumptions used in the Girsanov theorem systematically, and relate them to previously discussed examples. We also show their relevance to concepts in financial models.

We begin with the function ξ_t

$$\xi_t = e^{\frac{1}{\sigma^2}[\int_0^t X_u\,dW_u - \frac{1}{2}\int_0^t X_u^2\,du]}, \tag{87}$$

where we explicitly factored out the (constant) σ^2 term from the integrals. Alternatively, this term can be incorporated in X_u.

Suppose the X_u was constant and equaled μ:

$$X_u = \mu. \tag{88}$$

Then, taking the integrals in the exponent in a straightforward fashion and remembering that $W_0 = 0$,

$$\xi_t = e^{\frac{1}{\sigma^2}[\mu W_t - \frac{1}{2}\mu^2 t]}, \tag{89}$$

which is similar to the $\xi(z_t)$ discussed earlier. This shows the following important points:

1. The symbol X_t used in the Girsanov theorem plays the same role μ played in simpler settings. It measures how much the original "mean" will be changed.
2. In earlier examples, μ was time independent. Here, X_t may depend on any random quantity, as long as this random quantity is known by time t. That is the meaning of making X_t I_t-adapted. Hence, much more complicated drift transformations are allowed for.
3. The ξ_t is a martingale with $E[\xi_t] = 1$.

Next, consider the Wiener process $\tilde{W}_t$. There is something counterintuitive about this process. It turns out that *both* $\tilde{W}_t$ and W_t are standard Wiener processes. Thus, they do not have any drift. Yet they relate to each other by

$$d\tilde{W}_t = dW_t - X_t\,dt, \tag{90}$$

which means that at least *one* on these processes must have nonzero drift if X_t is not identical to zero. How can we explain this seemingly contradictory point?

The point is, $\tilde{W}_t$ has zero drift under $\tilde{P}$, whereas W_t has zero drift under P. Hence, $\tilde{W}_t$ can be used to represent unpredictable errors in dynamic systems *given that* we switch the probability measures from P to $\tilde{P}$.

Also, because $\tilde{W}_t$ contains a term $-X_t dt$, using it as an error term in lieu of W_t would reduce the drift of the original SDE under consideration exactly by $-X_t dt$. If the X_t is interpreted as the time-dependent risk premium, the transformation would make all risky assets grow at a risk-free rate.

Finally, consider the relation

$$\tilde{P}_T(A) = E^P[1_A \xi_T]. \tag{91}$$

What is the meaning of 1_A? How can we motivate this relation?

1_A is simply a function that has value 1 if A occurs. In fact, we can rewrite the preceding equation as

$$\tilde{P}_T(A) = E^P[1_A \xi_T] = \int_A \xi_T\,dP. \tag{92}$$

In the case where A is an infinitesimal interval, this means

$$d\tilde{P}_T = \xi_T\,dP, \tag{93}$$

which is similar to the probability transformations seen earlier in much simpler settings.

5.1 Application to SDEs

We give a heuristic example.

Let dS_t denote incremental changes in a stock price. Assume that these changes are driven by infinitesimal shocks that have a normal distribution, so that we can represent S_t using the stochastic differential equation driven by the Wiener process W_t

$$dS_t = \mu\,dt + \sigma\,dW_t, \qquad t \in [0, \infty), \tag{94}$$

with $W_0 = 0.$[12] The W_t is assumed to have the probability distribution P, with

$$dP(W_t) = \frac{1}{\sqrt{2\pi t}} e^{-\frac{1}{2t}(W_t)^2} dW_t. \tag{95}$$

Clearly, S_t cannot be a martingale if the drift term $\mu \, dt$ is nonzero. Recall that

$$S_t = \mu \int_0^t ds + \sigma \int_0^t dW_s, \qquad t \in [0, \infty) \tag{96}$$

or

$$S_t = \mu t + \sigma W_t. \tag{97}$$

We can write

$$E[S_{t+s}|S_t] = \mu(t+s) + \sigma E[W_{t+s} - W_t|S_t] + \sigma W_t \tag{98}$$

$$= S_t + \mu s, \tag{99}$$

since $[W_{t+s} - W_t]$ is unpredictable given S_t. Thus, for $\mu > 0, s > 0$:

$$E[S_{t+s}|S_t] > S_t. \tag{100}$$

S_t is not a martingale.

Yet we can easily *convert* S_t into a martingale by eliminating its drift. One method, discussed earlier, was to subtract an appropriate mean from S_t and define

$$\tilde{S}_t = S_t - \mu t. \tag{101}$$

Then $\tilde{S}_t$ will be a martingale.

One disadvantage of this transformation is that in order to obtain $\tilde{S}_t$, one would need to know μ. But μ incorporates any risk premium that the risky stock return has. In general, such risk premiums are not known *before* one finds the fair market value of the asset.

The second method to convert S_t into a martingale is much more promising. Using the Girsanov theorem, we could easily switch to an equivalent measure $\tilde{P}$, so that the drift of S_t is zero.

To do this, we have to come up with a function $\xi(S_t)$, and multiply it by the original probability measure associated with S_t. S_t may be a *sub*martingale under P

$$E^P[S_{t+s}|S_t] > S_t, \tag{102}$$

---

[12]This formulation again permits for negative prices at positive probability. We use it because it is notationally convenient. In any case, the geometric SDE will be dealt with in the next chapter.

but it will be a martingale under $\tilde{P}$:

$$E^{\tilde{P}}\left[S_{t+s}|S_t\right] = S_t. \tag{103}$$

As usual, the superscript of the $E[\cdot|\cdot]$ operator represents the probability measure used to evaluate the expectation.

In order to perform this transformation, a $\xi(S_t)$ function needs to be calculated. First recall that the density of S_t is given by

$$f_s = \frac{1}{\sqrt{2\pi\sigma^2 t}}e^{-\frac{1}{2\sigma^2 t}(S_t - \mu t)^2}. \tag{104}$$

This defines the probability measure P.

We would like to switch to a new probability $\tilde{P}$ such that under P, S_t becomes a martingale.

Define

$$\xi(S_t) = e^{-\frac{1}{\sigma^2}[\mu S_t - \frac{1}{2}\mu^2 t]}. \tag{105}$$

Multiply f_s by this $\xi(S_t)$ to get

$$d\tilde{P}(S_t) = \xi(S_t)\,dP(S_t)$$
$$= e^{-\frac{1}{\sigma^2}[\mu S_t - \frac{1}{2}\mu^2 t]}\frac{1}{\sqrt{2\pi\sigma^2 t}}e^{-\frac{1}{2\sigma^2 t}(S_t - \mu t)^2}\,dS_t. \tag{106}$$

Or, rearranging the exponents:

$$= \frac{1}{\sqrt{2\pi\sigma^2 t}}e^{-\frac{1}{2\sigma^2 t}(S_t)^2}\,dS_t. \tag{107}$$

But this is a probability measure associated with a normally distributed process with zero drift and diffusion σ. That means we can write the increments of S_t in terms of a *new* driving term $\tilde{W}_t$:

$$dS_t = \sigma d\tilde{W}_t. \tag{108}$$

Such an S_t process was shown to be a martingale. The Weiner process $\tilde{W}_t$ is defined with respect to probability $\tilde{P}$.

6 Conclusions

As conclusions, we review some of the important steps of transforming the S_t into a martingale process.

- The transformation was done by switching the distribution of S_t from P to $\tilde{P}$. This was accomplished by using a new error term $\tilde{W}_t$.
- This new error term $\tilde{W}_t$ still had the same variance.

- What distinguishes representation (108) from (94) is that the mean of S_t is altered, *while* preserving the zero mean property of the error terms. This was accomplished by changing the distributions, rather than "subtracting a constant" from the underlying random variable.
- More importantly, in this example, the transformation was used to convert S_t into a martingale. In financial models, one may want to apply the transformation to $e^{-rt}S_t$ rather than S_t. $e^{-rt}S_t$ would represent the discounted value of the asset price, where the discount is done with respect to the (risk-free) rate r. Obviously, the $\xi(S_t)$ function has to be redefined in order to accomplish this.

7 References

Transforming stochastic processes into martingales through the use of Girsanov theorem is a deeper topic in stochastic calculus. Hence, the sources that provide the technical background of this method will all be at an advanced level. Karatzas and Shreve (1991) provides one of the more intuitive discussions. Liptser and Shiryayev (1977) is a comprehensive reference.

CHAPTER 15

Equivalent Martingale Measures

Applications

1 Introduction

In this chapter we show how the method of equivalent martingale measures can be applied. We use option pricing to do this. We know that there are two ways of calculating the arbitrage-free price of a European call option C_t written on a stock S_t that does not pay any dividends.

1. The original Black–Scholes approach, where (1) a riskless portfolio is formed, (2) a partial differential equation in $F(S_t, t)$ is obtained, and (3) the PDE is solved either directly or numerically.
2. The martingale methods, where one finds a "synthetic" probability $\tilde{P}$ under which S_t becomes a martingale. One then calculates

$$C_t = E^{\tilde{P}} e^{-r(T-t)}[\max(S_T - K, 0)] \tag{1}$$

again, either analytically or numerically.

The first major topic of this chapter is to provide a step-by-step treatment of the martingale approach. We begin with the assumptions set by Black and Scholes and show how to convert the (discounted) asset prices into martingales. This is done by finding an equivalent martingale measure $\tilde{P}$. This application does not use the Girsanov theorem directly.

The Girsanov theorem is applied explicitly in the second half of the chapter, where the correspondence between two approaches to asset pricing is also discussed. In particular, we show that converting (discounted) call prices into martingales is equivalent to forcing the $F(S_t, t)$ to satisfy a particular partial differential equation, which turns out to be the Black–Scholes PDE introduced earlier. We conclude that the PDE and the martingale approaches are closely related.

2 A Martingale Measure

The method of forming risk-free portfolios and using the resulting PDEs was discussed in Chapter 12, although a step-by-step derivation of the Black–Scholes formula was not provided there.

The method of equivalent martingale measures adopts a different way of obtaining the same formula. The derivation is tedious at points, but rests on straightforward mathematics and consequently is conceptually very simple. We will provide a step-by-step derivation of the Black–Scholes formula using this approach.

First, some intermediate results need to be discussed. These results are important in their own right, since they occur routinely in asset pricing formulas.

2.1 The Moment-Generating Function

Now let Y_t be a continuous-time process[1]

$$Y_t \sim N(\mu t, \sigma^2 t), \tag{2}$$

with Y_0 given.

We define S_t as the geometric process

$$S_t = S_0 e^{Y_t}. \tag{3}$$

Note that S_0 is the initial point of S_t and is given exogenously.[2] We would like to obtain the moment-generating function of Y_t.

Recall that the moment-generating function denoted by $M(\lambda)$ is a specific expectation involving Y_t

$$M(\lambda) = E[e^{Y_t \lambda}], \tag{4}$$

where λ is an arbitrary parameter. The explicit form of this moment-generating function is useful in asset pricing formulas. More importantly, the types of calculations one has to go over to obtain the moment-generating function illustrate some "standard" operations in stochastic calculus. The following section is useful in this respect as well.

---

[1] Y_t is sometimes called a generalized Wiener process, because it obeys a normal distribution, has a nonzero mean, and has a variance not necessarily equal to one.

[2] S_0 may be random, as long as it is independent of Y_t.

2.1.1 Calculation

Using the distribution in (2), $E[e^{Y_t\lambda}]$ can be calculated explicitly. Substituting from the definition in (4), we can write

$$E[e^{Y_t\lambda}] = \int_{-\infty}^{\infty} e^{Y_t\lambda} \frac{1}{\sqrt{2\pi\sigma^2 t}} e^{-\frac{1}{2}\frac{(Y_t-\mu t)^2}{\sigma^2 t}} \, dY_t. \tag{5}$$

The expression inside the integral can be simplified by grouping together the exponents:

$$E[e^{\lambda Y_t}] = \int_{-\infty}^{\infty} \frac{1}{\sqrt{2\pi\sigma^2 t}} e^{-\frac{1}{2}\frac{(Y_t-\mu t)^2}{\sigma^2 t}+\lambda Y_t} \, dY_t. \tag{6}$$

In this expression, the exponent is not a perfect square, but can be completed into one by multiplying the right-hand side by

$$e^{-(\lambda\mu t+\frac{1}{2}\sigma^2 t\lambda^2)} e^{(\lambda\mu t+\frac{1}{2}\sigma^2 t\lambda^2)} = 1. \tag{7}$$

Then the equality in (6) becomes

$$E[e^{Y_t\lambda}] = \int_{-\infty}^{\infty} \frac{1}{\sqrt{2\pi\sigma^2 t}} e^{(\lambda\mu t+\frac{1}{2}\sigma^2 t\lambda^2)} e^{-\frac{1}{2}\frac{(Y_t-\mu t)^2}{\sigma^2 t}+Y_t\lambda-(\lambda\mu t+\frac{1}{2}\sigma^2 t\lambda^2)} \, dY_t. \tag{8}$$

The exponent of the second exponential function can now be completed into a square. The terms that do not depend on Y_t can be factored out. Doing this we get

$$E[e^{Y_t\lambda}] = e^{(\lambda\mu t+\frac{1}{2}\sigma^2\lambda^2 t)} \int_{-\infty}^{\infty} \frac{1}{\sqrt{2\pi\sigma^2 t}} e^{-\frac{1}{2}\frac{(Y_t-(\mu t+\sigma^2 t\lambda))^2}{\sigma^2 t}} \, dY_t. \tag{9}$$

But the integral on the right-hand side of this expression is the area under the density of a normally distributed random variable. Hence, it sums to one. We obtain

$$M(\lambda) = e^{\lambda\mu t+\frac{1}{2}\sigma^2 t\lambda^2}. \tag{10}$$

The moment-generating function is a useful tool in statistics. If its kth derivative with respect to λ is calculated, and evaluated at $\lambda = 0$, one finds the kth moment of the random variable in question.

For example, the first moment of Y_t can be calculated by taking the derivative of (10) with respect to λ:

$$\frac{\partial M}{\partial \lambda} = (\mu t + \sigma^2 t\lambda)e^{\lambda\mu t+\frac{1}{2}\sigma^2 t\lambda^2}. \tag{11}$$

Now substitute 0 for λ in this formula to get

$$\frac{\partial M}{\partial \lambda}\bigg|_{\lambda=0} = \mu t. \tag{12}$$

For the second moment, we take the second derivative and set λ equal to zero:

$$\left.\frac{\partial^2 M}{\partial \lambda^2}\right|_{\lambda=0} = \sigma^2 t. \tag{13}$$

These are useful properties. But they are of secondary importance in asset pricing. The usefulness of the moment-generating formula in asset pricing is tied to Equation (10). We exploit the relationship

$$E[e^{\lambda Y_t}] = e^{\lambda \mu t + \frac{1}{2}\sigma^2 t \lambda^2} \tag{14}$$

as a result by itself. At several points later we have to take expectations of geometric processes. The foregoing result is very convenient, in that it gives an explicit formula for expectations involving geometric processes.

2.2 Conditional Expectation of Geometric Processes

In pricing financial derivatives using martingale methods, one expression that needs to be evaluated is the conditional expectation $E[S_t | S_u, u < t]$, where S_t is the geometric process discussed earlier. This is the second intermediate result that we need before proceeding with martingale methods.

We use the same assumptions as in the previous section and assume that

$$S_t = S_0 e^{Y_t}, \qquad t \in [0, \infty), \tag{15}$$

where Y_t again had the distribution

$$Y_t \sim N(\mu t, \sigma^2 t). \tag{16}$$

By definition, it is always true that

$$Y_t = Y_s + \int_s^t dY_u. \tag{17}$$

Define ΔY_t by

$$\Delta Y_t = \int_s^t dY_u. \tag{18}$$

Note that, by the definition of generalized Wiener processes,

$$\Delta Y_t \sim N(\mu(t-s), \sigma^2(t-s)). \tag{19}$$

Thus, ΔY_t is a normally distributed random variable as well. According to calculations of the previous section, its moment-generating function is given by

$$M(\lambda) = e^{\lambda \mu (t-s) + \frac{1}{2}\sigma^2 \lambda^2 (t-s)}. \tag{20}$$

Using these, we can calculate the conditional expectation of a geometric Brownian motion. Begin with

$$E\left[\frac{S_t}{S_u}\Big|S_u, u < t\right] = E[e^{\Delta Y_t}|S_u],\tag{21}$$

since S_u can be treated as nonrandom. Recall that ΔY_t is independent of Y_u, $u < t$. This means that

$$E[e^{\Delta Y_t}|S_u] = E[e^{\Delta Y_t}].\tag{22}$$

But $E[e^{\Delta Y_t}]$ is the moment-generating function in (10) evaluated at $\lambda = 1$. Substituting this value of λ in (10), we get

$$E[e^{\Delta Y_t}] = e^{\mu(t-s)+\frac{1}{2}\sigma^2(t-s)}\tag{23}$$

$$= E\left[\frac{S_t}{S_u}\Big|S_u\right].\tag{24}$$

Or, multiplying both sides by S_u,

$$E[S_t|S_u, u < t] = S_u e^{\mu(t-s)+\frac{1}{2}\sigma^2(t-s)}.\tag{25}$$

This formula gives the conditional expectation of a geometric process. It is routinely used in asset pricing theory and will be utilized during the following discussion.

3 Converting Asset Prices into Martingales

Suppose we have as before

$$S_t = S_0 e^{Y_t}, \qquad t \in [0, \infty),\tag{26}$$

where Y_t is a Wiener process whose distribution we label by P. Here, P is the "true" probability measure that is behind the infinitesimal shocks affecting the asset price S_t.

Observed values of S_t will occur according to the probabilities given by P. But this does not mean that a financial analyst would find this distribution most convenient to work with. In fact, according to the discussion in Chapter 14, one may be able to obtain an equivalent probability $\tilde{P}$ under which pricing assets becomes much easier. This will especially be the case if we work with probability measures that convert asset prices into martingales.

In this section we discuss an example of how to find such a probability measure.

Recall that the "true" distribution of S_t is determined by the distribution of Y_t. Hence, the probability P is given by

$$Y_t \sim N(\mu t, \sigma^2 t), \qquad t \in [0, \infty). \tag{27}$$

Now, assume that S_t represents the value of an underlying asset at time t, and let $S_u, u < t$ be a price observed at an earlier date u.

First of all, we know that because the asset S_t is risky when discounted by the risk-free rate, it cannot be a martingale. In other words, under the true probability measure P, we *cannot* have

$$E^P[e^{-rt}S_t|S_u, u < t] = e^{-ru}S_u. \tag{28}$$

In fact, because of the existence of a risk premium, in general, we have

$$E^P[e^{-rt}S_t|S_u, u < t] > e^{-ru}S_u, \tag{29}$$

and, under the "true" probability measure P, the discounted process Z_t defined by

$$Z_t = e^{-rt}S_t \tag{30}$$

cannot be a martingale.

Yet, the ideas introduced in Chapter 14 can be used to change the drift of Z_t and convert it into a martingale. Under some conditions, we might be able to find an equivalent probability measure $\tilde{P}$, such that the equality

$$E^{\tilde{P}}[e^{-rt}S_t|S_u, u < t] = e^{-ru}S_u \tag{31}$$

is satisfied. This can also be expressed using Z_t:

$$E^{\tilde{P}}[Z_t|Z_u, u < t] = Z_u. \tag{32}$$

The drift in dZ_t will be zero as one switches the driving error term from the Wiener process W_t to a new process $\tilde{W}_t$ with distribution $\tilde{P}$.

The question is how to find such a probability measure $\tilde{P}$. We do this explicitly in the next section.

3.1 Determining $\tilde{P}$

Our problem is the following. We need to find a probability measure $\tilde{P}$ such that expectations calculated with it have the property

$$E^{\tilde{P}}[e^{-rt}S_t|S_u, u < t] = e^{-ru}S_u. \tag{33}$$

That is, S_t becomes a martingale.[3]

How can we find such a $\tilde{P}$? And what is its form?

---

[3]As usual, we assume that S_t will satisfy other regularity conditions for being a martingale.

The step-by-step derivation that follows will answer this question. We know that

$$S_t = S_0 e^{Y_t}, \tag{34}$$

where Y_t has the distribution denoted by P:

$$Y_t \sim N(\mu t, \sigma^2 t). \tag{35}$$

Now, define a *new* probability $\tilde{P}$ by

$$N(\rho t, \sigma^2 t), \tag{36}$$

where the drift parameter ρ is arbitrary and is the only difference between the two measures P and $\tilde{P}$. In particular, note that both probabilities have the same variance parameter.

Now, we can evaluate the conditional expectation

$$E^{\tilde{P}}[e^{-r(t-u)}S_t | S_u, u < t] \tag{37}$$

using the probability given in (36). In fact, the formula for such a conditional expectation was derived earlier in Equation (25). We have

$$E^{\tilde{P}}[e^{-r(t-u)}S_t | S_u, u < t] = [S_u e^{-r(t-u)}]e^{\rho(t-u)+\frac{1}{2}\sigma^2(t-u)}. \tag{38}$$

Note that because the expectation is taken with respect to the probability $\tilde{P}$, the right-hand side of the formula depends on ρ instead of μ.

Recall that the parameter ρ in (36) was *arbitrary*. We can select it as desired, as long as the expectation under $\tilde{P}$ satisfies the martingale condition. In particular, define ρ as

$$\rho = r - \frac{1}{2}\sigma^2. \tag{39}$$

The parameter ρ is now fixed in terms of the volatility σ and the risk-free interest rate r. The important aspect of this choice for ρ is that the exponential on the right-hand side of (38) will equal one, since with this value of ρ,

$$-r(t - u) + \rho(t - u) + \frac{1}{2}\sigma^2(t - u) = 0. \tag{40}$$

Replacing this in (38):

$$E^{\tilde{P}}[e^{-r(t-u)}S_t | S_u, u < t] = S_u. \tag{41}$$

Transferring e^{ru} to the right,

$$E^{\tilde{P}}[e^{-rt}S_t | S_u, u < t] = e^{-ru}S_u. \tag{42}$$

This is the martingale condition. It implies that $e^{-rt}S_t$ has become a martingale under $\tilde{P}$.

Note that by determining a particular value for ρ, we were able to find a probability distribution under which expectations of asset prices had the martingale property. This distribution is normal in this particular case, and its form is given by

$$
N\left(\left(r - \frac{1}{2}\sigma^2\right)t, \sigma^2 t\right).
\tag{43}
$$

Clearly, this probability is different from the "true" probability measure P given in (35). The difference is in the mean.

3.2 The Implied SDEs

The previous section discussed how to determine an equivalent martingale measure $\tilde{P}$, when the "true" distribution of asset prices was governed by the probability measure P. It is instructive to compare the implied stochastic differential equations (SDE) under the two probability measures.

S_t was given by

$$
S_t = S_0 e^{Y_t}, \qquad t \in [0, \infty),
\tag{44}
$$

where Y_t was normally distributed with mean μt and variance $\sigma^2 t$. In other words, the increments dY_t have the representation

$$
dY_t = \mu\,dt + \sigma\,dW_t, \qquad t \in [0, \infty).
\tag{45}
$$

To get the SDE satisfied by S_t, we need to obtain the expression for stochastic differentials dS_t. Since S_t is a function of Y_t, and since we have a SDE for the latter, Ito's lemma can be used

$$
dS_t = [S_0 e^{Y_t}][\mu\,dt + \sigma\,dW_t] + [S_0 e^{Y_t}]\frac{1}{2}\sigma^2\,dt,
\tag{46}
$$

or, after substituting S_t and grouping:

$$
dS_t = \left[\mu S_t + \frac{1}{2}\sigma^2 S_t\right]dt + \sigma S_t\,dW_t.
\tag{47}
$$

Under the "true" probability P, the asset price S_t satisfies an SDE with

1. a drift coefficient $(\mu + (1/2)\sigma^2)S_t$,
2. a diffusion coefficient σS_t,
3. and a driving Wiener process W_t.

The SDE under the martingale measure $\tilde{P}$ is calculated in a similar fashion, with one major difference. The drift coefficient is now different.

To get this SDE we simply replace μ with ρ and W_t with $\tilde{W}_t$ in (47). By following the same steps, we obtain

$$dS_t = \left[\rho S_t + \frac{1}{2}\sigma^2 S_t\right] dt + \sigma S_t \, d\tilde{W}_t. \tag{48}$$

Here we emphasize, in passing, a critical step that may have gone unnoticed. By substituting $\tilde{W}_t$ in place of W_t, we are implicitly switching the underlying probability measures from P to $\tilde{P}$. This is the case because only under $\tilde{P}$ will the error term in Equation (48) be a *standard* Wiener process. If we continue to use P, the error terms $d\tilde{W}_t$ will have a nonzero drift.

In Equation (48), ρ can now be replaced by its value

$$\rho = r - \frac{1}{2}\sigma^2. \tag{49}$$

Substituting this in (48):

$$dS_t = \left[\left(r - \frac{1}{2}\sigma^2\right)S_t + \frac{1}{2}\sigma^2 S_t\right] dt + \sigma S_t \, d\tilde{W}_t. \tag{50}$$

The terms involving $(1/2)\sigma^2$ cancel out and we obtain the SDE:

$$dS_t = rS_t \, dt + \sigma S_t \, d\tilde{W}_t. \tag{51}$$

This is an interesting result. *The probability that makes S_t a martingale, switches the drift parameter of the original SDE to the risk-free interest rate r.* The μ contained a risk premium that is in general not known before S_t is calculated. The r, on the other hand, is the risk-free rate and is known by assumption.

Note the second difference between the two SDEs. The SDE in (51) is driven by a new Wiener process $\tilde{W}_t$, which has the distribution $\tilde{P}$. This $\tilde{P}$ has nothing to do with the actual occurrence of various states of the world. The probability measure P determines that. On the other hand, $\tilde{P}$ is a very convenient measure to work with. Under this measure, (discounted) asset prices are martingales, and this is a very handy property to have in valuing derivative assets. Also, we know from finance theory that under appropriate conditions, the existence of such a "synthetic" probability $\tilde{P}$ under which asset prices are martingales is guaranteed if there is no arbitrage.

4 Application: The Black–Scholes Formula

The Black–Scholes formula gives the price of a call option, $F(S_t, t)$, when the following conditions apply:

1. The risk-free interest rate is constant over the option's life.

2. The underlying security pays no dividends before the option matures.

3. The call option is of the European type, and thus cannot be exercised before the expiration date.

4. The price S_t of the underlying security is a geometric Brownian motion with drift and diffusion terms proportional to S_t.

5. Finally, there are no transaction costs, and assets are infinitely divisible.

Under these conditions, the Black–Scholes formula can be obtained by solving the following PDE analytically:

$$0 = -rF + F_t + rS_t F_s + \frac{1}{2}\sigma^2 S_t^2 F_{ss}, \qquad 0 \le S_t, \qquad 0 \le t \le T. \qquad (52)$$

The resulting formula is given by

$$F(S_t, t) = S_t N(d_1) - Ke^{-r(T-t)}N(d_1 - \sigma\sqrt{T-t}) \qquad (53)$$

with

$$d_1 = \frac{\ln(S_t/K) + r(T-t) + \frac{1}{2}\sigma^2(T-t)}{\sigma\sqrt{T-t}}. \qquad (54)$$

In these expressions, T is the expiration date of the call option, r is the risk-free interest rate, K is the strike price, and σ is the volatility. The function $N(x)$ is the probability that a standard normal random variable is less than x. For example, $N(d_1)$ is given by

$$N(d_1) = \int_{-\infty}^{d_1} \frac{1}{\sqrt{2\pi}} e^{-\frac{1}{2}x^2} \, dx. \qquad (55)$$

Let S_t be an underlying asset, and C_t the price of a European call option written on this asset. Assume the standard Black–Scholes framework, with no dividends, a constant risk-free rate, and no transaction costs.

Our objective in this section is to derive the Black–Scholes formula directly by using the equivalent martingale measure $\tilde{P}$.

The basic relation is the martingale property that the $e^{-rt}C_t$ must satisfy under the probability $\tilde{P}$,

$$C_t = E_t^{\tilde{P}}[e^{-r(T-t)}C_T], \qquad (56)$$

where $T > t$ is the expiration date of the call option.

We know that at expiration, the option's payoff will be $S_T - K$ if $S_T > K$. Otherwise, the call option expires with zero value. This permits one to write the boundary condition

$$C_T = \max[S_T - K, 0], \qquad (57)$$

and the martingale property for $e^{-rt}C_t$ implies

$$C_t = E_t^{\tilde{P}}[e^{-r(T-t)}\max\{S_T - K, 0\}].\tag{58}$$

In order to derive the Black–Scholes formula, this expectation will be calculated explicitly. The derivation is straightforward, yet involves lengthy expressions. Hence, it is best to simplify the notation. We make the following simplifications:

- We let $t = 0$ and calculate the option price as of time zero.
- Accordingly, the current information set I_t becomes I_0. This way, instead of using conditional expectations, we can use the unconditional expectation operator $E^{\tilde{P}}[\cdot]$.

We now proceed with the step-by-step derivation of the Black–Scholes formula by directly evaluating

$$C_0 = E^{\tilde{P}}[e^{-rT}\max\{S_T - K, 0\}]\tag{59}$$

using the probability measure $\tilde{P}$.

The probability $\tilde{P}$ is the equivalent martingale measure and was derived in the previous section,

$$d\tilde{P} = \frac{1}{\sqrt{2\pi\sigma^2 T}}e^{-\frac{1}{2\sigma^2 T}(Y_T - (r - \frac{1}{2}\sigma^2)T)^2}\,dY_T,\tag{60}$$

with:

$$S_T = S_0 e^{Y_T}.\tag{61}$$

Using this density we can directly evaluate the expression

$$C_0 = E^{\tilde{P}}[e^{-rT}\max\{S_T - K, 0\}],\tag{62}$$

which can be written as

$$C_0 = \int_{-\infty}^{\infty} e^{-rT}\max[S_T - K, 0]\,d\tilde{P},\tag{63}$$

where we also have:

$$S_T = S_0 e^{Y_T}.\tag{64}$$

Substituting these in (63):

$$C_0 = \int_{-\infty}^{\infty} e^{-rT}\max[S_0 e^{Y_T} - K, 0]\frac{1}{\sqrt{2\pi\sigma^2 T}}e^{-\frac{1}{2\sigma^2 T}(Y_T - (r - \frac{1}{2}\sigma^2)T)^2}\,dY_T.\tag{65}$$

To eliminate the *max* function from inside the integral, we change the limits of integration. We note that, after taking logarithms, the condition

$$S_0 e^{Y_T} \geq K\tag{66}$$

is equivalent to

$$Y_T \geq \ln\left(\frac{K}{S_0}\right). \tag{67}$$

Using this in (65):

$$C_0 = \int_{\ln(\frac{K}{S_0})}^{\infty} e^{-rT}(S_0 e^{Y_T} - K) \frac{1}{\sqrt{2\pi\sigma^2 T}} e^{-\frac{1}{2\sigma^2 T}(Y_T - (r - \frac{1}{2}\sigma^2)T)^2} \, dY_T. \tag{68}$$

The integral can be split into two pieces:

$$C_0 = S_0 \int_{\ln(\frac{K}{S_0})}^{\infty} e^{-rT} e^{Y_T} \frac{1}{\sqrt{2\pi\sigma^2 T}} e^{-\frac{1}{2\sigma^2 T}(Y_T - (r - \frac{1}{2}\sigma^2)T)^2} \, dY_T$$

$$- K e^{-rT} \int_{\ln(\frac{K}{S_0})}^{\infty} \frac{1}{\sqrt{2\pi\sigma^2 T}} e^{-\frac{1}{2\sigma^2 T}(Y_T - (r - \frac{1}{2}\sigma^2)T)^2} \, dY_T. \tag{69}$$

We can now evaluate the two integrals on the right-hand side of this expression separately.

4.1 Calculation

First we apply a transformation that simplifies the notation further. We define a new variable Z by

$$Z = \frac{Y_T - (r - \frac{1}{2}\sigma^2)T}{\sigma\sqrt{T}}. \tag{70}$$

This requires an adjustment of the lower integration limit, and the second integral on the right-hand side of (69) becomes

$$K e^{-rT} \int_{\ln(\frac{K}{S_0})}^{\infty} \frac{1}{\sqrt{2\pi\sigma^2 T}} e^{-\frac{1}{2\sigma^2 T}(Y_T - (r - \frac{1}{2}\sigma^2)T)^2} \, dY_T$$

$$= K e^{-rT} \int_{\frac{\ln(\frac{K}{S_0}) - (r - \frac{1}{2}\sigma^2)T}{\sigma\sqrt{T}}}^{\infty} \frac{1}{\sqrt{2\pi}} e^{-\frac{1}{2}Z^2} \, dZ. \tag{71}$$

But the lower limit of the integral is closely related to the parameter d_2 in the Black–Scholes formula.[4] Letting

$$-\ln(K/S_0) = \ln(S_0/K), \tag{73}$$

---

[4]To see why the limits of the integration change, note that when Y_T goes from $\ln(\frac{K}{S_0})$ to ∞, the transform Z defined by (70) will be between

$$\frac{\ln(\frac{K}{S_0}) - (r - \frac{1}{2}\sigma^2)T}{\sigma\sqrt{T}} \tag{72}$$

and infinity.

we obtain the d_2 parameter of the Black–Scholes formula:

$$-\frac{\ln(\frac{S_0}{K}) + (r - \frac{1}{2}\sigma^2)T}{\sigma\sqrt{T}} = -d_2. \tag{74}$$

Finally, we recall that the normal distribution has various symmetry properties. One of these states that with $f(x)$ *standard* normal density, we can write

$$\int_L^\infty f(x)\,dx = \int_{-\infty}^{-L} f(x)\,dx. \tag{75}$$

Using the transformations in (74) and (75), we write

$$Ke^{-rT} \int_{-d_2}^\infty \frac{1}{\sqrt{2\pi}} e^{-\frac{1}{2}Z^2}\,dZ = Ke^{-rT} \int_{-\infty}^{d_2} \frac{1}{\sqrt{2\pi}} e^{-\frac{1}{2}Z^2}\,dZ \tag{76}$$

$$= Ke^{-rT} N(d_2). \tag{77}$$

Hence, we derived the second part of the Black–Scholes formula, as well as the value of the parameter d_2.

Finally, we are left to derive the first part, $S_0 N(d_1)$, and show the connection between d_1 and d_2. This requires manipulating the first integral on the right-hand side of (69). As a first step, we again use the variable Z defined in (70):

$$\int_{\ln(\frac{K}{S_0})}^\infty e^{-rT} S_0 e^{Y_T} \frac{1}{\sqrt{2\pi\sigma^2 T}} e^{-\frac{1}{2\sigma^2 T}(Y_T - (r - \frac{1}{2}\sigma^2)T)^2}\,dY_T$$

$$= e^{(r - \frac{1}{2}\sigma^2)T} e^{-rT} S_0 \int_{-d_2}^\infty e^{\sigma Z\sqrt{T}} \frac{1}{\sqrt{2\pi}} e^{-\frac{1}{2}Z^2}\,dZ. \tag{78}$$

We transform the integral on the right-hand side, using properties of the normal density:

$$= e^{-rT} e^{(r - \frac{1}{2}\sigma^2)T} S_0 \int_{-\infty}^{d_2} \frac{1}{\sqrt{2\pi}} e^{-\frac{1}{2}(Z^2 + 2\sigma Z\sqrt{T})}\,dZ. \tag{79}$$

Next, we complete the square in the exponent by adding and subtracting

$$\frac{\sigma^2 T}{2}. \tag{80}$$

This gives:

$$= e^{-rT} S_0 e^{\frac{T\sigma^2}{2}} e^{(r - \frac{1}{2}\sigma^2)T} \int_{-\infty}^{d_2} \frac{1}{\sqrt{2\pi}} e^{-\frac{1}{2}(Z + \sigma\sqrt{T})^2}\,dZ. \tag{81}$$

Note that the terms in front of the integral cancel out except for S_0.

Finally, we make the substitution

$$H = Z + \sigma\sqrt{T} \tag{82}$$

to obtain

$$= S_0 \int_{-\infty}^{d_2 + \sigma\sqrt{T}} \frac{1}{\sqrt{2\pi}} e^{-\frac{1}{2}H^2} dH = S_0 N(d_1), \tag{83}$$

where

$$d_1 = d_2 + \sigma\sqrt{T}. \tag{84}$$

This gives the first part of the Black–Scholes formula and completes the derivation. We emphasize that during this derivation, no PDE was solved.

5 Comparing Martingale and PDE Approaches

We have seen two contrasting approaches that can be used to determine the fair market value of a derivative asset price. The first approach obtained the price of the derivative instrument by forming risk-free portfolios. Infinitesimal adjustments in portfolio weights and changes in the option price were used to replicate unexpected movements in the underlying asset, S_t. This eliminated all the risk from the portfolio, at the same time imposing restrictions on the way $F(S_t, t)$, S_t and the risk-free asset could jointly move over time. The assumption that we could make infinitesimal changes in positions played an important role here and showed the advantage of continuous-time asset pricing models.

The second method for pricing a derivative asset rested on the claim that we could find a probability measure $\tilde{P}$ such that under this probability, $e^{-rt}F(S_t, t)$ becomes a martingale. This means that

$$e^{-rt}F(S_t, t) = E^{\tilde{P}}[e^{-rT}F(S_T, T)|I_t], \qquad t < T, \tag{85}$$

or, heuristically, that the drift of the stochastic differential

$$d[e^{-rt}F(S_t, t)] \qquad 0 \le t \tag{86}$$

was zero.

The Black–Scholes formula can be obtained from either approach. One could either solve the fundamental PDE of Black and Scholes, or as we did earlier, one could calculate the expectation $E^{\tilde{P}}[e^{-rT}F(S_T, T)|I_t]$ explicitly using the equivalent measure $\tilde{P}$. In their original article, Black and Scholes chose the first path. The previous section derived the same formula using the martingale approach. This involved somewhat tedious manipulations, but was straightforward in terms of mathematical operations concerned.

Obviously, these two methods should be related in some way. In this section we show the correspondence between the two approaches.

The discussion is a good opportunity to apply some of the more advanced mathematical tools introduced thus far. In particular, the discussion will be another example of the following:

- Application of differential and integral forms of Ito's lemma,
- The martingale property of Ito integrals,
- An important use of the Girsanov theorem.

We show the correspondence between the PDE and martingale approaches in two stages. The first stage uses the symbolic form of Ito's lemma. It is concise and intuitive, yet many important mathematical questions are not explicitly dealt with. The emphasis is put on the application of the Girsanov theorem. In the second stage, the integral form of Ito's lemma is used.

In the following, Ito's lemma will be applied to processes of the form $e^{-rt}F(S_t, t)$. This requires that $F(\cdot)$ be twice differentiable with respect to S_t, and once differentiable with respect to t. These assumptions will not be repeated in the following.

5.1 Equivalence of the Two Approaches

In order to show how the two approaches are related, we proceed in steps. In the first step, we show how $e^{-rt}S_t$ can be converted into a martingale by switching the driving Wiener process, and the associated probability measure. In the second step, we do the same for the derivative asset $e^{-rt}F(S_t, t)$.

These conversions are done by a direct application of the Girsanov theorem. (The switching of probabilities from P to $\tilde{P}$ during the derivation of the Black–Scholes formula did not use the Girsanov theorem explicitly.)

5.1.1 Converting $e^{-rt}S_t$ into a Martingale

We begin with the basic model that determines the dynamics of the underlying asset price S_t. Suppose the underlying asset price follows the stochastic differential equation

$$dS_t = \mu(S_t)\, dt + \sigma(S_t)\, dW_t, \qquad t \in [0, \infty), \tag{87}$$

where the drift and the diffusion terms depend on the observed underlying asset price S_t only. It is assumed that these coefficients satisfy the usual regularity conditions. W_t is the usual Wiener process with probability measure P.

We simplify this SDE to keep the notation simple. We write it as

$$dS_t = \mu_t\, dt + \sigma_t\, dW_t. \tag{88}$$

In the first section of this chapter, $e^{-rt}S_t$ was converted into a martingale by directly finding a probability measure $\tilde{P}$. Next, we do the same using the Girsanov theorem.

We can calculate the SDE followed by $e^{-rt}S_t$, the price discounted by the risk-free rate. Applying Ito's lemma to $e^{-rt}S_t$, we obtain

$$d[e^{-rt}S_t] = S_t d[e^{-rt}] + e^{-rt}\, dS_t. \tag{89}$$

Substituting for dS_t and grouping similar terms:

$$d[e^{-rt}S_t] = e^{-rt}[\mu_t - rS_t]\, dt + e^{-rt}\sigma_t\, dW_t. \tag{90}$$

In general, this equation will not have a zero drift, and $e^{-rt}S_t$ will not be a martingale,

$$[\mu_t - rS_t] > 0, \tag{91}$$

since S_t is a risky asset.[5]

But, we can use the Girsanov theorem to convert $e^{-rt}S_t$ into a martingale. We go over various steps in detail, because this is a fundamental application of the Girsanov theorem in finance.

The Girsanov theorem says that we can find an I_t-adapted process X_t and a new Wiener process $\tilde{W}_t$ such that

$$d\tilde{W}_t = dX_t + dW_t. \tag{92}$$

The probability measure associated with $\tilde{W}_t$ is given by

$$dP = \xi_t d\tilde{P}_t, \tag{93}$$

where the ξ_t is defined as

$$\xi_t = e^{\int_0^t X_u\, dW_u - \frac{1}{2}\int_0^t X_u^2\, du}. \tag{94}$$

We assume that the process X_t satisfies the remaining integrability conditions of the Girsanov theorem.[6]

The important equation for our purposes is the one in (92). We use this to eliminate the dW_t in (90). Rewriting, after substitution of $d\tilde{W}_t$:

$$d[e^{-rt}S_t] = e^{-rt}[\mu_t - rS_t]\, dt + e^{-rt}\sigma_t[d\tilde{W}_t - dX_t]. \tag{95}$$

---

[5]Here $rS_t\, dt$ is an incremental earning if S_t dollars were kept in the risk-free asset, and $\mu_t\, dt$ is an actual expected earning on the asset during an infinitesimal period dt.

[6]This means, among other things, that the drift and diffusion parameters of the original system are "well behaved."

Grouping the terms:

$$d[e^{-rt}S_t] = e^{-rt}[\mu_t - rS_t]\,dt - \sigma_t\,dX_t + e^{-rt}\sigma_t\,d\tilde{W}_t. \tag{96}$$

According to the Girsanov theorem, if we define this SDE under the new probability $\tilde{P}$, $\tilde{W}_t$ will be a *standard* Wiener process. In addition, $\tilde{P}$ will be a *martingale measure* if we equate the drift term to zero. This can be accomplished by picking the value of dX_t as

$$dX_t = \left[\frac{\mu_t - rS_t}{\sigma_t}\right]dt. \tag{97}$$

We assume that the integrability conditions required by the Girsanov theorem are satisfied by this X equaling the term in the brackets.

This concludes the first step of our derivation. We now have a martingale measure $\tilde{P}$, a new Wiener process $\tilde{W}_t$, and the corresponding drift adjustment X_t such that $e^{-rt}S_t$ is a martingale and obeys the SDE

$$d[e^{-rt}S_t] = e^{-rt}\sigma_t d\tilde{W}_t. \tag{98}$$

We use these in converting $[e^{-rt}F(S_t, t)]$ into a martingale.

5.1.2 Converting $e^{-rt}F(S_t, t)$ into a Martingale

The derivation of the previous section gave the precise form of the process X_t needed to apply the Girsanov theorem to derivative assets. To price a derivative asset, we need to show that $e^{-rt}F(S_t, t)$ has the martingale property under $\tilde{P}$. In this section, the Girsanov theorem will be used to do this.

We go through similar steps. First we use the differential form of Ito's lemma to obtain a stochastic differential equation for $e^{-rt}F(S_t, t)$, and then apply the Girsanov transformation to the driving Wiener process.

Taking derivatives in a straightforward manner, we obtain

$$d[e^{-rt}F(S_t, t)] = d[e^{-rt}]F + e^{-rt}\,dF. \tag{99}$$

Note that on the right-hand side we abbreviated $F(S_t, t)$ as F. Substituting for dF using Ito's lemma gives the SDE that governs the differential $d[e^{-rt}F(S_t, t)]$:

$$d[e^{-rt}F(S_t, t)] = e^{-rt}[-rF\,dt]$$
$$+ e^{-rt}\left[F_t\,dt + F_s\,dS_t + \frac{1}{2}F_{ss}\sigma_t^2\,dt\right]. \tag{100}$$

The important question now is what to substitute for dS_t. We have two choices. Under $\tilde{W}_t$ and $\tilde{P}$, $e^{-rt}S_t$ is a martingale. We can use

$$d[e^{-rt}S_t] = e^{-rt}\sigma_t\,d\tilde{W}_t. \tag{101}$$

Or we can use the original SDE:

$$dS_t = \mu_t \, dt + \sigma_t \, dW_t. \tag{102}$$

We choose the second step to illustrate once again at what point the Girsanov theorem is exploited. Eliminating the dS_t from (100) using (102):

$$d[e^{-rt}F(S_t, t)]$$
$$= e^{-rt}[-rF \, dt] + e^{-rt}\left[F_t \, dt + F_s[\mu_t \, dt + \sigma_t \, dW_t] + \frac{1}{2}F_{ss}\sigma_t^2 \, dt \right]. \tag{103}$$

Rearranging:

$$d[e^{-rt}F(S_t, t)] = e^{-rt}\left[-rF + F_t + F_s\mu_t + \frac{1}{2}F_{ss}\sigma_t^2 \right] dt$$
$$+ e^{-rt}\sigma_t F_s \, dW_t. \tag{104}$$

Now we apply the Girsanov theorem for a second time. We again consider the Wiener process $\tilde{W}_t$, defined by:

$$d\tilde{W}_t = dW_t + dX_t \tag{105}$$

and transform the SDE in (104) using the Girsanov transformation:

$$d[e^{-rt}F(S_t, t)] = e^{-rt}\left[-rF + F_t + F_s\mu_t + \frac{1}{2}F_{ss}\sigma_t^2 \right] dt$$
$$- e^{-rt}\sigma_t F_s \, dX_t + e^{-rt}\sigma_t F_s \, d\tilde{W}_t. \tag{106}$$

Again, note the critical argument here. We know that the error term $d\tilde{W}_t$ that drives Equation (106) is a standard Wiener process only under the probability measure $\tilde{P}$. Hence, $\tilde{P}$ becomes the relevant probability.

The value of dX_t has already been derived in Equation (97):

$$dX_t = \frac{\mu_t - rS_t}{\sigma_t} \, dt. \tag{107}$$

We substitute this in (106):

$$d[e^{-rt}F(S_t, t)]$$
$$= e^{-rt}\left[-rF + F_t + F_s\mu_t + \frac{1}{2}F_{ss}\sigma_t^2 - \sigma_t F_s\left(\frac{\mu_t - rS_t}{\sigma_t} \right) \right] dt \tag{108}$$
$$+ F_s e^{-rt}\sigma_t d\tilde{W}_t.$$

Simplifying:

$$d[e^{-rt}F(S_t, t)]$$
$$= e^{-rt}\left[-rF + F_t + \frac{1}{2}F_{ss}\sigma_t^2 + F_s rS_t \right] dt + e^{-rt}\sigma_t F_s \, d\tilde{W}_t. \tag{109}$$

But, in order for $e^{-rt}F(S_t, t)$ to be a martingale under the pair $\tilde{W}_t, \tilde{P}$, the drift term of this SDE must be zero.[7] This is the desired result:

$$-rF + F_t + \frac{1}{2}F_{ss}\sigma_t^2 + F_s rS_t = 0. \tag{110}$$

This expression is identical to the fundamental PDE of Black and Scholes. With this choice of dX_t, the derivative price discounted at the risk-free rate obeys the SDE

$$d[e^{-rt}F(S_t, t)] = e^{-rt}\sigma_t F_s\, d\tilde{W}_t. \tag{111}$$

The drift parameter is zero.

5.2 Critical Steps of the Derivation

There were some critical steps in this derivation that are worth further discussion.

First note the way the Girsanov theorem was used. We are given a Wiener process–driven SDE for the price of a financial asset discounted by the risk-free rate. Initially, the process is not a martingale. The objective is to convert it into one.

To do this we use the Girsanov theorem and find a new Wiener process *and* a new probability $\tilde{P}$ such that the discounted asset price becomes a martingale. The probability measure $\tilde{P}$ is called an *equivalent martingale measure*. This operation gives the drift adjustment term X_t required by the Girsanov theorem. In the preceeding derivation this was used twice, in (95) and in (106):

This brings us to the second critical point of the derivation. We go back to Equation (106):

$$d[e^{-rt}F(S_t, t)] = e^{-rt}\left[-rF + F_t + F_s\mu_t + \frac{1}{2}F_{ss}\sigma_t^2\right]dt \\ - e^{-rt}\sigma_t F_s\, dX_t + e^{-rt}\sigma_t F_s\, d\tilde{W}_t. \tag{112}$$

Here, substituting the value of dX_t means adding

$$dX_t = \frac{\mu_t - rS_t}{\sigma_t}\, dt \tag{113}$$

to the drift term. Note the subtle role played by this transformation. The dX_t is defined such that the term $F_s\mu_t\, dt$ in Equation (104) will be eliminated and will be replaced by $F_s r\, dt$.

---

[7]We know that if there are no arbitrage possibilities, the same $\tilde{P}$ will convert all asset prices into martingales.

In other words, the application of the Girsanov theorem amounts to *switching the drift term* μ_t *into* r, the risk-free rate. Often, books on derivatives do this mechanically, by replacing all drift terms with the risk-free rate. The Girsanov theorem is provided as the basis for such transformations. Here, we see this explicitly.

Finally, a third point. How do we know that the pair $\tilde{W}_t$, $\tilde{P}$ that converts $e^{-rt}S_t$ into a martingale will also convert $e^{-rt}F(S_t, t)$ into a martingale? This question is important, because a function of a martingale need not itself be a martingale.

This step is related to equilibrium and arbitrage valuation of financial assets. Hence, it is in the domain of dynamic asset pricing theory. We briefly mention a rationale. As was discussed heuristically in Chapter 2, under proper conditions, arbitrage relations among asset prices will yield a *unique* martingale measure that will convert all asset prices, discounted by the risk-free rate, into martingales.

Hence, the use of the *same* pair $\tilde{W}_t$, $\tilde{P}$ in Girsanov transformations is a consequence of asset pricing theory. If arbitrage opportunities existed, we could not have done this.

5.3 Integral Form of the Ito Formula

The relationship between the PDE and martingale approaches was discussed using the symbolic form of Ito's lemma, which deals with stochastic differentials.

As emphasized several times earlier, the stochastic differentials under consideration are symbolic terms, which stand for integral equations in the background. The basic concept behind all SDEs is the Ito integral. We used stochastic differentials because they are convenient, and because the calculations already involved tedious equations.

The same analysis can be done using the integral form of Ito's lemma. Without going over all the details, we repeat the basic steps.

The value of a call option discounted by the risk-free rate is represented as usual by $e^{-rt}F(S_t, t)$. Applying the integral form of Ito's lemma:

$$e^{-rt}F(S_t, t)$$
$$= F(S_0, 0) + \int_0^t e^{-ru}\left[-rF + F_t + \frac{1}{2}F_{ss}\sigma_u^2 + F_s rS_u\right] du \qquad (114)$$
$$+ \int_0^t e^{-ru}\sigma_u F_s \, d\tilde{W}_u.$$

Note that we use $\tilde{W}_t$ in place of W_t, and consequently "replace" μ_t by r, the risk-free interest rate.

We assume σ_t is such that

$$E^{\tilde{P}}[e^{\int_0^t (F_s e^{-ru}\sigma_u)^2 \, du}] < \infty. \tag{115}$$

This is the Novikov condition of the Girsanov theorem and implies that the integral

$$\int_0^t e^{-ru}\sigma_u F_s \, d\tilde{W}_u \tag{116}$$

is a martingale under $\tilde{P}$.

But the derivative asset price discounted by e^{-rt} is also a martingale. This makes the first integral on the right-hand side of (114),

$$\int_0^t e^{-ru}\left[-rF + F_t + \frac{1}{2}F_{ss}\sigma_u^2 + F_s r S_u\right] du, \tag{117}$$

a (trivial) martingale as well. But this is an integral taken with respect to time, and martingales are not supposed to have nonzero drift coefficients. Thus, the integral must equal zero. This gives the partial differential equation

$$-rF + F_t + \frac{1}{2}F_{ss}\sigma_t^2 + F_s r S_t = 0 \qquad t \geq 0, \ S_t \geq 0. \tag{118}$$

This is again the fundamental PDE of Black and Scholes.

6 Conclusions

This chapter dealt with applications of the Girsanov theorem.

We discussed several important technical points. In terms of broad conclusions, we retain the following.

There is a certain equivalence between the martingale approach to pricing derivative assets and the one that uses PDEs.

In the martingale approach, we work with conditional expectations taken with respect to an equivalent martingale measure that converts all assets discounted by the risk-free rate into martingales. These expectations are very easy to conceptualize once the deep ideas involving the Girsanov theorem are understood. Also, in the case where the derivative asset is of the European type, these expectations provide an easy way of numerically obtaining arbitrage-free asset prices.

It was shown that the martingale approach implies the same PDEs utilized by the PDE methodology. The difference is that, in the martingale approach, the PDE is a *consequence* of risk-neutral asset pricing, whereas in the PDE method, one begins with the PDEs to obtain risk-free prices.

7 References

The section where we obtain the Black–Scholes formula follows the treatment of Ross (1993). Cox and Huang (1989) is an excellent summary of the main martingale results. This is true, of course, of the treatment of Duffie (1996).

CHAPTER 16

Tools for Complicated Derivative Structures

1 Introduction

The types of derivative securities traded in financial markets are much more complicated than "plain vanilla" call options. Simple assumptions used by Black and Scholes, although often reasonable approximations, sometimes fall short of the requirements. New assumptions introduced in their place require more complicated tools.

These new tools are similar in broad terms to the ones already discussed. However, some of the complications are nontrivial and they need to be discussed separately.

First, recall the pricing of a call option in a Black–Scholes framework. The underlying security S_t was a non-dividend-paying stock. The risk-free interest rate r was constant; the call option was European, and could not be exercised early. Finally, there were no transaction costs or indivisibilities.

The examples discussed in previous chapters were, by and large, in line with the basic Black–Scholes assumptions. In particular, two aspects of the Black–Scholes framework were always preserved.

1. The early-exercise possibilities of American-style derivative securities were not dealt with.
2. The risk-free interest rate r was always constant.

These are serious restrictions for pricing a large majority of financial derivatives.

First of all, a majority of financial derivatives are of the American-style, containing early exercise clauses. A purchaser of financial derivatives often does not have to wait until the expiration date to exercise options that he or she has purchased. This often complicates derivative asset pricing significantly. New mathematical tools need to be introduced.

Secondly, it is obvious that risk-free interest rates are not constant. They are subject to unpredictable, infinitesimal shocks just like any other price. For some financial derivatives, such as options on stocks, the assumption of a constant risk-free rate may be incorrect, but is still a reasonable approximation. However, especially for interest rate derivatives, such an assumption cannot be maintained. It is precisely the risk associated with the interest rate movements that makes these derivatives so popular. Introducing unpredictable Wiener components into risk-free interest rates leads to some further complications in terms of mathematical tools.

In this chapter we discuss these new mathematical tools.

2 New Tools

This chapter deals with three separate issues. They all have practical implications in terms of pricing more complicated derivative structures.

The first topic that we discuss introduces concepts and formulas associated with the "term structure of interest rates" and yield curve. Our main interest in this topic is to use it for motivating most of the mathematical results to be introduced later. Otherwise, interest rate derivatives and associated yield curves are too broad to be dealt with here.

The major topic of this chapter is introduced next. It consists of a fundamental relationship between some expectations of stochastic processes and partial differential equations. Once this correspondence is established, a financial market participant gains a very important tool with practical implications.

Using this correspondence, one can work either with conditional expectations taken with respect to martingale measures, or with the corresponding PDEs. The analyst could take the direction that promises simpler (or cheaper) calculations.

The new concepts introduced in this chapter are the *generator* of a stochastic process, Kolmogorov's backward equation, and the Feyman–Kac formula.

Finally, at the end of this chapter we introduce the notion of *stopping times*, which is useful in dealing with American-style derivatives. Stopping times are random variables whose outcomes are some particular time periods. For example, an American-style put option can be exercised before the expiration date. Initially, such execution times are unknown. Hence, the execution *date* of an option can be regarded as a random variable. Stopping times provide the mathematical tools to handle such phenomena.

These mathematical tools are particularly useful in the case of interest rate derivatives. Thus, we need to introduce the notion of a yield curve in order to motivate these abstract concepts. This is done next.

2.1 Interest Rate Derivatives

One of the earliest and most important class of derivative instruments that violate the assumptions of Black-Scholes environment is the class of interest rate derivatives.

Some well-known interest rate derivatives are the following:

- *Bond options.* A call option written on a bond gives its holder the right to buy a bond with price B_t at the strike price K.[1]

  Introducing options on bonds leads to two complications. The price of a bond B_t depends on the level of interest rates in the economy. Hence, two new assumptions are required. (1) The bond price B_t must be a function of the interest rates, and (2) the rate of interest r_t cannot be constant as before, since this would amount to saying that B_t will be completely predictable, which would mean that the volatility of the underlying security is zero.

  The second complication is that bond options are, in general, of the American style, and may be exercised before the expiration date, if so desired.

  Finally, the payouts of the underlying security may be different for bond options. If the bond has a coupon, the underlying security B_t is different from a non-dividend-paying stock, S_t. At some (known) instants the bond has known payoffs.

  The Black–Scholes framework must be reformulated to take into account these changes.
- *Caps and floors.* Some of the more popular interest rate derivatives are caps and floors. Caps can be used to hedge the risk of increasing interest rates. Floors do the same for decreasing rates.

  Suppose t denotes the *present* and let t_0 be the *starting date* of a leg of an interest rate cap. Let t_1 be the *ending date* of the leg.[2] Then this portion of the interest cap is equivalent to a put option with expiration

---

[1]The holder of a bond *put* will have the right to sell the bond at a price K.

[2]We assume that $t < t_0 < t_1$.

date t_0, written on a (discount) bond with maturity date t_1.[3] Similarly, an interest rate floor can be shown to be equivalent to a basket of options on (discount) bonds.

Clearly, this very broad class of interest rate derivatives cannot be treated using the assumptions of the Black–Scholes environment. Interest rates cannot be assumed constant.

· *SW options*. These instruments can again be replicated using discount bonds and options written on bonds, in a way similar to interest rate caps.

Some of these complications can be handled within the Black–Scholes framework either by making small modifications in the assumptions, or by "tricking" them in some ingenious ways. But the early exercise possibility of interest rate derivatives and stochastic interest rates are two modifications that have to be incorporated in derivative asset pricing using new mathematical tools. In this chapter, we introduce these tools.[4]

3 Term Structure of Interest Rates

There are many classes of bonds in financial markets. For example, we can restrict ourselves to various risk classes, such as Treasury bonds, municipal bonds, corporate bonds, or junk bonds. Given the class of Treasury bonds, we still see Treasury bills that mature within a year, Treasury notes with maturities between one and five years, and Treasury bonds with maturities extending to 30 years.

In the remainder, we restrict ourselves to Treasuries only.

If risk-free instantaneous interest rates were constant at r, the time t price of a pure discount bond[5] with maturity u would be given by

$$B(u, t) = 100e^{-r(u-t)}, \tag{1}$$

where $B(\cdot)$ denotes the present value of 100 discounted at a rate r. The function $e^{-r(u-t)}$ at time t plays the role of a discount factor. At

$$t = u, \tag{2}$$

---

[3]See Hull (1993) for further details on interest rate caps. In particular, the face value of this discount bond will be $1 + R_{cap}\Delta_{cap}$, where R_{cap} is the cap rate, and Δ_{cap} is the length of the relevant leg of the cap.

[4]Pricing interest rate derivatives is a broad area that is beyond the scope of this book. We only introduce some basic formulas routinely used in pricing interest rate derivatives. These formulas have to do with the *yield curve* and are provided as motivation for the abstract mathematical results to be discussed.

[5]A pure discount bond does not make any coupon payments, does not contain any implicit options, and has a par value of 100.

the bond matures and the exponential function equals 1. At all $t < u$, it is less than 1.

When interest rates become stochastic, the formula would change. r_t would represent the risk-free rate earned instantaneously, and to obtain the price of a discount bond with par value equal to 100, we would have to use

$$B(u, t) = 100E\big[e^{-\int_t^u r_s \, ds}\big|I_t\big].\tag{3}$$

Some comments about this formula are in order. [See Jarrow (1996).]

First of all, we need to use the conditional expectations operator $E[\cdot|\cdot]$, since r_s represents the instantaneous rate at some *future* date $s > t$, and consequently is not known with certainty at time t. It can only be predicted.

Secondly, there is the issue of *which* probability measure is used to calculate these expectations. One can argue that Treasury bonds are risk-free assets, and that there is no need to use the equivalent martingale measure. This would not be correct. As interest rates become stochastic, prices of Treasury bonds with longer maturities are subject to more shocks, and, everything else being the same, longer maturities are "riskier." In order to eliminate the corresponding risk premia, we need to use equivalent martingale measures in evaluating the expressions shown in (3).

Third, note a heuristic explanation for where the integral in (3) comes from. Consider the case of a three-year bond. Recall that in a discrete time framework, the price of a three-period discount bond will be given by

$$B(3, 1) = E\left[\frac{100}{(1 + r_1)(1 + r_2)(1 + r_3)}\,\bigg|\,I_1\right],\tag{4}$$

where r_1 is the known current short rate, r_2 is the (unknown) short rate during year 2, and r_3 is the (unknown) short rate during year 3. According to Equation (4), the bond's price is equal to the expectation under risk-neutral probabilities of the discounted value of the par value. The discount factor is obtained by multiplying the one-period discounts during the present and the two future years. Since future discounts are unknown, an expectations operator needs to be used.

This example may be useful in interpreting the continuous-time bond price given in (3). As time becomes continuous, discrete-time discount factors need to be replaced by the exponential function. But because interest rates are continuously changing, an integral has to be used in the exponent.

The bond price formula given in (3) has a very important implication. The bond price depends on the whole spectrum of future short rates r_s, $t < s < u$. It turns out that the yield curve at time t contains all the available information concerning future short rates. Hence, bond prices depend on the whole "yield curve" or on the "term structure of interest rates," which we define formally next.

DEFINITION: Assume that at time t there exists zero coupon bonds with a full spectrum of maturities $u \in [t, T]$. Let their price $B(u, t)$ and their yield be given by R_t^u. Then the spectrum of yields $\{R_t^u, u \in [t, T]\}$ is called the term structure of interest rates.

Here the yield R_t^u is defined as the number that satisfies the equality

$$B(u, t) = 100e^{-R_t^u(u-t)}, \qquad t < u, \tag{5}$$

with $B(u, t)$ given by the expectation under risk-neutral probabilities:

$$B(u, t) = 100E[e^{-\int_t^u r_s ds}|I_t]. \tag{6}$$

In other words, to get the yield of a bond, we first calculate its price. This is obtained from (3). Then, Equation (5) is used to get the yield as

$$R_t^u = \frac{\log B(u, t) - \log(100)}{t - u}. \tag{7}$$

The definition just given is an extension of the yield curves observed in practice. Observed yield curves provide the spectrum of yields on Treasuries at a finite number of maturities. Here we assume that time is continuous, and at any time t, it is assumed that there are uncountably many zero coupon bonds. Their maturities extend from the immediate instant

$$u = t + dt \tag{8}$$

to the longest possible maturity

$$u = T. \tag{9}$$

This gives a continuous yield curve.

Under these conditions, note that we can look at two different changes. At any instant t we can ask what happens to R_t^u as u changes by du. Here, we are increasing the maturity of a bond by du. We can do this because we assumed a continuous spectrum of maturities. Such a change would not involve any unknown random shock. It is an experiment involving different maturities at the same time t, and at time t every R_t^u is known. This way we can obtain the derivative

$$dR_t^u/du = g_u. \tag{10}$$

This is simply the slope of the yield curve $\{R(u, t), u \in [t, T]\}$. (We assume that the yield curve is differentiable.) This slope has important implications in practice.

The change in R_t^u due to a change in time t, on the other hand, *does* involve random shocks. As t changes, the yield curve would *shift* because of random shocks.

3.1 Relating r_s and R_t^u

The r_s represented the instantaneous interest rate paid on a dollar borrowed at time s, where $t < s < T$, and held an infinitesimal period of time. For $s > t$, this *spot rate* is not observed as of time t, although its expectation can be formed.

We can relate future short rates to the yield curve of time t using the two equations in (3) and (5). Equating the right-hand sides:

$$e^{R_t^u(u-t)} = E[e^{-\int_t^u r_s ds}|I_t]. \tag{11}$$

Taking logarithms:

$$R_t^u = \frac{\log E[e^{-\int_t^u r_s\, ds}|I_t]}{u - t}. \tag{12}$$

Finally, we need to define *forward* rates. We let

$$F(t, u, T) = \frac{\log B(u, t) - \log B(T, t)}{T - u}, \qquad t < u < T, \tag{13}$$

be the forward rate at t, on a loan that begins at time u and matures at time T. By letting $T \to u$, we get the *instantaneous* forward rate $f(t, u)$:

$$f(t, u) = \lim_{T \to u} F(t, u, T). \tag{14}$$

This assumes that the bond prices are differentiable. Using Equation (13) and assuming that some technical conditions are satisfied, we see that

$$f(t, t) = r_t. \tag{15}$$

From these expressions it is clear that the yield curve contains all relevant information concerning forward rates.

3.1.1 Examples of Yield Curves

In practical situations, there are two different ways of proceeding. Often a market participant assumes a functional form for the yield curve or for the spot rate, and from there obtains the implied forward rates. A second method is to go the opposite direction. One can assume a dynamic behavior for the forward rates, and from there obtain a yield curve.

This is a broad topic beyond the scope of this book. We summarize some examples to introduce some functional forms routinely used in this field. In the most common case, one assumes that the yields $R(\cdot)$ depend on one state variable r_t, which represents the short rate observed now, and that they are given by the functional form

$$R(r_t, u, t) = A(u, t) - C(u, t)r_t. \tag{16}$$

Functions $A(u, t)$ and $C(u, t)$ can be constructed in various ways, so that the yield curve can be upward, downward-sloping, or hump-shaped.

The model is determined by assuming a SDE that gives the dynamics of the r_t:

$$dr = a(r_t, t)\, dt + \sigma(r_t, t)\, dW_t. \tag{17}$$

In this model, the movements of the yield curve will be stochastic, because r_t would have an unpredictable component and would move over time randomly.

This way of proceeding is straightforward but comes at a cost. There is a single factor behind the shifts in the yield curve; hence, the yields $R(r_t, u_1, t)$ and, say, $R(r_t, u_2, t)$ will be perfectly correlated. This is clearly not a realistic property of observed yields. To alleviate this problem, one can use *two* stochastic state variables, one representing a short rate, the other a long rate. Such models are called two-factor models.

A completely different approach is to model the dynamic behavior of instantaneous forward rates $f(t, u)$ at the outset, and then determine the corresponding yields from there. For example, one can let, for some fixed $u \in [0, T]$,

$$df(t, u) = a(f, t)\, dt + \sigma(f, t)\, dW_t^u. \tag{18}$$

From here one can use the relationship in (13) to determine the yields. One interesting modification, which often must be made here, is in the definition of the drift and diffusion terms. The drift and the diffusion terms of the SDEs describing forward rate dynamics will depend on u.

4 Characterization of Expectations Using PDEs

Interest rate derivatives introduced new complications in pricing derivative asset prices. In earlier chapters, Black–Scholes assumptions led to the fundamental PDE

$$0 = -Fr + F_t + rF_s S_t + \frac{1}{2}F_{ss}\sigma_t^2, \tag{19}$$

where r was constant. It was also shown that this PDE corresponded to the risk-neutral expectation

$$F(S_t, t) = E^{\tilde{P}}[e^{-r(T-t)}F(S_T, T)], \tag{20}$$

for an equivalent martingale measure $\tilde{P}$. We can ask two questions:

- Do we get similar PDEs in the case of interest rate derivatives? For example, what type of PDE would the price of a bond satisfy?
- Given a PDE involving an interest rate derivative, can we obtain a corresponding expectation similar to (20)?

When we investigate such questions, we are led to an interesting mathematical regularity, which we discuss in this section.

Suppose r_s is stochastic, and $\tilde{P}$ is an equivalent measure. It turns out that there is a very close connection between a representation such as

$$B(u, t) = E_t^{\tilde{P}}[100e^{-\int_t^u r_s \, ds}] \tag{21}$$

and a certain class of partial differential equations.

In stochastic calculus, these topics come under the headings of generators for Ito diffusions, the Kolmogorov backward equation, and, more importantly, of the Feyman–Kac formula. The following section gives a motivation for why such tools are useful in continuous-time finance.

4.1 Risk-Neutral Bond Pricing

Consider the price $B(u, t)$ of a bond with maturity u at time t. Assume that we have the spectrum of yields for all maturities $u \in [0, T]$, represented by the yield curve at time t.

We saw earlier in this chapter that under some conditions the price of this bond can be written using the equivalent martingale measure and the instantaneous interest rates of time s, $t < s < u$

$$B(u, t) = E_t^{\tilde{P}}[100e^{-\int_t^u r_s \, ds}], \tag{22}$$

where r_t obeys

$$dr_t = a(r_t) \, dt + \sigma(r_t) \, dW_t, \tag{23}$$

W_t being a Wiener process. The drift and diffusion components of this SDE are assumed to satisfy all regularity conditions. Note the special aspect of the drift and diffusion coefficients. They are not a function of t, as was the case for the general SDEs.

Now, consider the expression (22). On the right-hand side we have the expectation of a function of a stochastic process r_t. In particular, we see that the expectation is taken with respect to equivalent martingale measure, and the random variable in question has the form

$$e^{-\int_t^u r_s \, ds}. \tag{24}$$

It is an exponential function of the future instantaneous interest rates r_s, where $t < s < u$. The instantaneous interest rate is stochastic and changes constantly; its future values are unknown beyond a drift $a(r_t)$. The continuous changes in r_s force us to put the integral in the exponent. The fact that future r_s are unknown forces us to keep the exponential function inside the expectation operator $E_t^{\tilde{P}}[\cdot]$.

This expectation is not always easy to calculate. It will be nice to have an alternative representation for the bond price $B(u, t)$. In particular, if we obtained a PDE that represented the bond price, we could use numerical schemes to calculate $B(u, t)$ or the price of any derivative that relates to the bond.

In fact, suppose we showed that, each time a process $B(u, t)$ obeys

$$B(u, t) = E_t^{\tilde{P}}[100e^{-\int_t^u r_s \, ds} f(r_u)], \tag{25}$$

where $f(\cdot)$ is some twice differentiable function, $B(u, t)$ would automatically satisfy a particular PDE. And suppose we derived the general form of this PDE. This would be very convenient.

All interest rate derivatives have to assume that instantaneous rates are random. At the same time, arbitrage-free asset pricing would always permit writing this asset price as

$$B(u, t) = E_t^{\tilde{P}}[100e^{-\int_t^u r_s \, ds} f(r_u)], \tag{26}$$

where $f(r_u)$ is some boundary value. As a result, such representations are natural in asset pricing theory. This is especially the case for interest rate derivatives. If one could establish a PDE that corresponded to this representation, one would obtain a straightforward numerical method for obtaining the fair market price $B(u, t)$.

In the next section we provide the Feyman–Kac formula, which establishes precisely this correspondence and gives the corresponding PDE.

5 Random Discount Factors and PDEs

The Feyman–Kac formula will be obtained in several steps. In the process, we will see the important steps concerning Ito diffusions, generators of Ito diffusions, and Kolmogorov's backward equation.

We do not provide proofs, although we do try to explain various steps involved in obtaining the important results.

5.1 Ito Diffusions

A continuous stochastic process S_t which has finite first- and second-order moments is shown to follow the general SDE

$$dS_t = a(S_t, t) dt + \sigma(S_t, t) dW_t, \qquad t \in [0, \infty). \tag{27}$$

We now assume that the drift and diffusion parameters depend on S_t only.[6] The SDE can be written as

$$dS_t = a(S_t) dt + \sigma(S_t) dW_t, \qquad t \in [0, \infty), \tag{28}$$

where $a(\cdot)$ and $\sigma(\cdot)$ are the drift and diffusion parameters. Processes that have this characteristic are called time-homogenous *Ito diffusions*. The following results apply to these processes, whose instantaneous drift and diffusion are not dependent on t directly. The usual conditions apply to $a(\cdot)$ and $\sigma(\cdot)$, in that they are not supposed to vary "too fast."

We now discuss two properties of Ito diffusions.

5.2 The Markov Property

Let S_t be an Ito diffusion satisfying the SDE

$$dS_t = a(S_t) dt + \sigma(S_t) dW_t, \qquad t \in [0, \infty). \tag{29}$$

Let $f(\cdot)$ be any bounded function, and suppose that the information set I_t contains all S_u until time t. Then we say that S_t satisfies the *Markov property* if

$$E[f(S_{t+h})|I_t] = E[f(S_{t+h})|S_t], \qquad h > 0, \qquad \text{for all } t. \tag{30}$$

According to this, future movements in S_t, given what we observed until time t, are likely to be the same as starting the process at time t. In other words, observations of S_t from the distant past do not help to improve forecasts, given S_t.

This result is not unexpected. The SDE in (29) shows that changes in this process do not depend on time directly. These changes are a function of dW_t, which is independent of the present and the past; of $a(S_t)$; and of $\sigma(S_t)$, which for Ito diffusions depends on S_t only. Under such conditions, it is normal to expect that future forecasts are independent of S_u observed before time t.

---

[6]In almost all cases of interest where there are no jumps involved, the SDEs utilized in practice are either of the geometric or of the mean reverting type. The latter is especially popular with interest rate derivatives, since the short rate is widely believed to have a mean reverting character. Under these conditions, the drift and diffusion parameters would be functions of S_t only. However, often dependence on time is allowed to match the initial term structure.

5.3 Generator of an Ito Diffusion

Let S_t be the Ito diffusion given in (29). Let $f(S_t)$ be a twice differentiable function of S_t, and suppose the process S_t has reached a particular value s_t as of time t.

We may wonder how $f(S_t)$ can move starting from the current *state* s_t. We let the operator A be defined as the *expected rate of change* for $f(S_t)$:

$$Af(s_t) = \lim_{\Delta \to 0} \frac{E[f(S_{t+\Delta})|f(s_t)] - f(s_t)}{\Delta}. \tag{31}$$

Here the lowercase letter s_t indicates an already observed value for S_t. The numerator of the expression on the right-hand side measures expected change in $f(S_t)$. As we divide this by Δ, the A operator becomes a *rate* of change. In the theory of stochastic processes, A is called the *generator* of the Ito diffusion S_t.

Some readers may wonder how we can define a *rate* of change for $f(S_t)$, which indirectly is a function of a Wiener process. A rate of change is like a derivative, and we have shown that Wiener processes are not differentiable. So, how can we justify the existence of an operator such as A?

The answer to this question is simple. A does not deal with the *actual* rate of change in $f(S_t)$. Instead, A represents an *expected* rate of change. Although a Wiener process may be too erratic and nondifferentiable, note that expected changes in $f(S_t)$ will be a smoother function, and under some conditions a limit *can* be defined.[7]

5.4 A Representation for A

First note that A is an expected rate of change in the *limit*. That is, we consider the immediate future with an infinitesimal change of time. Then, it is obvious that such a change would relate directly to Ito's lemma. In fact, in the present case where S_t is a univariate stochastic process,

$$dS_t = a(S_t) dt + \sigma(S_t) dW_t, \qquad t \in [0, \infty), \tag{32}$$

the operator A is given by[8]

$$Af = a_t \frac{\partial f}{\partial S} + \frac{1}{2} \sigma_t^2 \frac{\partial^2 f}{\partial S^2}. \tag{33}$$

---

[7] Every expectation represents an average. By definition, averages are smoother than particular values.

[8] In the following, we simplify the notation for $a(S_t)$ and $\sigma(S_t)$, and write a_t, σ_t, respectively.

It is worthwhile to compare this with what Ito's lemma would give. Applying Ito's lemma to $f(S_t)$ with S_t given by (32):

$$df(S_t) = \left[a_t \frac{\partial f}{\partial S} + \frac{1}{2} \sigma_t^2 \frac{\partial^2 f}{\partial S^2} \right] dt + \sigma_t \frac{\partial f}{\partial S} dW_t. \qquad (34)$$

Hence, the difference between the operator, A, and the application of Ito's lemma is at two points:

1. The dW_t term in Ito's formula is replaced by its drift, which is zero.
2. Next, the remaining part of Ito's formula is divided by dt.

These two differences are consistent with the definition of A. As mentioned earlier, A calculates an *expected rate* of change starting from the immediate state s_t.

5.4.1 The Multivariate Case
For completion, we should provide the multivariate case for A.
Let X_t be a k-dimensional Ito diffusion given by the (vector) SDE

$$\begin{bmatrix} dX_{1t} \\ \vdots \\ dX_{kt} \end{bmatrix} = \begin{bmatrix} a_{1t} \\ \vdots \\ a_{kt} \end{bmatrix} dt + \begin{bmatrix} \sigma_t^{11} & \vdots & \sigma_t^{1k} \\ \cdots & \cdots & \cdots \\ & \vdots & \\ \sigma_t^{k1} & \cdots & \sigma_t^{kk} \end{bmatrix} \begin{bmatrix} dW_{1t} \\ \vdots \\ dW_{kt} \end{bmatrix}, \qquad (35)$$

where a_{it} are the diffusion coefficients depending on X_t, and where σ_t^{ij} are the diffusion coefficients possibly depending on X_t as well. This equation is written in the symbolic form

$$dX_t = a_t \, dt + \sigma_t \, dW_t, \qquad t \in [0, \infty), \qquad (36)$$

where a_t is a $k \times 1$ vector, and σ_t is a $k \times k$ matrix.

The corresponding A operator will then be given by

$$Af = \sum_{i=1}^k a_{it} \frac{\partial f}{\partial X_i} + \sum_{i=1}^k \sum_{j=1}^k \frac{1}{2} (\sigma_t \sigma_t^T)^{ij} \frac{\partial^2 f}{\partial X_i \partial X_j}, \qquad (37)$$

where the term $(\sigma_t \sigma_t^T)^{ij}$ represents the ijth element of the matrix $(\sigma_t \sigma_t^T)$.

The difference between the univariate case and this multivariate formula is the existence of cross-product terms. Otherwise, the extension is immediate.

In most advanced books on stochastic calculus, it is this multivariate form of A that is introduced. The expression in (37) is known as the *infinitesimal generator* of $f(\cdot)$.

5.5 Kolmogorov's Backward Equation

Suppose we are given an Ito diffusion S_t with drift and diffusion parameters a_t and σ_t, respectively. Also, assume that we have a function of S_t, denoted by $f(S_t)$. Consider the expectation

$$\hat{f}(S^-, t) = E[f(S_t)|S^-], \qquad \text{for all } t \geq 0, \qquad (38)$$

where $\hat{f}(S^-, t)$ represents the forecasted value, and S^- is the latest value observed before time t. Heuristically speaking, S^- is the immediate past. Then, using the A operator, we can characterize how the $\hat{f}(S^-, t)$ may change over time. This evolution of the forecast is given by *Kolmogorov's backward equation*:

$$\frac{\partial \hat{f}}{\partial t} = A\hat{f}. \qquad (39)$$

Remembering the definition of A:

$$A\hat{f} = a_t \frac{\partial \hat{f}}{\partial S} + \frac{1}{2}\sigma_t^2 \frac{\partial^2 \hat{f}}{\partial S^2}. \qquad (40)$$

It is easy to see that the equality in (39) is nothing else than the PDE:

$$\hat{f}_t = a_t \hat{f}_s + \frac{1}{2}\sigma_t^2 \hat{f}_{ss}. \qquad (41)$$

Thus, we see an important correspondence between equations such as

$$\hat{f}(S^-, t) = E[f(S_t)|S^-] \qquad (42)$$

and the PDE in (40). This correspondence can be stated in two different ways:

- $\hat{f}(S_-, t)$ satisfies the PDE in (39).
- Or one can say the opposite: given the PDE in (39), we can find an $\hat{f}(S^-, t)$ such that (42) is satisfied.

This result means that $\hat{f}(S^-, t)$ is a solution for the PDE in (39). Kolmogorov's backward equation gives the first correspondence between an expectation of a stochastic process and PDEs.

Note that the types of expectations in question, namely expressions such as

$$\hat{f}(S^-, t) = E[f(S_t)|S^-], \qquad (43)$$

are not very useful in financial markets the way they are stated. In particular, the function $f(\cdot)$ depends on S_t only, and a (random) discount factor is not allowed.

In the next section we extend the types of functions allowed inside the expectation sign. This permits a direct application to interest rate derivatives.

However, first we show a simple example of Kolmogorov's backward equation.

5.5.1 Example
Consider the function

$$p(S_t, S_0, t) = \frac{1}{\sqrt{2\pi t}} e^{-\frac{(S_t - S_0)^2}{2t}}. \tag{44}$$

An inspection shows that this is the conditional density function of a Wiener process, which starts from S_0 at time $t = 0$ and moves over time with zero drift and variance t.

If we were to write down a stochastic differential equation for this process, we would choose an SDE with a drift parameter 0 and a diffusion parameter 1. The dS_t would satisfy

$$dS_t = dW_t. \tag{45}$$

We would like to apply Kolmogorov's formula to this density. We know that a twice-differentiable function $\hat{f}(\cdot)$ of S_t would satisfy Kolmogorov's backward equation:

$$\hat{f}_t = a_t \hat{f}_s + \frac{1}{2}\sigma_t^2 \hat{f}_{ss}. \tag{46}$$

But according to (45), in this particular case we have

$$a_t = 0 \tag{47}$$

and

$$\sigma_t = 1. \tag{48}$$

Substituting these, Kolmogorov's backward equation becomes

$$\hat{f}_t = \frac{1}{2}\hat{f}_{ss}. \tag{49}$$

It turns out that the conditional density $p(S_t, S_0, t)$ is one such function $\hat{f}$. To see this, take the first partial derivative with respect to t and the second partial with respect to S_t and substitute in (49). The equation will be satisfied.

According to this result, the conditional density function of a (generalized) Wiener process satisfies Kolmogorov's backward equation. This PDE tells us how the probability associated with a particular value of S_t and with the "initial" condition S_0, will evolve as time passes.

5.6 The Feyman-Kac Formula

Kolmogorov's backward equation seems to establish a very convenient correspondence between conditional expectations such as (42) and some PDEs. This has several potential uses because arbitrage-free asset prices are given by conditional expectations of some functions of S_t with respect to an equivalent martingale measure. Establishing such correspondences will give a choice to practitioners in terms of numerical calculation methods of arbitrage-free asset prices.

It turns out that one can do this in more general settings as well. We generalize Equation (42) in a very interesting way. In fact, let the Ito diffusion be denoted by r_t instead of S_t. Then consider the generalized version of the conditional expectation in (42):

$$\hat{f}(t, r_t) = E[e^{-\int_t^u q(r_s)ds} f(r_u)|r_t]. \tag{50}$$

Note that the main difference with (42) is the function

$$e^{-\int_t^u q(r_s)\,ds} \tag{51}$$

that multiplies $f(r_t)$. This makes the formula more interesting to a financial market participant. What we have on the right-hand side is very much like a discounted value of an expiration payoff for some derivative instrument. More importantly, the formula permits a stochastic interest rate to be used as well.

The reader may have already seen the importance of this change from the point of view of asset pricing. In fact, a close examination of (50) indicates that with

$$q(r_s) = r_s \tag{52}$$

and $f(\cdot)$ selected as expiration payoff, the formula gives the price of an instrument that matures at time u under the condition of no arbitrage possibilities. If the probability used to calculate the expectation is the equivalent martingale measure, then Equation (50) gives the arbitrage-free price of an interest rate derivative at time t.

The Feyman–Kac formula is an extension of Kolmogorov's backward equation. The formula provides a PDE that corresponds to $\hat{f}$ defined by (50).

DEFINITION: The Feyman-Kac formula. Given

$$\hat{f}(t, r_t) = E[e^{-\int_t^u q(r_s)\,ds} f(r_u)|r_t], \qquad \text{all } t \geq 0, \tag{53}$$

we have

$$\frac{\partial \hat{f}}{\partial t} = A\hat{f} - q(r_t)\hat{f}, \tag{54}$$

where the operator A is as usual given by

$$A\hat{f} = a_t \frac{\partial \hat{f}}{\partial r_t} + \frac{1}{2}\sigma_t^2 \frac{\partial^2 \hat{f}}{\partial r_t^2}. \tag{55}$$

Hence, the Feyman–Kac formula provides a PDE that corresponds to conditional expectations obtained with equivalent martingale measures. These PDEs can be solved using numerical methods. The result gives $\hat{f}(r_t, t)$, which, in financial applications, is the arbitrage-free price of an interest rate derivative that matures at time u.

5.6.1 Example: A PDE for Bond Prices
Consider the time t price of a discount bond that matures at time u

$$B(u, t) = E[e^{-\int_t^u r_s ds} 100 | r_t], \qquad t \in [0, u], \tag{56}$$

where r_s is the instantaneous interest rate at time s, 100 is the par value, and the expectation is taken with respect to the equivalent martingale measure. The r_t satisfies

$$dr_t = a(r_t)\, dt + \sigma(r_t)\, dW_t, \qquad t \in [0, \infty). \tag{57}$$

It is clear that this conditional expectation in (56) is of the form assumed in the Feyman–Kac formula. Then $B(t, u, r_t)$ must satisfy:

$$\frac{\partial B}{\partial t} = AB - r_t B. \tag{58}$$

Substituting for the generator A, and simplifying the notation, this becomes

$$B_t = a_t B_r + \frac{1}{2}\sigma_t^2 B_{rr} - r_t B, \qquad r \geq 0;\ 0 \leq t \leq u. \tag{59}$$

Hence, discount bond prices will satisfy this PDE with the boundary condition

$$B(u, u) = 100. \tag{60}$$

The following is another way of looking at the same problem. The formula given by (56) is a solution to the PDE in (59) with boundary condition (60).

Again, we see the correspondence between a conditional expectation representation for an asset price and an implied PDE. The financial analyst may work with the representation that he or she prefers.

6 American Securities

American-type derivative securities contain implicit or explicit options which can be exercised before the expiration date, if desired. This often causes significant complications, both at the theoretical level where one has to characterize the fair-market value of the security, and at the practical level where one has to calculate this price.

The main mathematical concept that needs to be introduced to deal with American securities is the notion of a *stopping time*.

6.1 Stopping Times

Stopping times are special types of random variables that assume as values a particular time period t. For example, let τ be a (finite) stopping time. This means that τ is random and that the range of its possible values is the same as $t \in [0, T]$. When an outcome is observed, it will be in the form

$$\tau = t. \tag{61}$$

The outcome is a particular time period.

Now consider an American-style option written on a bond. The option can be exercised at any time between the present $t = 0$ and the expiration date of the option, denoted by T. The option holder will exercise this option if he or she thinks that it is better to do so, than to wait until the expiration date of the contract. Clearly, when the option is purchased, the occurrence date of such an early exercise is unknown.

Hence, we are dealing with a "possible date," which nevertheless is of great importance from the point of view of pricing the asset. In fact, the right to exercise *early* in general has some value, and pricing an American security must take this into account.

Thus, we let τ represent the early exercise date. It is obvious that given the information set I_t, we will be able to tell whether the option has already been exercised or not. In other words, given I_t, we can differentiate between the possibilities

$$\tau \leq t, \tag{62}$$

which means that option has already been exercised, or

$$\tau > t, \tag{63}$$

which means that the early exercise clause of the contract has not yet been utilized.

In fact, this property of τ is exactly what determines a *stopping time*.

DEFINITION: A stopping time is an I_t-measurable nonnegative random variable such that

1. Given I_t we can tell if

$$\tau \leq t \tag{64}$$

   or not.
2. We have

$$P(\tau < \infty) = 1. \tag{65}$$

In the case of derivative securities, we in general have a finite expiration period. So the options will either be exercised at a finite time, or will expire unexercised. This means that the second requirement, that τ be finite with probability 1, is always satisfied.

6.2 Use of Stopping Times

How are the stopping times τ utilized?

The most obvious use of τ is to let them denote the exercise date of an option. With European securities, there was no randomness in exercise dates. The security could only be exercised at expiration. Hence,

$$P(\tau = T) = 1. \tag{66}$$

With American-type securities, τ is in general random.[9]

Consider an American-style call option $F(S_t, t)$ written on the underlying security S_t, where S_t follows a SDE

$$dS_t = a(S_t, t)\, dt + \sigma(S_t, t)\, dW_t, \qquad t \in [0, \infty), \tag{67}$$

where the drift and diffusion coefficients satisfy the usual regularity conditions.

The price of the derivative security can again be expressed using the equivalent martingale measure $\tilde{P}$. But this time, there is an additional complication. The security holder does not have to wait until time T to exercise the option. He or she will exercise the option as soon as it is more profitable to do so than to wait until expiration.

We now want to express these notions in more precise terms. If one waits until expiration, a call option will be worth

$$F(S_t, t)^T = E_t^{\tilde{P}}[e^{-r(T-t)} \max\{S_T - K, 0\}], \tag{68}$$

---

[9]In some special cases, it is never worth exercising the American style option early, and the corresponding τ will again equal T.

now. If the option with expiration date T can be exercised early, we can compare this with

$$F(S_t, t)^* = \sup_{\tau \in \Phi_{t,T}} [E_t^{\tilde{P}}[e^{-r(T-t)}F(S_t, t, \tau)]], \tag{69}$$

where $\Phi_{t,T}$ is the set of all possible stopping opportunities. That is, it is the set of possible outcomes for τ.

Here, τ represents a possible date where the option holder decides to exercise the call option.

Hence, at time t, we can calculate a spectrum of possible prices $F(S_t, t, \tau)$ indexed by τ using the possible values for the stopping time τ.

To find the correct price, we pick the supremum of these prices.

7 Extending the Results to Stopping Times

Most of the results discussed in this book can be extended to stopping times. We simply give two such results, without commenting extensively on them.

7.1 Martingales

Suppose M_t represents a continuous-time martingale with

$$E[M_{t+u}|I_t] = M_t, \qquad u > 0. \tag{70}$$

Would this martingale property be preserved if we consider *randomly* selected times as well?

The answer is yes under some conditions. Let τ_1 and τ_2 be two independent stopping times measurable with respect to I_t and satisfying

$$P(\tau_1 < \tau_2) = 1. \tag{71}$$

Then the martingale property will still hold:

$$E[M_{\tau_2}|I_{\tau_1}] = M_{\tau_1}. \tag{72}$$

This property is clearly important to us in modeling asset prices using equivalent martingale measures. The fact that the exercise date of a derivative is random does not preclude the use of equivalent martingale measures. With random τ, randomly stopped asset prices will still be martingales under the probability $\tilde{P}$.

7.2 Dynkin's Formula

Let B_t be a process satisfying

$$dB_t = a(B_t)\,dt + \sigma(B_t)\,dW_t, \qquad t \geq 0. \tag{73}$$

Let $f(B_t)$ be a twice-differentiable bounded function of this process.
Now consider a stopping time τ such that

$$E[\tau] < \infty. \tag{74}$$

Then we have

$$E[f(B_\tau)|B_0] = f(B_0) + E\left[\int_0^\tau Af(B_s)\,ds|B_0\right]. \tag{75}$$

This expression is called *Dynkin's formula*. It gives a convenient representation for the expectation of a function that depends on a stopping time. The operator A is, as usual, the infinitesimal generator.

8 Conclusions

This chapter elaborated on an important correspondence already seen in Chapter 14. We showed that there was an important equivalence between some expectations of stochastic processes and certain classes of PDEs.

These results are important in practice as well as in theory. They enable the practitioner to choose the more convenient (or cheaper) method between two equivalent numerical approaches.

The chapter also introduced the notion of stopping times. This concept was useful in pricing American-style derivative products.

9 References

This section dealt with important issues in a very brief way. The correspondence between PDEs and a certain class of conditional expectations is very important for asset pricing. Interested readers should read Karatzas and Shreve (1991) and Revuz and Yor (1994) for the theory of generators and for Feyman–Kac type results. Applications in finance are best discussed in Duffie (1996).

BIBLIOGRAPHY

Bhattacharya, S., and **Constantinides, G.** *Theory of Valuation*. Rowmand and Littlefield, 1989.

Black, Fisher, and **Scholes, Marion**. "The Pricing of Options and Corporate Liabilities," *Journal of Political Economy*, **81**, 637–654, 1973.

Black, F., Derman, E., and **Troy, W.**. "A One-Factor Model of Interest Rates and Its Application to Treasury Bond Options," *Financial Analysts Journal*, **46**, 33–39, 1990.

Bremaud, Pierre. Bremaud (1979) p. 181. *Point Processes and Queues, Martingale Dynamics*, Springer-Verlag, New York, 1981.

Cinlar, E. *Stochastic Processes*. Prentice-Hall, New York, 1978.

Cox, J., C., and **Huang, C.** "Option Pricing and Its Applications," in *Theory of Valuation*: (Bhattacharya, S. and Constantinides, G., eds.). Rowman and Littlefield, 1989.

Cox, J., and **Rubinstein, M.** *Options Markets*. Prentice-Hall, New York, 1985.

Cox, J. C., Ingersoll, J. E., and **Ross, S.** "An Intertemporal Asset Pricing Model with Rational Expectations," *Econometrica* **53**, 363–384, 1985.

Das, Satyajit. *Swap and Derivative Financing*, Revised Edition. Probus, 1994.

Dattatreya, R. E., Venkatesh, R. S., and **Venkatesh, V. E.** *Interest Rate and Currency Swops*. Probus, Chicago, 1994.

Dellacherie, C., and **Meyer, P.** *Theorie des Martingales*. Hermann, Paris, 1980.

Duffie, Darrell. *Dynamic Asset Pricing*, Second Edition. Princeton University Press, 1996.

Gihman, I., and **Skorohod, A.** *Stochastic Differential Equations*. Springer-Verlag, Berlin, 1972.

Gihman, I., and **Skorohod, A.** *The Theory of Stochastic Processes*, Vol. I., Springer-Verlag, Berlin, 1974.

Gihman, I., and **Skorohod, A.** *The Theory of Stochastic Processes*, Vol. II., Springer-Verlag, Berlin, 1975.

Harrison, J. M. *Brownian Motion and Stochastic Flow Systems*, Wiley, New York, 1985.

Harrison, M., and **Kreps, D.** "Martingales and Multiperiod Securities Markets," *Journal of Economic Theory*, 1979.

Harrison, M., and **Pliska, S.** "Martingales and Stochastic Integrals in Theory of Continuous Trading," *Stochastic Processes and their Applications*. **11**, 313–316, 1981.

Hulls, John. *Options, Futures and Other Derivative Securities*. Prentice Hall, 1993.

Ingersoll, J. *Theory of Financial Decision Making*. Rosman and Littlefield, 1987.

Jarrow, R. J. *Modelling Fixed Income Securities and Interest Rate Options*. McGraw Hill, New York, 1996.

Jarrow, R. J. and **Turnbull, S.** *Derivative Securities*. South Western, Cincinnati, 1996.

Kapner, K., and **Marshall, J. F.** *The Swops Handbook*. NYIF, New York, 1992.

Karatzas, I., and **Shreve, S. E.** *Brownian Motion and Stochastic Calculus*. Springer-Verlag, New York, 1991.

Klein, R. A., and **Lederman, J.** *Derivatives and Synthetics*. Probus, Chicago, 1994.

Kloeden, P. E., and **Platen, E.** *Numerical Solution of Stochastic Differential Equations*. Springer-Verlag, Berlin, 1992.

Kloeden, P. E., Platen, E., and **Schurz, H.** *Numerical Solution of SDE Through Computer Experiments*. Springer-Verlag, Berlin, 1994.

Kuhsner, A. J. *Numerical Methods for Stochastic Control Problems in Continuous Time*. Springer-Verlag, New York, 1995.

Liptser, R., and **Shiryayev, A.** *Statistics of Random Processes I: General Theory*. Springer-Verlag, New York, 1977.

Liptser, R., and **Shiryayev, A.** *Statistics of Random Processes II: Applications*, Springer-Verlag, New York, 1978.

Lucas, R. "Asset Prices in an Exchange Economy," *Econometrica* **46**, 1429-1445, 1978.

Malliaris, A. G. "Ito Calculus in Financial Decision Making," *SIAM Review* **25**, 481–496, 1983.

Merton, R. "An Intermporal Capital Asset Pricing Model," *Econometrica*, **41**, 867–888, 1973.

Merton, R. *Continuous Time Finance*. Blackwell, Cambridge, 1990.

Merton, R. "On the Mathematics and Economic Assumptions of the Continuous Time Models," in *Financial Economics: Essays in Honor of Paul Cootner*, (William Sharpe and Cathryn Cootner, eds.). Prentice-Hall, 1982.

Milstein, G. N. *Weak Approximation of Solutions of Systems of Stochastic Differential Equations, Theory of Probability and Applications*, 1985.

Oksendal, Bernd. *Stochastic Differential Equations*, Third Edition. Springer-Verlag, Berlin, 1992.

Protter, P. *Stochastic Integration and Differential Equations*. Springer-Verlag, Berlin, 1990.

Revuz, Daniel, and **Yor, Marc.** *Continuous Martingales and Brownian Motion*, Second Edition. Springer-Verlag, Berlin, 1994.

Rogers, C., and **Williams, D.** *Diffusions, Markov Processes and Martingales: Ito Calculus*. Wiley, New York, 1987.

Ross, S. "A Simple Approach to Valuation of Risky Streams," *Journal of Business*, 1978.

Ross, S. *Probability Models.* Academic Press, San Diego, 1993.

Shiryayev, A. Optimal Stopping Rules, Springer-Verlag, New York, 1978.

Shiryayev, A. "Theory of Martingales," *International Statistical Review*, 1983.

Shiryayev, A. *Probability Theory*. Springer-Verlag, New York, 1984.

Smith, G. D. *Numerical Solution of Partial Differential Equations*: *Finite Difference Methods*, Third Edition. Oxford University Press, 1985.

Sussman, H. J. "On the Gap between Deterministic and Stochastic Ordinary Differential Equations," *Annals of Probability*, 1978.

Thomas, J. W. *Numerical Partial Differential Equations*: *Finite Difference Methods*. Springer-Verlag, New York, 1995.

Williams, David. *Probability with Martingales*, Cambridge University Press, 1991.

INDEX

Boundary conditions
  lattice models, 28
  numerical methods, 271–272
  ordinary equations, 68
  partial differential equations, 73–74,
    241, 242–243
Brownian motion, *see also* Wiener
    process
  defined, 148–149
  transformation into martingale,
    113–114

  ♦

Calls, *see also* Pricing methods
  defined, 7
Caps, interest rate, 321–322
  Doob-Meyer decomposition,
    121–122
  exotic types
    barrier, 263–265
    dual strike, 265
    portfolio, 265
    spread, 265
  expiration date, 7
  premium, 7, 56
  strike price, 7
Cash-and-carry goods
  defined, 3–4
  holding cost, 67
Cash market instruments, 2
Central limit theorem, 92–93
Chain rule
  deterministic, 47–48, 195
  stochastic, *see* Ito's Lemma
Circle, equation, 249–250
Commodities
  classes, 3
  derivatives based on, 3
Completing the square, 250
Composite functions, 47–48
Contingent claim, 2
Continuous time, 29–31, 35–36, 101
Convergence
  almost surely, 96–97
  mean square, 95–96, 177
  ordinary, 42

pathwise, 192
weak, 97–99
Convexity (bond), 62
Cost, holding, 67
Counterparties, 10
Covariance, 286
Currencies, 2

  ♦

Delta, 71
Delta hedging, 68–71, 195
Delta neutral portfolio, 71
Density function, probability
  conditional, 84
  defined, 81
  joint, 286
  normally distributed random variable,
    274
Derivative (calculus), *see also* Stochastic
    calculus
  as approximation, 44–47
  deterministic
    chain rule, 47–48
    defined, 43
  stochastic, 127–142
  total, 194, 195
Derivatives (asset), *see* Futures; Options
Differential
  deterministic, 53, 57–58
  stochastic, 169–171, 195, 196–197
  total, 57–58
Differential equations
  ordinary, 62–63
  stochastic, 132–142, 216–236
Diffusion coefficient, 128, 218
Discontinuity, in process trajectories,
    149–153
Discount, risk-free, 21, 280
Discount in riskless borrowing, 34
Distribution function, 80–81
Dividends, 15, 240, 260, 261–263
Doob-Meyer decomposition, 120–122
Doob-Meyer theorem, 121
Down-and-in option, 264
Down-and-out option, 264–265, 266
Downtick, 15, 87